JOURNAL FOR THE STUDY OF THE OLD TESTAMENT
SUPPLEMENT SERIES
400

Editors
Claudia V. Camp, Texas Christian University
and
Andrew Mein, Westcott House, Cambridge

Founding Editors
David J.A. Clines, Philip R. Davies and David M. Gunn

Editorial Board
Richard J. Coggins, Alan Cooper, John Goldingay,
Robert P. Gordon, Norman K. Gottwald, John Jarick,
Andrew D.H. Mayes, Carol Meyers, Patrick D. Miller

BIBLE IN THE TWENTY-FIRST CENTURY SERIES
3

Editor
Athalya Brenner

Sanctified Aggression

Legacies of Biblical and Post Biblical
Vocabularies of Violence

edited by

Jonneke Bekkenkamp
and Yvonne Sherwood

T & T CLARK INTERNATIONAL
A Continuum imprint
LONDON • NEW YORK

Copyright © 2003 T&T Clark International
A Continuum imprint

Published by T&T Clark International
The Tower Building, 11 York Road, London SE1 7NX
15 East 26th Street, Suite 1703, New York, NY 10010

www.tandtclark.com

British Library Cataloguing-in-Publication Data
A catalogue record for this book is available from the British Library

Typeset and edited for Continuum by Forthcoming Publications Ltd
www.forthcomingpublications.com

Printed on acid-free paper in Great Britain by Cromwell Press

ISBN 0-567-08070-6 (hardback)
        0-567-08060-9 (paperback)

CONTENTS

Athalya Brenner

This volume is the third in the 'The Bible in the 21st Century' series. This is the title of our collective research project in the Biblical Studies Section, within the Department of Art, Religion and Culture at the University of Amsterdam, with the support of NOSTER (Netherlands School for Advanced Studies in Theology and Religion) and ASCA (Amsterdam School of Cultural Analysis). In this research program, as can be seen from its Internet formulations,[1] together with our international research partners, we endeavour to problematize contemporaneous authoritative and cultural meanings of bibles by focusing upon the processes of transmission, readership and actualization of biblical texts up to and including the Twenty-First Century.

We started the project together with our corresponding department at the University of Glasgow in 2000. The first book of the BTC series, *Bible Translation on the Threshold of the Twenty-First Century: Authority, Reception, Culture and Religion* (A. Brenner and J.W. van Henten [eds], 2002), is a collection of papers problematizing contemporary biblical translations as cultural phenomena. Subsequent BTC volumes, be they collections or monographs by single authors, have followed and will follow a similar pattern and present work done locally as well as by international research partners and colleagues.

The present volume, *Sanctified Aggression*, is edited by Jonneke Bekkenkamp (University of Amsterdam) and Yvonne Sherwood (University of Glasgow). It constitutes an engagement with the highly topical issues pertaining to bible usage, religion and aggression. It doesn't take the easy route of assuming that religion is inherently violent or, on the contrary, an expression of humanity's best. Rather, as the editors write on the back cover, the book

> works from the premise that biblical, Jewish and Christian vocabularies continue to resonate, inspire and misfire... The collective conclusion is that it is not possible to control biblical and religious violence by simply identifying canonical troublespots, then fencing them off with barbed wire or holding peace summits around them. Nor is it always possible to draw clear lines between problem and nonproblem texts, witnesses and perpetrators, victims and aggressors and 'reality' and 'art'.

---

1. Visit <http://www.theo.uu.nl/noster/> for the Dutch version, and <http://cf.hum.uva.nl/bijbelwetenschappen/english/index.html> for the English (following the 'Research' link).

To quote from our local research program,

> The cultural-historical significance of 'the bible' results from the fact that bibles
> function as canons, i.e. networks or collections of intensely mediated texts that are
> considered sources for forms, values and norms by people. The canonical status of
> these texts leads to an ongoing process of re-interpretation and actualization, during
> which the biblical text is read selectively… Elements that are considered meaning-
> ful are being connected with actual views of life. Fragments of biblical texts func-
> tion as a source of common values and interests. They form a point of attachment
> for the formulation of common identities and a reservoir of images, archetypes,
> topoi and model texts that inspire new texts and other forms of expression.

Broadly speaking, this is the mission of the present series. Hopefully, this volume
as well as others will explore features and issues that are oriented to contemporary
culture and the bible's (and religion's) place within it, issues that are gaining ground
but—perhaps—still get less academic attention than they deserve.

ACKNOWLEDGMENTS

We would like to thank NOSTER, the Dutch research school for Theology and Religious Studies for supporting the project 'Vocabularies Relating to Views of Life and Religion: Tanakh, Bible and Qur'an in the Twenty-First Century'. Yvonne Sherwood would like to thank Richard Davie for his help with proofreading and further 'Englishing' the essays. (She would also like to thank her Dutch and Hebrew-speaking colleagues for having the grace and skill to bow to the demands of the linguistic Empire.)

ABBREVIATIONS

ANRW	Hildegard Temporini and Wolfgang Haase (eds.), *Aufstieg und Niedergang der römischen Welt: Geschichte und Kultur Roms im Spiegel der neueren Forschung* (Berlin: W. de Gruyter, 1972–)
BETL	Bibliotheca ephemeridum theologicarum lovaniensium
BHS	*Biblia hebraica stuttgartensia*
BibInt	*Biblical Interpretation: A Journal of Contemporary Approaches*
BJS	Brown Judaic Studies
EncJud	*Encyclopaedia Judaica*
ExpTim	*Expository Times*
HDR	Harvard Dissertations in Religion
Int	*Interpretation*
JPSV	*Jewish Publication Society Version*
JSJ	*Journal for the Study of Judaism in the Persian, Hellenistic and Roman Period*
JSJSup	*Journal for the Study of Judaism in the Persian, Hellenistic and Roman Period*, Supplement Series
JSNT	*Journal for the Study of the New Testament*
JSNTSup	*Journal for the Study of the New Testament*, Supplement Series
JSOT	*Journal for the Study of the Old Testament*
JSOTSup	*Journal for the Study of the Old Testament*, Supplement Series
KJV	King James Version
LCL	Loeb Classical Library
LXX	Septuagint
MGWJ	*Monatsschrift für Geschichte und Wissenschaft des Judentums*
NIB	*New Interpreter's Bible*
NJB	*New Jerusalem Bible*
NovT	*Novum Testamentum*
NRSV	New Revised Standard Version
RSV	Revised Standard Version
SBLDS	SBL Dissertation Series
SPB	Studia postbiblica
TDNT	Gerhard Kittel and Gerhard Friedrich (eds.), *Theological Dictionary of the New Testament* (trans. Geoffrey W. Bromiley; 10 vols.; Grand Rapids: Eerdmans, 1964–)
WBC	Word Biblical Commentary
ZAW	*Zeitschrift für die alttestamentliche Wissenschaft*
ZTK	*Zeitschrift für Theologie und Kirche*

Timothy K. Beal is Harkness Professor of Biblical Literature and Director of the Baker-Nord Center for the Humanities at Case Western Reserve University in Cleveland, OH. He is author, most recently, of *Religion and Its Monsters* (2002) and *Theory for Religious Studies* (2004).

Jonneke Bekkenkamp is Senior Lecturer in Religion and Literature at the University of Amsterdam. She published on the biblical Song of Songs, on the bible as literature and on literature as bible. Her recent research focuses on the religious vocabulary of the Mennonites.

Athalya Brenner is Professor of Hebrew Bible/Old Testament at the University of Amsterdam. She is the editor of the Feminist Companion to the Bible Series. Her main fields of interest are Semitic philology and feminist and literary criticism of the Hebrew bible.

Elizabeth Leigh Gibson published on the history of early Christianity, ancient Judaism and the interaction between the two. Her co-edited volume *Violence Amongst Jews and Christians* is forthcoming in 2005. She received her PhD in Religion from Princeton University, and is an independent scholar based in Princeton, NJ.

Jan Willem van Henten is Professor of New Testament and head of the Department of Art, Religion and Culture at the University of Amsterdam. His field includes Second Temple Period Judaism, with special emphasis on the issues of martyrdom, apocalyptic literature and Josephus.

Alastair Hunter is Senior Lecturer in Old Testament Studies at the University of Glasgow, the author of *Psalms* (Readings in the Old Testament Series, 1999). He is working on a major study of science, culture and religion, and researches and teaches in the areas of Bible and Literary Theory, Judaism and the Holocaust, and Biblical Wisdom Literature.

David Jasper is Professor of Literature and Theology at the University of Glasgow. The author of numerous books and articles, he has recently completed *The Sacred Desert* (2004), and is joint editor of the forthcoming *Oxford Handbook of English Literature and Theology*. His interests have recently moved more into the field of theology and visual culture.

Tod Linafelt is Associate Professor of Biblical Literature at Georgetown University in Washington, DC. He is the author of *Surviving Lamentations* (2000) and a commentary on the book of Ruth (Berit Olam, 1998). He is currently at work on a commentary on the Song of Songs.

Malachie Munyaneza came to Britain from Rwanda in 1993. He is currently writing his PhD dissertation on 'A Comparative Study of the Book of Proverbs and Rwandan Proverbial Wisdom' at the University of Surrey, Roehampton, and is working as a minister in the United Reformed Church.

Todd Penner did his PhD at Emory University in New Testament and Christian Origins. He teaches at Austin College (Sherman, TX) and currently focuses on analyzing early Christian texts in terms of their ancient gendered contexts. He also has an interest in the cultural reception of the bible in contemporary visual media.

Jeremy Punt is the author of 'Peace, Conflict and Religion in South Africa: Biblical Problems, Possibilities and Prospects' (1999) and 'Empire, Messiah and Violence: A Contemporary View' (2002). Among other projects, he is currently working on postcolonial biblical hermeneutics, focusing on issues of identity, representation and power in the New Testament, and which relates to his interest in cultural studies approaches to biblical texts.

Hugh Pyper is Senior Lecturer in Biblical Studies at the University of Leeds. He has written widely on the bible and postmodernism and on Kierkegaard and was co-editor of the *Oxford Companion to Christian Thought*. He is currently working on the concept of survival as a unifying theme in biblical studies.

Yvonne Sherwood is Senior Lecturer in Old Testament/Tanakh and Jewish Studies at the University of Glasgow. Previous publications include *The Prostitute and the Prophet* (1996) and *A Biblical Text and Its Afterlives: The Survival of Jonah in Western Culture* (2000). She is currently working on a monograph on the 'sacrifice' of Abraham's beloved son in Judaism, Christianity and Islam and on anthologies based on the conference 'Other Testaments: Derrida and Religion' (Toronto 2002).

Klaas Spronk is Lecturer in Old Testament Studies at the Theologische Universiteit Kampen. Previous publications include studies on the religions of ancient Israel and Ugarit and commentaries on the books of Joshua and Nahum. He is presently working on monographs about the (history of) interpretation of the of Judges and about the New Dutch Bible Translation

Caroline Vander Stichele received her PhD in New Testament Studies from the University of Leuven and currently teaches biblical studies at the University of Amsterdam. Her research focuses on the cultural reception of the bible in modern media and on the rhetoric of gender in biblical texts.

INTRODUCTION: THE THIN BLADE OF DIFFERENCE
BETWEEN REAL SWORDS AND WORDS ABOUT 'SHARP-EDGED
IRON THINGS'—REFLECTIONS ON HOW PEOPLE USE THE WORD

Yvonne Sherwood and Jonneke Bekkenkamp

Jesus: By sword I don't mean a sharp-edged thing.
        It's a figure of speech
John: But if you set a man against his father
        It may lead to a sharp-edged iron thing.
        Think of how people use words…

—Edwin Morgan

'Words'
Axes
After whose stroke the wood rings,
And the echoes!

—Sylvia Plath

When we ('we' being participants from the University of Amsterdam and the University of Glasgow and associates) first presented these papers to one another in Amsterdam in May 2002, the topic of violence was hanging heavy in the cultural, political and academic air. The world was still attempting to come to terms with 11 September and its aftermath—not least the 'war' on the abstract noun 'terrorism' that is now, as we are writing this introduction, rapidly turning into a war on the far more geographically determinable terrain of Iraq—and the Dutch participants were still in shock following the shooting of the LPF leader Pim Fortuin. Though the 1990s witnessed the horror of genocide in Rwanda, the death of tens of thousands in Chechnya, the murder of thousands of the Shi'ite Herzara minority by the Taliban in 1998 and the declaration of the current Intifada in Israel/Palestine in late 2000, it was '9/11' that brought the shock of violence home to the United States, just as it was the war in Bosnia and Kosovo that had brought the trauma of war home to Europe. In the debates that followed, it became increasingly difficult to draw firm lines between what the English and French termed 'violence'—a word that implies (illegitimate, always condemnable) violation from outside 'us'—and what the Dutch (and Germans) term *Geweld* or *Gewalt*, in words that cross the boundaries between what French and English segregate as 'violence' and 'power'.[1]

---

1. This distinction between '*Geweld/Gewalt*' and 'violence', as it relates to questions of violence and identity is discussed in detail in Samuel Weber's 'Wartime', in Hent de Vries and

At some deep level it suddenly seemed true, confusingly, that *violence/Geweld/
Gewalt* was attacking 'us' *and* happening in the very heart of 'us', that it could erupt
within our own identities, homes and liberal democracies, as well as in chronological or geographical elsewheres.

This blurring of boundaries between violence inside and outside mirrored what
had been gradually happening within studies of the Bible: the book still vaunted,
together with the 'Judaeo-Christian' tradition and 'ethical monotheism', as the
ancient root of liberal democracy and of that which we call the 'West' (and by
which we still often mean the 'Best'). To speak roughly, in the kind of brutalizing
generalizations that all these surveys must inevitably resort to, if the '70s and '80s
in Biblical Studies had been about supplementing historical study with rhetorical
and literary studies (still largely orientated around apostrophes to the beauty and
richness and [artistic] worthiness of the Bible[2]), by the '90s and 'noughties' criticism had turned increasingly to ideologically *critical* criticism, and was prepared to
analyze biblical violence not only as violation/abuse of essentially good material,
but as something that took place at the very heart of the biblical text. One of the
most powerful and important treatments of this topic—Elaine Scarry's *The Body in
Pain* (1985)—came too early, and from too far outside the discipline, to be widely
read among theologians and biblical scholars (and still has not received the wide
readership that it deserves), while earlier critiques of biblical violence, such as
Trible's *Texts of Terror* were still perceived as marginally 'feminist', interpreted by
many as non-essential. But in the '90s the topic moved towards the centre of the
disciplines with publications such as Regina Schwarz's *The Curse of Cain*, while,
in a parallel movement in theology, recent publications such as Anthony Bartlett's
Cross Purposes testify to the influence of (again originally feminist) critiques of the
violent grammar of the atonement. It is a mark of how far the topic has moved to
the centre of the disciplinary agenda that the 2002 annual meeting of the Society of
Biblical Literature in Toronto included not only a special session on 'Violence and
Representations of Violence among Jews and Christians', but a presidential address
by John J. Collins on 'The Zeal of Phineas: The Bible and the Legitimation of
Violence'. Although many still want to place violence firmly outside, in a historical, geographical or textual elsewhere (such as the primitive world before ethical
monotheism, the Middle East, or the Qur'an), many of us more accustomed than we
once might have been to the spectre of what could be called *domestic* violence, that
is, violence on the home-ground of the 'Judeo-Christian' (though new analogies
between the Bible and the contemporary, such as Klaas Spronk's suicide terrorist
Samson, responsible for the death of 3000 victims, still have the power to Shock).

Samuel Weber (eds.), *Violence, Identity and Self-Determination* (Stanford, CA: Stanford University
Press, 1997), pp. 80-105 (82-83).
    2.   For further discussion of the idealizing and apologetic direction of early literary studies of
the Bible, see Yvonne Sherwood, '"Darke Texts Needs Notes": On Prophecy, John Donne and the
Baroque', *JSOT* 27.1 (2002), pp. 47-74, and 'Prophetic Scatology: Prophecy and the Art of Sensation', in S.D. Moore (ed.), *In Search of the Present: The Bible through Cultural Studies* (Semeia,
82; Atlanta: Scholars Press, 2000), pp. 183-224.

These days, a collection like this now comes not as a new gospel, but as a supplementary discourse to an increasingly established critique of religious violence. But if we want to remind ourselves of how far our disciplines have come in this respect, we need only to consult Alastair Hunter's essay in this volume, and see what Albright and Bright once said so easily, and automatically, about the Canaanites...

Sanctified Aggression extends and supplements an existing debate in important, and we think timely, ways. Though there are papers here on what might be called 'the usual suspects'—Jephthah's daughter, Psalm 137, the 'sacrifice' of Isaac, Esther, Phineas, the destruction of the Canaanites/Amalekites, the anti-Judaism of Matthew, the Apocalypse and post-biblical constructions of the 'martyr'—our purpose here is not to identify key minefields or troublespots in the biblical and post-biblical landscape and then to attempt to diffuse them, put barbed wire around them, or hold peace summits around them; rather, we start from the premise that this violent 'canon-within-a-canon' is already well known, and that in fact this image of a separable sub-canon is a rather comforting idea, suggesting as it does that we can disentangle the victim from the aggressor, the witness from the perpetrator, and the 'good' texts from the 'bad'. In our treatment of the relations between the biblical, the Jewish, the Christian, and violence, we ally ourselves neither with the rather facile secular truism that the religious is by definition violent and dangerous and only the secular/humanist/humane offers a safe place of refuge from the ravages of religious authority, nor with the equally facile opposite view that religion, by definition, expresses the 'best' of human aspiration and that this 'best' is always capable of diffusing and sublating the worst. We also work from the assumption that biblical, Jewish and Christian vocabularies are not sealed off in hermetic worlds unto themselves, answerable only to themselves, but that biblical, Jewish and Christian words, figures, scripts and themes are recycled, appealed to, exploited, banalized, as they circulate as part of ongoing vocabularies, and that analyzing these vocabularies can help us understand what the title of this project terms 'The Future of the Religious Past'.[3] Our main motivation has been to explore how these vocabularies *play out on the ground*, particularly in relation to specific events and dates such as Jedwabne, Poland 1941, Columbine, New York 2001, Rwanda 1994, or particular phenomena such as anti-Semitism in Europe or the White Supremacist movement in the United States. But at the same time we realize that no firm lines can be drawn between art and reality, and that the lines between myths/fears/metaphor/symbols/acts/events are permeable, which is why we also look at films (*Twelve Monkeys, Outbreak, Terminator 2, The Matrix, Breaking the Waves, Dancer in the Dark*); plays (Edwin Morgan's *A.D.*, dramas on Jephthah's daughter by Buchanan, Vondel and Barnard); music (a Händel oratorio); the 'virtual' world of the Web; and texts/myths of Columbine (for example, *Rachel's Tears: The Spiritual Journey of Columbine Martyr Rachel Scott*).

---

3. The title 'The Future of the Religious Past' is the title of the project funded by the Netherlands Research Council for the Humanities and the Social Sciences (2003).

The collection opens with three essays that take wounding, sacrifice and circumcision as their central themes. Klaas Spronk takes one of the most infamous and shocking narratives of human sacrifice—the sacrifice of Jephthah's daughter—and analyzes four (per)mutations of the biblical narrative: George Buchanan's play of 1543; Vondel's play of 1659; Händel's 1751 oratorio (libretto by Morell); and a play by the contemporary Dutch playwright Benno Barnard (1998). The construction of God, man, woman and violence shift. In Buchanan's play (and Vondel's later retelling) the daughter surrenders herself for the sake of the father, and so, by in effect committing suicide, in a certain twisted sense, as Vondel says, 'surpasses Isaac'; in Händel/Morell's version, an angel intervenes to say that death is not required and that the sacrifice can be commuted to the 'sacrifice' of perpetual virginity—the move from sacrifice to 'sacrifice' making this Jephthah's daughter more like biblical Isaac (though the emphasis on her virginity does suggest that gender makes a considerable difference to how 'sacrifice' is conceived). In Benno Barnard's modern version, Jephthah's vow to 'sacrifice' his daughter is transformed into a vow to compel her to marry, but even though the 1990s father appropriates his right to take/control the daughter's life in a less overt—more metaphorically 'violent'—manner, the daughter rebels in no uncertain terms: 'I kick you, scratch you, bite you... You, my father and my traitor'—and so shows herself far less *in hoc* to the *pater familias* and God than her earlier prototypes. Yvonne Sherwood takes up the story of the son who is in many ways the male counterpart of Jephthah's daughter (except for the crucial fact that *he* does not have to wait for a contemporary playwright to get *him* up from the sacrificial altar): she looks at the sacrifice, or more properly 'sacrifice', or binding, of Isaac, and examines how Jewish tradition has bound itself to—and unbound itself from—the story that it knows as the Akedah. She argues that Jewish tradition holds the story in an ambiguous recoil-embrace: on the one hand it has Isaac die, or at least be wounded, and makes considerable use of Isaac's blood and Isaac's ash, but on the other it resists the efficacy of sacrifice through eloquent ethical discourses expressed by the scar of Isaac and the bodies and words of Isaac, Sarah and Satan.[4]

Sherwood discusses the difference between two kinds of wound—the good (productive) wound, and the bad (scandalous) wound—and this theme of the good/bad wound is taken up, in a broader sense, in Hugh Pyper's paper, 'Fleshing the Text'. Rather than looking at a specific biblical text, this paper explores the biblical in general, and looks at how the biblical relates to cutting and circumcision, which

---

4.   The resistance of the mother and the woman, fascinatingly, is a motif that has already been touched on in Spronk's essay (where the daughter rebels against the sacrificial religion of the fathers) and will also re-emerge later in Munyaneza's aside about women's/mothers' resistance to the ideology of *umutabazi*. Far from being an exclusively feminist concern or one that only emerges in Barnard's feminism-influenced (1998) play, the theme of the resistance of the mothers is one that emerges in ancient Rabbinic reading and early Rwandan mythology. Though gender is not a foregrounded concern in this collection, these observations suggest that constructions of masculinity and femininity are hardly incidental to the question of religion and violence. The gender theme recurs again, more explicitly, in 'The Tyranny of the Martyr' by Vander Stichele and Penner.

is a mark of love but also of loss/self-limit/mutilation. For Pyper, the contested and complex figure of circumcision is a sign for a Bible that constructs itself around anguish and loss (the loss of the temple, the loss of the land, the loss of the body of Jesus), and that is pulled apart by the tensions that it seeks to embody, as it works on the line/slash/cut between hope and dread, promise and betrayal, life and death. Pyper's paper explores the danger and also the allure of the wound/cut, which is also a 'memory of contact, a substitute for the caress'.

'Is there a volcano waiting to erupt in the inarticulacy of our spiritual vocabularies which can, as it is only too possible, seize on the biblical text and use it as a weapon?' asks Hugh Pyper, and the answer from the next three writers in this collection is an emphatic 'yes'. Malachie Munyaneza, Athalya Brenner and Alastair Hunter look at how the lava of this volcano clearly spills over into specific atrocities or vocabularies of hate. Munyaneza documents how biblical vocabularies, grafted onto indigenous myths and terms, helped to prepare the Rwandan cultural stage for genocide—a genocide conducted by a 'Committee for National Salvation' in which the perpetrators came largely from an area known as the 'Galilee of the Nations'. His article may come as something of a shock for those of us in the 'West' who learnt about the genocide through Western media and Western filters that confusingly combined discussion of Western guilt (in terms of the non-intervention of the UN) with a dominant narrative about the inexplicable upsurge of violence, that could only be 'explained' by the volatility of Africa, on which Westerners could only look in helpless sympathy and horror. Munyaneza tells a different story of the relationship between Rwanda and the West: he documents the Church and colonialist idealization of the *Abatutsis*; the calculating shift in sympathy towards the ascendant *Abahutus* in 1959; the appropriation of the dangerously loaded term *umutabazi* as a translation of Jesus' role as 'saviour'; and the legacy of the mapping of Rwanda as a kind of African Israel. But the story he tells is not all West- and Bible-centred—not one that would enable us to appropriate this story simply as a story of colonialist or European (German/Belgian) guilt, still fundamentally about 'us' and our texts. On the contrary, his discussion of the appropriation of the biblical also introduces us to a dense, and for many of us 'foreign', web of Rwandan myth. Munyaneza's account of the ancient Rwandan myth of the ascendant *Abatutsi* sounds very like the Genesis myths that affirm the superiority of the Israelites over the Ammonites, Moabites, Canaanites, Ishmaelites and Edomites. And the fact of this striking similarity, in the absence of historical dependence, suggests that there are also relations of analogy between Rwandan and biblical myth.

There is nothing forensic or, as that strange idiom goes, purely 'academic' about Munyaneza's analysis of the Bible and Violence—as a moderate Abahutu and advocate of peace between Abatutsis and Abahutus, he sheltered in a hiding space while those with machetes went on the rampage, knowing that he could die at any moment—and his presence at the colloquium was the most eloquent counter to any temptation to indulge in a detached 'verbal tourism of catastrophe', to use Brenner's phrase. Brenner's essay 'On the Rivers of Babylon' weaves a close textual reading of Psalm 137 with a historical event that, as text, only came to light in 2001—the murder of 1600 Jews in 1941 by the Polish Catholic citizens of Jedwabne. Like Munyaneza's, Brenner's own story is entwined with the genocides of the twentieth century: Brenner's parents emigrated to 'Palestine' in the '30s, leaving the rest of the extended family in Jendjziov in Poland, and the photographs of Jedwabne Jews published in Jan Gross's *Neighbours* are very like those of her non-immediate family who perished in Europe during the Shoah. Brenner reads Gross's account of the destruction of the Jedwabne Jews against Psalm 137, with its expressions of exiled abjection, individual nostalgia, and the horrible coda of wished-for revenge. She looks at this 'Jewish'/biblical song against the song of the Jedwabne Jews who were commanded to sing on their way to destruction; she explores the dual role of the Catholic Poles as at once victim and perpetrator; she touches on the complex relations between the Jewish diaspora and 'Israeli' identity and their relation to the Shoah; and she ends with reflections on current perceptions of the Israeli/Jew as both victim and aggressor.

Hunter's essay looks at the historically fraught terms 'Palestine', 'Israel' and 'Jew' (as well as 'Pharisee' and 'Amalek') in a way that suggests dialogue with Athalya Brenner's essay. Like Brenner, Hunter looks at how the Bible has contributed to Christian anti-Semitism, and looks at the tangled identities of victim and aggressor. If Westerners can now—as they habitually do—refer to 'Israel/Palestine' in a way that seems to do easy justice to competing vocabularies and competing spaces, that violent 'slash' is so much more difficult actually to work out on the contested and limited ground. (Hunter refers to a piece of grafitti written on the wall by an Israeli solider after the incursion into Jenin: '*Ein Li Eretz Acheret*' ['I do not have another land'], a statement which, as a British newspaper reader pointed out, would have perfectly summarized the deadlock of the situation if it had have been repeated in Arabic, alongside). His '(De)nominating Amelek' takes three key items of biblical vocabulary—'Palestine', 'Pharisees', 'Amalek'—and analyzes the violence that has been committed, literally, in (as well as through and against) their name(s). Interestingly, he notes how 'Pharisee' and 'Amalek' continue to function as useful hate terms precisely because there are no living Pharisees or Amalekites to represent their case to the anti-defamation league or to take to the streets with banners—an observation that suggests that when they are *loosed* from their original historical referents, biblical vocabularies of violence may in fact become *more* dangerous.

Hunter's essay concludes with a metaphor of a viral Bible, or at least potentially viral components of the Bible:

> We ignore at our peril the potential for violence built into the Bible. This is not something abstract, occupying a virtual space in which metaphor and rhetoric are safely confined, like computer viruses imprisoned in an IT lab. There is no shortage of those who cannot separate metaphor from reality, rhetoric from *Realpolitik*...

These issues—and metaphors—resonate with two essays written by two contributors from the United States: Tod Linafelt and Timothy K. Beal. Linafelt picks up on Hunter's metaphor of a viral Bible but sends it in a different direction as he charts the shift in American popular culture from nuclear to *viral* apocalypse as the new dominant strain of apocalyptic fear. 'Purity and Danger at the End of the World' charts the movement from the fear of nuclear holocaust to the purity and viral-obsessed world of *Outbreak* and *Twelve Monkeys*, a paradigm that has less in common with Daniel and the Apocalypse of John than with the biblical priestly literature. Like Hunter, Linafelt shows how metaphor slips seamlessly into 'reality' when he discusses, on one hand, the anthrax scares in Florida and Washington DC (comparable to growing fears about Ricin in Europe) and, on the other, the story of a professor of Cell Biology at Duke University who refused the applications of three Pakistani medical students because he thought that 'they were potentially [as] lethal as anthrax or HIV'.

Linafelt's argument is not that the relationship between the Bible and this par-ticular apocalyptic mutation is straightforwardly causal: he is not saying that the fear of the viral apocalypse could not have happened without the Bible, or that it draws explicitly on the Bible (though it sometimes does), but rather that the viral apocalypse seems to be a declension of the same paradigm of purity that is found in priestly literature. A similar position is taken by Beal in his paper, 'The White Supremacist Bible and the Phineas Priesthood', where he does not argue that the White Supremacist movement straightforwardly *derives* from the stories of Phineas in Numbers 25 and Psalm 106, but rather that the two were woven together recently, and explicitly, by Richard Kelly Hoskins's *Vigilantes of Christendom: The Story of the Phineas Priesthood* (1990). Beal's is a chilling account of the interweaving of ideals of racial purity and religious purity, and of a racist reading of Genesis where the Israelites are white and the Others are black (in a way that resonates, at a dis-tance, with Munyaneza's account of the division between [black] *Abahutus* and [almost-white] *Abatutsis*). In a way that vexes the Israeli/Palestinian 'slash' even further, and that should give pause to those who come down too easily on one side or the other, Beal notes that American White supremacists see themselves as en-gaged in a fight against the Zionist Occupied Government (the ZOG) and actively celebrate the success of Palestinian suicide bombers.

In a fascinating aside in 'Purity and Danger at the End of the World', Linafelt makes the point that the 'atomic bomb' first appeared as a phrase in H.G. Wells's *The World Set Free* (1913) and was read by Leo Szilard a year before he developed the scientific basis for the real atomic bomb—an observation that clearly demon-strates the very permeable borders between 'reality' and literature, art or film. These borders are opened further in essays on *The Matrix* (1999), *A.D: A Trilogy in the Life of Jesus* (2000), *Breaking the Waves* (1996) and *Dancer in the Dark* (2000), and in Leigh Gibson's discussion of the relationship between the 'reality' of Columbine (April 1999) and Columbine martyrology myths. David Jasper and Jeremy Punt both treat the question of the 'messiah' and the different inflections that the word is given in the contemporary world by analyzing the now-famous film by the Wachowski brothers and the Glaswegian poet Edwin Morgan's distinctive take on the life and legacy of Jesus. Morgan's *A.D.* provides what Jasper terms a 'deconstructive or pre-constructive backdrop to the systematic and justifying theology of Christianity' by imagining a pre-christological, pre-'messianic' Jesus who is something of an *ingenu* (this Jesus simply cannot conceive of the possibility of massacres perpetrated in his name and thinks that it is enough to clarify to his friend John, as he writes everything down, that 'By sword I don't mean a sharp-edged thing. It's a figure of speech'). Perhaps he should know better—this Jesus has, after all, seen a performance of *Antigone* and has probably heard Socrates' warning that 'a writing cannot distinguish between suitable and unsuitable readers' —but he simply does not anticipate the dangers involved in his transition from 'real' actor/human being to Word/*Logos* and has to be told by John 'But if you set a man against his father/It may lead to a sharp-edged iron thing'. Jeremy Punt also explores the relationship between the 'messiah' and violence in his analysis of *The Matrix* (a film which has drawn a great deal of attention from scholars of religion, unlike Morgan's lesser-known *A.D.*). Whereas Christianity has traditionally placed the emphasis on the violence inflicted on Jesus, Punt explores how violence has been fuelled by the idea and mission of Jesus and indeed the very notion of the 'messianic'—a concept that, in its turn, is interrogated by the role of the filmic messiah called the One, or 'Neo'. In the vision of *The Matrix*, as in certain strands of the New Testament, the true self is achieved only by overturning the present world, or in the film's terms escaping from the computer-generated illusion that is *The Matrix*. This quest for that which is more than seeming-life involves the sacrifice of life: in a familiar religious structure, the followers of Neo give up their lives in order to escape from a pseudo-life into one where one can really, truly *live*.

The cluster of essays by David Jasper, Jeremy Punt, Elizabeth Gibson and Todd Penner and Caroline Vander Stichele explore the seemingly counter-intuitive idea of the *dangers* of conventional ways of imagining *salvation*. As Jasper and Punt jointly focus on the legacy of the messianic, so Leigh Gibson and Vander Stichele and Penner jointly approach the figure of the martyr as portrayed in contemporary martyr texts. Leigh Gibson's essay resonates with the other two 'letters from America' by Beal and Linafelt, as well as with Michael Moore's recent film *Bowling for Columbine* (2002) in which he explores a culture of media-hyped fear constructed around an image of identity under siege. Gibson probes the martyrologies constructed around two Columbine schoolgirls (as well as one might-have-been-martyr) and asks what fuelled the development, elaboration and repetition of these martyr-texts in the vacuum of evidence that either girl was indeed murdered for her faith. Her analysis shows how the denominational commitments of the girls' families provided both the religious vocabularies for the creation of the martyr-stories and the institutional support for their propagation. And, by documenting a virtually instantaneous leap from myth to fact, she makes it clear that modern martyrologies, like ancient ones, gain no intrinsic truth from their proximity to the actual moment of death. In 'The Tyranny of the Martyr', Vander Stichele and Penner explore how Lars von Trier's *Breaking the Waves* and *Dancer in the Dark* reinscribe the traditional image of the passive, voluntary martyr and also, instinctively, gender that role as female—thus replaying the gender stereotype of self-sacrificial womanhood (a stereotype that may help us to reflect back on the difference between Jephthah's daughter, who dies, and Abraham's son, who is saved). But their conclusion goes beyond simply affirming, and lamenting, female passivity. Drawing on studies of early Christian martyrs, they argue that the martyrs in these films gain power—indeed that the martyr functions as a kind of 'tyrant'—whose death has the power to reverse insider–outsider distinctions and to impose her decisions on the other characters.

The final two essays are broader in their scope and move towards a more general survey of religious vocabularies. Jan Willem van Henten offers a perspective on martyrdom that complements—and extends in a different direction—the studies of Leigh Gibson and Vander Stichele/Penner, by analying the use of the term 'martyr' on the internet. Interestingly, historical martyrs still dominate contemporary websites; contemporary martyrs are less frequently referred to and where there are references to contemporary 'martyrs' the term is broadened, so that is has political, ethnic and national dimensions, with or without religious connotations. Martyrs are always part of a definable group; they are always victims of an overtly condemnable injustice (but not necessarily one that results in death—they must only be 'victimized' to qualify as a martyr); and the appellation 'martyr' tends to elevate the martyr's actions to a level beyond all criticism. The image that Vander Stichele and Penner show to be so crucial in the movies of Lars von Trier—that of the voluntary martyr, which in turn draws on classical formulations of Jewish and Christian martyrdom—fades in many contemporary designations of the 'martyr', where the word martyr can effectively be replaced with the term the '(unwilling) *victim*'. The mutations of meaning of the word 'martyr' show how biblical and Christian vocabularies still circulate in contemporary culture but as elements of an amalgam of different vocabularies and traditions. The issue treated by Jonneke Bekkenkamp is the problem of defining religious studies in a world where beliefs are becoming more eclectic and diffuse. Using Richard Rorty's concept of final vocabularies, she explores the problem of mapping personal and cultural vocabularies and asks how such vocabularies, and the hopes and beliefs that they express, can be analyzed and defined. Her point of reference is Elfride Jelinek's *The Piano Teacher*, which she uses to explore personal vocabularies of self-creation, in this case (in a way that resonates with several other essays in the collection) through acts of violence committed against the central character's own life.

THE DAUGHTER OF JEPHTHAH:
CHANGING VIEWS ON GOD, MAN, AND VIOLENCE IN PLAYS AND ORATORIOS SINCE GEORGE BUCHANAN

Klaas Spronk

Introduction

Modern actors and scenes of violence are often found to be mirrored in biblical stories. One may note, for instance, the many parallels between the story of Samson's death taking 3000 Philistines with him as recounted in Judges 16 and the terrorist action on 11 September 2001 with the same number of casualties in the Twin Towers. Should we now call Samson a suicide terrorist *avant la lettre*? In the same book of Judges we come across the story of Jephthah's daughter. We can compare her sorry fate to what happens to Bess in Lars von Trier's 'Breaking the Waves' (see the article by Penner and Vander Stichele). Both women give their life for a man, a father and husband respectively, albeit that Bess does so voluntarily whereas Jephthah's daughter only gives in to the whim of her father. Are these comparisons justified? Do they help us to achieve a better understanding of violence by and against people of our own time? A closer look at both the biblical stories and their modern counterparts shows that ancient biblical characters hardly fit into our modern categories. The survey presented here of the history of reading and interpreting the biblical story of Jephthah and his daughter shows that the works of Buchanan, Vondel, Händel and Barnard teach us much about the authors and their time, but hardly contribute to a better understanding of the biblical text. To put it positively, the biblical story functions as a mirror of the world in which it is being interpreted. The comparison with the modern texts will show changing views, primarily with regard to the role of the daughter. More than in the biblical story she shall be portrayed as not only a victim but also as a woman who takes her fate in her own hands.

Buchanan

George Buchanan (1506–82) was a Scottish scholar who spent many years in France. As was customary in this period of the Renaissance, he had great interest in the Classical Greek literature and translated, as did Erasmus, plays from Euripides and other ancient Greek writers. In his own plays he related biblical themes to the Greek tragedies. He wrote them in Latin, the academic language of the time, as learning material for the school where he was working as a teacher. Afterwards they became popular and influenced later writers, as will become clear when we come to the work of Händel and Vondel. The play on Jephthah and his vow, *Jefphtes sive votum*, was first performed by his pupils in Bordeaux in the year 1543 and was published in 1554.[1]

The play starts with a prologue by an angel preparing the hearer for the events to come. They are presented as a lesson: God wants to teach the people of Israel humility by punishing them via the Ammonites and saving them by means of Jephthah, 'an exile from his father's house, despised by his brothers and sprung from a lowborn mother'. In his turn Jephthah should not make the mistake of being too proud of himself: 'so that Jephthah too may not assess himself by the outcome of this battle, and grow proud and arrogant with success, he will at once be overwhelmed with domestic loss, and his arrogant airs will be shattered and retreat'. He is pitied: 'Poor man, what a mountain of ills overhangs you!'; and so is his daughter: 'great will be the interest with which the poor child will discharge and with her throat's blood pay for the premature joy of that success'. So, it is not Jephthah's vow that is called premature, but only his daughter's happiness on his return. Jephthah is not accused. Like his daughter, he is a victim in a tragedy.

In the first scene of his play Buchanan introduces a new character, absent from the biblical story: the wife of Jephthah. She is called Storge, a Greek name meaning 'love' (especially of parents for their children). She suffers an anxious presentiment of her daughter's fate: in a dream she sees a pack of wolves attacking a flock; there are no shepherds; a dog drove off the wolves but tears a wounded lamb from her arms and 'mangle[s] it with merciless teeth'. For anyone familiar with Judges 11, this dream hardly needs explanation: the dog symbolizes Jephthah, who protects his people against the enemy but also causes his daughter's death.

The daughter reproaches her mother for being too worried: 'fear uncontrolled readily lends credence to unpropitious prophecies'. The daughter is named Iphis; in this way Buchanan relates her to Iphigeneia, well-known from Euripides's drama 'Iphigeneia in Aulis' in which the girl is sacrificed by her father Agamemnon, and in this Classical play we find a similar conversation between mother and daughter.

A messenger reports the successes of Jephthah on the battlefield and announces his return when he has dealt with the enemy. Shortly before his homecoming Jephthah appears on stage speaking to God. As with his wife's dream, albeit less obviously, his words are ominous—a listener familiar with the biblical story finds many hints to the coming events. To begin with Jephthah addresses his God, praising him as

> ruler of the world, one true God, unique deity of mercy, power and strength, harsh avenger but kindly father, fearsome to your foes, gentle bearer of salvation to your friends, figure of dreadful anger yet willing to be appeased, warm in love yet goaded to wrath.

---

1. P. Sharrat and P.G. Walsh (eds.), *George Buchanan Tragedies* (Edinburgh: Scottish Academic Press, 1983), pp. 21-94.

Indirectly Buchanan formulates here the theological problem of the story: how in the name of this merciful God and kindly father was it possible that a pious man like Jephthah came to his deed. Jephthah himself confesses that the Israelites have sinned by abandoning their God and therefore deserve the penalty of being delivered into the hands of the Ammonites: 'we poured out foolish prayers to dumb rocks, and made empty vows to deaf logs'. His own vow is of a different nature. It is not made to idols and it comes from a faithful man: 'Mindful of the contract with you, be pleased to receive in kindly fashion this vow of your servant. Though insignificant, it stems from a grateful heart and is freshly owed to you.' When formulating the vow Buchanan does not use the words he knew from the Vulgate, the common Latin translation, and in this way he leaves open the possibility that Jephthah was thinking of sacrificing an animal not of a person:

> The first thing [*quod primum*; Vulgate: *quicumque primus*] to encounter me on my safe return to my house will be your welcome victim and will steep your altar with its blood, even though no victim can be counted equal to your kindnesses. But you must with good will consider this as the gift of a mindful heart. You both redeem your promises faithfully and rejoice that vows are faithfully paid to you.

These last words add an aspect one misses in the biblical text: there we hear nothing of God's attitude towards the vow made by Jephthah. One can interpret this silence as approval, but this is by no means certain, especially not in this special case resulting in the offering of a human being.

The next scene describes the meeting between father and daughter when Jephthah returns safely from the battlefield.

Iphis:	I am come forth. How glad and happy I am to see the face of my sire back with us! Father whom I must revere second only to God, allow me to enjoy your embrace. Why, father, do you turn your frowning eyes from me?
Jephthah:	Wretched am I.
Iphis:	May God divert this omen on the enemy!
Jephthah:	That is my wish too, but it rebounds on me.
Iphis:	Alas, what is this I hear?
Jephthah:	The most wretched father of a wretched daughter.

Jephthah does not yet reveal the vow he has made, although Iphis urgently tries to find the reason for his sadness. As in the Euripides' play, the father gradually prepares his daughter for things to come. Iphis comes close to the truth when she remarks that with the favourable outcome of the war 'it is right to pray and pay our vows. We should not coax the deity with prayers when the fickle breeze of fortune blows against us, and then abandon ceremonies in thoughtless negligence when we are prosperous.' Jephthah agrees and asks her to attend the sacrifice, without telling her its nature.

Iphis is unhappy with the situation. She keeps asking herself why her father has reacted so strangely. Is she to blame? She makes an interesting observation on the fate of women in general:

> What a harsh fate the breed of women experiences when brought forth into the
> world! Though free of blame, they are bitten by the envious tooth of malevolent
> gossip. The fictions invented by the anger of the talkative servant, the lies uttered
> by the suspicious husband himself, or by malicious neighbours, are regarded as
> fact. I cannot control the suspicions of my sire; the safest remedy, I think, is enjoy-
> ment of an unspotted conscience.

She gets help from Symmachus, whose name means 'fellow fighter', as befits his
role in the story: he fought next to Jephthah on the battlefield and is a friend of the
family. He offers to try to clarify the situation. Jephthah reveals to Symmachus
that he is forced to sacrifice Iphis, 'the sole surviving hope of my family'. More
important than his fatherly love is his conviction that 'promised vows demand un-
flinching observance'. He clearly suffers under this heavy burden, but there is no
way out, not even in death:

> O sun, creator of the light of day, O ancestors, O all you men who have no part in
> sin, turn your faces from this accursed sacrifice. Or you earth which is to drink in
> the innocent blood of the maiden, suck me into your open caverns and devour me
> in your boundless womb. As long as I can die in innocence, bury me anywhere. I
> do not refuse to enter Tartarus itself, so long as I do not dwell in Tartarus as slayer
> of my kin. But why do I mention Tartarus? For me Tartarus is my home!

In Classical Greek mythology Tartarus is the place of punishment in the nether-
world. The hell Jephthah is facing in his home is the coming confrontation with his
wife.

Before he meets his wife he is admonished by an unnamed priest who points to
higher values than to keeping one's vow:

> How is it open to you to carry through what our sacred mother nature forbids, what
> our love of kin struggles against, and what God loathes?… Our God is not offered
> gory victims of the blood of cattle; but hearts defiled by no pollution, a mind
> refined by ingenuous truth, and a chaste conscience are to be offered to him.

He commands Jephthah to 'cease to anger God in your wish to placate him'. Jephthah is not impressed by the lengthy theological expositions. (The way Buchanan
portrays the priest can be regarded as criticism of a theology that adapts God's
words to our wishes.) He decides to keep to the harsh but simple truth: 'I prefer
foolish and simple truth to impious wisdom gleaming with deceit'. He compares
himself to Abraham obeying God's command to offer his only son.

His wife complains that while she has been preparing herself for their daughter's
wedding, she now is confronted with 'a criminal sacrifice conducted with barbaric
ritual'. The reference to the coming marriage of Iphis is another new element in
Buchanan's version of the story. Again, it seems to be inspired by Euripides. In his
play Iphigeneia goes to Aulis on the assumption that she is going there to marry
Achilles.

After Jephthah has told Iphis that she has not committed any crime, but that her
coming death is due to his 'impious sacred vow', she accepts her fate. In fact, she
appears to be the only one who shows understanding for her father:

> Whatever the fate which necessity impels, I readily consent to suffer, and I gladly
> offer my life which I owe to my father and my land. I ask you, mother, for this
> final favour, and will demand nothing hereafter—do not on my account be angry
> with my father, nor cause friction.

Jephthah offers to take her place on the altar, but she rejects his proposal: she
prefers to keep to the letter of the vow. In the chorus following this scene Iphis is
praised as a 'maiden with a spirit truly manly' and comforted with the prospect of
immortal fame:

> Though the injustice of the fates has deprived you of your more serviceable years,
> and though the monstrous savagery of Fortune has plucked the blossom of your
> youthful life, your renown after death will add to your glory that portion of life of
> which chance has deprived you.

It is remarkable that we do not hear one word of accusation against Jephthah. Both
she and her father are presented as powerless victims of fate.

In the final scene a messenger reports to Storge about the last hours of her
daughter. It can be compared to another play of Euripides, namely *Hekabe*, in
which the woman Hekabe is informed about the death of her daughter Polyxene.
We hear nothing of the delay the girl asked for according to the story in the book of
Judges: two months in which she and her friends 'bewailed her virginity'. The
reason for this probably has to be sought in the Classical (Aristotelian) insistence
on unity of time in one and the same play. Moreover, this long period of weeping
would not fit the picture Buchanan wanted to give, that Iphis bore her fate with
dignity: 'Whilst others wept, she alone was dry-eyed as she stood with features
relaxed, constant and untroubled about her fate'. She looks more beautiful than ever
and she appears to be even more devout. This girl 'of manly spirit' utters a prayer,
'her voice unbroken by her evil fortunes': 'Eternal Begetter of the universe, Father
of men, now finally show mercy and pardon the sin of your race, and receive this
victim with gentle heart'. She encourages the trembling priest to do his duty: 'Draw
near, and remove this life of mine from the light of day; loose the hindering barrier
of my body. Discharge from the vow the people, my father and myself'. The act of
the offering is not extensively described, only the reaction of her father: 'he was
suffused with tears and he covered his eyes with his garment and condemned both
himself and his rash vow'; the reaction of the priest: 'he was overwhelmed with
weeping and could scarcely loose the passage of her breath'; and of the crowd: 'for
long numb in sorrowful silence'.

The people are said to feel sorry for her mother Storge, but she is also regarded
as blessed with such a daughter. She answers that this cannot comfort her: 'This
consolation is more painful than the ill itself… The braver the spirit with which my
daughter bore her death, the sorer the anguish which gnaws my heart.'

In Buchanan's version the story of Jephthah and his daughter bears the hallmarks
of a Classical tragedy. People are governed by fate: what seems to be most important is the way they react to things that cannot be changed. Jephthah is torn by
the struggle between fatherly love and pious conviction: he shows character by
keeping to his vow and resisting the temptation from those around him to see things

in a different way now the consequences have become so bitter. He does not evade his responsibility; although he admits his foolishness and although he more than anyone else regrets the outcome. As a mortal he knows his place: he is not God and cannot shape his own life.

In Judges 11 Jephthah's daughter is praised for being not a passive victim but one who deliberately subordinates herself to a religious system in which God and man are to be held to their word. Buchanan presents her as an example for the spectator of one who is able to distinguish between what is essential and what is of secondary importance in life and death. Life may be violent to her and her death may seem untimely and undeserved yet she does not want to resist fate as the divinely set order of things. More than in the original story in the book of Judges Buchanan describes her death as a self-sacrifice based on her own choice.

Buchanan's play was translated into English, French and German. It greatly influenced the way the biblical story was later recounted, for instance in an oratorio by Händel and a play by Vondel.

Vondel

The famous Dutch dramatist Joost van den Vondel (1587–1679) in 1659 published a play entitled *Jeptha of Offerbelofte* ('Jephthah and His Promise to Sacrifice').[2] In many respects his approach can be compared to that of Buchanan. Both wrote according to the rules of Classical drama and, as in Buchanan's play, the entire action takes place on one day. At variance from Buchanan, however, and more in line with the biblical text is that this day is placed after the daughter's return from a period of two months of mourning in the mountains. In the meantime Jephthah has settled affairs with the rebellious tribe of Ephraim, an episode which is recounted in the Bible *after* the story of the sacrifice. Like Buchanan, Vondel adds a number of other characters: in addition to Jephthah and his daughter—who, as in Buchanan, is given the name Ifis—we meet the wife of Jephthah (named Filopaie, a Latin translation of Buchanan's Storge, 'she who loves her child'), the head of the royal household, the governor of the city, the royal priest, and a jurist.

Filopaie knows nothing of Jephthah's vow and is ignorant of the reason for Ifis's absence. Jephthah hopes to fulfil his vow before he meets his wife and before the two women themselves have the chance to meet. In this way he seeks to prevent Filopaie resisting his plans. As a consequence he does not give in to his daughter's wish to say goodbye to her mother. Only after Jephthah has left for the sanctuary at Shilo does Philopaie hear of the death of her daughter.

Vondel characterizes Jephthah's vow as an inconsiderate, rash action: Jephthah declares that it was never his intention to bring a human sacrifice, let alone his only child, 'the hope of my life, my crown'. In his desperation Jephthah consults a priest and a jurist who try to stop him, but he is not impressed by their flood of words— he does not find in them the purity and obedience to God which should come from

---

2.   N.C.H. Wijngaards (ed.), *Vondels Jeptha of offerbelofe. Treurspel* (Zutphen: W.J. Thieme, 2nd edn, 1976).

the heart. He does consent, however, to go to the high priest at Shilo for advice, but, in the end, time does not permit him to do so before the sacrifice. Jephthah proves unshakeable in his conviction that a vow made to God has to be fulfilled: there can be no doubt that this is the will of God, as his victory over the Ephraimites has shown, and it seems clear that Jephthah's vow had pleased him. Only after the sacrifice does Jephthah realize that he has made a terrible mistake and reproach himself for not having listened to the jurist and the priest.

Ifis, by contrast, accepts with happiness the fact that she has to give her life for father and fatherland. She does not fear death and compares herself to a bride offering her youth on the altar to God and she goes to the altar wearing a wedding dress not mourning garb. For her father she feels only sorrow and tries to comfort him by saying that her death is a blessing and not a punishment. She makes a comparison with the story of Abraham offering Isaac: like Isaac she is prepared and is not hoping, as Jephthah himself cries out, for an angel to prevent the killing. The choir, reacting to her words, praises her as one surpassing Isaac, as she offers her life without objection. In the prologue Vondel himself calls her an example and his play 'a mirror to youth'.

Vondel ends his play more positively than Buchanan. Jephthah is reconciled with God, does penance and finds forgiveness for his rash vow and is able to cope with the death of his daughter. Whereas Buchanan ends with the bitter words of an inconsolable mother, Vondel puts the final words in the mouth of the priest explaining to Filopaie that there is great comfort for her in Jephthah being reconciled with God and with his people, and in her daughter being praised year after year in a solemn feast on her behalf.

Händel

Georg Friedrich Händel (1685–1759) wrote an oratorio on Jephthah in 1751.[3] It was his last great composition, written in a period of growing problems with his physical health, and it is not unlikely that his personal difficulties left their marks on the way he composed the music to the libretto written by Thomas Morell.

Morell himself was clearly influenced by Buchanan's play. He uses the same names for Jephthah's daughter and wife. In addition to them he introduces Zebul, a half-brother of Jephthah, and Hamor, soldier and lover of Iphis. Morell generally follows the biblical account and abandons the unity of time, unlike Buchanan and Vondel who concentrate the events on one day. In this version of the story, as Hamor departs to serve in the army of Jephthah, Iphis shows him out, promising a fitting reward on his return and hinting at their coming marriage. In a lovely duet they sing of happiness to come:

> These labours past, how happy we!
> How glorious will they prove!
> When gathering fruit from conquest's tree
> we deck the feast of love!

---

3.   V. Novello (ed.), *Jephtha: An Oratorio in Vocal Score* (London: Novello).

Jephthah speaks of strange feelings, but eventually he ascribes these to the spirit of God and then he makes his vow:

> What mean these doubtful fancies of the brain?
> Visions of joy rise in my raptured soul.
> There play awhile and set in darksome night
> strange ardour fires my breast; my arms seem strong
> with tenfold vigour, and my crested helm
> to reach the skies.—Be humble still, my soul.—
> It is the spirit of God; in whose great name
> I offer up my vow:
> If, Lord, sustained by thy almighty power,
> Ammon I drive, and his insulting bands
> from these our long-uncultivated lands
> and safe return a glorious conqueror,
> what of whoever shall first salute mine eyes
> shall be for ever thine or fall a sacrifice.

In the book of Judges, the gift of God's spirit to Jephthah is reported prior to the story of his vow. In the plays of Buchanan and Vondel this element is not mentioned. Morell's libretto introduces a version of the vow which leaves open a possible interpretation other than human sacrifice. Speaking of 'what of whoever' suggests that Jephthah may be thinking of an animal; promising that this 'shall be for ever thine or fall a sacrifice' indicates that, in any case, he shall have the choice of sparing the life of the victim.

After the ominous words of Jephthah it comes as no surprise that mother Storge has a more negative presentiment than her daughter. When Jephthah returns it becomes clear that Storge is right. In this scene everyone around Jephthah tries to make him change his mind. In a dramatic quartet, beautifully scored by Händel, Zebul, Storge, Hamor and Jephthah discuss the matter:

Zebul:	O spare thy daughter!
Storge:	Spare my child!
Hamor:	My love!
Jephthah:	Recorded stands my vow in heaven above.
Storge:	Recall the impious vow, 'ere it is too late.
Hamor/Zebul:	And think not heaven delights
	in Moloch's horrid rites.
Jephthah:	I'll hear no more; her doom is fixed as fate.

One may note that here, as with Buchanan, we also encounter the element of fate. At the beginning of the oratorio this idea is stressed: the first words, sung by Zebul describing Israel's situation, are 'It must be so'. There are things human beings cannot change or comprehend, as is articulated by the choir following the quartet: 'How dark, O Lord, are thy decrees'. Apparently Händel had his difficulties in simply putting God on a par with fate. At the end of the oratorio he changed the words of Morell 'what God ordains is right' into 'whatever is, is right'. This phrase, from the famous British philosopher John Locke (1632–1704), is given extra emphasis by repetition of a theme in the music.

Iphis obediently accepts fate and prepares for her coming departure. The priests who have to execute the offering appeal to God, whereupon an angel appears declaring that the vow can be fulfilled if Iphis devotes the rest of her life to heaven in virginity:

> Rise, Jephthah, and, ye reverend priests, withhold
> the slaughterous hand. No vow can disannul
> the law of God. Nor such was its intent
> when rightful scanned; and yet shall be fulfilled.
> Thy daughter, Jephthah, thou must dedicate
> to God, in pure and virgin-state for ever;
> as not an object meet for sacrifice,
> else had she fallen an holocaust to God.
> The holy spirit, that dictated thy vow,
> bade thus explain it, and approves your faith.

Everyone happily welcomes this 'escape', which brings Jephthah's vow and its outcome into accord with the story of Abraham offering Isaac. It offers a plausible answer to the theological questions left open in the biblical story. Now there is no longer any tension between Jephthah having received the spirit of God and making his vow. In addition, the contradiction between the vow and the prohibition of human sacrifice is resolved.

Listening to the oratorio one gets the impression that Händel was particularly fascinated by the personal tragedy of Jephthah. The music at the end sounds somewhat perfunctory, and out of keeping with the apotheosis in Morell's text. Händel was more inspired by the preceding story of Jephthah wrestling with incontrovertible fate. Next to the aforementioned quartet, the most impressive piece is sung by the choir at the end of the second part of the oratorio. It begins hesitantly on a note of protest, followed by an emotionally turbulent passage as joy turns to sadness, and ends with a clear acceptance of reality:

> How dark, O Lord, are thy decrees,
> all hid from mortal sight!
> All our joys to sorrow turning
> and our triumphs into mourning.
> As the night succeeds the day.
> No certain bliss,
> no solid peace.
> We mortals know
> on earth below,
> yet on this maxim still obey:
> whatever is, is right.

Barnard

In 1998 Benno Barnard published a new version of Vondel's 'Jeptha', a free adaptation called 'Jephthah or Semitic Loves'.[4] In the play, which was staged in

---

4.   Benno Barnard, *Jefta of Semitische liefdes* (Amsterdam: Het Toneel Speelt, 1998).

numerous Dutch theatres, there are many echoes of Vondel's interpretation. Everything happens in the same place and on the same day, namely, at the moment of Iphis's return from her stay in the mountains and of Jephthah's return from the battle against the Ephraimites. Alongside Jephthah and Iphis we encounter Jephthah's wife, Filopaie, a steward called Ruben, who is also Iphis's lover, Jephthah's military adviser called Tariq, and Rabbi Silberblatt. Barnard also uses a similar plot: Jephthah has to sacrifice his daughter because of a rash vow he made to ensure military success. Although he is distraught at the outcome and although many attempts are made to withhold him from fulfilling his vow, he keeps to his word. He also tries to avoid the confrontation with his wife.

Barnard placed the story in a 'mythic present' with all kinds of modern elements featured—a tank and a pistol, and modern words like 'Playboy', 'ecstasy', and references to Freud, Einstein, and Brooklyn. Barnard also 'modernizes' Jephthah's vow: 'The first woman that on my return floats out of the door of Masfa to meet me I shall surely give in marriage to my excellent advisor'. He excuses himself by remarking that he knows for certain that dancers (or women of that kind) would never oppose this proposal. When things turn out differently he says:

> I was thinking of a prize of victory, not of a human being; not of Ifis, because no Ifis did cross my mind. But she was the first. And I tried to settle this among gentlemen, because this one scaled with medals could be her father. But no, Tariq wishes to be promoted to my son-in-law.

Unlike the daughter as she is presented in Vondel's play, Ifis does not accept the consequences of her father's promise. She is in love with Ruben and together they look for a way out. Ifis is angry with her father and when, after her return from the mountains, they meet and Jephthah speaks, 'O, child', Ifis cries out: 'I kick you, scratch you, bite you… You, my father and my traitor!'[5] This scene recalls the meeting as described in Judg. 11.35-36 and underlines the completely different relationship between father and daughter in Barnard's play. But in addition to these reproaches Ifis also shows tender feelings for her father based on sweet memories from her childhood. At the same time she realizes that this period is definitely past. The harsh reality is that her father has ruined her life. He still is the most powerful man in her life—she calls him 'second god'—this man, however, who previously protected her, is now the man who uses his power to force her into an intolerable situation.

All the men in this play are pictured negatively. Tariq may be a hero on the battlefield, but in the dialogues with Ruben and the rabbi he proves to be no match for his opponents. Ruben is verbally strong, but when it comes to deeds he does not have the nerve to see things through to the end. At the moment the arranged marriage seems inescapable Ruben grabs Jephthah's pistol to force him to change his intentions. With such power in his hands he becomes scared and even falls back into childish behaviour.

5.   In Dutch the words 'father' and 'traitor' rhyme: '*vader*'/'*verrader*'.

Ruben:	Death has the solution!
	(*Starts sucking at the pistol*)
Silberblatt:	No solution
	is better than life. Deep inside of Ruben
	there is fear: fear of death and fear of life
	and fear of that pistol and bang…
Ifis (*furious*):	Now shoot!
	Ejaculate! That stupid thing
	isn't your mother, is it?

She takes the pistol out of Ruben's hands. He has shown himself to be no different from the other men: 'Now you are like them; now you know the feeling of power'. They are all like her father, alike in their fear of 'our second sex'. Sarcastically she greets all the men around her. 'Goodbye god', she says to each of them, but a moment later her last words are: 'we are all dead'. Then she takes the pistol and kills herself.

In the final scene all the characters are together, including Filopaie. They find no comfort from each other, nor can they give an explanation of what has happened. As a conclusion they say, one after another: 'We are silent and shall sleep no more. We are not close to ourselves [*Wij zijn ons niet nabij*].' This accords with the tragic lines previously expressed by Ruben:

> Countless people are looking for themselves
> and find nobody: there is nobody
> for them, nobody that can be them.
> Said someone. Said someone. A human being.

God does not play a role, not even in connection with the vow. This becomes clear in a dialogue between Ruben and Jephthah where Ruben suggests asking the rabbi for advice—perhaps he can help change the situation.

Ruben:	That oath of yours has religious roots.
	This orthodoxy asks for a black,
	a Bible-black rabbi…
Jephthah:	My oath
	does not need God nor rabbis, because my oath
	is made in front of my most intimate men,
	my general staff, steward—
	my oath cannot be broken.

Rabbi Silberblatt is not asked to solve the problem, he is only invited to make up the marriage contract. The only thing he can do for Ifis is to spend time with her. He appears to be better at telling jokes than in finding convincing theological arguments against Jephthah's plan. Jephthah himself is far from the pious man portrayed by Vondel. At the moment Silberblatt begins a fine theological-philosophical discourse Jephthah rudely interrupts..

Silberblatt:	And God?
Jephthah:	The god of Masfa has been asleep for centuries.
	His book is finished.

Silberblatt:	You will occupy yourself
	with the question why something is and why not?
	The god...
Jephthah:	Rabbi, I must!
Silberblatt:	Alright, alright.
	(I have tried, but now his spring snaps.)

At the end of Vondel's play the priest speaks words of comfort to the mother of Iphis. Not so with Barnard. Silberblatt starts repeatedly with pious truisms, but they sound unconvincing, even to himself.

I, a Jew,
say to you: through this Red Sea of blood
there also is a passage. No, that doesn't sound right.[6]
But I have to talk, say that your daughter...
(*moved*)...that Ifis has chosen peace
above, O above the dream. For peace
that goes beyond my understanding...

Nobody listens. When he tries again, Jephthah indicates his antipathy: once again he interrupts Silberblatt, this time with a blasphemous wordplay:

Silberblatt:	The god of Abraham and of...
Jephthah:	...God vomits.[7]

In a way, when it comes to the role of God in the story of Jephthah and his daughter, Barnard remains close to the biblical text. In Judges 11 God is remarkably absent. He is spoken to, but he does not react. It is as if the words of Jephthah fall back upon himself and his family.

As in the plays of Buchanan and Vondel, as well as in the oratorio of Händel/Morell, Jephthah is pictured as a tragic character. He is torn by the dilemma he is confronted with because of his own inconsiderate vow. Barnard portrays his daughter as a passionate, intelligent and wayward young woman, discovering the truth about men in general and her father in particular. She is not a passive, slavishly obedient girl who gladly offers her life for father and fatherland. She does not accept the macho-like behaviour of the men around her and in the end proves to be more courageous and active. She does not let others take her life, she takes it herself. It is by this deed, by her own initiative, that she is the only one in this play who saves his/her honour. In so doing she follows the trajectory already set out by Buchanan, but blurred in the works of Vondel and Händel by an effort to make the biblical story acceptable to the readers/hearers of their time.

---

6. In Dutch the words for 'blood' and 'right' rhyme: '*bloed*'/'*goed*'.
7. In Dutch the last word ('*braakt*') sounds like the second syllable of the name Abraham.

Textual Carcasses and Isaac's Scar, or What Jewish Interpretation Makes of the Violence that Almost Takes Place on Mt Moriah

Yvonne Sherwood

This paper is part of a study in progress looking at how Judaism, Christianity and Islam incorporate the story of the sacrifice of Isaac/Ishmael into the body of religious tradition, but at the same time recoil, as any ethically responsible religion must, from the celebration of Abraham's/Ibrahim's willingness to sacrifice the son at God's command.[1] Though all three religions are bound to the text in a paradoxical recoil-embrace, the double movement is most powerfully articulated in Judaism, where the story known as 'the binding' (the Akedah) is unravelled, even as it is bound to the very heart of what is meant by the Jewish understanding of religion (from *religare*, 'to be bound'). In a curiously bodied metaphor, Judah Goldin claims that Genesis 22 is 'central to the nervous systems of Christianity and Judaism',[2] and the metaphor of the nervous system (as opposed to, say, the heart) is intriguing, suggesting a text that lies at the centre of a capillary-network of interpretation and tradition, but also a text that makes us nervous and sets the nerves on edge. This article looks at how this vital text permeates the body of Jewish tradition, then looks at how midrash conscripts the human body—particularly the body of Isaac and the mother, Sarah—to dramatize the instinctive recoil from the text/test.

1. Good (Productive) Wounds, Or How the Bones of Whatever/Whoever is Sacrificed on Mt Moriah Form the Backbone of Jewish Liturgy and Life

> Thus says the Lord God to these bones: I will cause breath to enter you, and you shall live. I will lay sinews on you, and will cause flesh to come upon you, and cover you with skin and put breath on you, and you shall live. (Ezek. 37.5)

One of Marc Chagall's most striking Akedah paintings (Fig. 1) is simply, starkly, red, yellow and blue, as if to evoke something of the *primary* (or maybe *funda-*

---

1. For preliminary work on the three 'Abrahamic' religions, see my 'Binding-Unbinding: Divided Responses of Judaism, Christianity and Islam to the "Sacrifice" of Abraham's Beloved Son', *JAAR* 72.4 (forthcoming 2004).

2. Judah Goldin, 'Introduction' to Shalom Spiegel, *The Last Trial: On the Legends and Lore of the Command to Abraham to Offer Isaac as a Sacrifice* (Woodstock, VM: Jewish Lights, 1993 [1st edn Hebrew 1950, ET 1967]), pp. xi-xxx (xxi).

mental) importance of the story and to set up a tension between the tranquility of blueness and the red and yellow of blood and flame.

Figure 1. *Marc Chagall, 'Le sacrifice d'Isaac'*
(Musée Chagall, Nice. Copyright Réunion des Musees Nationaux, ADAGP, 1995)

Figure 2. *Marc Chagall, 'Le Songe de Jacob' (Note the mini-Akedah in the right hand corner)*
(Musée Chagall, Nice. Copyright Reunion des Musees Nationaux, AGADP, 1995)

Throughout Chagall's biblical sequences the Akedah keeps recurring, as in 'Jacob's Dream' (Fig. 2) where Abraham and Isaac crouch in the right hand corner (shadowing the cross of the crucifixion that floats above them), as if to say that this 'sacrifice' is the basis and predicate of so much that comes after both in the biblical corpus and in the body of Jewish interpretation.

A similar point seems to be made by the midrashic collection known as the *Pirke de Rabbi Eliezer* or *The Chapters of Rabbi Eliezer*, one of the more esoteric and magical of the midrashim that seems to be crying out for an edition illustrated by Chagall. The midrash is based around the rich, juicy metaphor of the ram's carcass and all the things that Jewish tradition has *made* from the ram's carcass:

> Rabbi Hanina ben Dosa said: From that ram, which was created at the twilight, nothing came forth that was useless. The ashes formed the foundation of the inner altar used for the expiatory offering on the Day of Atonement. The sinews of the ram were the strings of the harp on which David played. The ram's skin was the girdle around the loins of Elijah... The horn of the ram of the left side was the one which marked the revelation at Mount Sinai... The horn of the right side, which is larger than that of the left, is destined in the future to be sounded in the world that is to come and at the ingathering of the exiles, as it is said 'And it shall come to pass in that day, that a great trumpet shall be blown' (Isa. 37.13) and it is said 'And the Lord shall be king over all the earth' (Zech. 14.9).[3]

The metaphor is attributed to Rabbi Hanina ben Dosa, a first-century Rabbi who, in the gallery of rabbinic caricatures, is known chiefly for being poor.[4] With the air of one who knows what he is talking about, Hanina ben Dosa compares the resource-fulness of midrash to the pragmatism of the peasant family, as they pick every piece of meat from the bone, then use the sinew, skin and horns for shoes and clothes, and boil up the bones for soup. The passage reminds me of a similar saying in the mediaeval midrashic collection, the *Seder Eliyahu Zuta*, where the Holy One is described as giving Torah to Israel in the form of 'wheat for us to make flour from it, and flax for us to make a garment from it':[5] both proclaim Torah as raw material, provocative in its rawness, and both proclaim the utilitarian nature of interpretation as putting the text to work in as many ways as you possibly (and impossibly) can. But whereas the *Seder Eliyahu Zuta* passage is about making Torah into food and clothing *for* the body—about creating life for the body—the *Pirke de Rabbi Eliezer* passage is about making life *from* the body and describes the productive synergy *between life and death*. The Jewish appropriation of the ram-carcass is not unlike the Christian appropriation of the body of the God-lamb in the eucharist, since both proclaim the power of sacrifice: the reason that these particular bones, ash, sinews, horns are so productive, implies the midrash, is because someone, in obedience to

---

3.   *Pirke de Rabbi Eliezer* (trans. G. Friedlander; New York: Sepher-Hermon Press, 4th edn 1981), pp. 229-30. I have simplified and glossed the text in places, partly taking my cue from Louis Ginzberg, *The Legends of the Jews* (Philadelphia: Jewish Publication Society of America, 1937), pp. 282-83.

4.   According to legend, Hanina ben Dosa was so poor that his wife did not have flour to bake Sabbath loaves, so in order to avoid embarrassment she put burning wood in the stove so that smoke would appear. For this and other stories of Hanina ben Dosa's legendary poverty, see *b. Ta'an.* 24-25.

5.   *Seder Eliyahu Zuta* 2 cited by B.W. Holz (ed.), *Back to the Sources: Reading the Classic Jewish Texts* (New York: Simon & Schuster, 1992), p. 29. I discuss this text in more detail in *A Biblical Text and Its Afterlives: The Survival of Jonah in Western Culture* (Cambridge: Cambridge University Press, 2000), p. 1.

God, offered up the gift of death. It is this gift that sets Genesis 22 apart as more than just any piece of Torah-flour or Torah-flax for Jewish interpreters to cook and spin with, and that marks it as a special piece of Torah—an existential event.

Because it has been sacrificed, the body of the ram lives again, and lives irrepressibly, like the dry bones of Ezek. 37.4-10. So important is it, that the carcass is presented as providing crucial bits and pieces of the Bible (David's harp, Elijah's girdle, the ashes of the temple altar), as if to say that this piece of text from Genesis/ *Bereshit*/the Beginning forms the substance of so many of the pages and stories that follow that it is as if the horn, skin, and sinews become the very woodpulp, papyrus or vellum of Torah. The process by which the ram's body supplies parts of Samuel, Exodus and the Prophets seems to be a special case of the general midrashic practice of the grafting of one text onto another: the process is, as Daniel Boyarin observes, generally 'disruptive and regenerative',[6] but this special case takes us beyond common tropes of textual 'afterlives' or textual 'reanimation' and describes nothing less than *textual resurrection*, making new life from death. In fact, this meta-midrash perfectly conjures up the way in which the Akedah is actually put to work in midrash and Jewish liturgy as *that which has the power to make life from death*.

Because the Torah is rather more full than anyone would like of cataclysmic scenes of death, defeat and rejection, one of the main functions of midrash is to convert catastrophe into promise and to turn textual base metal into gold. The Akedah is perceived as the philosopher's stone that makes this alchemy possible, and is constantly shuffled around the canon as the predicate of all good stories and the antidote to all bad. According to the testimony of midrash, the Akedah is the reason why Balaam's curse was converted to blessing and the reason why the destroying angel and the pestilence in 1 Chron. 21.15 were turned aside.[7] According to the third century *Mekilta de Rabbi Ishmael*, when God passed over the Israelite firstborn because he 'saw the blood' (Exod. 12.13), the blood that he saw was the blood of the paschal lamb mingling with 'the blood of the binding of Isaac';[8] while according to the *Mekilta de Rabbi Simeon ben Yohai*, God commissioned Moses saying 'I can be trusted to pay out the reward of Isaac son of Abraham, who gave a quarter of his blood upon the altar'.[9] Historically, the Akedah was originally associated with Passover and was only later moved to Rosh Hashanah. In midrash, scenes from Mt Moriah are interlaced with scenes from the Exodus: the waters of the Red Sea part because God sees Abraham-with-knife-raised-over-his-son standing behind Moses-with-staff-raised-over-the-waters; God cleaves the sea for Moses and the Israelites because Abraham cleaved the wood for

---

6.   Daniel Boyarin, *Intertextuality and the Reading of Midrash* (Bloomington: Indiana University Press, 1990), p. 25.

7.   *Midrash Aggadah Vayera* 51; *Mek.* Pisha 57 and 88. In each case the link hinges on a single narrative echo: Abraham's 'saddling' combats Balaam's 'saddling' and the Genesis angel's 'Do not raise your hand against the boy' (Gen. 22.12) is concealed in the Chronicler's angel's 'Enough! Stay your hand' (1 Chron. 21.15).

8.   *Mek.* Pisha 7.

9.   *Mek. SbY. Vayera* on Exod. 6.2 and 4.13.

the offering; and Mt Sinai is said to have been broken off from Mt Moriah as a piece of dough is broken off from the batch.[10]

Just as the Akedah functions as the predicate and background of Israel's greatest story of salvation, so, conversely, it becomes the antidote to Israel's greatest disaster. *Lamentations Rabbah* reports how Abraham and Isaac were transported to the carcass of the ruined temple in order to plead with God to have mercy on '[their] children' and to lead a whole host of biblical characters in dissuading the Torah and its letters from joining the case for the prosecution, one by one.[11] The transportation of the Akedah altar to the site of the ruined temple is a very physical image of Akedah-portability, while the drama of Abraham and Isaac repulsing bad Torah letters clearly demonstrates how father and son are used as a crack team to combat pestilence, curses, bad letters, Babylonians, death, violence—and with them all the associated problems of theodicy—wherever they occur. It is as if, though the Rabbis have the ingenuity, Abraham and Isaac are needed to provide the *justification* for textual manipulation because through their submission they have earned the right to put physical pressure on God and the letters of God. Through this textual manipulation, the Akedah becomes a text of comfort that anticipates all future national crises and releases a thicket of reassurances from God. The Akedah is the reason why the God of *Leviticus Rabbah* can say: '[As the ram was tangled in the thicket] in a similar way are your children destined to be caught by the nations and entangled by troubles, being dragged from empire to empire, from Babylon to Media, from Media to Greece, and from Greece to Edom [Rome], but they will ultimately be redeemed through the horns of the ram'.[12]

Redemption through the horns of the ram leads us to the key thing that Jewish tradition makes from the ram's carcass—the shofar, itself a visual image of Rosh Hashanah. Though technically a shofar can be any horn, according to Saadia Gaon a ram's horn is preferable since its purpose is 'to remind us of Isaac who offered his life to Heaven' and to exhort us to 'also offer our lives to Heaven'.[13] The twofold purpose of the shofar is to trigger Jewish memory and exhort Jews to metaphorical sacrifice, *and* to trigger God's memory and release the benefits of the sacrifice, which is why the Holy One in the Talmud commands 'Blow the shofar before me so that I may remember for your benefit the binding of Isaac, son of Abraham, and *account it to you as if you yourselves had been bound*'.[14] The dominant message of the shofar and the Rosh Hashanah liturgy is one of reciprocal love, obligation and reassurance: the binding in some way pulled taut the cords of the covenant; because

10.   *Yal.* 98; *Midr. Teh.* 68, 17.

11.   *Lam. R.* Petiha 24. I am indebted to Tod Linafelt's translation and discussion in *Surviving Lamentations: Catastrophe, Lament and Protest in the Afterlife of a Biblical Book* (Chicago: Chicago University Press, 2000), pp. 100-16, and to Alan Mintz's discussion in *Hurban: Responses to Catastrophe in Hebrew Literature* (Syracuse: Syracue University Press, 2nd edn 1996), pp. 49-83.

12.   *Lev. R.* 29 on Gen. 22.13 and 23.14.

13.   Saadia Gaon (882–942), 'Reasons for Sounding the Shofar', in P. Goodman (ed.), *The Rosh Hashanah Anthology* (Philadelphia: Jewish Publication Society of America, 1992), pp. 38-40 (39).

14.   *b. Ros. Has.* 16a (my italics).

Abraham bound his son, God is bound (in every sense of the English word) to redeem his people, or, as Nahum Sarna puts it, Abraham's and Isaac's obedience created an 'inexhaustible store of spiritual credit on which future generations could draw'.[15] The sacrifice of Isaac is woven into Rosh Hashanah's three key liturgical themes: God's kingship (*Malkhuyot*), God's remembrance (*Zikhronot*) and God's revelation (*Shofarot*). Mediaeval Machzorim (festival liturgies) depict Isaac bowed on the altar in the shadow of the final ך of מלך ('king') and demonstrating the paradoxically liberating submission to God that is at the heart of Jewish tradition (Fig. 3),[16]

Figure 3. *The sacrifice taking place beneath the canopy of the final* ך *of* מלך *('king')*
(Klm. Ms. Reggio 1, folio 159v. Machzor, Germany, first half of fourteenth century.
Copyright Bodleian Library, Oxford)

or show Isaac and the ram on the altar flanked by Abraham and the angel above (and imitating the shapes of) the word *Zikhrenu* ('Remember us') from the famous Rosh Hashanah prayer, *Zikhrenu leḥayyim*, 'Remember us into life, O King, who delights in life, and inscribe us in the book of life' (Fig. 4 [next page]). Midrashically, the power of the Akedah is proclaimed through miraculous effects on the body, both God's body and our bodies: because of this, reports of Israel's sin will go in one of God's ears and out the other like a breath of air through the shofar, and the body of Israel will be sustained by food/sustenance (אכלות, *akhilot*) because of the Akedah knife (מאכלת, *ma'akhelet*)[17]—yet another intimation that it is the presence of the *knife* that makes this text so much richer than the average piece of Torah flour or flax. Ultimately the gift of Isaac's body becomes the prooftext for the resurrection of the whole body: according to one tradition, Isaac on the altar discovers the truth of resurrection and recites the second benediction of the *Amidah/*

15. Nahum Sarna (ed.), *Torah Commentary: Genesis* (Philadelphia: Jewish Publication Society of America, 1989), p. 354.

16. Compare the traditional Jewish reading of the Exodus, where the Israelites are liberated from slavery to Pharaoh into slavery to God.

17. *Gen. R.* 56.3; *Midrash haGadol* 352; *Lam. R.* (Proem).

Shemoneh esreh concerning the *loosening of the bond* (of death). According to another tradition, Isaac is not just the first to experience resurrection but the inaugurator of all resurrection, since 'by the *merit* of Isaac who offered himself upon the altar, the Holy One Blessed be He will in future resurrect the dead'.[18]

Figure 4. *The word* זכרינו *('remember us'), with the Akedah above,
and imitating the shape of, the Hebrew letters. The angel stands on the left,
Abraham on the right, Isaac prone on the altar, with the ram above.
(Machzor, Germany, fourteenth century. Ms. Parma 3518 fol. 25v
Courtesy of Biblioteca Palatina, Parma)*

It is really not so surprising that a biblical text that ends with such a burst of star-sons, such a promise of more life (Gen. 22.17) should have become, for post-biblical Judaism (as for Christianity), a prooftext for the resurrection—more life in the most superlative, spiritualized, sense. But despite the bold assertions of post-Enlightenment Jewish apologists, who are far more happy with the idea of offering God the 'cows of our lips' (Hos. 14.2) than with offering him real cows, let alone real sons, it is clear that, in Jewish *tradition*, the Akedah *does not mean life because Isaac is spared.*[19] In a clear trajectory that could not be further from that peculiarly

18. *PRE* 31; *Pes. K.* Piska 32, 200a.
19. Clutching at apologetic straws borrowed from Christian commentators, Julius Greenstone affirms that the Akedah was 'one of the great moral contributions made to mankind by the Jewish conceptions of God, at the time when idolatry, even in the most advanced countries of antiquity, still exacted its toll of human sacrifices', while Judah Goldin proclaims that 'nothing could be more repugnant to the God of Israel than human sacrifice' (*Jewish Feasts and Fasts* [Philadelphia: Jewish Publication Society of America, 1945], pp. 14-16; Judah Goldin, in Spiegel, *The Last Trial*,

stretched piece of modern apologetic which claims that Genesis 22 functions as a piece of anti-child sacrifice polemic, traditional Judaism affirms that the text is so productive precisely because a body was offered and *perhaps even taken, or part taken, by God*. Curiously, the Rosh Hashanah liturgy proclaims that God 'deals with his children in accordance to the attribute of Mercy' when he sees, 'heaped on top of the altar', the *'ashes of Father Isaac'*[20]—a clear indication that the alchemical life-making power of this very special text is all bound up with a very special, liminal substance known as *Isaac's ash* or alternatively *Isaac's blood*.

2. *Wonder-Working Ash and Blood*

> But cinders remain: and there is no cinder without fire, without memory of what was sacrificed...[21]

> Why cinders there? The place of burning, but of what, of whom?[22]

Our midrash from the *Pirke de Rabbi Eliezer* makes it clear that this text is so productive because it leaves us with a corpse/carcass—the only question is to what or whom does it belong? If we confine ourselves to the biblical frame of reference the answer is obvious, but in Jewish tradition it becomes more complicated; indeed, we have already seen how at least one of the images that we have looked at complicates the issue by putting Isaac and the ram together on the altar (see Fig. 4). Midrash also conflates Isaac and the ram who, according to tradition, was also called Isaac,[23] and the result of this deliberate confusion is that the midrashic 'Slaughtered Ram', like Rembrandt's 'Slaughtered Ox', begins to show considerable resemblance to the body of a man (Fig. 5 [next page]). Indeed the special, liminal life-form is sacrificed on Mt Moriah bears some striking resemblances to the man-lamb Jesus: not only are they both *adult* men who give themselves as a self-offering but, as if to drive home the analogy, Jewish Isaacs are prone to say things like 'Let a quarter of my blood be a redemption for my people Israel', or to take the woodpile on their shoulder 'like one who carries a cross'.[24] As Jon Levenson has argued (in an important book that deserves far more attention than it has

---

p. xvii). Nor is this recoil from sacrifice simply a post-Enlightenment, and particularly post-Holocaust phenomenon: compare the protests of Josephus who was at pains to maintain that 'God has no craving for human blood' (*Ant.* 1.233).

20. 'Traditional supplication for the one who sounds the shofar', Heidenheim (ed.), *Vienna Machzor* (1827), cited by Spiegel, *The Last Trial*, p. 38; *Tanh. Vayikra* 23; *Sifra* and *Lev. R.* on Lev. 26.42. Cf. *Ta'an* 2.1 and *b. Ber.* 62b, where ashes are placed on the head as a 'reminder of the ashes of Isaac'.

21. Jacques Derrida, *Cinders* (trans. and ed. Ned Lukacher; Lincoln: University of Nebraska Press, 1991), p. 37.

22. Derrida, *Cinders*, p. 37.

23. *Midrash haGadol* on Gen. 22.13, p. 356; 'Midrash Composed Under the Holy Spirit' in Jacob Mann, *The Bible as Read and Preached in the Old Synagogue* (Cincinnati: published by the author, 1940), p. 67.

24. The Isaac who sheds a quarter of his blood comes from *Midrash haGadol* 353. Cross-carrying Isaac can be found in *Gen. R.* 56.3; *Pes. R.* 31, 143b, and *Midrash Sekhel Tov* 61.

received to date), both Judaism and Christianity have incorporated the 'ancient, protean, strangely resilient story'[25] of the 'death and resurrection of the beloved son' deep into the bodies of tradition: both proclaim, in their own idioms, that 'there can be no expiation without the shedding of blood [or ash]' (*b. Yom.* 5a) and both affirm the power of death-defeating, curse-reversing, wonder-working blood. While not quite unique in the same sense as the blood of Jesus, Isaac's blood is clearly no humdrum A, O, B, rhesus negative, or rhesus positive, and certainly comes close to that particular theological blood group that we could call S for salvific, P for Propitiatory, M for meritorious, or maybe A* for Atoning.

Figure 5. *Rembrandt, 'Slaughtered Ox'*
(Copyright Glasgow Museums, reproduced with permission)

Because the blood/ash/merit is so precious, midrash underscores its preciousness by presenting Abraham and Isaac as muscular athletes of the spirit, doing whatever a man has to do to get the precious vial of blood/ash/merit down from Mt Moriah. As Brian Hook and R. Reno have argued, the biblical text presents us with an idea of obedience that 'involves giving up our very selves' even to the point of allowing ourselves to be 'absorbed or annihilated'; it does not and cannot present Abraham

25.   Jon D. Levenson, *The Death and Resurrection of the Beloved Son: The Transformation of Child Sacrifice in Judaism and Christianity* (New Haven: Yale University Press, 1993), p. 232.

and Isaac as heroes, for this a story about giving up all personal significance, pos-
terity and life.[26] The biblical Abraham and Isaac are not heroes, but religion needs
heroes and a tradition that goes at least as far back as the book of *Jubilees* responds
to this need by presenting the Akedah as the last and most climatic of hero-
Abraham's 'ten trials'. Having left his homeland and endured (among other things)
famine, the taking of Sarah, the battle with the three kings, the expulsion of Hagar
and Ishmael and the roaring pain of circumcision, the Akedah comes as the final
bout in the ring for Father Abraham, the final test of the father's mettle as he passes
through the furnace of the trial. This time is the knife-edge, crisis time—the moment
on which everything is balanced—so much so that just before the trial commences
the Holy One approaches Abraham and says to him 'I have tried you with many
trials and you have passed them all successfully. Now I beg of you, for my sake
[and for Israel's sake] withstand also this trial, so that men will not say that all the
earlier ones were without true worth.'[27] This time is like the final (double or quits)
round in a game show when, depending on the result, what has gone before will
count for everything or count for nothing; this time his opponent is no less than
Satan (a.k.a. Prince Mastema, Sammael or the Wicked Angel) who knows that the
sacrifice is to become the lifeblood and maybe even the *raison d'être* of the Jewish
people and so does everything he can to prevent the successful completion of the
crucial test that is Moriah. Numerous midrashim report, for example, how Satan
blocked the path up Mt Moriah; how he made himself into a river and almost
drowned Abraham; how he attempted to throw stones at the Isaac-lamb to damage
his perfect sacrificial body; and how, at the crucial moment, he tried to knock the
knife out of the patriarch's hand.[28] The large part given to Satan—usually nothing
more than a bit player in Jewish theology—is clearly a corollary of the test's vital
importance: his role is to play the fairytale opponent who highlights by contrast the
absolute value of the princess/the treasure/the blessing, while Abraham's role is to
ensure that 'Prince Mastema [Satan] was shamed' (*Jub.* 181.12).

To overcome all the forces of darkness, sin and death that encroach on Israel and
humanity, Abraham must be of one mind: he must, as Philo puts it, 'be mastered by
his love for God and mightily overcome all the fascination expressed in the fond
terms of family affection',[29] and midrash uses all kinds of narrative hyperbole to
show how perfectly, and extremely, this is the case. In *Genesis Rabbah*, Abraham's
response to the command 'Take your only son…and burn him as a holocaust' is an
expression of anxiety about his lack of training as a priest or shochet (will the
sacrifice not therefore be invalid?);[30] and hero-Abraham cunningly conceals his son
from Satan in a bush (or thicket?) to stop Satan damaging his perfect flesh.[31] Both

26. See Brian S. Hook and R.R. Reno, 'Abraham and the Problems of Modern Heroism', in
Leonard J. Greenspoon and Bryan F. LeBeau (eds.), *Sacred Text, Secular Times* (Studies in Jewish
Civilization, 10; Omaha, NA: Creighton University Press, 2000), pp. 135-61 (136, 142).
27. *b. Sanh.* 89b
28. *Midrash Aggadah Vayera*, 51; *Tanh. Vayera* 81.
29. Philo, *On Abraham* 170 (following F.H. Coulson's LCL translation).
30. *Gen. R.* 55.7
31. *Gen. R.* 56.5.

Genesis Rabbah and *Ecclesiastes Rabbah* describe how Abraham is so resolutely committed to sacrifice that when the angel says 'Do not do anything to the lad', he begs 'Then may I strangle him; may I burn him; may I cut him up in pieces before you?', or pleads 'Let me bruise him, let me extract some blood from him, let me remove from him one drop of blood', so that the angel has to say again 'Don't do anything (מאומה, *meumah*) to him; don't you bruise (מום, *mum*) him'.[32] The Abraham who must be told to desist twice develops partly from the *double* biblical command 'Do not lay your hand upon the lad, *nor* do anything to him' (Gen. 22.12; for according to midrashic logic, the angel cannot simply be talking this way for banal stylistic reasons or because he has taken elementary courses in Hebrew parallelism), but also develops in response to the need to inflate Abraham's heroism and so magnify his right and power to intercede on Israel's behalf. It is only from his exalted place at the very pinnacle of absolute submission *in extremis* that Abraham can say to God 'May it be Your will...that your compassion suppress your anger, just as I suppressed my compassion'[33] or audaciously argue, using the midrashic principle of *qal vehomer* (from the smaller case to the larger, or from the human case to the divine), 'When Isaac's children therefore are on trial before you, even as I held my peace and made no retort to you, so you make no retort to them'.[34]

Isaac, too, has the power to intercede because he is no mere pawn, or ram, in the drama of the Fathers, but an enthusiastic martyr who simply longs to convert himself into the blood/ash/potential blessing that God requires. We have already witnessed Isaac crying, by way of prologue to Genesis 22, 'O that God would appear to me and cut off my limbs!'—a cry that makes him sound uncannily like the early Christian martyrs (compare, for example, Ignatius of Antioch's impassioned cry 'Let fire and the cross; let the crowds of wild beasts; let tearings, breakings and dislocations of bones; let cutting off members; let shatterings of the whole body...come upon me').[35] Generally speaking, Judaism tends not to give martyrdom the full-blooded affirmation that it receives in early Christianity, but, as I plan to argue elsewhere, Jewish Isaac seems to develop into a safely iconic Jewish martyr, enclosed within the realm of the past and the biblical text. The Isaac of *Genesis Rabbah* who longs to cut off his limbs is joined by the Isaac of *Pesikta Rabbati* who 'rejoices to have his throat cut';[36] Josephus's Isaac who 'rushes to the altar and his doom';[37] and the Isaacs of the Targums who exhort their fathers 'Bind me properly, lest I start suddenly, and there will be a blemish in your offering'.[38]

32. *Qoh. R.*; *Gen. R.* 56.7

33. *Gen. R.* 56.10

34. *Bereshit Rabbati*, cited and translated by Spiegel, *The Last Trial*, p. 94.

35. Ignatius of Antioch, *Epistle to the Romans* in Alexander Roberts and J. Davidson (eds.), *The Anti-Nicene Fathers: Translations of the Writings of the Fathers Down to AD 325* (10 vols.; Buffalo, NY: The Christian Literature Publishing Company, 1885–96), V, pp. xx.

36. *Pes. R.* 40.

37. Josephus, *Ant.* 1.232.

38. *Targum Jonathan* and *Targum Yerushalmi* on Gen. 22.9.

Figure 6. *Howard Lerner, 'Binding of Isaac' (oil and charcoal, 1992)*
(Congregation Adas Israel Synagogue, Permanent Art Collection, donated by the artist.
With personal thanks to Howard Lerner)

Strange things happen to the body of Isaac in Jewish tradition: 'his soul leaves him...when his father's knife hits his neck...but then the Holy One restores him with the dew of resurrection';[39] his body is burnt to ash and lays piled on the altar;[40] his throat is cut by his father, he is resurrected and his throat is cut a second time;[41] his soul flees when the blade touches his neck, but when he hears the voice of the angel his soul returns to his body;[42] he leaves a quarter [a *log*] of his blood upon the altar[43]—a *log* being all the blood a person has[44] but also just a quarter, as if he were somehow able to give one quarter of his life and keep three quarters back. (A *log* is also the amount of blood required for a ritually valid *shehitah*, reinforcing the sense that Isaac is the human animal being ritually sacrificed). Alongside the image of Isaac's ash, Jewish tradition enshrines the image of Isaac's scar or Isaac's wound and affirms that life comes from the wound: as Howard Lerner's contemporary painting of the Akedah (Fig. 6) suggests, a tree/a text/a nation grows from the hole

39. *Midrash Ha-Hafetz* 166.

40. 'Traditional supplication for the one who sounds the shofar', *Vienna Machzor* (1827); *b. Ta'an.* 2.1; *b. Ber.* 62b; *Lev. R.* 36.5; *Gen. R.* 94.5, and Rashi on Gen. 22.14, 'On the Mount of the Lord will be seen Isaac's ashes in a heap set for atonement' (cited and translated by Spiegel, *The Last Trial*, p. 42).

41. *Midrash haGadol* 360.

42. *PRE* 31.

43. *Mek. SbY. Vayera; Tanh. Vayera.*

44. *b. Sot.* 5a

in the body of traditional Jewish Isaac, just as plants/life/salvation grows from the mediaeval Jesus' stigmata.

The power of the wound is the power to testify to what Maimonides calls '*the extreme limits* of the love and fear of God',[45] the love that turns you inside out and goes deep beneath the skin. Indeed, so crucial is Isaac's scar to Jewish tradition that *Genesis Rabbah* presents Isaac and Ishmael competing fiercely over who bears the deepest love-scar and who is therefore entitled to receive the richest gush of blessing:

> Isaac and Ishmael were engaged in a controversy: the latter argued, 'I am more beloved than you, because I was circumcised at the age of thirteen' while the other retorted 'I am more beloved than you because I was circumcised at eight days'. Ishmael said to him: 'I am more beloved because I could have protested, and yet I did not'. At that moment Isaac exclaimed 'O that God would appear to me and bid me cut off my limbs! then I would not refuse'. God said, 'Even if I bid you to sacrifice yourself, you will not refuse'.

> Another version: Ishmael said to him: 'I am more beloved than you, since I was circumcised at the age of thirteen, but you were circumcised as a baby and could not refuse'. Isaac retorted: 'All that you did was to lend to the Holy One, Blessed be He, three drops of blood. But I am now thirty-seven years old yet if God desired of me that I be slaughtered, I would not refuse.'[46]

The Akedah is interpreted as a *hypercircumcision* that trumps all previous acts of bloodshed—an interpretation that becomes somewhat clearer when we realize that rabbinic tradition sees the blood shed in circumcision as salvific and interprets circumcision as a 'covenant of blood'.[47] Indeed, the *Pirke de Rabbi Eliezer* attributes to the 'blood of the covenant of Abraham's circumcision' precisely the same kinds of properties as those ascribed to the Akedah blood (or ash): just like the ashes of the ram (Isaac) the blood of Abraham's circumcision became the foundation of the temple altar, and because Abraham was circumcised on the Day of Atonement, 'every year the Holy One, blessed be He, looks upon the blood of circumcision and forgives all our sins'.[48]

The obvious question, and one raised rather huffily by the mediaeval literalist Abraham Ibn Ezra,[49] is why does midrash perversely persist in claiming that Isaac was damaged when the text says, quite clearly, that he was spared? The reasons for Isaac's death or half-death are, I suggest, mainly (though not exclusively) *textual*.[50]

---

45. Moses Maimonides, *The Guide for the Perplexed* (trans. S. Piries; Chicago: University of Chicago Press, 1964), pp. 500-501.

46. *Gen. R.* 55.7.

47. See Lawrence A. Hoffman, *Covenant of Blood: Circumcision and Gender in Rabbinic Judaism* (Chicago: University of Chicago Press, 1996). On possible connections between circumcision and sacrifice, see also Howard Eilberg-Schwartz, *The Savage in Judaism* (Bloomington: Indiana University Press, 1990), p. 175.

48. *PRE* 29.

49. Ibn Ezra on Gen. 22.19, cited by Levenson, *The Death and Resurrection of the Beloved Son*, p. 196.

50. The reasons are also, to some degree contextual, in that they increase—*though do not*

They are an attempt to capture something of the biblical paradox whereby sacrifice is both suspended *and* rewarded, and to gloss the existential crisis of Isaac suspended on a knife-edge. According to the words of God's blessing in Gen. 22.16-18 (*'Because* you have done this, and have not withheld your son, your only son, I will indeed bless you'), sons scattered across the sky and seashore and the dissemination of blessing are attendant on Abraham giving (or 'not withholding') Isaac, and so the gift of sacrifice is given and accepted (in a sense). Pseudo-Philo expresses the paradox perfectly as the God of *Biblical Antiquities* recalls: 'And he brought him to be placed on the altar, *but I gave him back to his father*', and 'his offering was acceptable before me, and *on account of his blood I chose them*'.[51] Not only does Jewish tradition reinforce the biblical conundrum that, as R. Joshua puts it, 'though Isaac did not die, scripture regards him as though he did so',[52] but it goes on finding ingenious ways of visually reproducing the paradox in stark images of a beloved son suffering partial, virtual or momentary death. The paradox is reproduced *spatially*, in graphic images of Isaac's *wounded* body (a wound being a mini-death or death in a part of the body) and in the partial letting of the blood, which is the life of the body, and it is written *temporally* in the body that dies for that smallest conceivable sliver of time and that is almost simultaneously resurrected.

This sense of pervasive liminality leads us back to the meta-midrash from the *Pirke de Rabbi Eliezer* with which we started, and in which the carcass/corpse is linked to those provocatively liminal 'substances'—twilight and ash. In rabbinic tradition the 'twilight' is shorthand for the eve of the first shabbat and those very last, liminal things that God created just before he rested: the inventory of these special biblical 'things' traditionally includes the mouth of the earth that swallowed the sons of Korah (Num. 16.32); the mouth of the well that provided the Israelites with water in the desert (Num. 21.16-18); the mouth of Balaam's (miraculously speaking) ass; the rainbow; the manna; writing and the writing instrument; Jonah's fish; Moses' grave (the location of which only God knows); and Abraham's ram. What the twilight 'things' seem to have in common is that they represent an opening out (or mouth) between the natural and the supernatural, either as a hollowing out of presence or the miracle of something bursting out of nothing (water and manna in the desert; Jonah kept alive in the womb/tomb of the fish; the ram that delivers Isaac from death). They also share a certain non-permanence, a flimsiness in the solid world of being—you cannot keep manna for more than a day, a rainbow fades, no-one knows where to find Moses' grave, writing is always precarious— and they share this flimsiness with ashes, those curiously intangible (non)substances.

---

begin—in the mediaeval period and reflect the Ashkenazi experience of martyrdom during the Christian Crusades.

51. Philo, *Bib. Ant.* 18.5.

52. *Gen. R.* 55.5; cf. Maimonides, *More Nebuchim* 3.24. Compare also David Kimhi: 'Although ▸ the thing was not accomplished and Isaac was not slain, before God the willingness was reckoned as equal to the deed'.

Like the image of part-dead or wounded Isaac or momentarily-dead Isaac, cinders flicker between presence and absence and occupy the impossible place between life and death. As Jacques Derrida reflects, ashes or cinders testify to a cremation that has already taken place (something/someone must have been burnt for there to be cinders) but they are also 'what remains from what is not',[53] a testimony to a certain ineradicability of being, and also intimate the possibility of a rekindling or a resurrection, the 'incubation of…fire lurking beneath the dust'.[54] Jewish midrash and liturgy exploit this liminality in the way in which they stage and interpret Genesis 22: the ram's carcass midrash situates the text somewhere between the solid world of current Jewish practice (study, shofars, liturgy), and the more distant worlds of biblical memory (Moriah/altars) and personal and communal eschatology, while the liturgy places it precisely in the *twilight* (the temporal equivalent of 'cinders') between the old year and the new. And the overriding message of Rosh Hashanah is one of liminality and transition: the congregation tread the precarious path between sin and redemption, death and life, in an attitude of *teshuvah* (turning/repentance); the shofar blast communicates impotence, fear, danger and trembling (the blast of the ram's horn quivers and a ram's horn by its very nature defies complex orchestration and delight in human skill[55]) and all of this ties in with this text—or existential test—and the image of Isaac lying (dying?) on the altar. Indeed it seems to me that the power of this text or test is bound up with its power to communicate something of the precariousness of mortality—the sense of human being as being located on a knife-edge—and that this sense of inbetweeness contributes to the text's appeal. In his study of Psalm 23, playfully titled 'The Triumph of the Lamb', Hugh Pyper argues that the most well-used biblical texts, the ones that Jews and Christians tend to make most (out) of, are those that straddle fear and promise and enact the 'anxiety of survival'.[56] Perhaps in a similar vein we could argue that our *Pirke de Rabbi Eliezer* midrash (that we could, perhaps, playfully call 'The Triumph of the Dead Lamb') makes it clear that this text matters so much because it articulates the absolute jeopardy of life/matter and the redemption of matter—in fact the creative explosion of matter—and because it somehow keeps us in suspense and in suspension between dry bones, skin, sinews, ash and the promise of the regeneration of flesh.

Rather than resolving the tension, Jewish midrash and liturgy work hard to *maintain* this sense of suspension by using the motifs of a part-dead (scarred) Isaac or a momentarily soul-vacated Isaac; by writing about 'blood' and 'ash' in such a way that they may or may not be in scare quotes; or by intimating that the Isaac who is sacrificed is a human being and also (just) a ram. Rather than negating sacrifice and inviting us to relax in an affirmation of resurrection, or claiming, like

53. Derrida, *Cinders*, p. 39.
54. Derrida, *Cinders*, p. 59.
55. For a discussion of the multiple resonances of the shofar, see Goodman, 'The Shofar', pp. 113-18.
56. Hugh S. Pyper, 'The Triumph of the Lamb: Psalm 23, Darwin and Textual Fitness' (unpublished paper presented at the Reading, Theory and Bible section of the Society of Biblical Literature Annual Meeting, Orlando, 21-24 November 1998).

modern commentators, that this text signals the cessation of sacrifice, they instead exploit the rich ambiguities of sacrifice and acknowledge the text's indebtedness to sacrifice (just as we do when, unthinkingly, we refer to the story of the sacrifice of Isaac rather than the *near* sacrifice of Isaac). Problems arise, however, when this sense of pervasive liminality is allowed to seep into the realm of ethics because the only logical ethical deduction from the fact that the sacrifice does and does not happen is that *it should and should not happen*. Engaging with the ethical implications of Isaac's wounds and Isaac's ash leads midrash to say both that these are good, in fact absolutely *vital*, wounds but also that they are prone to turn ethically messy and s(c)eptic, as soon as you look at them closely enough.

3. Bad (Festering) Wounds, or the Counter-Testimony of Isaac's Foot, Sarah's Coffin and Isaac's Scar

Because your language does not follow one thread, one course, we are in luck.
—Luce Irigaray

But Isaac would not be human if he didn't put up some kind of resistance—after all, even Jesus, who has the very will of God in his veins, cries out 'Eloi Eloi lema sabachthani' and 'Take this cup away from me', as well as 'Not my will but yours be done' (Mk 14.36; 15.33). Similarly there are other modulations of the voice of Isaac than that which swoons in masochistic frenzy, and often masochistic frenzy and uncertainty collide in the same breath. *Pesikta Rabbati* expands Isaac's speech in the Targums to 'Father bind my hands and my feet, *for the instinct of life is so strong* that when I see the knife coming towards me, I may move convulsively and have you cut me in a place that will disqualify me as an offering';[57] *Midrash Tanhuma* goes further and has Isaac say 'Father bind my hands and my feet *so I will not kick you* and thus be desecrating the commandment of honouring the father, since the soul of a person is impudent/uncowable, not to be intimidated'.[58] The rebellious foot or the resurgent life instinct of Isaac constitute a viable narrative counterforce, a grist to the mill of Satan, even though they are carefully wrapped in the language of submission to the fathers and only happen in the 'what if' sphere of the subjunctive tense. It is only much later in secularized twentieth-century Akedot that Isaac actually gets down from the altar—for the time being his rebellion is couched in the desire to keep the Third Commandment but that the kick never (actually) happens is about as certain as the fact that the sacrifice never (actually) takes place.

The interesting thing about a kick or an irrepressible surge of *nephesh* is that it belongs to the involuntary reflex of the body—it is part of the neural and muscular system outside the control of the brain. Perhaps the kick is simply an accidental product of imagining how a sacrificial animal would react—a way of envisaging

---

57. *Pes. R.* 40.

58. *Tanh.* on Gen. 22.9; cf. *Midrash Bereshit Rabbati* 55, 90. For a discussion and translation of the Tanhuma passage see Yaakov Elbaum, 'From Sermon to Story: The Transformation of the Akedah', *Prooftexts* 6 (1986), pp. 97-116 (106).

how the instinct of self-preservation would, as it were, kick in—but, more probably, the kick is a way of raising the question of damage to the son and the justi-
fiability of damage to the son, mutedly, obliquely, so that the thing is said and yet
not quite said. By warning his father that he *may* kick him and expressing anxiety
that the instinct of self-preservation *may* spoil the act of sacrifice, Isaac does not
mount a midrashically validated mutiny so much as take up a position inside and
slightly outside the narrative of prescribed obedience unto death. 'Isaac's kick'
(kept as firmly in scare quotes as 'Isaac's blood') is a way of speaking silently, cor-
poreally against the violence of the fathers; it is a way of using the depths of the
body to inflict a counter-aggression on the text.

Midrash lashes out a little more overtly in curious retrospectives that ask what
happened to the body of the son at the end? A number of midrashim ostensibly deal
with the curious absence of Isaac in 22.19, where Abraham and his young men
seem to return Isaac-less to Beersheba, and seem deliberately to interpret the lacuna
as a textual wound that opens up the question of damage inflicted by the test/text.
Some midrashim speculate that Isaac is absent because he was spirited away, by the
angels, to the Garden of Eden, which seems to function here as a kind of intensive
care unit then convalescent home: 'And the angels bore him to Paradise, where he
tarried three years, to be healed from the wound inflicted on him by Abraham on
the occasion of the Akedah'.[59] Rather than healing the wound, they keep it open
(for three years) and salt it with questions, as if to make it clear that even when it is
finished (*tetelestai*), even when that precious spiritual credit has been stored up for
future generations, you can still see the marks of damage epitomized by Isaac's scar.

Instead of ameliorating the narrative or applying the salve of modern apologetic,
traditional Jewish interpreters *exacerbate* ethical pain and employ various strategies for exploring the ethical quagmire that is Moriah. One of the most surprising devices that they use is the voice of Satan, modulated in such a way that he
becomes, shockingly, a spokesman for 'humanity, compassion, and elementary
ethics'.[60] In a speech to 'old-man' Abraham, Satan suggests that he has gone senile,
'lost his wits' and then points out the rift between ethics and religion, murder and
sacrifice (as if he's somehow got his hands on a preview copy of Søren Kierkegaard's *Fear and Trembling*): 'Today God says sacrifice your son but tomorrow he
will say "You are a *murderer* and you are guilty" or "You will lose your son given
to you in old age, your soul will perish, you will be *judged*"'.[61] Skulking up to
Isaac he asks 'How many fasts did your mother fast and how many prayers did she
pray until you came to her? And yet this old man, gone mad in his old age, is about
to cut your throat', and then urges 'Do not listen to him, for he is a silly old man,
and let not your precious soul and beautiful figure be lost from the earth'.[62] This
compassionate therapist-Satan addresses Isaac as the 'helpless son of a helpless
mother' and the 'son of an unhappy mother'—reinforcing the connection between

---

59. See *Paaneah Raza, Yal.* and *Midrash haGadol* on Gen. 22.19.
60. Elbaum, 'From Sermon to Story', p. 109.
61. *Yal.* 98; *Gen. R.* 56.4.
62. *Gen. R.* 56.4.

son and mother on the grounds of helplessness in the face of the decisions of the fathers—and he empathizes with Sarah: 'Oh you poor old woman, your teeth will be set on edge on account of your son'.[63]

Appropriately enough the devil plays the role of devil's advocate: '[*L. advocatus diaboli*], one who advocates the wrong side, or injures a cause by his advocacy' (*Shorter Oxford English Dictionary*). As any good student of Aristotelian narrative knows, all plots need some kind of 'complication' or devilish counterplot to over-come, but here the counterplot becomes too eloquent and too compassionate to function purely as a straw man for the plot to exert itself against, and seems to function in its own right and indeed righteousness. To compound the moral confu-sion, Satan's roles multiply so that, for example, he becomes the opposer of the text *and* its initiator—for example in *Jubilees* where the trial of Abraham begins in precisely the same manner as the trial of Job, making Satan and not God the in-augurator of the text. Moreover, the opposing tactics attributed to Satan in some midrashim are attributed to the angels in others, where it is the *angels* who attempt to knock the knife out of Abraham's hand, who melt it with their tears, and who proclaim the text as 'abnormal/anomalous'.[64] As primary ownership of the text shifts between God and Satan and the demonic and the angelic blur, midrash man-ages, confusingly, to tell the Akedah as the supreme religious adventure story in the manner of conventional fairytale *and* to make the point that Abraham's 'quest' is in fact the antiquest, the biblical equivalent of finding the beloved princess and stick-ing a knife in her heart. It proclaims doubly that the Akedah is like a fairytale or adventure story, and that Judaism is founded on no fairytale and that there is some-thing rather dark about the Akedah.

Two major ethical stumbling blocks stand in the way of a simple heroic run up Mt Moriah to obtain the precious vial of ash/blood/merit: the fact Abraham and God do not live in a vacuum where the hero can deal directly with his God without inflicting damage on others in the process, and the fact this is not a narrative about martyrdom but about *martyrdom at one remove*. These objections are most power-fully expressed by the body of the mother which becomes, in effect, an extension of the son's body and a giant footnote to the wordless rebellion already 'expressed' by Isaac's foot. Genesis 23 begins with the death of Sarah and several Jewish inter-preters decide that this is a simple case of cause and effect. The very plausible thesis that a mother's response to the test would have been (in all likelihood) terminal *could* be dismissed as nothing more than an arbitrary consequence of midrashic technique—where sequence is usually interpreted causally—were it not for the numerous midrashim that seem so keen to explore how the text begins to darken when read under the shadow of Sarah's grave. There is a perverse tendency to encourage Isaac to conjure up the very solid presence of the mother at the moments

---

63. *Gen. R.* 56.4.

64. *Pes. R.* 40: *R. Berechiah* commented: 'The angels cry without (הצוח)'. This word can also be read *hisah* meaning 'an anomalous act'. The angels cried out, 'It is an anomaly on your part to have Isaac slaughtered...' Cf. *Pes. R.* 40: 'Where was the knife? Tears had fallen from the angels upon it and dissolved it'; and *Gen. R. Vayera* 56.7.

Figure 7. *Marc Chagall, 'Le Sacrifice d'Isaac' and 'Abraham pleurant Sarah'*
(Copyright Réunion des Musees Nationaux, ADAGP, 1995)

when her appearance will most cause the text to *suffer*: *Midrash Tanhuma* imagines Isaac warning his knife-wielding father not to 'tell my mother when she is standing by a pit or when she is on the roof because she will fall and die',[65] and *Midrash Bereshit Rabbati* scripts him instructing the father to 'gather the ashes' and put

65.   *Tanh. Vayera* 81.

them in a casket in my mother's chamber so that 'at all hours, whenever she enters her chamber, she will remember her son Isaac and weep'.[66] When the Abraham of *Genesis Rabbah* tells Isaac 'You are the lamb', Isaac tears his hair and asks: 'Is this what you have told my mother?'[67] as if to drive home the point that this is not a plot that you can take home and show your mum (or indeed anybody's mum). It's as if the Rabbis were asking us to imagine Chagall's Akedah (where Sarah looks on anxiously in the background from her place among those other minor players, the ram and the 'thicket') set directly up against Chagall's painting of Abraham mourning Sarah (Fig. 7)—as if to drive home the point that the Akedah leaves us with two dead bodies: 'Isaac's body', which may or may not be human, and the body of Sarah. It is hard not to be struck by the corporeality of these midrashic images—the way in which they draw on the silent rebellion of the body, as the mother falls from a roof or into a pit and breaks her body, or sheds tears over the ashes of her son's body, or as Isaac responds to Abraham's sacrifice—which is of course in a different and more crucial sense the sacrifice of Isaac (as object not as subject)—by tearing out his hair. So deeply, it seems, is Sarah's 'soul bound to [Isaac's] soul'[68] by an umbilical cord of empathy that the damage done to Isaac's body, the momentary death or the partial-death from which he must go to the Eden-hospital to recover, becomes for her actual whole-body death (without a coda of resurrection).

Figure 8: *Sarah's gravestone, as imagined by the Rabbis, in the manner of Phyllis Trible's* Texts of Terror

Let's be clear: the Rabbis are not exactly setting up Sarah's gravestone as proto-feminist gesture, as Phyllis Trible sets up Hagar's or Jepthah's daughter's gravestone in *Texts of Terror* (Fig. 8), nor are they using Sarah's body as a way of saying

66. *Midrash Ber. R.*55, 90.
67. *Gen. R.* 56.4.
68. Ginzberg, *The Legends of the Jews*, pp. 274-75.

'Mothers will let sacrifices like this happen over their dead bodies', as if they were a bunch of female peace protestors holding banners at the foot of Mt Moriah. Rather, they are using Sarah's body as a useful midrashic tool that, precisely because it is outside the crucial text, can be used to say—*at a distance*—absolutely anything that needs to be said. Just as you can say anything through the mouth of Satan, so you can do anything with the body or voice of the mother, because placing ethical reservations in the mouths of devils and women is a way of saying something and not saying it, for when the demonic/the female accuses the text of unnaturalness, the accusation is made and retracted in the same breath. The alliance between devils and women is not new: what is strange here is the credence and power given to their voices/bodies as they become vehicles for asserting the primary Jewish principle of the sanctity of life over and against all that threatens it.

The fact that the Rabbis make so much of Sarah even though they are not under any compulsion to operate a textual quota system or equal opportunities policy (in which women have an equal right to participate in the Bible, as they have an equal right to drive trains or give lectures or sermons), adds force to a contemporary feminist critique. It confirms that it has always been impossible to think the Akedah without sparing some, and often several, thoughts for the mother, and at the same time challenges any condescending ghetto-ization/periodization of thinking in which we imagine that 'feminist' or 'ideological' post-Enlightenment critics were the first to feel discomfort with this most excruciatingly difficult test/text. In fact, it seems that, both midrashically and liturgically, Jewish tradition channels its critique of the Akedah largely through the body of the mother, not least in the Torah and haftarah readings for Rosh Hashanah. Here, just as in the midrash, Genesis 22 is effectively swaddled/stifled by a compendium of stories about mothers weeping for/longing for/grieving over their children—Hagar, Hannah and Rachel refusing to be comforted for her children 'because they are not' (literally כי אננו *ki ennunu*, 'because or as if he or *we* were not') and even the God-mother speaking of her son Ephraim, 'Is Ephraim my dear son? Is he my darling child? For as often as I speak against him, I do remember him still' (Jer. 31.20).

These very contemporary, corporeal responses to the Akedah read for all the world as if they were written by post-second wave Jewish feminists such as Rachel Adler or Miriam Peskowitz or a group of Jewish feminists working on liturgical reform. It is as if they were written deliberately to expose the limits of second-wave feminist readings based on equality (for example Phyllis Trible's 'The Sacrifice of Sarah'[69] where she argues that Sarah should have equal rights to sacrifice without ever putting sacrifice in question), and they seem to resonate with so much contemporary feminist Christian theology/thealogy with its critique of the power of blood to redeem and save us, and its fear of the transcendent, supra-natural principles that so often jeopardize bodies. The difference is that while contemporary Christian thinkers have to work actively to earth a tradition that, by definition, privileges spirit over body and does its most important work in the realm of theological

69. Phyllis Trible, 'Genesis 22: The Sacrifice of Sarah', in Alice Bach (ed.), *Women in the Hebrew Bible: A Reader* (London/New York: Routledge, 1999), pp. 271-90.

abstraction, Judaism, as Daniel Boyarin argues, has always been more 'carnal' and more oriented towards the human and to flesh.[70] Moreover, Jewish tradition has always shown a predilection for a sacrificial logic in which even the most important stories and concepts can interrogatively be put to death. Putting ideas to the knife and the fire results in a burst of thoughts scattered like stars through the heavens; resourceful husbandry of the text carcass puts it to use in multiple, contradictory ways. The result is a splatter of midrashim which say, effectively, 'we recoil from this debt to blood, ash, fire even as we enter into the legacy of this gift of blood, ash, fire', and 'We feel profoundly ambiguous about the violence of a story in which death is not eradicated, but only displaced'.

70.   See Daniel Boyarin, *Carnal Judaism: Reading Sex in Talmudic Culture* (Berkeley: University of California Press, 1993).

FLESHING OUT THE TEXT

Hugh S. Pyper

In his recently published essay 'The Eyes of Language: The Abyss and the Volcano',[1] Derrida reacts to an extraordinary letter found among Gershom Scholem's papers after his death. It is addressed to Franz Rosenzweig, and dated 26 December 1926. In it, Scholem warns Rosenzweig of the dangers of the attempted secularization of Hebrew as the language of Israel. 'Hebrew is pregnant with catastrophes', he writes, and, earlier, 'This country is a volcano. It houses language.' The mistake is to imagine that the 'apocalyptic thorn' of the language has been pulled. 'Each word which is not newly created but taken from of [sic] the "good old" treasure is full to bursting'.

Scholem continues, 'We do live inside this language, above an abyss, almost all of us with the certainty of the blind. But when our sight is restored, we or those who come after us, must we not fall to the bottom of this abyss? And no one knows whether the sacrifice of individuals who will be annihilated in this abyss will suffice to close it.' And further, 'After evoking the ancient names daily, we can no longer hold of their power. Called awake they will appear since we have evoked them with great violence... Those who called the Hebrew language back to life did not believe in the judgement that was thus conjured upon us.'

This warning of the uncanny power of Hebrew, rooted in its inescapable but unrecognized connection to the symbolics of the biblical text, is startling, although the relevance or credibility of Scholem's underlying assumptions about language and its significance as yet another diagnosis of the endlessly ramifying complexities of Israeli politics is still to be tested. It is certainly a highly idiosyncratic view. What struck me in reading his letter was the volcanic metaphor of the potentially catastrophic repressed violence of biblical language, and its foreboding that this repression will have its consequences in real violence wreaked on real bodies. This repression is not confined to Hebrew, although Scholem's reaction is specifically so directed. All European languages rely on metaphors and vocabulary which draw their original power from the biblical text but which are now used indiscriminately and unwittingly in all sorts of contexts.

Let me now juxtapose this shattering text with another which also amazes me, for rather different reasons. 'Is there a relationship between the fact that every

---

1. In Jacques Derrida, *Acts of Religion* (ed. with an introduction by G. Andijar; London: Routledge, 2002), pp. 191-227. A translation by Andijar of Scholem's letter appears as an appendix on pp. 226-27. The quotations above are taken from this.

twenty-five seconds a male infant is circumcised and every fifteen seconds a man beats a woman?' asks Ronald Goldman MD in his book *Circumcision, The Hidden Trauma; How an American Cultural Practice Affects Infants and Ultimately us All*.[2] Circumcision is currently the subject of a fascinating and sometimes virulent debate centred mainly on the US, where the opponents of 'genital mutilation' and 'infant torture' marshal evidence to demonstrate the long-lasting traumatic effects of this procedure.[3] Goldman's book, sponsored by the Circumcision Resource Centre, Boston, is a good example of the genre. The topic brings into play a plethora of the discourses of the day: sexuality, masculinity, child violence and sexual abuse, human rights, torture, psychoanalysis, trauma, victimhood, body image, medical cover-up, medical authority, scientific discourse, conspiracy theory, cultural pressures and conformity, identity, Judaism and anti-Semitism, to name but a few. The biblical resonances are obvious, though the relationship of the contemporary debate to biblical discussions is an oblique one.

Goldman's argument is that circumcision, which its opponents insist is no minor operation, is not only the physical mutilation of an unconsenting infant, but the cause of a desensitizing of the male body which has lasting physiological consequences. The circumcised male is quite simply rendered less responsive to physical stimuli. Whatever the medical truth of this, we may note in passing that the rationale offered by Moses Maimonides for the practice of circumcision is 'to weaken the organ of generation as far as possible and thus cause man to be moderate'.[4]

Psychologically, Goldman argues, circumcision inflicts a traumatic betrayal on the infant, whose relationship of trust to the mother is terminally undermined. Goldman encapsulates his analysis in the following, somewhat ungainly, statement: '...the violent act of circumcision (what's done to children) may be an unrecognised perinatal factor that, in certain circumstances, increases the potential for adult violence (they will do to society)'.[5] Hence the link between the statistics of circumcision and male violence against women, he claims: desensitized and traumatized men wreak their vengeance for their affective crippling on the substitutes for the mother as betrayer. Adult male violence, particularly in the US, is exacerbated, at least, by the practice of circumcision.

The hypothesis, as Goldman presents it, would, I suspect, prove to be riddled with begged questions and unsupported statistics if further investigated. It is an extreme, but not unique, view, as the number of websites directed to 'circumcision

---

2. Ronald Goldman, MD, *Circumcision, The Hidden Trauma: How an American Cultural Practice Affects Infants and Ultimately us All* (Boston: Vanguard Publications, 1997), p. 163.

3. For a relatively balanced historical approach to a highly polemical debate, see David L. Gollaher, *Circumcision: A History of the World's Most Controversial Surgery* (New York: Basic Books, 2000). Aspects of the internal debate in the American Jewish community are discussed in Laurence A. Hoffman's *Covenant of Blood: Circumcision and Gender in Rabbinic Judaism* (Chicago: University of Chicago Press, 1996), particularly in the final chapter (pp. 209-20).

4. Moses Maimonides, *The Guide for the Perplexed* (trans. M. Friedländer; New York: Dover Books, 1956 [1904]), p. 378. Interestingly, Maimonides treats circumcision in his discussion of the laws to do with marriage.

5. Goldman, *Circumcision*, p. 171.

survivors' testifies. What even such a speculative hypothesis bears witness to, however, is a complex of issues about body and text, wounded bodies and wounded texts, the repression in language and the repressed memory of physical and psychic trauma, focused on the phenomenon of circumcision. Circumcision is a recurrent theme in contemporary critical debate, most notably in the work of Derrida himself, but also in the writings of Julia Kristeva, where it becomes displaced into the symbolic realm as a way of talking about features intrinsic to language. In this way, circumcision also resonates with the concerns of Scholem's letter. Is there a link to be made between the violence potentially intrinsic in biblical language and the trauma of circumcision?

Some such connection is certainly suggested by the concept of a 'hermeneutics of circumcision' which surfaces in a dialogue between three leading representatives of the school of Postmodern Jewish Philosophy—Steven Kepnes, Peter Ochs and Robert Gibbs—recorded in their jointly edited volume *Reasoning After Revelation*.[6] Kepnes introduces the idea that circumcision is 'an icon for the Jewish act of delimiting the logos'[7] in the context of a discussion of the distinctiveness of Jewish postmodernism in terms of its strategies for countering logocentric reductionism. Gibbs takes the analogy on, but conflates circumcision and castration as strategies for humbling the phallogocentric ego, wondering if Origen's self-castration bespoke 'an excess logocentrism in his hermeneutics'.[8]

Ochs takes Gibbs to task for this conflation and distinguishes between a *castrating* hermeneutic which attempts to sever the roots of logocentrism, which he regards as still a modernist strategy (given its logic of negation), and a hermeneutic of *circumcision*. 'For us…' he writes, 'circumcision, as opposed to castration, signifies a hermeneutic that preserves the text—or tradition or impulse—while delimiting its potential oppressiveness'.[9]

This comment is taken up at some length in Elliot Wolfson[10] in one of several reflections on the dialogue by distinguished commentators which make up the latter part of the work. Wolfson refers to Ochs's 'incisive'[11] remark (pun intended?) but puts it in the wider context of a kabbalistic view of Torah as a concrete manifestation of God which is the product of an act of 'self-constriction' by the divine, something which Wolfson himself describes as an 'incarnational theology' of Torah.[12] He takes issue with Ochs's rather sanguine characterization of circumcision as a release from oppression. Women and gentiles might take a different view, he reminds him. That said, he continues as follows:

6.   Steven Kepnes, Peter Ochs and Robert Gibbs (eds.), *Reasoning after Revelation: Dialogues in Postmodern Jewish Philosophy* (Boulder, CO: Westview Press, 1998).

7.   Kepnes, Ochs and Gibbs, *Reasoning after Revelation*, p. 37.

8.   Kepnes, Ochs and Gibbs, *Reasoning after Revelation*, p. 37.

9.   Kepnes, Ochs and Gibbs, *Reasoning after Revelation*, p. 37.

10.   Elliot R. Wolfson, 'Listening to Speak: A Response to Dialogues in Postmodern Jewish Philosophy', in Kepnes, Ochs and Gibbs, *Reasoning after Revelation*, pp. 93-104.

11.   Wolfson, 'Listening to Speak', p. 100.

12.   Wolfson, 'Listening to Speak', p. 99.

There is no question, however, that the analogy that Ochs draws resonates deeply with the rabbinic tradition. Expanding on his comments, I would emphasise that circumcision as a trope for the hermeneutical process underscores the painfulness of reading, a painfulness that relates to the opening of the flesh that both marks and seals the covenant relationship between God and Israel. Divine writing and human reading share in the suffering of the text.[13]

Wolfson goes on to draw the analogy between the restriction of possible meaning that the reader has to accept in order to be faithful to the text and the self-restriction of the God who becomes concrete in Torah.

The reader…must limit the range of possible meanings by learning how to decode the footprints that the author left behind in the text. In this sense, the hermeneutical process can be viewed as an emulation of the suffering of God that results in the constriction of the divine light into the form of the letters of the Torah. Reading, therefore, is a re-enactment of circumcision, an act of de-cision [his hyphenation], that brings the male Jew into a covenantal relationship with the God of Israel.[14]

This is a most intriguing discussion in our context, but note that Wolfson ends up with the male Jewish (religious) reader.[15] What of those readers whom the text excludes from the covenantal relationship, those whose circumcision is not being *re*-enacted, for whom the painful exercise of circumcised reading seems like oppression, precisely because they feel excluded from or indeed are unaware of the covenantal embrace of the text? Wolfson himself notes the potential oppressiveness of the kabbalistic concept of the homology between the 'covenant of the foreskin' and the 'covenant of the tongue'.[16]

This leads me to the following questions: Is Scholem's warning not related precisely to the fact that the language forged in a covenant predicated, in Wolfson's terms, on the painful self-limitation, or repression, of both God and the reader is now circulating with no consciousness of its underlying trauma? Or is Goldman not witness to a culture where circumcision is performed with no sense of covenant, desacralized and medicalized, where its trauma cannot be set against the gift of identity and the promise of restoration?

In this article I can do no more than trace some of these resonances and draw on some of the theoretical resources which Derrida and Kristeva offer in an attempt to illuminate how biblical metaphors and narrative dynamics pervade and problem-

---

13.　Kepnes, Ochs and Gibbs, *Reasoning after Revelation*, p. 100.

14.　Kepnes, Ochs and Gibbs, *Reasoning after Revelation*, p. 101.

15.　For a fascinating discussion of a hermeneutics of circumcision in a Christian context, see Annexe 3, 'La lettre et la circoncision', in François Martin's *Pour une théologie de la lettre: l'inspiration des Ecritures* (Paris: Editions du Cerf, 1996), pp. 477-94. See also Michel de Certeau's fascinating correlation between circumcision as a conferral of meaning through removal and absence (of the foreskin) and the unpronounceable grapheme YHVH [*sic*], which also creates meaning by acting as an 'absence' in the text (in his *The Writing of History* [trans T. Conley; New York: Columbia University Press, 1975], p. 342).

16.　Kepnes, Ochs and Gibbs, *Reasoning after Revelation*, p. 100. Wolfson traces this concept to *Sefer Yetsirah* and cites a reference from the thirteenth-century Spanish kabbalist, Joseph Gikatilla.

atize contemporary discussions of violence. There is nothing novel in claiming that biblical tropes underpin the violence of the contemporary world. Regina Schwartz in her insightful study *The Curse of Cain: The Violent Legacy of Monotheism*[17] sees the principle of scarcity which underlies the dynamics of the biblical narratives as leading inevitability to a culture of violence. Monotheism and its ideology of one God, one land, one blessing, one chosen people: these pervasive ideas reinforce the conviction that survival depends on the domination or eradication of the other. Mark McEntire's *The Blood of Abel: The Violent Plot in the Hebrew Bible*[18] reaches similar conclusions, pointing out how even the prophetic vision of peace is predicated on God's actions in destroying Zion's potential enemies. Yet what Scholem points to, and what Derrida and Kristeva explore, is an implication at another level which may suggest that a simplistic rejection of the biblical tradition and its ostensible message may be inadequate to come to terms with the insight it may bring to our understanding of the roots and reasons for human destructiveness.

We will return to Schwartz's theory later in the discussion but immediately I shall turn for help in understanding the relationship between language, violence and circumcision in the biblical text to Elaine Scarry's fruitful and still neglected reading of the biblical tradition in *The Body in Pain*.[19] Scarry finds the biblical rejection of visual signs of the god's presence striking in a cultural milieu where idols were universally accepted. The God of the Hebrew Bible is a voice, not a vision, invisible, unembodied and so constantly escaping the efforts of the human imagination to encompass him. This is made explicit in Deut. 4.12 where Moses reminds the people that on Horeb 'you heard the sound of words, but saw no form, there was only a voice' and from this argues for the ban on graven images (Deut. 4.16-18).

Human beings, in contrast to God, are embodied, tied to the materiality, the vulnerability, changeability and ultimately the mortality of their bodies. How are voice and body to interact? The short answer, Scarry maintains, is by writing, by which she means the recording of the elusive voice in the transformation of the material world. God writes, literally, on the tablets of stone, but also, so Scarry claims, makes his mark on the world in his effect on human bodies. It is in the weapon and the wound that God is made known, through instruments which mark the changeable substance of the material world. The marks which are left are the evidence of his unseen power and presence.

Just such an alteration is demanded of Abraham and his descendants as the sign of the covenant in Genesis 18. No verbal agreement, no written pledge is sufficient. Instead, Abraham's genitals are to be wounded, and his body bears an indelible mark as a permanent reminder to himself, and to those who see him naked, that he

17. Regina Schwartz, *The Curse of Cain: The Violent Legacy of Monotheism* (Chicago: University of Chicago Press, 1997).

18. Mark McEntire, *The Blood of Abel: The Violent Plot in the Hebrew Bible* (Macon, GA: Mercer University Press, 1999).

19. Elaine Scarry, *The Body in Pain: The Making and Unmaking of the World* (Oxford: Oxford University Press, 1985).

stands in relation to God. This mark is to be transmitted to all who bear the promise as his descendants. The continuity of the ungraspable God is etched into the flesh of the succeeding generations who bear the mark of circumcision. The mutability of the body is what enables it to become a record of memory, but also the bearer of a pledge for the future. The circumcised penis is a reminder of a past act of wounding, an act within the community, but also a promise: a promise that the bearer of the scar will be bound up in the destiny of the community and its otherwise unseen God.

This physical inscription of the presence of God by human wounding runs much wider than circumcision, of course. Jacob, wrestling with the angel, bears away not only a blessing, but also a limp, a permanent wound. Others are blinded or blasted with leprosy as a sign of God's presence. The firstborn of Egypt are killed, Amalek is annihilated. Throughout the Hebrew Bible it is the wounding and scarring of human bodies that serves as the sign of God's presence with Israel. Either Israel or their enemies are smitten with plague or devastated by famine or war, and the promise that is awaited is a promise of more violence, either of punishment vented on the people, or the destruction of their enemies.

Confirmation that the wound's importance is as a sign of God's action comes from the fact that in the Hebrew Scriptures modification of the body by humans is frowned upon. Leviticus 19.27-28 is blunt: 'You shall not round off the hair on your temples or mar the edges of your beard. You shall not make any cuttings in your flesh on account of the dead, or tattoo any marks on you'. Deuteronomy 14.1 confirms this: 'You shall not cut yourselves or make any baldness on your head for the dead'. Of course, one only forbids what is a temptation, and wider cultural comparisons indicate that self-mutilation was a common counterpart of mourning. Ugaritic sources, which testify to a highly developed cult of the dead, bear this out and even the high God El gashes himself and 'ploughs his chest like a garden and harrows his back like a plain' in mourning for the dead Baal.[20]

---

20. See H.L. Ginsberg's translation of Ugaritic tablet V AB in the section on 'Poems about Baal and Anath', in James B. Pritchard (ed.), *The Ancient Near East*. I. *An Anthology of Texts and Pictures* (Princeton NJ: Princeton University Press, 1958), p. 110. There is evidence that such practices were not unknown in Israel itself. Jer. 41.5 describes the aftermath of the murder of the governor Gedaliah by Ishmael son of Nethaniah: 'The day after Gedaliah's assassination, before anyone knew about it, eighty men who had shaved off their beards, torn their clothes and cut themselves came from Shechem, Shiloh and Samaria, bringing grain offerings and incense with them to the house of the Lord.' No-one seems to disapprove of their actions or their appearance in the temple. Seventy of them are indeed killed in their turn by Ishmael but this seems to be more for their political opinions than for their mourning practices. In Jer. 16.6 the writer seems to take it for granted that people gash themselves and shave their head for the dead, in a context where the whole point is the suspension of what are implicitly normal mourning practices, and this is borne out in similar passages in Ezek. 7.18 and Mic. 1.16. These practices may not simply have been mourning rituals, however. The prophets of Baal gash themselves with knives in their vain attempt to compete with Elijah on Mount Carmel in 1 Kgs 22. The connection of self-wounding with prophecy in Israel as well as in Baalide circles is hinted at in the odd passage in Zech. 13.6 where the prophet, now ashamed of his calling, will have to answer the question 'What are these wounds on your body?' Other bodily marks—perhaps what Leviticus condemns as 'tattooing'—are also referred to in

This at least suggests that the legal material of the Torah is countering a set of accepted cultural practices which it seeks to redefine as abuse. It seems jealous to reserve the power of modifying the human body to God alone. Deuteronomy 32.9 could not put this more starkly. 'See now that I, I am he [or: I am the one]: and there is no other God beside me: I shall kill and I have brought to life; I have wounded [or smashed] and I shall heal [or repair] and there is no-one to save you from my hand'. Wounding is God's business. It is also significant that, as clearly as Hebrew grammar can convey it, the point is made that what God has already done is to wound; it is healing which is held out as the uncompleted act of the future. Wounding and healing, death and the bringing of life are for God's hands.

Circumcision is the exception that proves the rule, in that the modification of the human body by human action is explicitly enjoined. God's presence is not directly visible, but his action in the world is readable from wounded bodies. However, this licit action itself serves to repress through the biblical text a complex of cultural practices related to wounding and violence. Circumcision becomes the permissible remnant of a now forbidden and denied cultural impulse. In its biblical form it is a trope which severs Israel from a widespread cultural and religious set of signifiers in its ancient Near Eastern context which depend on the wounding of the body.

Circumcision carries a particular significance because it intersects not only with the wound, but with procreation and with the marking out of gender. There are pragmatic aspects to this: there are not so many possibilities of marking the male body indelibly and yet without inflicting major physical disability. Israel is by no means unique in its practice of circumcision either within the global context of anthropology or indeed among its ancient Near Eastern neighbours. Herodotus credits the Egyptians with the invention of circumcision and indeed Freud argues that it was introduced by the Egyptian Moses not as a mark of distinction, but as a mark of respectability.

However, in most other cultures where it is practised, it is a rite associated with puberty, performed by older men on the boys of the tribe. Where Israel is unusual is in the fact that the rite is performed on infants. One traditional line of justification for this depends on an association with the story of the Akedah which is often interpreted as a prohibition of another widely attested practice in the ancient Near East, the sacrifice of children. This too is a practice which biblical texts seem to acknowledge in Israel, even as something that at one time was construed as a divine requirement (Ezek. 20.25-26), but which the explicit rhetoric of the text condemns fiercely. Once again, in biblical thought, the killing of children becomes a divine prerogative—Egypt's firstborn, the unnamed child of Bathsheba and David, the children of Babylon in Psalm 137 all attest to a possibility of the displaced action of God. If circumcision substitutes for the practice of child sacrifice, it also acts as a metonymic reminder of it. Each male child is put to the knife. Circumcision becomes the acceptable sign of a troubling discourse in this case of the violence of fathers against their sons which otherwise is excluded from the text.

passing. Isa. 44.5, for instance, describes without condemnation one who writes on his hand '*l^eyhwh*' ('belonging to Yahweh').

Julia Kristeva offers a further insight into the exceptional nature of biblical circumcision. She points out that the purity of the cult explicitly demands the exclusion of anything deformed or wounded, including a specific prohibition of men with damaged genitals:

> The body must bear no trace of its debt to nature: it must be clean and proper in order to be fully symbolic. In order to confirm that, it should endure no gash other than that of circumcision, equivalent to sexual separation and/or separation from the mother. Any other mark would be the sign of belonging to the impure, the non-separate, the non-symbolic, the non-holy.[21]

Circumcision here, to coin a pseudo-Lacanianism, is 'the wound which is not one'. Its function, Kristeva explains, is, like food taboos, to mark separation without the need for sacrifice.

> ...what the male is separated from, the other that circumcision carves out on his very sex, is the other sex, impure, defiled. By repeating the natural scar of the umbilical cord at the location of sex, by duplicating and thus displacing through ritual the pre-eminent separation, which is that from the mother, Judaism seems to insist in symbolic fashion—the very opposite of what is 'natural'—that the identity of the speaking being (with his God) is based on the separation of the son from the mother.[22]

In Kristeva's reading, this dynamic reflects the pain yet possibility of the development of the human subject, which entails the abjection of the maternal as the price for access to the paternal gift of the word. Here we come closer to a connection between circumcision and language.

What she does not mention, however, is what might seem the counter-argument represented by Howard Eilberg-Schwartz[23] and others that circumcision represents a feminization of the Jewish male, and the anger expressed by some American men who regard themselves as 'circumcision survivors' who resent what they experience as a theft of some aspect of their masculinity. Circumcision may be a displacement of the navel, but it is more commonly read as a displacement of castration. There are Jewish commentators who see it precisely as a form of assurance to the boy that the undeniable aggression of the father, which Freud sees as manifest in the child's fear of castration, can be acknowledged, but will proceed no further.[24]

---

21. Julia Kristeva, *New Maladies of the Soul* (trans. Ross Guberman; New York: Columbia University Press, 1995), p. 102.

22. Kristeva, *New Maladies*, p. 100.

23. See, e.g., Chapter 6, 'Unmanning Israel', in his *God's Phallus and Other Problems for Men and Monotheism* (Boston: Beacon Press, 1994), pp. 137-62, and a recurrent theme in the work of Daniel Boyarin.

24. Hoffman (*Covenant of Blood*, p. 2) cites a quotation from an article in the *New York Times* 'About Men' column by Joshua J. Hammerman, a conservative rabbi, who celebrates for each father 'this experience, even vicariously, of inflicting upon his child a ritualised blow so intense as to make him shake and recoil, yet so controlled that no damage is done, to signify that this will be the worst the child will ever know from his father's hand' ('About Men: Birth Rite', *New York Times Magazine*, 13 March 1994, p. 28).

However, what Kristeva may point to, and what Goldman suggests, is that performed before the child has entered into the linguistic community, on an eight-day old child, the trauma is experienced in a preverbal context where only the maternal is real. The trauma of this displaced wound is displaced onto the mother. The cut of castration and the severing of the umbilical cord are conflated. Hence Kristeva's insistence in *Powers of Horror* that the dynamic of biblical legislation expresses an abjection of the maternal. The centrality of circumcision, to the exclusion of any other modification of the body, is of a piece with this insight.

Paradoxically, this central function of circumcision is borne out by Paul's apparent rejection of it in the New Testament. In Phil. 3.2 he turns on what he calls 'these impure dogs', against these 'workers of evil, against those who make incision in their own bodies' (a periphrasis which masks the rather crude pun replacing *paratomes*, 'circumcisers', with *katatomes*, 'choppers'). Why is Paul so hard on the advocates of circumcision, when in the next few verses he is prepared to declare his own circumcision as at least a potential matter for boasting?

The answer may be because we are once again in a world where the believer's body is the visible site of divine action, the manifestation of an invisible agency. His objection chimes directly with the disapproval manifest in Leviticus and Deuteronomy of human alterations to the body. It is God's business to alter bodies, not ours. It is not circumcision which is the problem, but those who presume to circumcise. In Phil. 3.21 this divine prerogative is explicit. Paul tells us that we await a saviour 'who will change the fashion of this humbled body of ours, making it conformable to the body which is his in his glorified state, and who will accomplish this by exerting the very power which he has to make all things subject to himself'. The change is that this has now been carried further so that even the once licit wounding of the circumcision has become a trespass on the divine prerogative of altering the human body.

The marks that matter now are the apostolic signs of suffering.[25] This is made abundantly clear at the end of the letter to Galatians, where the issue of circumcision is particularly to the fore. Paul sums up his position in the final verses. 'As for circumcision or the want of it, they count for nothing. What counts is that there is a new *ktisis*' (*either* a new act of creation *or* a new creature; cf. 2 Cor. 5.17). Paul clinches this with an assertion of the basis for his claim to authority, which is also

25.   Writing to the Philippians, Paul hopes for 'sufficient courage so that now as always Christ will be exalted in my body, whether by life or death' (Phil. 1.20). The Philippians are privileged to join Paul in this witness by suffering. 'For it has been granted to you on behalf of Christ not only to believe in him, but also to suffer for him, since you are going through the same struggle you saw I had, and now hear that I still have' (Phil. 1.29-30). These final clauses are the important point. The Philippians may not have seen Christ, but they have seen Paul, and Paul's struggles. As they read his letter they are now hearing the narrative of his continuing sufferings. Their share in these sufferings, he has told them, is exactly the sign that paradoxically they, who seem to be in such trouble, will be saved, while their enemies, who no doubt are congratulating themselves on their superior strength, are actually confronted with the sign of their destruction. Once again we are in the world where destruction is intrinsic to the manifestation of God in the world—the only question is who will be for the chop.

his evidence for being himself a new creature: 'From this time onward let there be nobody who will be a cause of trouble for me; for I bear the marks of Jesus imprinted on my very body' (Gal. 6.17). Paul's body is now the sign of God. But, paradoxically again, these shared marks, on Paul's own body, include the sign of circumcision.[26]

Yet does this not leave modern Christian readers in a recurrent dilemma? What evidence do we have now here of the state of *Paul's* body? Somewhere in Rome, we may believe, that body is buried awaiting the resurrection Paul so confidently expected, but no longer bearing those marks which Jesus has laid on it. In this connection, it is surely telling that the final book of the New Testament, and one of the last to be adopted into the canon, the Revelation of St John, reverts to an apocalyptic picture of kingdom of God which is accompanied by the most comprehensive slaughter and drastic modification of the bodies of the enemies of the kingdom to be found in the biblical corpus. In the absence of the body of God or his disciples, the heaped bodies of his dead enemies become the sign to be awaited.

What the modern reader has, however, which neither biblical Israel nor the early Church had in its present form, is the Bible. The wound, God's writing on the mutable flesh of humanity, can be inscribed in writing. In this regard, we come close once more to the account of the Torah that Wolfson offered as a text which 'arises from God's own suffering' related to the 'opening of the flesh that both marks and seals the covenantal relationship between God and Israel. Divine writing and human reading share in the suffering of the text.'[27]

In a remarkable passage in *Moses and Monotheism*, Freud indicates how the biblical text can act as the bearer of the wound:

> The text, however as we possess it today will tell us enough about its own vicissitudes. Two mutually opposed treatments have left their traces on it. On the one hand it has been subjected to revisions which have falsified it in the sense of their secret aims, have mutilated [N.B.] and amplified it and have changed it into its reverse; on the other hand, a solicitous piety has presided over it and has sought to

---

26. Space does not permit an adequate treatment of the complex issues around Jesus' circumcision in Christian thought. Suffice it to say that the Feast of the Circumcision celebrates a proleptic wounding of Christ's body as a foretaste of the crucifixion. The fact that this Feast has been redesignated in recent years as the Feast of the Holy Family could open up a whole new layer of discussion of the repression and return of the maternal. For further discussion, see Leo Steinberg's groundbreaking work *The Sexuality of Christ in Renaissance Art and in Modern Oblivion* (Chicago: University of Chicago Press, 2nd edn, 1996), especially pp. 50-71. Steinberg tackles the question of the lack of the physical evidence of circumcision in Renaissance depiction of Jewish biblical figures, including Christ, in the context of his claim that there is a consistent trope of *ostentation genitalium*, the positive exhibition of Christ's genitals as a testimony to the incarnation. Steinberg sums up the artists' dilemma as follows: 'The honorific seal of a compact between man and God was manifestly a shameful scar. Between these conflicting positions the gulf was unbridgeable—deeper than the theological issue, wide as the divergence between, say, Hellenic sculptor and biblical prophet. Where the twain finally meet in Christianity they collide in a culture shock never quite overcome' (p. 158). That shock, it could be said, is what still resonates in the debates I am outlining.

27. Wolfson, 'Listening to Speak', p. 100.

preserve everything as it was, no matter whether it was consistent or contradicted itself. Thus almost everywhere noticeable gaps, disturbing repetitions, and obvious contradictions have come about—indications which reveal things to us which it was not intended to communicate.[28]

Critics and readers have, since antiquity, been aware of the seams and scars in the text, the pieces that seem to have dropped out, or become misplaced or disfigured, the duplications and the graftings, the distortions and disjunctions. The biblical text itself bears wounds, more or less healed. Higher criticism, like much medicine, in the interest of healing the patient has dissected it, stripping off layers, hacking off or transplanting bits and pieces, rather as if Dr Frankenstein took up employment as a plastic surgeon. The biblical text has been stripped and separated into layers, shown to be myopic in its view of women and of the cultures of Palestine. This process has proceeded apace throughout the last few decades, but to critical eyes it appears innocuous compared to the wholesale pillaging of the corpus of the Hebrew Scriptures by Paul and other early Christian writers, who pull the brightest threads out of the textile of the Hebrew Scriptures to weave them into their own books, dismembering it in order to rebuild its story, an activity blithely continued by its dissection into lectionaries and reading, and the search for sermon texts, dragged out of context.

All texts, Frederick Jameson has argued, involve effort in production, an effort which can only be justified if they offer some promise of resolution to the tensions of the community for whom they are produced. The pain of the exile, the destruction, the anxiety over the continuity of Israel and the promise, the pain of the withdrawal of the physical presence of Jesus, give rise to the texts of scriptures. That pain is expressed as wounding, notably in a book such as Lamentations, where the hope of the people is placed in the wounding Father, at the expense of the battered and sexually brutalised Mother Zion. A wound, a scar is a memory of contact, which at times stands duty for the longed-for caress.

The processes of fracture, rupture and fragmentation, so characteristic of so-called postmodernity, are not likely to cease, and media manipulation of the text will disseminate and dismember it with accelerating ease. Yet the text itself encodes and displays its own fracture and rupture. The Bible is pulled apart by the tensions it seeks to embody—hope and dread, life and death, inclusion and exclusion, choice and responsibility, promise and betrayal. It is a text in tension, the product of anguish and loss—the loss of the temple, the loss of the land, the loss of the body of Jesus. It is a battered survivor of a text, which bears the anguish and the guilt that are a survivor's lot. The Bible as sign is a sign of the rupture that leads to the wound as sign. It also bears witness, in the trace of the scar, to the agony of healing.

But can we finally close the loop and argue that the Bible is not simply a wounded but a circumcised text, and that it is as a result of this that it encodes a violence which Scholem detects? Here we can return to Derrida, who explores the

---

28. *Moses and Monotheism*, in *The Origins of Religion* (Penguin Freud Library, 13; Harmondsworth: Penguin Books, 1985), p. 283.

concept of the circumcised word in *Shibboleth*. He follows Celan in this semantic sideshift which seems to arise in response to a line of Maria Tsvetayeva quoted in the original Russian by Paul Celan as the epigraph of a poem in his *Die Niemands-rose*: 'All poets are Jews' or, more accurately, 'All poets are Yids'. Derrida takes this line as a pretext to develop the idea of circumcision as a diagnostic of poetic language. The original story of the use of the word '*shibboleth*' to single out and kill the fugitive Ephraimites (Judg. 12.5-6) brings the linguistic and the physical together—after all, Derrida reminds us, it is a physical incapacity to pronounce the word that dooms the Ephraimites, something that can be related to the odd expression Moses uses of himself in Exod. 6.12 and 6.30, when he claims to be of 'uncircumcised lips'. A physical incapacity brought to light by the failure to speak a word leads to death. Derrida meditates on the idea as follows:

> ...the circumcised word, the word turned *Shibboleth*, at once both secret and readable, mark of membership and of exclusion, the shared wound of division [*blessure de partage*], reminds us also of what I will call the *double edge* of every *Shibboleth*. The mark of an alliance, it is also an index of exclusion, of discrimination, indeed of extermination. One may, thanks to the *Shibboleth*, recognize and be recognized by one's own, for better and for worse, for the sake of partaking [*partage*] and the ring of alliance *on the one hand*, but also, *on the other hand*, for the purpose of denying the other, of denying him passage or life. One may also, because of the *Shibboleth* and exactly to the extent that one may make use of it, see it turned against oneself: then it is the circumcised who are proscribed or held at the border, excluded from the community, put to death, or reduced to ashes merely on the sight of, or in the name of, the *Wundgelesenes*.[29]

Paul, or more accurately later readings of Paul, it could be argued, turns the '*shibboleth*' of circumcision against Israel—what once marked out the chosen people now marks out those who are rejected. Scholem's warning is also directed to those who may find themselves on the wrong side of a divide they have mistakenly seen as a safeguard. Hebrew as a mark of a secular nationality may not lead to security but insecurity, he seems to imply, and the displacement of the sacred may lead to the rise of religious fanaticisms within and beyond the community marked by language. Something has been cut away from the language, some level of resonance hidden from the conscious life of the community.

This may be particularly true of Hebrew, though I feel in no place to comment further on that, but is it confined to Hebrew? Are not all European languages at least imbued not only with their own sacredness, but with a sacredness that comes from their being summoned into writing by the biblical word? Is there a volcano waiting to erupt in the inarticulacy of our spiritual vocabularies, an energy of violence which can, as is only too possible, seize on the biblical text itself and use it as a weapon?

---

29. 'Shibboleth', in G.H. Hartman and S. Budick (eds.) *Midrash and Literature* (New Haven: Yale University Press, 1986), pp. 307-48 (346). *Wundgelesenes* is the final word of Celan's poem *Dein Vom Wachen*, a typical neologism which might be translated 'wound-read'—in the present context, a pregnant term.

Reading the literature of those who liken the circumcision of American men to
a new holocaust exposes one to the inarticulate rage at what is perceived as an
irreparable injury and assault by some circumcised men. This, one cannot help feeling, has become the focus for some other, much wider sense of frustration which
simmers below language because the secularized language, which is all so many of
us have to express ourselves in, cannot speak deep enough. An aspect of this may
be ascribed to the fact that this rage stems from a prelinguistic trauma, but Derrida
points to another issue in his constant insistence in 'Shibboleth' on the uniqueness
and unrepeatability of circumcision. It can only happen once. Each man has only
one foreskin to be removed. There is both a particular irreparability implicit in this,
but also no possibility of retribution. The trauma of circumcision cannot be overcome by the *lex talionis*, a foreskin for a foreskin, when the circumcised father, or,
if Kristeva is to be believed, the mother who has no penis, is seen as the perpetrator. Where is the pain to go?

In an unpublished paper on 'Forgiveness and Resentment: Kierkegaard, Levinas
and Weil',[30] Patrick Sheil discusses the dynamics of revenge and points out that it
can never rest at the level of 'tit for tat', of strict reciprocity. If I respond to your
attack with an equal display of force, this still leaves the most important disparity
between us untouched. Your attack was an unprovoked assault on an innocent
victim; mine is a justified retaliation against a guilty party. We may sustain equal
physical injury, but you will not suffer the sense of outrage and betrayal that I
suffered. In order to even up the score, I have to go further by assaulting your innocence and provoking you to outrage, which then begins a new cycle as you now
feel the victim of an unjustifiable or even unforgivable attack.

History all too chillingly bears witness to the accuracy of this analysis. The discussion which followed Sheil's paper turned, interestingly, to Psalm 137. Its notorious blessing on those who dash the children of Babylon against a rock is a prime
example of the escalation of revenge which results from the fact that the initial
condition before the offence can never be restored. Babylon's innocence must be
assailed, its people must experience outrage, and how better than through an assault
on its innocent: its children. Further biblical examples could be multiplied.

As Sheil put it, the characteristic word of revenge is 'more'. It is here that an
assumption of plenitude, as Schwartz seems to advocate, can lead to violence—the
plenitude of the vendetta, where there are always more victims, and more ingenious
atrocities, to assail the innocence of the offender. The *lex talionis*, the 'eye for an
eye', is where the principle of scarcity can step in to limit the spiral of revenge.
'One for one' is its watchword. The law steps in to cut off the excess that revenge
demands. Yet the excess must be discharged somehow. The answer in the Hebrew
Scriptures is to displace it onto the divine. '"Vengeance is mine", saith the Lord, "I
will repay".' Human wounding, and the wounding of the innocent, as we have seen,
is God's business. So he demands the life of David's newborn son in recompense

---

30.   The paper was delivered at a one-day conference of the Søren Kierkegaard Society of the
United Kingdom on 'Kierkegaard and Modern European Thought', 11 May 2002, University of
Essex, and is cited with gratitude for the author's permission and useful further discussion.

for Uriah's life (2 Sam. 12) or the firstborn of Egypt for the lives of the Hebrew children slain at Pharaoh's orders. God, we might say, is the name for the non-reciprocal, for the excess which can injure innocence, or in terms which are drawn from a recent essay of Derrida's, the name of 'sovereign cruelty'.[31]

Part of the anger felt by the survivors of circumcision is precisely the sense that their innocence has been outraged and that helpless children have been made to suffer this irreparable damage. The helplessness is, as Philo made explicit, part of the point.[32] Who would consent to circumcision, even as the sign of the covenant, as an adult? American medical circumcision is thus, rather as Scholem warned about the Hebrew of his day, a sign without significance, one which has been cut adrift from the ritual context in which it found meaning. Its meaning is now given in medical terms, insofar as any justification is sought at all. The most common reason given by parents who are asked why they chose to have circumcision performed is that they did not want their son to have to endure the mockery of others in the locker room. It is a norm because it is a norm. Its effects, then, cannot be incorporated in a collective narrative of identity so that the loss and pain it inflicts can be seen to have a compensation. There is nowhere for the search for recompense to go.

This same sense of a void where there should be a point of discharge for human frustration, fear and pain is to be found in an essay by another great Jewish, indeed Israeli, writer, Haim Bialik. In his 'Revealment and Concealment in Language', Bialik discusses the constant renewal of words necessary because words are a talisman against the human fear of nothingness, but eventually themselves become tainted by the nothingness they exist to conceal. As he puts it:

> ...the word or system has been worn out by being manipulated and used, is no longer able to conceal and hide adequately, and can, of course, no longer divert mankind momentarily. Man, gazing for a moment through the open crack, finding to his terror that awesome void before him again, hurries to close the crack for a time—with a new word.[33]

31. In her recent collection of Derrida's writings entitled *Without Alibi* (Stanford, CA: Stanford University Press, 2002) Peggy Kamuf includes a text entitled 'Psychoanalysis Searches the States of Its Soul: The Impossible Beyond of a Sovereign Cruelty' (pp. 238-80). In this paper, Derrida argues that cruelty has to be distinguished from violence in that it is the infliction of suffering for its own sake. He argues that sovereignty and cruelty are co-implicated, but also that there is a beyond of cruelty which is also beyond all drives and principles—part of his ongoing concern with the Kantian notion of radical evil. This 'beyond' is another instance of the excess of revenge. Although Derrida does not take this line, the point where cruelty and sovereignty coincide at their absolute point is in the divine. On another tack, which Derrida does follow, it finds a resting point in the state's arrogation to itself of the death penalty. Derrida is particularly disturbed by the place of the death penalty in US society. There is a whole nexus of issues here which could be explored in a parallel paper.

32. Gollaher (*Circumcision*, p. 13) cites Philo's justification for infant circumcision as follows: 'It is very much better and more far-sighted of us to prescribe circumcision for infants, for perhaps one who is full-grown would hesitate through fear to carry out this ordinance of his own free will'.

33. Haim Nahman Bialik, *Revealment and Concealment: Five Essays* (Jerusalem: Ibis Editions, 2000). Bialik's essay is dated 1915.

Bialik's vision of the abyss beyond language is the negative image of Scholem's, but the effect and the danger is the same. In this context is Derrida's much-over-used phrase, '*Il n'y a pas hors texte*' a comfort or a terror—or symptom? Or—and here I admit that the metaphor takes on a heady uncanniness that I cannot yet quite grasp—rather than itself representing the wounded phallus, is the Bible the excised and disregarded foreskin of our phallic culture? Is it the text, the parchment, severed from the unseen phallus of the invisible God? In a post-Christian, post-Jewish, world, do we collectively live out the trauma of an unrecognized circum-cision?

Howard Eilberg-Schwartz[34] points out what he calls the 'irony' that though circumcision marks the covenant, Rabbinic Judaism defined it as a sign that is to be hidden when praying to God. In the biblical text, priests are not to run the risk of exposing their nakedness at the altar and in later Judaism it is forbidden to recite the Shema naked. There is a paradox in a sign that is to be hidden and a paradox too, that, simplistically, if a man is identified as a Jew, that gives anyone who meets him a knowledge of an detail of his anatomy that would otherwise only be revealed in intimate or carefully circumscribed social circumstances. Circumcision is a site of trauma and concealment, and the circumcised text is also one which conceals the trauma of its identity and gives voice to the concealed traumas of its circumcised producers.

Something of what I am grasping towards is to be found at the end of Kristeva's remarkable chapter 'Lire la Bible' in *Les nouvelles maladies de l'âme*. Kristeva encourages us to read the Bible again: 'Relisons, une fois de plus, la Bible. Pour l'interpréter certes, mais aussi pour y laisser se découper, se couper, nos propres fantasmes, nos délires interprétatifs.'[35] The published translation does not quite catch the double edge of this last sentence. We can translate the passage as follows: 'Let us, one more time, read the Bible. To interpret it, certainly, but also to let it cut out, cut for itself, our own fantasies, our interpretative deliriums [but note the allu-sion to *lire* itself in this word]': alternatively '…to let our own fantasies, our inter-pretative deliriums, cut themselves out, cut themselves, from it'.

Here the pivotal metaphor is of cutting but it is ambiguous in its reference. Does the Bible cut us or do we cut it? Earlier, Kristeva has described the Bible as 'a text which plunges its word into the side of my loss, but in order to allow me, in speak-ing of it, to face up to it in the knowledge of its cause'.[36] For Kristeva, reading the Bible can act as a prophylactic against violence: 'Never in any way better than in the Bible does one observe this transformation of sacrifice into language, this superseding or displacement of murder into the system of meanings'.[37] That system of meaning includes its own fracturedness, its own status as a text of survival, its witness through its wounding to the suffering of its readers and the suffering of

34. Eilberg-Schwartz, *God's Phallus*, pp. 208-209
35. Julia Kristeva, *Les nouvelles maladies de l'âme* (Paris: Fayard, 1993), p. 189.
36. Kristeva, *Les nouvelles maladies*, p. 179 (my translation).
37. Kristeva, *Les nouvelles maladies*, p. 180 (my translation).

its God.[38] Precisely because it attests textually to the trauma of circumcision, the irreparable assault on the innocent that severs from the mother in the name of the father, it offers the best hope of insight into the displaced fury of those who are circumcised physically or linguistically. The Bible, Kristeva insists, constitutes us as its readers as inhabitants of a borderland where our fragility and our solidity are confounded.

But by the same token, the Bible may always offer—or threaten—the possibility of reversal, of the transformation of language into sacrifice if its system of meanings is unravelled. The shibboleth cuts two ways. The offer of circumcision, as Dinah's rapist—or was he her lover?—and his people found out in Genesis 34, may not be an offer of identity, protection and community, but the foretaste of a fatal wounding and a fatal exclusion. As David Halperin reminds us in another context:

> We cannot suppose that the contents of the communal unconscious are necessarily bright and kindly. The contrary is far more likely to be true. There is much there that is dreadful and monstrous, which we nonetheless ignore at our peril. Access to these dark and terrible realms, however indirect, may be a necessary part of what religion means for us. A religious teacher or text that can grant us such access has the potential for doing us great service, as well as enormous injury.[39]

Access itself, however, may demand that injury as its price. Whether it is the loss is a foreskin, or loss of the union with the maternal that the move to language entails, the Bible both demands and mourns it. How we react to such loss, and where we displace the resentment that it can engender, is the challenge the Bible sets us.

---

38. See here Elliot Wolfson's essay 'Divine Suffering and the Hermeneutics of Reading: Philosophical Reflections on Lurianic Mythology', in Robert Gibbs and Elliot R. Wolfson (eds.), *Suffering Religion* (London: Routledge, 2002), pp. 101-62, where Wolfson cites a remarkable passage on 'textual circumcision' from Marc-Alain Ouaknin's *Mysteries of the Kabbalah* (trans. J. Bacon; New York: Abbeville Press, 2000), in which Ouaknin explains reading in terms of a process of cuts that the reader must make in the text: 'It is a circumcision of the text, but also the circumcision of God revealing Himself as text' (Gibbs and Wolfson, *Suffering Religion*, p. 137, citing Ouaknin, p. 321).

39. David J. Halperin, *Seeking Ezekiel: Text and Psychology* (University Park, PA: Pennsylvania State University Press, 1993), pp. 223-24.

GENOCIDE IN THE NAME OF 'SALVATION':
THE COMBINED CONTRIBUTION OF BIBLICAL
TRANSLATION/INTERPRETATION
AND INDIGENOUS MYTH TO THE 1994 RWANDAN GENOCIDE

Malachie Munyaneza

Rwanda's tragic history of violence culminated in one of the most terrible genocides of the twentieth century. In 1994, between April and July, within only three
months, up to a million innocent people were killed, mostly from the Abatutsi ethnic
group, but also, in some measure, from the moderate Abahutu.[1] Men, women (including pregnant women), babies, mentally handicapped, disabled, old and young
alike were massacred by the most terrible means, many in churches and church
compounds. Of the hundreds of thousands who fled, many were killed in the forests
of the Congo or remained in exile where many died in refugee camps of cholera.

The scale of the violence resulted from a number of institutional factors in
Rwanda which I will address in this paper, but it was also influenced by Christian
thinking and interpretation of the Bible. The key concept in this regard was the
ideology of *umutabazi* ('the deliverer', 'the saviour', or 'the rescuer' [plural *Abatabazi*]). This idea was central to the conquest wars both within Rwanda and without,
especially during the consolidation of the Abanyiginya dynasties, from the fifteenth
to the nineteenth centuries CE. With the introduction of Christianity under the
German and then the Belgian colonizers, *umutabazi* shifted in its application and
meaning. In 1973, after *a coup d'état* which overthrew the government of the first
Republic, General Habyarimana became president and formed a 'Committee for
Salvation and National Unity'. When he, together with the President of Burundi,
died on the 6 April 1994, following the shooting down of his plane, a self-appointed
government declared itself *Leta y'abatabazi* ('the Government of the Saviours')
and implemented a massacre so concerted and extensive that it has been compared
to 'the final solution'.[2]

---

1. The usual way of referring to the ethnic groups of Rwanda is 'the Tutsi', 'the Hutu' or 'the
Twa'. I have opted to use Abatutsi (singular, Umututsi), Abahutu (singular, Umuhutu) and Abatwa
(singular, Umutwa) because the definite article in English is also understood in the Kinyarwanda
equivalents.

2. The use of Nazi terminology 'the final solution' for the 'plan of extermination of the Jews
and the Tziganes' reflects the words of a high-ranking officer in the defeated former Rwandan
army, Colonel T. Bagosora who, at the end of the peace negotiations in Arusha, Tanzania, on 8
January 1993, publicly declared, 'I am going home to prepare the apocalypse' (Jean-Pierre Chrétien,
Rwanda: Les médias du génocide [Paris: Karthala, 1995], on photos inserted between pp. 128-29).

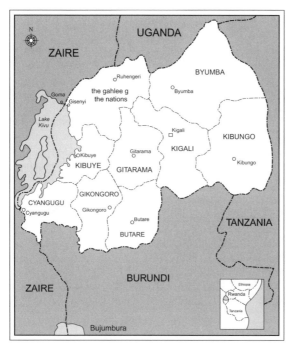

Figure 1. *Map of Rwanda (Reproduced, with permission, from Gérard Prunier,*
The Rwanda Crisis: History of a Genocide 1959–1994 *[London: Hurst & Co., 1995], p. xiv)*

The History and Origins of Abatutsi and Abahutu

Abatutsi clans are now believed to be descendants of Abahinda, a 'Nilotic' group
known as the Bito who exterminated the Cwezi to whom the sites of Bigo and
Ntusi[3] in Bunyoro (Uganda) are attributed, and who ruled the Buhaya kingdom,
probably between 1400 and 1500 CE.[4] Before the conquest, Rwanda was divided

As in the Nazi final solution, derogatory language was used to describe and humiliate Abatutsi:
they were *inyenzi* ('cockroaches'), *inzoka* ('snakes'), *abafalasha* ('falashas'), to be crushed or sent
back to their supposed place of origin, Ethiopia. As in the genocide of the Jews, the media also
played its part, stirring up the killers against Abatutsi and their *ibyitso* ('collaborators'). The
Rwandan final solution also had its extremist parties with their own youth wings who were used to
carry out the massacres.

3.   L. de Heuch, *Le Rwanda et la civilisation interlacustre: Etudes d'anthropologie historique
et structurale* (Brussels: Université Libre de Bruxelles, 1966), p. 17. These origins are themselves
interesting: the Cwezi are mentioned in Rwandan myths and stories in relation to the cult of *Lyangombe* (see below). The word *Ntusi* is equally significant linguistically because Abatutsi may be a
derivation ('people from *Ntusi*'), although Abatutsi could also be a euphonic form of *Abatunzi* ('the
ones who possess cattle and riches'; similarly, the clan name *Abanyiginya* [see below] denotes
those who possess riches, and reflects the power of the monarchs who founded their dynasty).

4.   De Heuch, *Le Rwanda*, p. 18.

into small entities called *ibihugu* ('countries' or 'territories') under Abahutu monarchs who reigned over their own clans and other people living in the same *ibihugu*.
From the tenth or twelfth centuries the east of Rwanda was conquered by Abatutsi
groups creating a number of kingdoms which, over the centuries, spread westward.
Among these the Abanyiginya clan became pre-eminent and one their rulers,
Mibambwe Mutabazi—a derived form of *umutabazi*[5]—advanced into the middle of
the country and defeated Mashira, Umuhutu king of Nduga, and captured his
empire which extended into the south and the west.[6] Mibambwe and successive
monarchs created a national army to guard the borders, to help in the administration
of territory and to pursue later conquests. The remnants of Mashira's kingdom fled
and settled in the northwest —an area today covered by the provinces of Gisenyi
and Ruhengeri—where their branches later founded two more kingdoms: Buhoma
and Rwankeri.[7]

The northwest continued to resist Abanyiginya administration until the twentieth
century, when, between 1923and 1931, they were subdued with the help of the
colonial powers Germany and Belgium. This policy of divide and rule, common
throughout the East African Middle Ages, with its wars, fratricidal conflicts and
expulsions fostered intrigues, exiles, acts of treachery and ongoing rivalry and
resentment between Abatutsi clans, between Abatutsi and Abahutu, and between
the south and the north, despite their common language, religious beliefs and
culture.

The Separating-Out of Identity:
An Indigenous Rwandan Myth of the Ascendant Abatutsi

Before the political and ideological stratification of Rwandan people, there had
been at least eighteen known clans (*ubwoko*, 'race' or 'ethnic group')—probably
more—and all Rwandan groups were represented within them.[8] With the consolidation of Abanyiginya dynasties, Rwandans were divided into three manageable
statutory casts: Abatutsi, Abahutu and Abatwa. Popular legends were invented at

5.   L. de Lacger, *Ruanda* (Kabgayi: Imprimatur, 1959), pp. 102-104. Mibambwe Mutabazi
reigned in the fifteenth century (Alexis Kagame, *Un abrégé de l'ethno-histoire du Rwanda* [Butare:
Editions Universitaires du Rwanda, 1972]), or in the sixteenth century (according to Jan Vansina's
revision of Kagame's chronology, *L'évolution du royaume rwandais des origines à 1900* [Brussels:
Academie Royale des Sciences d'outre-Mer, 1962], pp. 56, 85, cited in de Heuch, *Le Rwanda*,
p. 82). Already the concept of *Umutabazi* was so influential that the monarch bore the name
Mutabazi (the letter '*u*' is an augment which is omitted in the vocative, in names or before certain
prepositions).

6.   De Lacger, *Ruanda*, p. 103.

7.   F. Nahimana, *Le Rwanda: emergence d'un etat* (Paris: L'Harmattan, 1993), p. 84. Nahimana suggests that these people were under the leadership of Nkuba, son of Mashira (p. 83), while
Kagame suggests that Nkuba was the father of Mashira and that he had been killed by Kigeli I
Mukobanya's armies after his son Nkoko 'voluntarily died as a liberator on the battle field' (p. 75;
all translations, unless otherwise indicated, are my own).

8.   B. Muzungu, 'Ethnies et clans', in *Cahiers Centre Saint-Dominique: Ethnies au Rwanda
en 1995* (Kigali: Fraternité Saint-Dominique/Kacyiru, 1995), I, pp. 22-23.

the royal court to claim that Abatutsi had come from heaven and therefore were superior to the rest. According to these myths, God, their father Kazi ka Muntu[9] and the wise man called Gihe[10] put to the test the representatives of Abatutsi, Abahutu and Abatwa: Gatutsi, Gahutu and Gatwa respectively.[11] Gatutsi passed the test and was blessed with the rank of primacy and rewarded with cows; Gahutu half failed the test and was awarded second place and became the tiller of the land and the servant of Gatutsi. Gatwa utterly failed the test and was placed last—as a lowly potter and a beggar at the royal court.[12] Social caste was born in a way similar to so many other cultures: biblical scholars will recognize similarities between the stories of the ascendant Abatutsi and the stories of the ascendant Israelites in Genesis, genealogically superior to the Ammonites and Moabites, Canaanites, Edomites and Ishmaelites. It was only with the coming of the missionaries, however, that this type of comparison was made explicit.

The Impact of Colonization and the Missionaries: The Theory of the Non-African (Edenic) Abatutsis, Identity-Books and a Self-Styled Rwandan 'Moses'

After Rwanda, together with Burundi, became a German protectorate in 1884 and when missionary activities began in 1900, the Germans began the process of quelling the still quasi-independent, and insubordinate Abahutu kingdoms in the north and west. The Belgians completed the task after the First World War. Influenced by the nineteenth-century pre-occupation with race, the incoming Europeans believed and persuaded the tall, thin and relatively non-African looking Abatutsi that they were of a different racial extraction and shared nothing with Abahutu of Bantu stock. A 1925 report by the Belgian Ministère des Colonies described the typical Abahutu as 'short and thick-set, with a big head, a jovial expression, a wide nose and enormous lips' and described them as 'extroverts who like to laugh and lead a simple life'. The same report described Abatutsi as 'having nothing of the negro': their brows were 'fine', their noses 'thin', their teeth 'beautiful', and they were

---

9.   *Kazi ka Muntu* means 'Kazi son of Muntu', or 'Work of Person', from the words *akazi* ('work', 'job' or 'specialization'), and *umuntu* ('a person', plural: *abantu*, which gives the generic term *bantu* in words like 'Bantu people', Bantu languages...). Here we have an aetiology which sets out to explain why Abatutsi are cattle keepers, Abahutu are farmers and Abatwa are potters.

10.   Gihe simply means 'season' or 'time'. Wise Gihe is therefore the regulator of seasons, on whom depends the cycle of the seasons, harvests and prosperity.

11.   *Ga* normally indicates the diminutive class of substantives, as in *a-ga-ti* ('a small tree'). There are many names in Rwanda which take a diminutive form. Because of the mortality rate, it was commonly thought that by giving a diminutive name, death would not take such a 'small' human being. Diminutives can also be 'friendly', sometimes quite the contrary. For example, *akagabo* can mean a small or a very courageous man, according to the context.

12.   W. Mensching, *Ruanda: Eine Selbstdarstellung des Volkes in alten Ueberlieferungen* (Stadthagen: General-Anzeig-Verlag, 1987), pp. 28-34. I had the privilege of helping to produce this book based on manuscripts that W. Mensching brought from Rwanda during the First World War and left in his archives.

'gifted with a vivacious intelligence' and 'a refinement of feelings which is rare among primitive peoples' and which made him a 'natural-born leader, capable of extreme self-control and calculated good will'.[13] Their origin was sought in Ethiopia, Egypt, even Tibet (according to a rambling quasi-anthropological study by a French ambassador published in 1970 describing the Abatutsi as magi who had come from the far East[14]); it was even suggested, by the Dominican Father Etienne Brosse, that Abatutsi had come from the Garden of Eden, or, according to the theory of the Belgian administrator Count Renaud de Briery, from the lost continent of Atlantis.[15] Abatutsis received the rubber stamp of Indo-European blood, putting them on the same level as European colonialists. The Nilotic-Hamitic myth was born and exploited by the Abatutsi élite to their advantage. The Belgians, influenced by their experience of division at home between the Walloons and the Flemish, introduced *ibuku* (identity books) showing the ethnic group of the bearer and divided Abatutsi from Abahutu along purely economic lines. Everyone who had ten or more cows was classified as *umututsi*. Abatutsi who had no cows became Abahutu and Abahutu who had many cows became Abatutsi with all the attendant advantages, disadvantages and complexes of superiority and inferiority. During the 1994 genocide, as the private extremist Radio des Milles Collines incited Abahutu to exterminate the 'superior' and 'arrogant' Abatutsi 'foreigners', 'colonialists' and 'oppressors', these identity cards would play a key role in identifying those for slaughter.

As the Belgian administration applied the colonial principle of divide and rule, and supported the status quo, the Church too supported Abatutsi rule. This was done strategically and intentionally to secure a Constantine-type (top-down) conversion and to obtain the best tracts of land for their mission stations. King Musinga (1895–1931) resisted Christianity because of its threat to indigenous traditions and because of the competition between different denominations. He was forced to abdicate and died in exile in the Congo. His son Rudahigwa (1931–59) was converted into the Roman Catholic Church, which became de facto the official church, and Rwanda was dedicated to Christ the King. Special schools were built exclusively to give Abatutsi children an elementary education and train them as auxiliaries in colonial administration.[16]

13.	Ministère des Colonies, 'Rapport sur l'administration belge du Ruanda-Urundi' (1925), p. 34, quoted in Jean-Paul Harroy, *Le Rwanda, du féodalisme à la démocratie (1955–62)* (Brussels: Hayez, 1984), p. 26. For a discussion of the astonishing 'scientific' literature created by the colonialists of Rwanda, see Jean-Pierre Chrétien, 'Les deux visages de Cham', in P. Guiral and E. Témime (eds.), *L'idée de race dans la pensée politique française contemporaine* (Paris: Editions de CNRS, 1977), pp. 171-99.

14.	Paul del Perugia, *Les derniers rois-mages* (Paris: Phébus, 1970), p. 37. Babylon, Crete, and Noah and the Flood are also mentioned on p. 99. For a discussion of these race theories, see Gérard Prunier, *The Rwanda Crisis: A History of a Genocide* (London: Hurst & Company, 1995), pp. 5-16.

15.	See Prunier, *The Rwanda Crisis*, p. 8.

16.	In the aftermath of the Rwandan genocide, G. Mbonimana analyzed the social origin of the first Roman Catholic Christians and early schools and 'racial discrimination'. See his well-documented article 'Ethnies et église catholique', in *Cahiers Centre Saint-Dominique: Ethnies au Rwanda en 1995* (Kigali: Fraternité Saint-Dominique/Kacyiru, 1995), I, pp. 52-67.

The story and geography of the Bible were mapped onto the indigenous mythology and terrain of Rwanda, with the Abatutsi taking on the key roles of Abraham and Adam. The missionary-historian L. de Lacger called Mubari (a locality in the east) 'the place on which the Adam of mututsi descended from the clouds'.[17] Kigwa, 'the father of Batutsi', was Adam. Serwega, the eponymous ancestor of the Abega clan was 'a Tubal-Cain' who 'taught the aborigines iron work'.[18] Gihanga, the founder of Rwanda, was the 'Jabel of Genesis; because it is due to him or to his daughter that humanity acquired pastoral art'.[19] He was 'the Abraham of Batutsi: he is the one who is the stem of Hamite groups of Urundi, of Bunyabungo, of Gishari, of Mulera, of Ndorwa, of Bugesera, of Ruanda'.[20] The mausoleums in Rwanda were like the funeral sites in Israel where 'the deceased was reunited with his ancestors'.[21] The deliberate application of the books of Genesis and Kings to Rwandan history provided a strategic justification of the Abatutsi position and reinforced the sense of rivalry between Abahutu and Abatutsi by retelling and reinforcing it in terms of biblical myths—chiefly from Genesis and the succession narratives—concerning rivalry between siblings or between kinsmen and their progeny.

Mapping Ancient Israel onto Rwanda

The biblical paradigms were also applied to Rwanda's geography. The first major territory to be conquered, Nduga, became the 'Eden of Batutsi'.[22] This area, according to de Lacger, had the greater proportion of *eugéniques* and *métis*—that is, people of noble extraction and mixed race—than anywhere else, apart from Bigogo.[23] King Ruganzu Ndoli (1510–43), the 'legendary artisan' of Rwandan 'national unity', was compared to David.[24] The queen mothers were compared to Bathsheba, the mother of King Solomon.[25] According to this fusion of biblical myth and

17. De Lacger, *Ruanda*, p. 93.
18. De Lacger, *Ruanda*, p. 93. In fact, it is not true that Abatutsi introduced iron and metal work in Rwanda—it's prior existence is attested by archaeological findings—but the appropriation of this important resource was part of the whole political approach at that time of conquests.
19. De Lacger, *Ruanda*, p. 94. Again, as in the case of iron, it has been proven beyond doubt that cows existed in Rwanda before the arrival and consolidation of the Abanyiginya dynasties. Abahutu kings were using bulls' skins for their burials.
20. De Lacger, *Ruanda*, p. 94. The areas mentioned lie within the natural borders of Rwanda in the south, west, north and east, respectively. This shows that the court historians were surely reading history back into the events at a later stage with the benefit of hindsight, and in the light of the quasi-reunification of the country.
21. De Lacger, *Ruanda*, p. 96.
22. De Lacger, *Ruanda*, p. 104.
23. De Lacger, *Ruanda*, p. 104. It is difficult to see how even some missionaries could have been so biased in their analysis. The so-called *métis* were a meeting point between Abatutsi and Abahutu. Had the missionaries insisted on the value of the *métis* as an important element in their teaching, much violence and misery could have been avoided. Today, after the genocide and the widening divisions, people from mixed marriages are more perplexed than ever.
24. De Lacger, *Ruanda*, p. 107.
25. De Lacger, *Ruanda*, p. 126.

Rwandan history, Ndoli came back from exile as 'the redeeming messiah'[26] to re-store order after the chaos caused by his absence. The territories in the northwest of Rwanda (see above) which resisted the central Abanyiginya dynasty's authority, were described by de Lacger as the 'Galilee of Nations',[27] implying by this that the region was a mixture of different foreign groups (who had converged on the region in fleeing the advance of the Abanyiginya). It was in this region that another mis-sionary, Father Loupias, was killed: no wonder that his colleague de Lacger could affirm the proverb nothing good comes from 'the Galilee of nations' of Rwanda. The same region was ultimately home to most of the extremist leaders and the *interahamwe*, the perpetrators of genocide and the members of the so-called *Akazu* ('the small house'), which created chaos in the country in the 1980s, and lead to the 'final solution' of 1994.[28] Did the historical, political and religious marginalization of this region contribute to their paranoia? When the late president Habyalimana took power in 1973 and formed the *Comité du Salut et de l'Unité Nationale* ('Com-mittee for Salvation and National Unity'), the ideological fragmentation of the country had by then made such a goal impossible.

The Winds of Change: The Shift of Support from Abatutsi to Abahutu

The attempt to fit Rwandan myths and fables into biblical myths can be seen as an attempt on the part of the Church to curry favour with the ruling Abanyiginya aris-tocracy. In the period before 1959 the Church remained silent in the face of in-justices suffered mainly by Abahutu as a result of the absolute monarchy and the colonial system. When African revolutionaries and intellectuals raised their voices to call for independence for their countries, the wind of change[29] affected Rwanda. Political parties were founded. The Belgian colonial power became suspicious of the Royalist party, the Rwandese National Union, which allegedly received finan-cial and 'diplomatic backing' from the Communist countries in the UN Trusteeship Council.[30] This led to the collapse of the 1920s agreement between the Belgian administration and the 'Tutsi ruling caste'.[31] The Church also changed sides and approved of and supported the 1959 Abahutu revolution.[32] Subsequently it failed to speak out for justice for Abatutsi who were massacred or fled in 1959, 1964, 1967

26. De Lacger, *Ruanda*, pp. 106-107.

27. De Lacger, *Ruanda*, p. 110.

28. The ring leader of *Akazu* was the wife of President Habyalimana, who was compared to the infamous queen mother Kanjogera whose cruelty and political influence remained legendary in the Rwandan monarchy.

29. In Kinyarwanda (the language of Rwanda), the 1959 disturbances are called the *muyaga*: *muyaga* means a strong but variable wind, with unpredictable destructive gusts.

30. Prunier, *The Rwanda Crisis*, p. 47.

31. Harroy, *Rwanda, du féodalisme à la democratie (1955–1962)*, p. 241, quoted in Prunier, *The Rwanda Crisis*, p. 47.

32. Though it could be seen as a gesture in defence of justice, the Church wanted to safeguard its influence and interests. It succeeded in having a statement outlawing Communism included in the new Republican Constitution.

and 1972, and it was unable to facilitate their peaceful return. Later, the Church, crippled by its previous history and the political restrictions placed on it, could not succeed in its belated efforts to facilitate peace talks when the refugees returned by force in October 1990.

The return of Abatutsi exiles was led by General Rwigema, who was likened to Moses bringing his people back from Egypt to the Promised Land. Not all the returnees were exiles of the twentieth century: some had been exile families for more than 400 years, following fratricidal wars and feuds between rival princes. As we will see below, researchers and missionaries compared Abatutsi patriarchs to certain Israelite patriarchs. In patriotic songs and in some local papers, Rwigema was praised as Moses because he had mobilized all Abatutsi in the Diaspora, founded the Rwandese Patriotic Front and spearheaded their return. He was killed on the second day of hostilities and, like Moses, did not live to enjoy the 'Promised Land'. There is no doubt that in the eyes of many he was considered 'a liberator'.

The Ideology of Abatabazi: The Saviours, the Rescuers, the Deliverers, the Liberators

At the heart of the tangled skein of both politics, religion, indigenous myth and Christianity in Rwanda is the ideology of *abatabazi* (the saviours, the rescuers, the deliverers, the liberators), an ideology which is tied to the idea of self-sacrifice. In times of wars or natural calamities, human sacrifices were offered, usually by men offering themselves to be killed by the enemy on behalf of the king, with the blood of the *umutabazi* representing the blood of the king himself. The *umutabazi* offered himself up voluntarily or in response to a diviner's oracles, and usually submitted himself to death outside his own country in the belief that the land that swallowed the *umutabazi*'s blood would be easily conquered or affected by calamities. Alexis Kagame records that the first known person to die as such an 'offensive liberator' was Rwambali, in the reign of King Nsoro Samukondo (1279–1312). With its aura of magico-religious practice, this ideology began its lasting influence under the following king, Ruganzu Bwimba ('the victorious', 'the furious'), who reigned between 1312 and 1345.[33] Kimenyi I Musaya of Gisaka planned to annex Rwanda through a son by Robwa, Ruganzu's sister. A man named Nkurukumbi, of the Abasinga clan, from which the queen mothers came and who was a great favourite of the then queen mother, was designated by diviners' oracles to become *umutabazi*. But, with the support of the queen mother, he refused the great honour.[34] The spell then fell on the young king Ruganzu Bwimba himself. He went to Gisaka and was killed by their warriors. Learning of her brother's death, Robwa threw herself on the emblem-drum of Gisaka and killed herself and the son inside her womb. Both

---

33. Kagame, *Un abrégé*, p. 57.

34. Kagame, *Un abrégé*, p. 58. See also Perugia, *Les derniers rois-mages*, p. 202. As the blood of the chosen *umutabazi* mystically represented the blood of the king himself, after his death the family was honoured and received gifts and the 'hero' was recorded in historical annals.

Ruganzu and Robwa became the first models of self-sacrificial *abatabazi* ('liberators'; the plural form of *umutabazi*).[35] (No doubt, however, in reality this indirect form of killing was due partly to fear, and partly to conspiracy and intrigues at the royal court.)

Other *abatabazi* are also remembered in Rwanda. In order to annex the kingdom of Nduga, the prince Nkoko died there voluntarily as a liberator. King Yuhi II (1444–77) arranged a marriage between his own wife and King Samukondo of Bungwe. She returned pregnant and the child was later sent as 'a liberator' against his own country and was killed by his own father. Prince Gihana, son of King Cyilima II (1675–1708) died in Burundi as a liberator. His killer, the prince Rurinda, committed suicide over Gihana's body as a counter-liberator, thinking that his blood, as a prince himself, mixed with Gihana's, would nullify the latter. However, as Rurinda was not properly killed, that is, he was not killed by an enemy's hand and in a foreign land, Burundi suffered a severe drought as a result, until a satisfactory solution was found. The ingenious solution found by the Burundian court was to build a residence for Gihana in Burundi in a locality they named Muyange, the same name as the place of his residence in Rwanda, in order to mystify his spirit through assuming identity with Rwanda.

Kibogo, son of Ndahiro, became a liberator to avert a severe drought. The story is told that he went to the top of a mountain and was taken up by a cloud. His 'ascension' caused the rain to fall immediately.[36] This can be seen as a covert attempt to claim and supersede the magical powers of Abahutu kings whose functions included bringing rain in times of drought—a foe that could be as terrible as invading armies. The elevation of Kibogo to the rank of *umutabazi* could have been a machination of the court to explain the death of a prince tragically killed by lightening or by a rival prince.[37] When missionaries wanted to explain the translation into heaven of figures like Enoch, Moses, Elijah or Jesus' ascension or Mary's assumption they could appeal to the familiar example of Kibogo who went to heaven to plead with God for rain.

A Spiritual Umutabazi*: Lyangombe and the Non-Critical Appropriation of* Umutabazi *by European and Rwandan Christians*

If there were political *abatabazi*, a spiritual *umutabazi*, Lyangombe, should also be mentioned, although traditional oral literature has never recognized him as such.

35. Kagame, *Un abrégé*, pp. 57-59.
36. De Lacger, *Ruanda*, pp. 141-42.
37. Kagame indicates that his father Ndahiro II died in humiliating circumstances at the hand of a foreign enemy (Ntsibura I of Bunyabungo). Ndahiro's wives likewise died a cruel death (Kagame, *Un abrégé*, pp. 88-92). The same Kibogo is mentioned among the sixteen loyal men who had to ensure that Ndoli, son of Ndahiro II, who had fled to Karagwe (Tanzania) would return safely to Rwanda to succeed his father. It is possible that Kibogo did not survive the eleven years of occupation by Ntsibura I. Though Ntsibura had been made king of Bunyabungo (in the west), he had been born in Bugesera (in the east) and held Rwandans responsible for the death of his father. He was therefore exercising a vendetta.

There are different versions of the story concerning this mythical figure. In one account Lyangombe appears in the northwest. He disguises himself as a large rock reaching to the sky in order to cause confusion to a Rwandan monarch, King Ruganzu II (1510–43), who had lost his way back to Rwanda after a military expedition. He helped the king find the way back home, providing he promised that *umuhutu, umututsi* and *umutwa* would be united as followers of his mystery cult.[38] Other versions introduce Lyangombe from the south as a historical figure. His father was Babinga, son of Nyundo, a minor king of Nyakare.[39] Kagame asserts his historicity and traces his origin back to 'the region of Gitara in Muliro; which is now Toro in Uganda', adding that he was 'a wandering magician who was accompanied by his adepts called by the generic term *Ibicwezi*'.[40] In Rwanda, his followers were called *imandwa*. According to legend, he was a great hunter; his mother opposed one of his hunting adventures because of bad omens revealed to her in dreams. He disregarded the warning, went hunting, and was killed by a buffalo. As the buffalo tossed him into the air, he begged every kind of tree to receive him; most refused but the *umuko* tree[41] received him and he died in its branches. Before he expired, he sent a message to his mother that her premonition had come true, and that 'a child who does not listen to his father and his mother listens to the cicada'.[42] Lyangombe promised her that they would meet again and he instituted his mystery cult in which all ethnic groups would take part. Lyangombe became king of the spirits and reigned on the volcano Karisimbi,[43] which became paradise for his followers. Those who were not dedicated to his cult were considered Lyangombe's enemies and their spirits were banished to the volcano Nyiragongo.[44]

Whether entirely mythical or partly historical, Lyangombe corresponds to the idea of *umutabazi*. He opposed the existing social system, which was based on violence, stratification and exclusion. He attempted to create an inclusive society in which all ethnic groups had a place, united in life, death and beyond. In the northern tradition, he is presented as a mysterious foreigner who wanted to conquer

38. E. Johanssen, *Geistesleben afrikanischer Völker im Lichte des Evangeliums* (Munich: Chr. Kaiser Verlag, 1931), pp. 172-73.

39. De Lacger, *Le Ruanda*, p. 281.

40. Alexis Kagame, 'L'historicité de Lyangombe, Chef des "Immandwa"', in Tassa Okombe Lukumba (ed.), *Lyangombe mythe et rites: actes du deuxième colloque du CERUKI BUKAVU, 10-14 Mai 1976* (Bukavu: Centre de Récherches Universitaires du Kivu, 1976), pp. 17-28 (23). *Ibicwezi* (singular, *igicwezi*) is the term used to refer to the initiates of Lyangombe in Toro (Uganda)

41. The tree, called *érythrine* in French, has red flowers. They were used as shrines for the Lyangombe cult and received the cultic name *umulinzi* ('the protector', 'the watchman'; Mensching, *Ruanda*, pp. 312-34).

42. Mensching, *Ruanda*, p. 319.

43. At 4507 m, Karisimbi (or Kalisimbi) is the highest volcano in the north of Rwanda (now extinct). The area is rich in highly prized fresh water shellfish, which was the origin of its name: 'the mountain where pearls are found'.

44. Nyiragongo is situated in neighbouring Congo. By contrast with the paradisal Karisimbi, Nyiragongo is still active, as its eruptions early in 2002 have shown: clearly, the spirits of Lyangombe's enemies are still in torment there!

Rwanda with his spiritual powers. In this version, his religion would therefore be considered as an 'import'—probably from Uganda. The southern stories present him as a hero whose blood is shed not by a human enemy but by a beast. According to some of these versions the buffalo was a metamorphosed girl, Nyanzinge, daughter of King Ruganzu,[45] whom Lyangombe made pregnant and who was banished to the forest and later took her revenge. When Lyangombe's sons in turn killed Nyanzinge to avenge their father, it was she who was elevated to the rank of *umutabazi*.[46] This reinforces the suspicion that Lyangombe was denied the official 'honour' because he wanted an inclusive religious state, although more research is needed in support of this. Despite his death, his religion produced a revolution within, or at least offered an alternative to, the status quo.[47] In fact his religion outlived the monarchy and is still practised, and although there is much violence in the liturgy of the cult, this is attributable to its members and not to Lyangombe himself.

Membership of the cult of Lyangombe itself has two phases. The first is the process of initiation into the mystery cult called *kwatura* ('to confess', 'to make public') during which the candidate goes through the rituals of purification, symbolic death and salvation around the *umurinzi* tree. The candidate is then brought back into a hut where a symbolic ceremony of 'marriage' with Lyangombe is performed and the secret language of the cult is learned. A communal meal ends the first initiation. The second phase is called *gusubiraho* ('to return to the throne or seat of Lyangombe'). The candidates are permitted to sit on Lyangombe's throne, they are given a new name and they become qualified to incarnate Lyangombe or the spirits of his followers and to introduce other candidates into the cult. Sacrifices are offered, preferably bulls, but for the symbolic 'resurrection' itself two sheep are presented to the priest who incarnates Lyangombe. According to de Heuch, the first is refused. The second is accepted and is covered by a cow's skin. Once it stops writhing and lies still—as if dead—a pot of cold water is poured onto it. The sheep stands up and frees itself of its shroud and the people proclaim: 'It is risen. We have brought it back to life.'[48]

Missionaries witnessed these rites and exploited the similarities between the Lyangombe cult and Christianity. The Western Christian missionary-scholar Johanssen, for example, in his observations uses phrases such as 'giver of salvation' (*Heilsbringer*), 'unity' and 'fellowship', 'the new name', 'a kind of confirmation', 'welcome into the family of God', 'vows made and fulfilled', 'spiritual communication', 'act of piety', 'union of the person with the hero who has overcome the mysterious beast, that is, who has overcome death'[49]—all implying some kind of similarity with Christianity without ever making it explicit, probably for fear of seeming to approve of the Lyancombe cult. Johanssen argues that the cult

45. De Lacger, *Le Ruanda*, p. 282.
46. De Lacger, *Le Rwanda*, p. 282.
47. For a detailed diachronic and synchronic social-anthropologic approach, see de Heuch, *Le Rwanda*, pp. 201-362 (Chapters 4 and 5).
48. De Heuch, *Le Rwanda*, p. 194.
49. Johanssen, *Geistesleben*, pp. 180-82.

was similar to that of Mithras and claims that it must have been brought to Africa by the Hamites from Asia—thereby denying Africans the right to their own indigenous religious experience. He concludes: 'We see the soil ready for an understanding of the Gospel of the Giver of eternal life, of the Giver of the divine Spirit, whose Sonship and renewal can be attained by dying and radical purification'.[50] Johanssen's appropriation of the Lyangombe cult—while at the same time maintaining a decent distance from it—is a powerful illustration of how indigenous stories about 'liberators' and their redemptive sacrifices were used by a number of missionaries and preachers, including Rwandans, to explain the self-sacrificial meaning of Christ's death. However, these appeals were not made to the relatively non-violent cult of Lyancombe only, but to the ideology of *umutabazi* in general—appropriating and citing the history, while offering no critique of the concept of deliverance and the bloodshed and violence it involved.

Resistance to the Umutabazi *Ideology: The Opposition of Women, and the Fading of the Power of the Myth in the Nineteenth Century*

The only form of resistance that we can see in relation to the *umutabazi* ideology and the sacred violence that it sanctions was indigenous, and was expressed by mothers and women more generally. In the story of Nkurukumbi, who declines the honour of being *umutabazi* and who is substituted by Ruganzu and Robwa, the queen mother refuses to send her favourite, Nkurukumbi, to die in a foreign country. This opposition runs counter to the normal infallibility of oracular pronouncements on people's destinies. Another example of a female resisting sacrifice is the case of Nyamurunga, the daughter of a king, who was chosen to become another female 'liberator' during a Rwandan drought. According to tradition, a lion who was holding back the rain needed a victim to devour in order for rain to fall again. Nyamurunga was sent to the wilderness and climbed a tree and shouted, 'O, lion from the forest of Manyenye and Magage, come and devour Nyamurunga the king's daughter. She has come as a ransom for rain in her homeland Rwanda.'[51] When the lion came, Nyamurunga killed it with her axe and the rains returned. In mythical terms, Nyamurunga is Kibogo's counterpart—but whereas he climbs a mountain, sacrifices himself and ascends into the clouds, and so brings rain, she remains in and of the earth, and fights and kills the enemy rather than giving up her life. Logically, if Abanyiginya kings and their sons have succeeded in taking power from Abahutu and other Abatutsi clans, the superiority of their daughters should also have been justified by their readiness to sacrifice themselves—instead, the women are seen to exhibit a remarkable courage to resist and to fight.

An attentive observer can see in *umutabazi* myths political manoeuvres and tactics, attempts to establish and justify political systems, and the desire to boost warriors' morale by glorifying and sanctifying violence. But we should not assume the ideology was pervasive. In a small but important observation, de Lacger

50. Johanssen, *Geistesleben*, p. 182.
51. Mensching, *Ruanda*, p. 64.

observes how king Rwabugili (1853–95) could not rely on the morale produced by the effect of *abatabazi*, but recruited warriors among 'the humble bahutu' on account of their endurance and discipline.[52] This suggests that in the nineteenth century the mystical, magical and moral effect of the ideology of *abatabazi* was losing its weight. It did not die out, however, nor was it confined to the past. The concept was revived (resurrected) by the self-proclaimed government during the genocide of 1994. It called itself *Leta y 'Abatabazi* ('The Government of Saviours') —but with a radical new inflection of the myth. The government of saviours never sacrificed their own lives and they sanctified the spilling of blood on Rwanda's own soil.

Christian Appropriation of Umutabazi *Ideology*

The Christian appropriation of the *umutabazi* myth both changed and gave new currency to the idea. De Lacger, in his study of 'forgiveness', 'salvation' and 'rewards' from *Imana* ('God'), concludes that Rwandans see God[53] as by nature indulgent and forgiving, and as one who works via an intermediary, an *umutabazi*. He uses the example of the indigenous myth of Abatutsi Kigwa (the one who fell from above). Along with his brother and sister, he was expelled from heaven in expiation for an indiscretion committed by his mother, but also in order to help Abahutu who had been expelled, and settled in Mubari (a locality in the east of the country). After suffering sicknesses, hunger and cold, they prayed to 'Imana of Rwanda' to have mercy on them. He sent them grain, beans, pears, sorghum and bananas, and a few days later, iron, a billhook and a hoe fell from heaven and they started to cultivate. (An editorial parenthesis by de Lacger shows that three families of Abahutu—Abasinga, Abazigaba and Abatwa—were already living in the same area. They too had been chased from heaven for the grave sins of their own ancestor but, failing to ask for forgiveness, they were in a miserable state and so the newcomers gave to them from their own abundance. Again, this seems to be an aetiological ruse on the part of the Abatutsi to justify their supremacy over other groups who lived in the land before they came. The analogy with biblical Israel, in a different, more critical sense to the one used by the missionaries, is striking).[54] Telling the myth in his own quasi-indigenous terms, de Lacger writes: 'At the end, Imana, informed by the settlers of the problem of their future and the perpetuation of their race, pushed his indulgence to the point of dispatching on the wings of thunder an angel Raphaël—… a mutabazi—who said, "Do not be afraid. It is Imana who sent me to you. I will be your mediator".'[55] According to de Lacger's report, Father Loupias also compared *umutabazi* to the angel Raphaël who was sent by Imana to communicate his forgiveness to Kigwa and his brother and sister, saying,

---

52. De Lacger, *Ruanda*, p. 142.
53. De Lacger, *Ruanda*, p. 167.
54. De Lacger, *Ruanda*, pp. 167-68; he acknowledges P. Loupias (see above) as the source of this report.
55. De Lacger, *Ruanda*, p. 168.

'Fear not. It is Imana who sends me to you. I will be your mediator…'[56] Ironically, when the Roman Catholic Church changed sides to support the Abahutu revolution of 1959, it portrayed itself, in a sense, as an intervening/mediating *umutabazi*. This led the way for the use of lofty phrases such as the 'Committee for Salvation and National Unity' or 'the Government of Saviours' which had a clear theological as well as political content, through the hijacking of Christian vocabulary.

After the arrival of Christianity, the figure of the *umutabazi* assumed a new role. He was spiritualized and elevated to the level of an angelic being. God as helper became *umutabazi*. Jesus was given the same title in hymns. We can see how the concept of *umutabazi* affected religious life in Rwanda by looking at how freely it was applied to God and Jesus in the translation of the Bible and hymns, mainly by Protestant missionaries and their collaborators. The translators of the Bible into *Ikinyarwanda* ('the language of Rwanda') freely used the word *umutabazi* and other related terms, especially *umukiza* ('the saviour') and *umucunguzi* ('the redeemer' or 'the liberator' who achieves freedom for someone by paying a ransom). The term *umurokozi* ('the deliverer', from the verb *kurokora*) was the root of the term *abarokore*, meaning the 'saved ones', 'the born-again', and was mostly used from the time of the early revival movement of 1936. It was sometimes used as a popular alternative to *umutabazi*, as a form of unconscious opposition to the violent implications of the latter term (as set out above).

In Ps. 40.17, in Kinyarwanda, we read, *Ni wowe mutabazi wanjye n'umukiza wanjye…* (literally: 'It is you my liberator and my saviour'). The NRSV has 'You are my help and my deliverer…' The latter should have been translated, *Ni wowe Mufasha wanjye n'umukiza wanjye…* because the Hebrew word rendered *mutabazi wanjye* is עזרתי (v. 18 in *BHS*, correctly translated 'my help' in the NRSV). This is parallel to the phrase *n' umukiza wanjye* ('and my saviour') as it is in Ps. 70.5 (Kinyarwanda, v. 6 in *BHS*) and is the translation for the Hebrew ומפלטי, which has a more positive and general sense. However, according to the Psalter (17.13) the Lord will *save* by his הרב, his 'sword'. The Psalms are attributed to David and for him the sword is the instrument *par excellence* for extending his territory and taking the women and wealth of his defeated foes, the image of the divine sword masking the real aggression of the human sword and so bracketing out the question of personal responsibility and accountability. In Ps. 121.1-2, the passive form *gutabarwa* (infinitive passive from *gutabara*, from which the substantive *umutabazi* is derived—meaning to 'be rescued' or to 'be liberated') and the Lord is *umutabazi* but, since it is referring to the creator of heavens and the earth who does not need territory, there is no mention of a physical instrument of salvation. Here, the singer is inside the country, in the already possessed land, ascending to Jerusalem's temple. In Isaiah 49, which presents the 'state of the nation' and the need for a redeemer, the Kinyarwanda translation uses *ndagutabaye* (a present tense) for עזרתיך in v. 8. Paul uses this verse in 2 Cor. 6.2 and the translators have used the same archaic verb *naragutabaye* (perfect tense).

---

56. De Lacger, *Ruanda*, p. 168.

The translators of the New Testament used *umurokozi* ('deliverer') for God. For example, in 2 Cor. 1.10, we read in Kinyarwanda: [*Imana*] *Yaturokoy'urupfu rukomeye rutyo, na non'iracyaturokora, kandi twiringira yukw'izakomeza kuturokora* ('He who rescued us from so deadly a peril will continue to rescue us; on him we have set our hope that he will rescue us again', NRSV). It should be remembered that at the time of the translation, the KJV was using 'to deliver', not the later 'to rescue' used in the NRSV. Jesus is *umukiza* ('the Saviour'), suggesting one who deals with the total life of a human being (both his/her sin and his/her wellbeing). The term *umutabazi* was also applied to him in hymns, for example in:

Mutabazi wacu Yesu,	Our deliverer, Jesus,
Twese tuguhimbaze;	We all praise you;
Ni wowe wadupfiriye,	It is you who died for us,
Yesu Mwana w'Intama.	Jesus, the Lamb.[57]

Samson Inyarubuga, who was the first Rwandan to help Harold Guillebaud and other missionaries in the translation of the Bible (1929–32)—he is recognized as having been 'very critical'[58]—did not realize that the term *umutabazi* used instead of *umufasha* was ambiguous and had violent connotations in Rwandan history. He belonged to the royal family and is described by M. Guillebaud as a cousin of the king of Rwanda, a grandson of King Rutarindwa who spoke clear Kinyarwanda.[59] Because he was from the élite and knew the traditions and the role of *abatabazi*, Inyarubuga would naturally have preferred to use the archaic word *umutabazi* (with its strongly heroic overtones), when kings such as David (or Ndoli of Rwanda), are spoken of in Psalms, instead of *umufasha*, which is used of a woman (Eve is the *umufasha* of Adam in Genesis). The same word is used in Ps. 121.1-2 where the ability to be *gu-tabarwa* ('to be liberated', 'to be rescued') comes from the Lord.

In 'translating' Christianity into Inkinyarwanda the missionaries affirmed—and allied themselves with—the social and spiritual system of the elite, while their zeal to convert the Abanyiginya aristocracy through the strange mediation of Christian and Rwandan myth blinded many missionaries to the legacy of violence involved in the concept of *umutabazi*. It was precisely this ideology of *umutabazi* which encouraged the pursuit of war, annexation of territory, internal displacement, and thus the creation of a 'Galilee of nations' in the north of Rwanda as the only remaining stronghold where refugees could find security. The region became a time bomb for the future of the country.

---

57.   From Hymn 27 in the *Kinyarwanda Protestant Hymn Book* (Kigali: Editions Celtar, year not given). This was in turn translated from Hymn 170 of the *Keswick Hymn Book* (no details). I have given a literal translation.

58.   M. Guillebaud, *Rwanda, The Land that God Forgot? Revival, Genocide and Hope* (London: Monarch Books, 2002), p. 44.

59.   Guillebaud, *Rwanda*, p. 24. Rutarindwa reigned for one year (1895–96) and died in what is popularly known as the 'coup d'état de Rucuncu' following the treachery of the 'adoptive' queen mother who wanted her own son Musinga to become king.

Conclusion

This article has tried to show how the genocide in Rwanda had deep roots in its colonial history, social structure, and oral tradition, and also in the old ideology of *umutabazi*, as the cause and justification of violence, unthinkingly taken up by Christian missionaries and Bible interpreters and disseminated in political thought. Missionaries and their disciples were fascinated with the meeting of indigenous and Christian traditions, but by pursuing the analogy with certain Rwandan myths, they unwittingly emphasized violent undercurrents in Christianity, over and against other life-affirming or liberating motifs. Political, intellectual and religious leaders alike failed to challenge their own abuse of the central theme of salvation in order to justify their political and social positions, and used violence as a means to achieve or maintain power.

In order to break the cycle of violence in Rwanda (and in the region as a whole), we need to continue grappling with the magnitude of the genocide of 1994 and to investigate other faces of violence in the history of the nation. The church and theological institutions need to foster a new biblical hermeneutics for the post-missionary era: a hermeneutics which takes into account the realities of people and their history and the 'signs of the time'. Rwanda needs to hear other words from the stories and myths of its ancestors:

va i buzimu ujye i buntu

Quit the world of spirits and come to the world of the living!

'ON THE RIVERS OF BABYLON' (PSALM 137),
OR BETWEEN VICTIM AND PERPETRATOR*

Athalya Brenner

Psalm 137 charts a poetic-fictive journey from collective exiled abjection, to individual nostalgia for Jerusalem and what it symbolizes, to once again collective 'eye-for-eye' wishful revenge. This journey is undertaken in three 'stanzas' or strophes, in nine variously divided verses. The wishful revenge section, vv. 7-9, is problematic for interpreters and is often wished away, one way or another.[1] This article will re-problematize (1) the accepted setting of the psalm and/or its composition date as the Babylonian exile or immediately following it, and (2) the significance of the last section *vis-à-vis* the rest of the psalm, then to re-read the text through the post-Shoah lens of a recent non-biblical book.

Let me start by briefly presenting the two texts I would like to read together. The first is Psalm 137: to begin with in the original Hebrew, well known but worth repeating, then in English. In my translation the psalm is rendered in as low a register as possible, as un-poetically as possible, a counterbalance to the extremely poetic renderings one usually comes across for this celebrated psalm, at least for the first two stanzas (vv. 1-6) thereof. This is my preference since the linguistic usages of this psalm are simple enough: at times the choice of semantic stock may be problematic for readers and commentators, but the register seems far from high-

*   Heartfelt thanks to Toni Craven, who so generously fed me with relevant literature and let me see her work in progress on the Psalms (forthcoming in Walter J. Harrelson [gen. ed.] *The New Interpreter's Study Bible* [Nashville: Abingdon Press]). The Psalms section is co-authored by Toni Craven and Walter J. Harrelson.

1.   H. Gunkel, *Die Psalmen* (Göttinger Handkommentar zum Alten Testament, 2, Die poetischen Bücher, 2; Göttingen: Vandenhoeck & Ruprecht, 5th edn, 1968), pp. xxx, did not consider vv. 7-9 an integral part of the psalm. This view has since been dropped. Other commentators took the view that it is integral but tried to explain it or explain it away. The following cross-section of English-language commentaries have been consulted (for page numbers see the notes for specific verses and issues in the notes below): C.A. Briggs and E.G. Briggs, *A Critical and Exegetical Commentary on the Book of Psalms* (2 vols.; repr., Edinburgh: T. & T. Clark, 1969 [1906–1907]), II; E.J. Kissane, *The Book of Psalms*. II. *Psalms 73–150* (Dublin: Browne & Nolan, 1954); L.C. Allen, *Psalms 101–150* (WBC, 21; Waco, TX: Word Books, 1983); J.L. Mays, *Psalms* (Int; Louisville, KY: John Knox Press, 1994); H.-J. Kraus, *Psalms 60–150: A Commentary* (trans. H.C. Oswald; Minneapolis: Augsburg, 1989); H.J. Levine, *Singing Unto God a New Song: A Contemporary Reading of the* Psalms (Bloomington: Indiana University Press, 1995); J. Clinton McCann, Jr, 'The Book of Psalms', in Leander E. Keck (ed.), *The New Interpreter's Bible* (Nashville: Abingdon Press, 1996), IV, pp. 639-1280; K. Schaefer, *Psalms* (Berit Olam; Collegeville, MN: The Liturgical Press, 2001).

brow; on the other hand, while translating, I suppose that the imagined emotionalism and grandeur of the psalm suggests a higher register than presented by the Hebrew itself. Simplicity is then lost in favor of dramatic impact; I have tried to restore simplicity in my translation, while also taking into account accepted emendations, linguistic clarifications, and so on.

On the rivers[2] of Babylon	עַל נַהֲרוֹת בָּבֶל
There we sat, and cried	שָׁם יָשַׁבְנוּ גַּם־בָּכִינוּ
When we remembered Zion	בְּזָכְרֵנוּ אֶת־צִיּוֹן
On willows[3] within it we hung up our harps[4]	עַל־עֲרָבִים בְּתוֹכָהּ תָּלִינוּ כִּנֹּרוֹתֵינוּ
For there our captors asked us for words of song	כִּי שָׁם שְׁאֵלוּנוּ שׁוֹבֵינוּ דִּבְרֵי־שִׁיר
And our enemies,[5] for joy	וְתוֹלָלֵינוּ שִׂמְחָה
"Sing to us a song of Zion!"	שִׁירוּ לָנוּ מִשִּׁיר צִיּוֹן
How[6] can we sing Yhwh's song on foreign soil?	אֵיךְ נָשִׁיר אֶת־שִׁיר־יְהוָה עַל אַדְמַת נֵכָר
If I forget you, Jerusalem, let my right [arm] be forgotten,[7]	אִם־אֶשְׁכָּחֵךְ יְרוּשָׁלִָם תִּשְׁכַּח יְמִינִי
Let my tongue stick to my palate if I do not remember you,	תִּדְבַּק־לְשׁוֹנִי לְחִכִּי אִם־לֹא אֶזְכְּרֵכִי
If I do not remember Jerusalem first, in my joy	אִם־לֹא אַעֲלֶה אֶת־יְרוּשָׁלִַם עַל רֹאשׁ שִׂמְחָתִי
Remember, Yhwh, the day of Jerusalem to the sons of Edom,	זְכֹר יְהוָה לִבְנֵי אֱדוֹם אֵת יוֹם יְרוּשָׁלִָם
Who said, "Destroy, destroy[8] her down to her foundation"	הָאֹמְרִים עָרוּ עָרוּ עַד הַיְסוֹד בָּהּ
Daughter Babylon, the aggressor,[9]	בַּת־בָּבֶל הַשְּׁדוּדָה

2.   'Rivers' seems to me the simplest translation of a most common Hebrew word, rather than the 'watercourses' or 'canals' sometimes used. At any rate, the *positive* connotations of water sources, rather than the negative geopolitical connotations of exile, have largely escaped interpretative attention. Sitting on the 'rivers of Babylon' may indicate a *materially* comfortable position of abundance, in contrast to the *emotional* state expressed later in the psalm.

3.   Weeping willows, to echo the crying? For the 'hanging harps' motif see J.L. Kugel, *In Potiphar's House: The Interpretive Life of Biblical Texts* (Cambridge, MA: Harvard University Press, 2nd edn, 1994 [1st edn 1990]), pp. 184-89, and 209-10 n. 35, esp. in *Pes. R.* 144 and parallels but also in other sources.

4.   Or lyres?

5.   For the obscure Hebrew תּוֹלָלֵינוּ see *BHS*. 'Enemies', as well as the oft-used 'tormentors', is by analogy to 'captors' (שׁוֹבֵינוּ).

6.   The psalm does not state that one should not sing the song or songs on a foreign land; rather, it asks, literally, 'how' it should be done. Indeed, a 'song' is immediately produced in vv. 4-6, perhaps not the one asked for. On the problem this constituted for ancient exegetes see Kugel, *In Potiphar's House*, pp. 187-89.

7.   Or: 'forget its skills'; or, 'deny (from a metathesis of the Hebrew root שכח to כחש) its skills'.

8.   Literally 'lay bare', 'make nakedness seen', from the Hebrew root ערה, which is used in contexts of metaphorical 'nakedness', such as in a euphemism for sexual intercourse. Hence, the metaphor is in fact nullified by the well-mannered—albeit correct by implication and sense—translation as 'destroy'.

9.   The Hebrew officially is a passive form. Translating into the active, such as 'the aggressor' or 'cruel' implies either an emendation of the passive into an active form, necessitating a minimal metathesis, or viewing the seemingly passive as active in meaning, a late feature for Biblical Hebrew, which is the position adopted here.

Praised[10] be the one who pays you the reward   אשרי שישלם־לך את־גמולך שגמלת לנו
you rewarded us,

Praised be the one who holds your infants and   אשרי שיאחז ונפץ את־עלליך אל־הסלע
crushes them to the rock.

If I were to summarize the cognitive/emotive contents of this poem, I would say there are three dominant motifs in it: (1) exile experienced as captivity, complete with the captors' ironic (or simply curious?)[11] call for the captives to 'sing'; (2) memory is invoked as a marker of collective (first-person plural in vv. 1-4, then 8) identity, then of individual identity (first-person singular in vv. 5-6)—the particular memory referred to is that of 'Jerusalem/Zion', a locus antithetical to the present position experienced as at siege (see below); (3) verbal revenge, born out of the memory of war, is sought against the most defenseless of the enemy.

The second text is Jan T. Gross's book *Neighbors*, which appeared almost simultaneously with investigative newspaper reporting of the same events Gross describes in 1941 Poland, in 2001.[12] I feel strongly that the book, deceptively simple and even handed, could not have been written in the same way 20 years ago, perhaps not even 10 years ago—it had to wait for Shoah denials on the one hand, and for non-demonizing historical literature about the utter ordinariness of most Germans, Nazis and Nazi collaborators included, on the other hand. This is especially impressive since in this book Gross gives us, calmly and with reigned-in passion, a picture of *ḥurban*, a total annihilation of a Jewish community:

> One summer day in 1941, half of the Polish town of Jedwabne murdered the other half—1600 men, women, and children—all but seven of the town's Jews... Most arresting is the sinking realization that Jedwabne's Jews were clubbed, drowned, gutted and burnt not by faceless Nazis, but by people whose features and names they knew well... (From the book's front and back covers.)

A veritable carnivalesque event, horrifying in its explicitness. Here are some more moments from the story, as retold by Gross and the testimonials he used. While the Jews were herded into a barn and burned, they had

> to pick up a huge monument of Lenin... While carrying the monument, they also had to sing[13]... Newborn babies were killed at their mothers' breasts, people were beaten murderously and forced to sing and dance. In the end they proceeded in the main action—the burning... The Jews were ordered to line up in a column...and all were ordered to sing and were chased into the barn... Then the barn was

---

10.   On the Hebrew אשרי see the Excursus at the end of this article.

11.   This possibility, that the request attributed to the host community is motivated by curiosity rather than by mockery, has not (to the best of my knowledge) been entertained by commentators, who are quick to empathize with the textual speakers at this point. On the other hand, see Kugel, *In Potiphar's House*, p. 185: 'Now in the context of the psalm, this may have been a simple request for entertainment'.

12.   Jan T. Gross, *Neighbors: The Destruction of the Jewish Community in Jedwabne, Poland* (Princeton: Princeton University Press, 2001).

13.   And in another place: '...and the rabbi was told to walk in front with his hat on a stick, and all had to sing, "The war is because of us, the war is for us"' (p. 99).

doused with kerosene and lit, and the bandits went around to search Jewish homes, to look for the remaining sick and children. The sick people they found they carried to the barn themselves, and as for the little children, they roped a few together by their legs and carried them on their backs, then put them on pitchforks and threw them onto the smoldering coals.[14]

Let us start by looking at the events of that fateful day, 10 July 1941, from the emic viewpoint of Jedwabne Poles. Mostly devout Catholics, they had been hosts to a Jewish community larger than themselves for centuries. Differences of religion, supposed ethnicity, occupation and class were in most cases obvious: the Poles were largely producers of food (farmers); the Jews were largely service and trade people. In daily life necessity dictated tolerance and coexistence. Religiously, enmity was inescapable because of church teaching, although it was held in delicate balance in the interest of both groups' survival, in between outbursts of violence or intended violence. It is beyond dispute that—in spite of the long-standing co-exis-tence—most Poles were by and large ignorant of the essentials of Jewish life, jealous, uncomprehending, resentful and suspicious of Jewish segregationist iden-tity. Such an attitude, at least until recently, was unproblematically labeled as anti-Semitism.

The balance of co-existence was rudely disturbed by the introduction of a bal-ance of terror: the Russian/Communist and then the German/Nazi invasions, both occurring within months of each other and both causing the Poles great anguish and suffering.[15] Internal differences within the larger, Catholic/Jewish local community came to the fore. And the stronger, host Pole communities turned against their more numerous but less powerful neighbors, for changing balances require that accounts be settled by extraction and payment. The pogrom in Jedwabne, although the cruel-est, was by no means the only one in that geographical area around that time:[16]

> Where the initiative came from—whether it originated with the Germans…or with the town council members of Jedwabne—is impossible to settle once and for all. But it is also an academic matter, since both sides apparently quickly agreed on the matter, and on the method of its implementation'.[17]

While the Germans were the only ones who could decide the fate of the Jews, and while after 10 July 'Poles were no longer permitted to kill the Jews of Jedwabne at will',[18] nevertheless,

> Murderous intent toward their neighbors was manifested by the Polish population in Jedwabne *not just verbally*, when the town council members spoke with the Germans, but through actual deeds carried out by the town population.[19]

---

14. Testimony by Samuel Wasersztajn, one of the seven survivors, delivered on 5 April 1945 (Gross, *Neighbors*, pp. 19-20 in Gross).

15. Gross, *Neighbors*, pp. 41-53 (42-43).

16. Gross, *Neighbors*, pp. 54-71.

17. Gross, *Neighbors*, p. 74.

18. Gross, *Neighbors*, pp. 77, 103.

19. Gross, *Neighbors*, p. 75 (my emphasis).

In other words, *the so-called local population involved in the killing of Jews did so of its own free will.*[20]

That plunder, that is, economic gain, was one of the chief motives for the pogrom (as for earlier East European pogroms) is well established by various testimonies.[21] Gross states:

> ...I would think it very probable that the desire and unexpected opportunity to rob the Jews once and for all—rather than, or alongside, atavistic anti-Semitism—was the real motivating force that drove Korolak [the town mayor] and his cohorts to organize the killing.

And yet, the question remains: What can explain this horror, this monstrosity, committed by a 'bunch of ordinary men'[22] who were, at the same time, victims themselves? Gross hazards an educated guess: that, at least in the devout Catholic lands of Eastern Europe, Jew hatred—even among the intelligentsia and urban so-called elites, even after the war—was motivated not only by the overt suspicion of Jewish collaboration with the 'enemy' (communism?) or by jealousy/greed. It also was intimately bound up with the suspicion of ritual murder, the blood libel of Passover, a mediaeval anachronism in the midst of modernity.[23] In other words, when all is said and done, and after systemic respect for authority (of the town's mayor, of the priest, of the Germans) is taken into account, it was deeply rooted religious prejudice—according to Gross—that facilitated the cruelty of the pogrom, even if it did not serve as its only or even chief conscious motive. This act, writes Gross, should serve as a marker of Polish collective identity, even though it was committed by individuals.[24] Jedwabne was *not* an isolated episode; and the Polish supply a painful example of how one can be a victim and a perpetrator at the same time.[25] And ultimately the only remedy available, and the urgent task for historiography in general and for the New Historicism in particular (since its practitioners are so keen on historical re-evaluation), is to open the wounds and record what local people have known all along anyhow.

---

20. Gross, *Neighbors*, p. 133 (original emphasis).

21. Gross, *Neighbors*, pp. 105-10. The quote is from p. 110.

22. Gross, *Neighbors*, p. 111.

23. Gross, *Neighbors*, pp. 122-25, 150-51. Another example of a cultic libel against Jews that became historically important, this time from ancient times, might be in order here. Elias Bickerman emphasized that the oldest version of the widespread accusation that the Jews used to venerate a golden ass's head may go back to a story transmitted in Zabidus' tale about the stealing of the ass head that would have already circulated in Idumea in the fifth and fourth centuries BCE (E. Bickerman, 'Ritualmord und Eselskult', *MGWJ* 71 NS 35 [1927], pp. 171-87, 255-64). This is mere speculation, but the association of Jewish ass-worship was linked to (and became part of) the struggle between Jews and Idumeans in the second century BCE, possibly also in Egypt (where this libel originated), since Egypt hosted a Jewish/Judahite as well as an Idumean diaspora (*pace* M. Stern, *Greek and Latin Authors on Jews and Judaism*. I. *From Herodotus to Plutarch* [Jerusalem: Israel Academy of Sciences and Humanities, 1974], p. 98). I am indebted to Jan Willem van Henten for this reference, among others.

24. Gross, *Neighbors*, pp. 132-37.

25. Gross, *Neighbors*, p. 144.

And while on the issue of memory, let me return to Psalm 137. It has been accepted, from ancient times, as a *genuine* expression of the exiled state in Babylon, after the destruction of the first temple (567 BCE). This is the case in the Jewish tradition which, among other things, places the psalm on a par with Lamentations and Jeremiah as poetic responses to the Babylonian conquest of Jerusalem.[26] Also, it was and is recited in full on weekdays[27] just before the Blessing for Food in Orthodox Ashkenazi communities, and in Orthodox Sephardic communities as part of the Ninth of Ab liturgy, that is, the annual service for the destruction of the first and second Jerusalem temples (and more of that later).[28] The psalm's setting and composition date is accepted by most biblical scholars as exilic or early pre-exilic, although several of them ascribe the actual composition to a date later than the exile and a past perspective in relation to an assumed exile experience,[29] claiming that it shows recently remembered suffering while interpreting the verbs of the passage in keeping with its assumed subject matter.

With all respect due to traditional renderings and a straightforward understanding of scripture, the following arguments may be listed against such—or similar— allegedly concrete settings and/or composition dates.

1. *Linguistic Considerations*

(1) The verbs in the first verses—sit, cry, hang, ask—are consistently in the *qatal* (rather then *wayyiqtol*) formation. Biblical verb tenses, especially in poetry, do not have chronological meanings that are easily deciphered. They may indicate any narrated 'time'. Thus, the *qatal* formation may indicate past, present or future. It cannot be used with any confidence for a date in the past or the present, therefore.

---

26. *Lam. R., Petihtot*; *Zuta* for Lamentations (beginning); *Pes. R.* 26, 29; *b. Pes.* 118a; *Ag. Ber.*; *Eliyahu Rab.*; see also Rashi, Ibn Ezra, *Mezudat Zion* and *Yalkut Shimeoni* for the chapter. Cf. Kugel, *In Potiphar's House*, pp. 174-80, for Davidic and Jeremianic authorship of the psalm in rabbinic sources.

27. Excluding festivals and holidays, when the reversed Ps. 126 ('When Yhwh returned to Zion') is recited.

28. For a convenient summary of the Orthodox usage and its origin see Macy Nulman, *The Encyclopedia of Jewish Prayer: Ashkenazic and Sephardic Rites* (Northvale, NJ: Jacob Aronson, 1996), pp. 19-20. Note also the following quote: 'That the psalm relates to the destruction of both the First and the Second Temples is evident from verse one, which refers to the Babylonians, and verse seven, which mentions Edom (Rome)' (p. 19). For a possible Christian usage see McCann, 'The Book of Psalms', pp. 1228-30. See also Mays, *Psalms*, p. 423, on the textual singers: 'Whatever justifiable reservations may lead us to omit their prayers from our lections and prayers must not obscure *the question their passion and understanding places against ours*'. Let me add that Mays refrains from fully interpreting vv. 7-9, clearly recoiling from the task.

29. Briggs and Briggs, *Psalms*, II, p. 484; Allen, *Psalms 101–150*, following Weiser, p. 239; Kissane, *Psalms*, II, pp. 285-87; McCann, 'The Book of Psalms', p. 1227 (quoting Kraus, *Psalms*, p. 501: 'the only psalm in the psalter that can be dated reliably'); Levine, *Sing Unto God*, p. 184; Mays, *Psalms*, p. 421. Schaefer, *Psalms*, pp. 321-23, is somewhat more neutral about the date, although he is more than emotionally involved with the speakers' imagined fate elsewhere in his interpretation of the psalm.

(2) Such verb usage is nevertheless more characteristic of post-exilic texts than of pre-exilic and exilic texts, even in poetry, although in later texts (Qoheleth!) and post-Biblical Hebrew the *qatal* formation signifies, almost exclusively, a past tense. That, however, is not sufficient reason to ascribe a precise composition date in the sixth century; on the contrary, it indicates a later composition date.

2. *Semantic and Content Considerations*

(1) Babylon and its rivers, as mentioned in the first verse, receive lots of inter-pretative attention as the true geographical locus of the narration or the narrated setting. However, is Babylon here the real, historical Babylon of Nebuchadnezzar and his successors? Or is it no more so than the Nineveh of Jonah, or the Babylon of Daniel or of Revelation (especially in ch. 18, vv. 2, 10, 21). Thus 'Babylon' may be not a reference to the place itself but, rather, function much as in the New Testament and early church writings:

> As a symbol, Babylon embraces more than the empire, city, and culture of Rome. It is the sphere of idolatry and worldliness under the temporary control of Satan, a worldliness in opposition to the people and work of God, a worldliness epitomized first by Babylon and then by Rome. Babylon as the mother of harlots and abomi-nations in opposition to God (17.5) is the antithesis of the Church as the Bride of Christ, the New Jerusalem, and the Kingdom of God.[30]

If this seems a little far-fetched in relation to Psalm 137, let us read from Ibn Ezra on v. 7:

> 'Remember' [the call for revenge addressed to Yhwh]. This does not talk about the exile of Titus [the second, Roman exile] as many have thought, since afterwards the 'daughter of Babylon' is mentioned. Furthermore, Titus the Wicked was not of Edomean seed, since the Romans are Greek...

Ibn Ezra clearly polemicizes against an attribution of this psalm to the second, Roman exile. However, he knows of opinions to that effect, he seems to know of an identification of 'Babylon' (or 'Edom')—perhaps through Christian influence, who knows?—with Rome.[31] Or with any other oppressive political force that operates or operated in history against Jews. Or was perhaps the Christian symbol of 'Babylon' taken from Judaic texts, such as the Jeremiah oracles (chs. 50–51, for instance)?[32] Let's look at the *ABD* once more:

---

30. D.F. Watson, 'Babylon in the NT', in David Noel Freedman (ed.), *The Anchor Bible Dictionary CD-ROM* (New York: Doubleday, 1997).

31. And cf. Mireille Hadas-Lebel, *Jerusalem contre Rome* (Paris: Editions du Cerf, 1990), review by G. Stemberger, *JSJ* 23 (1992), pp. 111-14. Thanks again to J.W. van Henten for this reference.

32. C.H. Hunzinger, 'Babylon als Deckname für Rom und die Datierung des 1. Petrusbriefs', in H. Reventlow (ed.), *Gottes Wort und Gottes Land* (Göttingen: Vandenhoeck & Ruprecht, 1965), pp. 67-76.

Rome is identified with Babylon in early Judaism, for like Babylon it overthrew Jerusalem and destroyed the temple (*2 Bar.* 11.1-2; 67.7; 2 Esd. 3.1-2, 28; *Sib. Or.* 5.143, 155-61, 434, 440; Str-B 3.816).

(2) And this leads us to Edom (v. 7), another toponym that, if taken literally, would cause the commentator who attributes the psalm or its contents to the historical first exile (on 'internal evidence'![33]) an interpretative headache. Thus, vv. 7-9 too must be viewed as specifically directed against the Edomites and their *historical* behaviour during the destruction of Jerusalem,[34] with 'daughter of Babylon' as the work of a later glossator;[35] and similarly Allen[36] after Freedman[37] and Kellerman.[38] Mezudat Zion, ingeniously, interprets 'daughter of Babylon' as the Babylonian exiled community, thus killing two birds with one stone: solving the naming problem and the passive form of השדודה, seemingly 'the oppressed' in the same noun phrase.[39] Clearly, the introduction of Edom alongside Babylon is problematic—unless we accept Bert Dicou's position, namely, that 'Edom' too became a concept and a 'type':

> At the beginning of the exilic period...Edom abandoned Judah when the Baby-lonians came to punish Judah for its rebellion...[thereafter] 'Edom' became a cultic theme, and later a prophetic-literary theme. Edom served as Israel's special opponent and the representative of the nations.[40]

Thus Dicou, whose perspective is decidedly historical and text-critical, allows for a symbolic (that is, a-historical) evolution of 'Edom'. Furthermore Edom, or even more specifically 'Wicked Edom', is an occasional rabbinic code-name for the Hellenistic kingdom, or for Rome, or for any foreign oppressive regime, and so up to the Responsa literature of the twentieth century.[41] Moshe David Herr contends

33. Briggs and Briggs, *Psalms*, II, p. 484.
34. McCann, 'The Book of Psalms', p. 1228; cf. Kraus, *Psalms*, p. 503.
35. Briggs and Briggs, *Psalms*, II, pp. 484-87.
36. Allen, *Psalms 101–150*, p. 236.
37. D.N. Freedman, 'The Structure of Psalm 137', in H. Goedicke (ed.), *Near Eastern Studies in Honor of W.F. Albright* (Baltimore: The Johns Hopkins University Press, 1971), pp. 187-205, summarized by Allen, *Psalms 101–150*, pp. 239-40.
38. U. Kellerman, 'Psalm 137', *ZAW* 90 (1978), pp. 43-58.
39. Cf. n. 9 above for my understanding of the Hebrew form as a late formation—formally passive but functionally active.
40. B. Dicou, *Edom, Israel's Brother and Antagonist: The Role of Edom in Biblical Prophecy and Story* (JSOTSup, 169; Sheffield: JSOT Press, 1994), p. 199. One can also think of the Idumeans associated with Edom; forced to convert to Judaism by John Harcanus [Hyrcanus] I; anti-Judahite passages in Greek express Edomite hatred of Jews, see Bickerman, 'Ritualmond und Eselkult', and Stern, *Greek and Latin Authors*.
41. Some ancient transparent examples are: *Megillat Ta'anit*, for the twenty-eighth of Adar, *Num. R.* 7.10, *Pes. K.* 4.9, *Tanhuma* (three occurrences in both versions), *Midrash Tehillim* on Pss. 68, 69, 104 and 121; see too Eisenstein for several biblical passages (seven times), Rashi to *b. Sanh.* 97b; and there are more. That there is no injunction against singing Yhwh's songs per se in a foreign land; cf. Kugel, *In Potiphar's House*, pp. 173-213, especially pp. 188-89 on Sa'adia Ga'on's interpretation. As his commentary (and Kugel's discussion) implies, the conflation of

that the specific encoding of Rome (and later Christian Rome and Christianity itself) as Edom does not predate the late tannaitic period (that is, the time of the Bar Kochba revolt, mid-second century CE) or the early amoraitic times, although he too claims that the origin of this encoding is historical and harks back to biblical times.[42] The (probably later) extension of the name as code is telling. In other words, in Psalm 137 Edom too might be symbolic of *any* oppressive political/military power, much like Babylon, although its more common referent in rabbinic literature is indeed Rome.

(3) Commentators tend to read 'Jerusalem' as a symbol for the temple and cult, so much so that they speculate whether the 'songs of Zion' are Levite songs, cultic songs that by definition should not be sung on foreign soil.[43] This would concretize the psalm even further, of course, but I wonder how sure the commentators are: How sure can they be?

For Jerusalem is certainly itself, and can symbolize the temple by way of the general standing for the particular, the whole for a part. But more often, the part stands for the whole, and then Jerusalem functions as a symbol of the land of Israel, as antithetical to the exile. Is there any 'internal evidence' to read 'Jerusalem' in this psalm as indicative of 'temple', when the temple itself is nowhere explicitly mentioned? Would not this minimize, rather than maximize, the psalm's effect while serving the commentators' religious agendas? It seems to me that there's no way of justifying this optimistic quest for 'evidence', and the matter had better be left open.

(4) Is there in fact 'internal evidence' for specific *first-hand* suffering? Do vv. 1-6 contain such 'evidence'? There *is* evidence of suffering and being away from one's own territory, as symbolized by 'Jerusalem' and 'Zion'. There is a call for revenge for the murdered children in vv. 7-9 which is reminiscent of the children's fate in Lamentations. But, linguistically, it seems to be even closer to Jeremiah's call for revenge against the Babylonians (ch. 51, esp. vv. 20-25 and 53-59): in other words, there might be a case of literary re-adaptation here, less a case of spontaneous anguish than that of conscious literary borrowing. Perhaps it is better to agree with

music/cultic song and music/temple/possibly Levites song had already been made early on. This is of great historical interest, of course. However, it reflects historical Jewish needs while in itself containing no compelling intrinsic reason for its uncritical acceptance by bible scholars. Cf. also Kugel on p. 208 n. 29: 'Indeed, various modern exegetes, following (by and large unwittingly) the lead of both rabbinic and medieval Jewish commentators…have suggested that the putative speakers of this psalm are not run-of-the-mill Israelites, but Temple singers who might have been separated off from their countrymen…' While Kugel acknowledges the ancient Near Eastern custom of taking singers/musicians of both genders as booty, his presentation implies skepticism as to the 'levite-ness' of Ps. 137's 'singers'.

42.   M.D. Herr, 'Edom in the Aggadah', in *EncJud*, VI, pp. 379-80.

43.   McCann, 'The Book of Psalms', p. 1227; Levine, *Sing Unto God*, p. 186 ('…the psalm is pre-eminently a song of the Levite guilds entrusted with the nation's ritual memory'); Kraus, *Psalms*, p. 502; Schaefer, *Psalms*, p. 321.

Rogerson and McKay,[44] who proclaim mildly that the author of this psalm might not have participated personally in the Babylonian exile.

(5) Much interpretative distress could have been avoided had an understanding of אשרי as either 'confirmed in existence' or 'praised', as suggested in my translation and Excursus here, been adopted. At any rate, the mere possibility of understanding אשרי other than in the sense of 'happy' or in a way 'blessed' may introduce another 'story' to the psalm.[45]

(6) Furthermore, where have we found in the Hebrew bible that the 'enemies', or Babylonians, or Edomites for that matter, did throw infants against the rock, as is claimed in vv. 8-9? Biblical sources use the terrible trope of infants suffering and dying in war especially in connection with hunger, be it their own hunger (Lam. 2.11; 4.4) or the hunger of their mothers, who cook them for food (Lam. 2.20; 4.10; cf. 2 Kgs 6.24-30).[46] Other biblical texts (Nah. 3.9-10; Isa. 14.21; Jer. 51) wish that same fate on various enemies' infants, much as in this passage, but do not precisely claim that such cruelty was practiced on the Israelites or Judahites, or Jews. As we have seen even in Lamentations, when the death of young ones is so movingly mourned, such a claim is not made. Already the *Midrash Tehillim* (for Ps. 121.4) deals with this difficulty by asking, 'We have heard that they [the enemies] did many things…but we have not heard that they dashed the infants!' And the answer necessitates a midrash, reading all 'children of Israel' as 'infants' (my paraphrase). And yet modern commentators opine that killing children like this was 'a feature of ancient Near Eastern warfare', which is difficult to accept for 'Christian readers', but, within the given framework, represents the 'satisfaction of divine justice'.[47] This is a weak solution for a weighty moral problem, one that to my mind equals a virtual removal of vv. 7-9 from the original composition for reasons of professed delicacy.

Let us return for a minute to Jewish liturgy. I have mentioned the reading of Psalm 137, *in full*, every weekday by Orthodox Ashkenazim, and on the Ninth of Ab by Sephardim. However, Jewish Conservative, Liberal and Reform prayer

44. J.W. Rogerson and J.W. McKay, *Psalms 101–150* (Cambridge Bible Commentary; Cambridge: Cambridge University Press, 1977), p. 150.

45. I thank Toni Craven for encouraging me to develop the line of inquiry beginning with אשרי which, in her opinion, may be the key to understanding the whole psalm, not to mention other psalms from the very first word of Ps. 1 onwards.

46. On the other hand, references in 2 and *4 Maccabees* to mothers thrown by Greeks from a wall with their circumcised sons at their breasts may be relevant here—in 2 Macc. 6.10, 'two women were brought in for having circumcised their children. These women they publicly paraded about the city, with their babies hung at their breasts, then hurled them down headlong from the wall.' Or in *4 Macc.* 4.25, because they had circumcised their sons, women were thrown headlong from heights along with their infants, 'though they had known beforehand that they would suffer this'. Once again, thanks to J.W. van Henten for mentioning this source.

47. For instance Allen, *Psalms 101–150*, p. 237, after McKenzie (see there for fuller reference).

books—as they have evolved in the last 150 years, from Geiger onwards[48]—recommend a different practice. Variously, Psalm 137 may or may not be recited
on weekdays; it may or may not be read on the Ninth of Ab; but, significantly,
*whenever it is recited only the first six verses are recited. The offending vv. 7-9 are
removed from the relevant prayers and services.*[49] The symbolic Jerusalem remains
as such, memory and longing are upheld for their own sakes and as symbolic;
revenge, however, is rejected. Liturgy can and does use only parts of scripture. The
interpreter, however, has to account for a whole passage, and there is no ancient
witness that I know of that omits vv. 7-9 from the biblical text.

To give an interim summary at this point: What choices, then, do I make in the
matter of interpreting Psalm 137, in the light of the considerations advanced?
Partially in the face of interpretative tradition and liturgical tradition, I proceed
from these assumptions. The psalm/poem is, structurally, an integrated whole. Its
language is emotional, yet commonplace from the perspective of register (difficulties of a semantic or textual nature, such as תוללינו, notwithstanding). Its language
is relatively late, probably later than that of the exilic or early post-exilic period. It
does indeed deal with a situation of exile and longing for 'Jerusalem' and 'Zion' as
a symbolic reminder and antithesis to 'exile', not necessarily as a cultic centre. The
place of exile, while identical with at least one of the oppressing enemies' names
(Babylon) or both (also Edom), is either symbolic (I stop short of claiming that it
actually points to Rome) or else non-specific, referring to any political and military
oppressor. The cumulative effect of all these considerations will be to render the
poem/psalm historically non-specific, in so far as its composition and setting are
concerned: any exile situation, any memory of physical annihilation, will do as a
setting. Nevertheless, and having admittedly softened אשרי, the vehemence of the
last stanza (vv. 7-9), the cruel call of the powerless for revenge against their more
powerful neighbours in exile, still has to be accounted for or at least explained
more satisfactorily.

And this is my cue for returning to the story of Jedwabne and for comparing
these two superficially dissimilar texts. In the intertext of Jedwabne the supra-
historical, subjectively reported situation of Ps. 137.1-3 is objectively enacted with
specific historical vehemence. Jews are indeed required to sing about themselves,
en route to their death within the boundaries of their exiled community, encircled
by their 'captors', no escape, because of their collective religio-ethnic identity. Will

---

48. My thanks to Edward van Voolen on this point. We have consulted several prayer books
dated 1960–2000 from Dutch, Swiss-German, Israeli and American communities.

49. The choice to remove the last verses is undoubtedly motivated by the wish to remember
Jerusalem *sans* the revenge motif. However, on the removal or possible removal of the psalm
altogether, one must remember that, for example, Reform interpretation of the ninth of Ab is different from that of Orthodox Judaism. The variations (between daily recitation, when commanded
or recommended, and the ninth of Ab) are accounted for by the newer Judaisms' wish to transcend
the traditional Ashkenazi–Sephardic boundaries as well as the Liberal–Reform (and to an extent the
Conservative/Reconstructionist) attempt at reconstructing the ninth of Ab's significance (and
liturgy).

this enforced singing qualify as 'songs of Zion', I wonder? Will it, even if in neither source (according to my reading) cultic songs are implied? Will it be enough to agree that among the mixed motives for the Jedwabne pogrom Jewish identity as well as greed and the cultic blood libel played their parts, according to Gross, so that the singing can qualify as the singing of a Jerusalem song? Clearly, the singing does embody religious identity, as does the strongly invoked individual and collective memory of the not-necessarily cultic Jerusalem (vv. 4-6). It does so for the captors as well as for the victims; religious difference overrides neighbour-liness, friendliness, centuries-long co-existence. At the end of the day, mass murder is committed in both senses of the word: a mass is murdered by a murderous mass. Memory prevails—as it would, despite suppression.[50] Memory of the symbolic Jerusalem for the one orthodox group, of the religious difference for the other orthodox group. And the stronger victim group commits horrible violence on the weaker one. The Poles, a group conquered by the Russian and then (20 months later) by the German occupation forces but made carnivalesque kings for one day by the latter, are allowed—nay, encouraged by the Germans as well as the local Catholic clergy—to carry out a pogrom on the Jews in their midst, most of them orthodox-religious, with whom they have been coexisting in the same place for centuries. They do so, with exceptional hideousness and after premeditated prepara-tions. And this may serve, if you so wish, as a reminder for Jewish people that the symbolic Jerusalem stands not only for a concept but also for a land; that keeping it alive in collective memory is not just an identity marker, it is the only solution to 'the Jewish problem'—when and if it indeed exists. A reminder that diaspora existence, as recommended at least implicitly in another possible intertext for Psalm 137, the book of Esther, with 'Jerusalem' in past horizons but not in present and future horizons, can work up to a point and no more.

In Jedwabne and elsewhere, the wishful thinking of Psalm 137's final three verses becomes enacted reality, with a twist. In the psalm, *verbal* revenge against the enemies' babies is called for; this is horrible enough, it is horrible enough that in certain orthodox Judaisms these verses are liturgically recited daily. It is bad enough that similar verses are to be found also elsewhere in the Hebrew bible. However, and without minimizing this, as Toni Craven says,[51] how else can the powerless be rid of the poison of anger and hate, the frustrated wish for revenge, if not by giving verbal expression to it? 'Pour out your wrath on the nations that do not know you, and on the peoples that do not call on your name; for they have devoured Jacob; they have devoured him and consumed him, and have laid waste his habitation' (Jer. 10.25 NRSV; see also Ps. 79.6-7 and the Passover Haggadah) is

---

50. It is a curious phenomenon, but a dialectical situation has obtained for many years regard-ing Shoah memories: suppression of memories by victims exists side-by-side with remembrance made public voluntarily or institutionally (such as by the Yad Va-Shem in Jerusalem, or various Shoah museums). In other words, suppression of memory may have different roots for perpetrator and victim but both may indulge in it.

51. In an e-mail message dated 15 May 2002 she recounts how that exactly was the experience of a woman who studied the same psalm with her.

typical of this.[52] Granted, verbal violence may legitimize and incite physical violence, the danger of that cannot be denied. However, there is a great difference between expressing a sentiment and 'dashing the infants'—as, in a reversal of roles, the Poles were happy to turn verbal threats and plans into action and dash the Jewish children into the fire. Among other things, the liturgical recitation serves to keep memory of a catastrophe alive. In Gross's words, 'War is a myth-creating experience in the life of every society'.[53] Jewish communities that drop Psalm 137 —or parts thereof—from their prayer books have also dropped 'Jerusalem' in favour of creating a new Jewish identity in a diaspora of their choice.

All remembered the story of Jedwabne: the Jewish survivors and the Polish locals. The story was later suppressed: unlike the cry for memory to be preserved in Psalm 137, the opposite was attempted in this case. But Jan Gross went to the archives following a newspaper report, and dug further, and published his findings, thus reawakening memory. And the Catholic Bishops of Poland conducted a Sunday Mass apologizing to the Jews of Jedwabne and Poles and Jews in general. And the non-specific Jedwabne monument for World War II victims was removed to make way for one commemorating the Jews murdered on that day. Memory is ostensibly restored, as Psalm 137 requires, although the children are not. And the question for us should be one of how reading the two texts together can help us to come to any kind of terms with each—and with both.

And I cannot and do not wish to stop here. Let me continue while becoming even more personal.

On ethical grounds, since if the Poles can simultaneously be victims and perpetrators, everyone can function as both simultaneously or successively, including the successors of Jedwabne Jews and those who recite Psalm 137 on weekdays.[54]

On emotional grounds, since my parents were Ostjuden from Poland and my mother's family, based in Jendjziov, perished in the Holocaust. (Most of my father's family had immigrated to Palestine before World War II.) I grew up on memories of the Holocaust; the photographs of Jedwabne Jews in pp. 175-97 of *Neighbors* bring tears to my eyes, they are the twin images of photographs in our disorganized family album, all that is left (together with some memorial trees, planted in Israel) of that vanished world. The same formal postures, the same group arrangements, same clothing, same types, same physiognomies. Same fate.

And on political grounds. I first encountered Anti-Semitism, Anti-Judaism if you will, personally when I was 22 and left Israel for the first time to go to South Africa. I was extremely surprised: I did feel that it had died with the Shoah, that it belonged to memory and history books, certainly not to life as I experienced it.

---

52. See also Nah. 3.10 (and 1.2 on the nature of the Hebrew god concerning his enemies); Isa. 13.16; Hos. 10.14. Cf. the interesting discussion in the Jewish sources on attitudes of 'love' and revenge towards community (according to definition) members and out-of-boundary persons in Kugel, *In Potiphar's House*, pp. 214-46 (Chapter 8, 'Hatred and Revenge').

53. Gross, *Neighbors*, p. 143.

54. As acknowledged by Gross (*Neighbors*, pp. 1228-30), and by McCann ('The Book of Psalms') in his 'reflections' on Ps. 137 (if not in his 'commentary' section).

Laugh at me if you will. Now, coming back to Amsterdam from Haifa after Passover in April 2002, a suicide bombing you might have heard of, a new version of Passover offering invented in Netanya; and I see, in Amsterdam, in April 2002, street posters urging all who are against violence to come to a demonstration against Israel's racism and 'war crimes'; and a day later football fans from Utrecht chant in Amsterdam, 'Hamas, Hamas/All Jews to the Gas'; and British academics (to judge by names, some Jews in their number too) call for a boycott of Israeli academics on the pages of the *Manchester Guardian* in the same month; and the UN attempts to send a commission of inquiry to find out what happened in Jenin—then I know that for Europe, once again, the Jews (read especially Israelis, not simply the state of Israel as such) have become the perpetrator, the aggressor, the hated outsider. A nice twist yet again when read against the sentiments expressed in Psalm 137 and the Jedwabne text, to which I would like to respond in the light of the two texts just read alongside each other.

First, it must be emphasized again and again that the dialogic condition of being perpetrator as well as victim is a distinct human condition: we would prefer it not to be so, on moral grounds, of course. But it must be recognized nevertheless. Let me be specific: I'm not talking about a simplified change of roles, when a slave may become a master and a master a slave, when victim may mutate permanently into a perpetrator and vice versa over a stretch of time.[55] Neither would the platitude that 'violence breeds violence' be sufficient. No: I'm talking about potentially analogic situations, or simultaneous states of being. The recognition of that—in my thinking—should be borne in mind, together with the knowledge that every monotheistic religion, especially if missionary or elitist, is inherently violent, and thus potentially fosters perpetration/victimization. Such recognitions should form an *a priori* condition for any indulgence in a verbal tourism of catastrophe, which is what we're doing when discussing such topics academically (at least in part, our motives are certainly not restricted to voyeurism only). For example, we should extend this recognition for any sitting in judgment or entering a discussion of current events in the Middle East. Allotting a position of victim or of perpetrator exclusively to one party in the conflict, postcolonial or neo anti-Judaic style, or inverting the positions of the involved parties, is simply not adequate treatment.

Now, this recognition does not mean that anything goes or may be justified for either side in a violent conflict. It also does not mean that the banality of evil concept should be extended without due care, even though evil—and violence—holds such fascination even to the most pacifist of Western souls. It nevertheless means that an evaluation of retaliation, violence verbal/propagandistic or physical/armed, individual or collective, should start here; and, I beg to be excused, such a recognition should be valuable especially for Christians, whose canonical traditions of kindness and forgiveness stand in stark contrast to historical, religiously motivated praxis against Jews.

---

55. There is statistical knowledge and psychological insight concerning domestic abuse and incest: child abuse and incest victims tend to replay their injuries later as parents or parent figures. This is *not* what is here meant.

And, second: remember Jedwabne, Poland, on 10 July 1941, like the psalmic rivers of Babylon, like Edom, like Amsterdam, like Berlin, like Jerusalem—they are all real. Concurrently each is also meta-real, a *mashal*, a figuration, an *exemplum*. Remembering Jedwabne should be as essentially productive for Western consciousness as it is for Jewish and Israeli identity. Is it?

Excursus: The Hebrew Word אשרי

The Hebrew אשרי is usually translated as 'blessed' (for a list of occurrences in the book of Psalms and elsewhere see the Excursus on אשרי by Craven in Harrelson and Craven, *Psalms*[56]). This has been a dominant and conventional understanding of the term from Antiquity onwards (and certainly so in mainstream rabbinic literature, which must have influenced this understanding for biblical occurrences of the term and, in turn, its translations and Christian understanding). However, if examined philologically, another central or at least original meaning emerges.

The etymology ultimately harks back to a root sequence that means either 'walk [in the right path]' or 'exist' (see also the goddess name Asherah and terms for 'steps'; and cf. *HAL*); the analogical derivation of אשרי from the piel of the same root (itself a metonymy: 'walk in the right path/be content'), seems not to be formally valid. Alternative clues to the majority opinion ('be blessed, happy') are also to be found in some traditional Jewish commentaries. At least one commentator on the Hebrew bible, Mezudat Zion (a late compilation of mediaeval Jewish commentaries), insists that אשרי means 'praise'. For instance, in Ps. 1.1 they comment, 'praised be the man...', as in Gen. 30.13. See also *RaDaK* (Rabbi David Kimhi) on Josh. 1.1, discussing the form אחרי ('after, behind'): in his opinion, like אשרי, אחרי looks like a plural form, and would always, because 'a man is not confirmed in/by one good thing he finds, but by many'.

An interesting and comprehensive discussion of אשרי, which supports alternative understandings of it, is that of Mayer Gruber. Here is his treatment, as related to Rashi's commentary on Psalm 1, in full and with Gruber's own notes:[57]

> (HAPPY IS THE MAN).[1] THE LAUDATIONS OF THE MAN.[2] These are the commendations [*'ishshurayw*], i.e.,[3] the praises of a person [*'adam*].[4] WHO DID NOT WALK IN THE COUNSEL OF THE WICKED...[5]
>
> [1] Conventional rendering of the *lemma*.
> [2] Rendering of the *lemma* according to the understanding presupposed by Rashi's comment here.
> [3] Exegetical *waw*.
> [4] Rashi's point is that the difficult form *'ashre* with which the psalm opens is to be taken as the plural construct of a supposed singular *segholate* noun *'esher* 'laudation' derived from the *piel* verb *'ishsher* 'laud' which appears in synonymous parallelism with the verb *hll pi.* 'praise' in Prov. 31.28; Cant. 6.9 and in antithetic parallelism with the verb *baz qal*, 'insult' in Prov. 14.21. Cf. the supercommentary of Abraham Luria *Nisyonot Abraham* (Vilna, 1821), p. 10b. Rashi's comment here presupposes his recognition of the synonymous parallelism in Prov. 31.28 and

56. Harrelson and Craven, in Harrelson (ed.), *The New Interpreter's Study Bible* (Nashville: Abingdon Press, forthcoming).

57. Mayer I. Gruber, *Rashi's Commentary on Psalms 1–89 (Books I-III) with English Translation, Introduction and Notes* (South Florida Studies in the History of Judaism, 161; Atlanta: Scholars Press, 1998), p. 49 (Rashi's text in Gruber's translation) and p. 50 nn. 1-5. My thanks to Professor Gruber for letting me have the text of his analysis by e-mail.

Cant. 6.9. Concerning Rashi's recognition of synonymous parallelism see the discussion at Ps. 9, n. 12. Most interpreters (LXX, Vulgate, Kimhi, NJB, *et al.*) treat the word *'ashre* as an adjectival noun related etymologically and semantically to the noun *'osher* 'happiness' (Gen. 30.13); hence the conventional rendering 'Happy is the man who...' The latter interpretation is supported by various instances of the word *'ashre* in synonymous parallelism with other expressions meaning 'happy' (Ps. 128.2; Prov. 16.20).

[5] Most interpreters (see the previous note) take the word *'ashre* as an adjectival noun, the subject of a nominal sentence, whose predicate is the noun *'ish*, 'MAN'. Hence they take the clauses introduced by the relative particle *'asher*, 'who, that' as a relative clause modifying the predicate. Rashi, on the other hand, takes the construct pl. noun *'ashre* 'laudations of' (see previous note) as the subject of a nominal sentence, whose predicate is the noun clause 'WHO DID NOT WALK...'

In short, as can clearly be gleaned from Gruber's grammatical and exegetical notes on the very first word of the psalter, the אשרי that opens the whole collection, the translation 'happy, blessed' seems to be ideological, albeit honoured by many from Antiquity onwards. An age-old tradition can and should be honoured. On the other hand, such an understanding of the term in Psalm 137 is troublesome for reasons that are discussed in the body of my article. To be sure, to render אשרי as 'be praised' or 'confirmed' rather than 'be happy' does not remove the ethical issue; neither is it my intention, while adopting the latter, to do so or to be apologetic about the emotive contents of the utterance it expresses. It is for reasons of linguistic and interpretive accuracy that I have chosen with regret to defy tradition in this matter.

To summarize: Read in this manner, what does the vocabulary of revenge in Psalm 137 indicate? It indicates that a verbal assault on the most defenseless of the enemy constitutes affirmation, in the sense of 'righteousness' perhaps (see Ps. 1), and/or is 'praiseworthy' for the avenger. Not a comfortable moral notion, certainly. Nevertheless, such a linguistic usage within its context is, still, far removed from depicting the avenger as 'happy', or from actually enjoying exactly this kind of cruel sport, as both verbalized and enacted in Jedwabne.

(DE)NOMINATING AMALEK: RACIST STEREOTYPING IN THE BIBLE AND THE JUSTIFICATION OF DISCRIMINATION

Alastair G. Hunter

1. *Introduction*

In keeping with the aim of identifying and analyzing religious vocabulary as it relates both to the modern context and its biblical roots, this study is in essence an analysis of three words—three proper names. Methodologically it explores both the biblical usage (or, where relevant, the biblical *umwelt*) and the extension or mis-representation of that use leading up to contemporary interpretations.

The Bible has provided through the ages a rich source of significant names. The Pharisees, the Samaritans, the Philistines, the Canaanites, Sodom and Gomorrah, Egypt, Babylon, the Assyrians, the Amalekites, Ruth the Moabitess, Mary Mag-dalene, the widow with her mite, Susannah. In keeping with the aim of examining the role of the Bible in shaping the way that identity is construed so as to legitimize violence, I shall admit at the outset a bias towards negative aspects of the foregoing list. But it is a salutary bias, for we too often let the Bible off lightly in discussions of the contribution it undoubtedly makes, and has made, to human bigotry, preju-dice and cruelty. The blood of heretics, the suffering of women marked as witches, the dispossession of peoples in the name of God, the imposition of oppressive and cruel social constraints in the mistaken belief that biblical morality required them[1] —these wrongs and manifest injustices are not tangential to the Bible, they are not accidental consequences of human sinful misreadings: on the contrary, they are all too readily drawn from the literal text when it is not mediated through a broader humanity nor qualified by the insights derived from a clearer understanding of human nature and the physical world we inhabit. Demagogues throughout the Bible's history have never been shy of using its less inhibited passages to justify what more enlightened [*sic*][2] ages might see as victimization. Paul's reputed remarks on the nature and status of women may be dismissed today as either culturally

---

1.   For example, the incarceration until recently in mental institutions—often for life—of young girls who 'fell pregnant' while unmarried, and the abominable treatment of people of non-heterosexual inclination—which persists murderously to this day in many places. Not to mention attitudes to abortion, contraception, genetic research and possible cloning—just to remind ourselves that the past is still with us!

2.   The use of 'enlightened' to describe an era which includes the twentieth century is, to say the least, problematic!

conditioned or the result of some psychological limitations on the apostle's part. But the fear of women's natural bodily functions (those they do not share with men, of course) persists in both Jewish and Christian discourse. The mikveh is primarily for *women*: whence does that bias derive? The menstruating priest handling the sacrament is an object of fear/horror to certain Christians: What troubled atavistic world is that coming from? The immediate answer in both cases is: the Bible.

These are not merely academic questions. For, just as we allow religions the customary right to plead innocence of the charge of violence by saying something like 'Christianity (Islam, Judaism, Buddhism, Hinduism) are not inherently aggressive forces, it is just that human beings misuse them', so we claim that the Bible— if we read it aright—is a work of compassion and love, testifying to a merciful and caring God. *Per contra*, the Bible at many points (and not just in the 'Old' Testament) directly advocates the violent suppression of the enemy and preaches the eternal damnation of those who disagree. It was Jesus, was it not, who said, 'I come not to bring peace but a sword'? Yes, I'm quoting out of context—but so too do those who would elide the violence as though it did not exist, and (worse) had not caused grievous suffering to a great many people.

2. Pick a Name

Since it would be impossible to cover all the leads indicated by the opening sentences, I shall select just three terms for further analysis. They are not entirely arbitrary, since they represent three of the most potent sources of continuing controversy, contempt and callousness towards fellow human beings. Two are widely used in religious, social and/or political discourse, the third is in some ways more restricted—but nonetheless important since its use is malign and its influence to a considerable extent hidden. I refer to the terms Palestine/Palestinian, Pharisee/Pharisaism and Amalek/Amalekite. The term Pharisee, common in the New Testament, is not explicit in Tanakh, nor is Palestine found in either Tanakh or New Testament, though of course the Hebrew *peleset* (Philistine) from which it ultimately derives is common in the former. Pharisaic traditions are commonly traced back to Ezra, and early proto-Pharisaic texts (like the book of *Jubilees*) were produced contemporaneously with canonical or near-canonical biblical books (such as Daniel, Qoheleth and Ben Sira).

Misuse of these three proper names is spread across the experience of Jews, Christians and Muslims, but not equally in respect of the three categories of abuse. Thus Jews have suffered grievously from religious and social applications of the term 'Pharisee' used in contempt. All three have been caught up in the tangled political web woven around the word 'Palestine'. And both Christians and Muslims have been characterized as latter-day Amalekites, with all that that entails. In each case use of the term in question tends to racist stereotyping and deliberate dehumanizing: a process of alienation of the other which permits us to treat them with a kind of inhumanity which would be shocking were it to be found *within* our respective groups.

a. *Palestine*

In the aftermath of the Bar Kochba revolt the Romans ejected the Jews from Judaea. They renamed Jerusalem Aelia Capitolina and banned the Jews from setting foot in it—in effect it became a Roman city. But they also banished the Jews from the territory of Judaea, and Jewish land was given to retired Roman soldiers as bounty. The land, too, was renamed—or rather, they went into the past and chose a name which was calculated (though whether the Romans intended this I do not know) to enrage their rebellious Jewish subjects. For they designated it *Palaestina*, the Greek form of the ancient appellation *Philistia*. The territory of Philistia, in the region of Gaza, had of course continued to exist as a region separate from Israel and Judah from the time of its establishment in the twelfth century BCE, not long after the first hints of the name 'Israel' enter the archaeological record, and it is clear that the cities of Ashdod, Ashkelon and Gaza were well established some considerable time before the foundation of either Hebrew kingdom. Both the biblical record, and to some extent archaeological finds, suggest that at one stage the Philistines had ambitions to control much more of the territory than the city states of Gaza; the Roman choice of *Palestine*, therefore, had considerable ironic force.

In the modern period Israeli displacement of Palestinians, and the quite specific re-designation of the land as a whole and its individual topography,[3] constitute a highly effective example of the process which I hope to illustrate in this paper. For one of the most effective ways of controlling a subject people's spirit, culture and freedom, is to disempower their language. The English and lowland Scottish ascendancy in North Britain[4] from the late eighteenth century employed a rigorous ban on the use of Gaelic which, together with the highland clearances and the concentration of economic and political power in the Glasgow–Edinburgh axis, effectively impoverished Celtic culture and society in Scotland for the best part of two centuries. Only in the latter part of the twentieth century did Gaelic once again become a teaching medium—arguably too late to save it as a living language. And it is supremely ironic that the 'Scottish culture' vigorously marketed throughout the world today is a lowland sham which is parasitic on the very culture lowland Scotland did its best to eradicate.

The parallels with Israel and Palestine today are instructive, though also significantly different. Those Scots who were dispossessed formed a diaspora in the relatively promising territories of the New World, and now form part of the white elite in North America, Australia and New Zealand, while their original homelands are to this day significantly under-populated. Dispossessed Palestinians have found no such alternative, and in consequence the pressure on the land is intense. What is fascinating, nevertheless, is that in both cases a strong sense of cultural identity has persisted—and this despite the passing of a significant period of time in the Scottish

---

3.   See Meron Benvenisti, *Sacred Landscape: The Buried History of the Holy Land Since 1948* (Berkeley: University of California Press, 2001).

4.   The designation regularly given to Scotland at the height of British imperialism—an imperialism, it should be noted, which the Scottish elite enthusiastically endorsed and its peasant classes fought for.

case. Those who imagine that either violence or cultural dominance will reduce Palestinian self-awareness might learn from that example; as indeed they might learn from the much more immediate case of the Jews themselves, the survival of whose religious and cultural identity is regularly (and justifiably) celebrated. Jonathan Freedland, in a thoughtful piece written shortly after the Israeli army incursion into Jenin, reflects on the irony that two peoples are equally in no doubt that their future in their own land is threatened:

> Of all the stories and testimonies emerging from the ruins of Jenin, one detail, picked up by the *Guardian*'s Suzanne Goldenberg, captures completely the strange tragedy unfolding in the Middle East. It does not convey the horror wrought in that West Bank town, nor the suffering of its victims. But it says everything about why this disaster is happening.

Goldenberg describes a line of graffiti, written in 'neat blue ink', on a wall in the home of Aisha Salah. She is a Palestinian whose house was seized by Israeli soldiers, for use as a base of operations. Before they left, one of them took up his pen and wrote on the wall: 'I don't have another land'.

That was no spur of the moment doodle. That is a phrase ingrained in the Israeli, and wider Jewish, consciousness. *Ein Lee Eretz Acheret* is even the title of a favourite Hebrew folk song, the kind of standard that will be performed regularly at Israeli Independence Day celebrations.

At the end of the article, in which he attempts to show how both sides have justification for their sense of victimhood, he uses a vivid metaphor to describe the situation:

> These are the two universes, now living in parallel. In Washington, thousands gather to demand justice for the endangered people of Israel. In London, 36 hours earlier, 50,000 gather demanding justice for the endangered people of Palestine. Both sides believe they are the victim, both sides are fighting for their very lives. And, like parallel lines, they never touch.[5]

The next day the following letter was published, poignantly confirming the dilemma:

> Jonathan Freedland says the tragedy of the Israel–Palestine conflict is summed up by the Israeli soldier's scrawl on a wall in Jenin: 'I don't have anywhere else to go to'. The picture is only complete if we add the words of a Palestinian: 'Neither do I'.
> Sophie Richmond
> London

Who, where, or what, then, is Palestine? Or, to ask a parallel question: Who, where, or what is Israel? The latter question is ironically the more difficult to answer, since the term Israel (as both Whitelam and Davies show)[6] has from the beginning been

---

5.   *The Guardian* (17 April 2002).

6.   Philip R. Davies, *In Search of 'Ancient Israel'* (JSOTSup, 148; Sheffield: Sheffield Academic Press, 1992); Keith W. Whitelam, *The Invention of Ancient Israel* (London: Routledge, 1996).

fraught with more religious than geographical significance. In an earlier piece (1994),[7] I examined some of the difficulties surrounding both the idea of the land as sacred and the defining of the extent of that land. To speak of 'the Holy Land' or 'Ancient Israel' as if these were unproblematic base-points from which to construct a politically feasible modern state called Eretz Yisrael is to ignore history, religion and personal tragedy, and to guarantee a fatal clash of interests. There is no easy way to reconcile the claims and hopes of settlers who believe that God has dedicated the entirety of the territory to Jews, Orthodox Jews who would (from their fastness in Me'ah She'arim) impose rabbinic religious control on the personal lives of their fellow Israelis, secular Jews who want only the freedom to party in the cafés of Tel Aviv and Ben Yehuda Street, and Arab Israelis who would welcome basic equal opportunities as citizens of Israel. Yet this is the challenge which must be met *at the same time* as the matter of Palestine is taken up. For the true complexity of the situation lies in the fact that for every Jewish story there is an Arab parallel; for every Israeli claim there is a perfectly understandable Palestinian counter-claim; for every horror story of sudden innocent death in the streets of Jerusalem or Haifa or Tel Aviv there is an equally harrowing narrative from Hebron or Nablus or Jenin or Bethlehem.

Palestine, on the other hand, has two obvious definitions: as the region of Judaea and Jerusalem renamed by the Romans after the failure of Bar Kochba, and as the territory designated as a British mandate after the First World War, the successor to the former province of the now defunct Ottoman Empire.[8] Ironically, prior to the twentieth century little religious significance was vested in this geographical fact beyond the Muslim recognition of Al Quds (Jerusalem) as a place of importance in the life of the Prophet. Now, of course, in a mirroring of the religious Zionist position *vis-à-vis* Israel, Palestinian rhetoric takes on an increasingly possessive tone. The escalation of the religious value invested in Jerusalem, for example, is clearly shown in Bernard Wasserstein's excellent *Divided Jerusalem*.[9] It might not be putting it too strongly to suggest that the genie of 'the Holy Land', having been let out of the bottle to enhance Jewish claims, is now uncontrollable. While Jewish wishes *may* have been granted, the price (as is usual with these arrangements) has been much higher than anyone would have expected to pay.

The Jewish experience of the Roman re-designation of their land and cities and towns in the second century must have been a bitter one. Thus Clayton Miles Lehmann:

> In the aftermath of the Bar Kochba Revolt, the Romans excluded Jews from a large area around Aelia Capitolina, which Gentiles only inhabited. The province

---

7.   'Whose Land is it Anyway?', in Robert P. Carroll and Alastair G. Hunter (eds.), *Words at Work: A Festschrift for Robert Davidson* (Glasgow: Trinity St Mungo Press, 1994), pp. 44-56.

8.   The question of the propriety of using the term 'Palestine' to relate to Philistine territory in the late second and early first millennium is hotly debated. Suffice it to say that the etymological link between *peleset* and *palaestina* does not imply a political continuity.

9.   Bernard Wasserstein, *Divided Jerusalem: The Struggle for the Holy City* (London: Profile Books, 2001).

now hosted two legions and many auxiliary units, two colonies, and—to complete the disassociation with Judaea—a new name, Syria Palaestina. The centre of Jewish settlement moved northward to Galilee and Gaulanitis. The number of Jewish communities elsewhere declined, and many once-Jewish towns became Gentile or received large numbers of Gentile inhabitants. They lost their old Jewish names to new Roman names; e.g., Sepphoris became Diocaesarea, Lydda Diospolis, and Beth Guvrin Eleutheropolis. Sebaste became a colony, like Caesarea and Aelia Capitolina.[10]

Just as bitter, surely, as the Palestinian experience of Israeli re-designation of their land and cities and towns in the twentieth century as described by Meron Benvenisti. Until those involved can become sensitive to each other's pain, it seems likely—sadly—that this biblical legacy will continue to impose its harsh inheritance as both Jews and Palestinians use the etymology of the past to undermine any hope for the future.

b. *Pharisees*

Perhaps there is no need, in the context of a scholarly and informed readership, to dwell at much length on the matter of the Pharisees. But there is still much lazy treatment of them from Christian pulpits and in popular understanding. Given the pervasiveness of English usage of terms like 'pharisaic'—which has strangely not attracted the same opprobrium that attaches to words from the field of colour racism—and the simplistic syllogism 'Pharisee = Jew' therefore 'Jew = hypocrite', it is not surprising that there is a continuing problem here.

Part of the explanation (which is certainly not an excuse) is that 'Pharisee' is seen as a historic term, rather like 'Amalekite' and 'Canaanite', so that there appears not to be the same need to be careful. There are no Pharisees left (nor Amalekites either) to be offended, so both scholars and lay writers feel free to use language which would see them in a court of law if applied to a contemporary group. This is profoundly mischievous on a number of counts. First of all, it encourages, by analogy, contemporary forms of repression (if a commentator regards it as acceptable to recommend genocide as a way of dealing with supposedly immoral Canaanites, it is but a short step to the application of similar punishments to contemporaries who are deemed immoral). Secondly, it reflects a lack of serious commitment to justice and equality on the part of the commentator. If someone imagines that violent discrimination is acceptable if it is safely confined to the Bible, that speaks volumes about their own underlying attitudes. And thirdly, at least in the case of the Pharisees (but also, as we shall see, with the Amalekites) historical remoteness is neither a correct analysis nor a safe protection. For history has a habit of leaking into the present (who would have thought that ancient German folk traditions could have become one of the inspirations of a murderous fascist regime in the enlightened twentieth century?), and those who have been less than careful when they gave account of the past may find they have left an unfortunate debt to the future.

---

10.   <http://www.usd.edu/erp/Palestine/history.htm>, p. 6

The claim that the Pharisees belong to the past is precisely not sustainable because the link-idea 'hypocrite' and the fact that everyone 'knows' that the Pharisees were Jews establishes a connection into the present. Every time a preacher makes a lazy remark about hypocritical Pharisees and the superiority of Jesus, he or she is guilty of anti-Semitism (of the inadvertent kind) because everyone in the congregation is capable of making, and almost certainly does make, the connection which is surely implied. Thus de-nomination works twice. Historical Pharisees are turned into dictionary 'pharisees', and real Jews are read as hypocrites because Pharisees are/were Jews.

There is another canard which is less acutely offensive, but every bit as effective in robbing real Jews of their identity. For what lies behind the charge of hypocrisy is of course Matthew 23, and what that violent passage is about is the denunciation of those the writer takes to be devoted to legal niceties in the place of love and compassion. Hence the 'legalistic Judaism' myth, which like many such generalities is not devoid of a portion of truth. No doubt the law matters to an observant Jew, no doubt the halakhah takes an interest in judicial matters which can at times appear obsessive. But the canons of Church Law are no less pettifogging, and the history of the Reformation no less replete with oppressive insistence on rule-bound observance, without drawing down upon Christianity the charge of 'legalism'. Conversely, the annals of Judaism are replete with examples of love and joy and human compassion, but these are systematically ignored in favour of an ill-informed stereotype. It is no wonder that many regard the Gospel of Matthew (for all the Jewishness of its discourse) as being the most anti-Semitic of early Christian works.

In the same way that the place-name 'Palestine' has more than once been re-defined—de-nominated—as a means of excluding peoples from their natural place, so the word 'Pharisee', however ambiguous it may originally have been, now exists preserved in a purely negative vacuum from which all historical and sociological reference has been removed. It thus becomes available as a term of abuse which first removes all that was honourable from a key religious group in Roman Palestine and then applies the negative residue to a whole people.

c. *Amalek*
In the preceding sections I have tried to show how the traditions to which we subscribe have found support for diverse forms of stereotyping and discrimination in various aspects of the biblical materials, and that this has typically taken place by means of a process which I have chosen to call *de-nomination*. By this neologism I mean that specific proper names are de-historicized, emptied of their original content, and re-appropriated in ways which on the one hand effectively disenfranchise their original owners and on the other implicate contemporary groups in a negative discourse which they have no means of countering. The enormous cultural influence of the Bible, even in a highly secularized Western Europe, means that these processes acquire an authority which makes challenging them all the more contentious.

My third case study deals with Amalek. The Amalekites could well be regarded as the archetypal victims in the Pentateuch, in that divine instructions to dispose of this people are given on more than one occasion. No doubt other peoples were to be eliminated from the 'Promised Land', but no single group acquired quite the same status as them. They also symbolize a further classic device: the rhetorical move— very familiar from the twentieth century—of portraying the victim as aggressor in order to justify his/her elimination. This resonates, surely, with the experiences of Jews in Germany and Poland, Blacks in North America and South Africa, Asians in Africa, Muslims in Bosnia, Armenians in Turkey, Christians in Pakistan, Algerians in France, Pakistanis in Britain, and innumerable others—all labelled as a threat and a danger to the dominant culture and then victimized as a punishment. The biblical evidence is unambiguous: thus Exod. 17.14-16 (after Moses' defeat of the Amalekites), reports that

> the Lord said to Moses, 'Write this as a reminder in a book and recite it in the hearing of Joshua: I will utterly blot out the remembrance of Amalek from under heaven'. And Moses built an altar and called it, The Lord is my banner. He said, 'A hand upon the banner of the Lord![11] The Lord will have war with Amalek from generation to generation.'

The more frequently quoted passage, in Deut. 25.17-19, is where the denunciation of the victim as the aggressor is most explicitly found:

> Remember what Amalek did to you on your journey out of Egypt, how he attacked you on the way, when you were faint and weary, and struck down all who lagged behind you; he did not fear God. Therefore when the Lord your God has given you rest from all your enemies on every hand, in the land that the Lord your God is giving you as an inheritance to possess, you shall blot out the remembrance of Amalek from under heaven; do not forget.

Almost every commentary on this passage (including a range of Christian websites which would try the patience of a saint) (1) assumes that the Bible's account is factual, and (2) reads that account as an unproblematic description of unprovoked attack. But surely even in the Bible's own terms the story is of a vast army of people making incursions into a territory which is not theirs and no doubt making huge demands on the economic resources of a region not famous for agricultural surpluses. The Amalekites' *defence* of their *home territory* is hardly surprising: how odd, then, that we should so readily accept the Deuteronomists' claim that the victim is the aggressor. And yet, in the general discourse of the West it is a not unfamiliar pattern. First blame your chosen victims, then you are free to exploit or criminalize them. Every petty racist in Marseilles, in Oldham, in Rotterdam does this, and we condemn them for it. But when we find this in the Bible we are silent.

This is a phenomenon frequently and offensively found in the writings of scholars of the modern period. Here are just a few of the more startling arguments found in standard works. Thus Eichrodt:

---

11. The word *yad* here might indicate 'remembrance' or 'power'; the word translated 'banner' might be an abbreviated form of 'throne'. We might therefore read this sentence as referring to the memory of this oath being preserved at the throne of God.

The introduction of this custom of war into the worship of Yahweh was linked with the Mosaic demand for unqualified devotion to the cause of God. The fact that it was the wrath of Yahweh himself raging in the slaughter of battle made even the giving up of the enemy to annihilation an act of worship.[12]

Bright:

There is no reason to doubt that it was, as the Bible depicts it, a bloody and brutal business. It was the Holy War of Yahweh by which he would give his people the Land of Promise. At the same time, it must be remembered that the *cherem* was applied only in the case of certain Canaanite cities that resisted; the population of Palestine was by no means exterminated. Indeed, there is every reason to believe that large elements of that population—specifically Hebrews, but others as well—made common cause with the Israelites and rendered them willing assistance.[13]

No doubt, having seen the benefits of the 'ban', sensible Canaanites would have quickly recognized the benefits of making 'common cause with the Israelites'!

Perhaps most chilling of all is de Vaux's dispassionate analysis of the meaning of *cherem*:

...the word *cherem* denotes the fact of 'separating' something, of taking it out of profane use and reserving it for a sacred use; alternatively, it may stand for the thing which is 'separated' in this way, forbidden to man and consecrated to God. The term...originally...belonged to the ritual of the holy war: it meant leaving to God the fruits of Victory... In theory, it admits of no exception whatsoever: at Jericho, all living things, men and beasts, had to be put to death, the town and all its movables were burnt, the metal objects consecrated to Yahweh (Jos. 6.18-24)... The *cherem* was to be applied with the utmost rigour against any Israelite town which had denied Yahweh.[14]

It is even argued by von Rad that these wars involving the ban were purely defensive;[15] and one writer[16] even argues that the ban was a moral act: 'God's justice needed to be signally vindicated against them [the Amalekites] to emphasise the supreme place of the moral element in life'. Perhaps I am naive, but I am honestly vexed to understand how a policy of genocide can be held to be evidence of supreme morality. When we find ourselves excusing mass slaughter in the name of morality

12.   Walther Eichrodt, *Theology of the Old Testament* (2 vols.; London: SCM Press, 1961), I, p. 139

13.   John Bright, *A History of Israel* (London: SCM Press, 2nd edn, 1972), p. 138.

14.   Roland de Vaux, *Ancient Israel: Its Life and Institutions* (London: Darton, Longman & Todd, 2nd edn, 1965), p. 260.

15.   Gerhard von Rad, *Old Testament Theology* (2 vols.; Edinburgh: Oliver & Boyd, 1962), I, p. 17: 'Only when the Amphictyony itself was threatened or when its vital interests were involved—when, for example, the existence or non-existence of a whole clan was at stake—did it take action in a military capacity. These wars were then holy wars, in which Jahweh himself fought in defence of his own people; they were sacral operations, before which men sanctified themselves—submitted, that is, to abstention from sexual intercourse—and whose termination was the ban (*cherem*), the assignment of the spoil to Jahweh.'

16.   In F. Davidson *et al.* (eds.), *The New Bible Commentary* (London: The Inter-Varsity Fellowship, 1953), p. 270.

we have reached a serious pass—though not one, perhaps, entirely unfamiliar to the twentieth century. This kind of twisted logic is not greatly different to that used in the Third Reich to legitimate the murder of the Jews.

A second persistent theme relates to the tendency of tyrants to blame the victims of their tyranny. Whitelam refers to an astonishing statement which Edward Said reports as having been made in a speech by the Bishop of Salisbury in 1903: 'Nothing, I think, that has been discovered makes us feel any regret at the suppression of Canaanite civilisation by Israelite civilisation…the Bible has not misrepresented at all the abomination of Canaanite culture which was superseded by the Israelite culture'.[17] And Albright, in an astonishing outburst, declares that:

> It was fortunate for the future of monotheism that the Israelites of the Conquest were a wild folk, endowed with primitive energy and ruthless will to exist, since the resulting decimation of the Canaanites prevented the complete fusion of the two kindred folk which would almost certainly have depressed Yahwistic standards to a point where recovery was impossible. Thus the Canaanites, with their orgiastic nature worship, their cult of fertility in the form of serpent symbols and sensuous nudity, and their gross mythology, were replaced by Israel, with its pastoral simplicity and purity of life, its lofty monotheism, and its severe code of ethics.[18]

Note once again how this brutal dismissal of whole peoples as being incorrigibly corrupt is seen as part of the moral agenda of Israel with 'its severe code of ethics'. Certainly the adjective is appropriate! Eichrodt is equally dismissive of the Canaanites, and equally blithe about their extermination:

> It is because the Canaanites are ripe for judgment and the Amalekites are cruel plunderers, or because the idolatry of their enemies might become an occasion of stumbling to Israel, that they are delivered to destruction. Thus the ban becomes the execution of Yahweh's sentence, and by means of it he takes vengeance on his enemies; to deliver up to the ban and to punish are the same thing. Hence even here the rite undergoes a change of meaning based on the nature of the covenant God.[19]

Others speak more particularly of the Amalekites, but with similar venom. Thus Gordon,[20] while noting that 'the "ban", like the whole concept of the holy war, is far removed from the Christian code of the New Testament and must be seen in the context of the provisional morality of the Old Testament', still finds it morally acceptable, in that 'it is not simply a pagan idea that has nothing to say to the Christian believer, for within the Old Testament it is viewed strictly as the execution of God's judgment on nations and societies that are morally irredeemable'. It is strange and disturbing to find a mainstream scholar writing as recently as 1986 of the moral irredeemability of whole nations and societies. Hertzberg[21] brings it

---

17. Whitelam, *Ancient Israel*, p. 57.
18. Quoted in Whitelam, *Ancient Israel*, p. 83.
19. Eichrodt, *Theology*, p. 140.
20. Robert P. Gordon, *1 & 2 Samuel* (Exeter: Paternoster Press, 1986), p. 147.
21. H.W. Hertzberg, *1 & 2 Samuel* (London: SCM Press, 1964), pp. 236-37.

down to individual terms, when speaking of the lad who brought news to David of Saul's death (2 Sam. 1):

> His description of himself as an Amalekite, twice repeated, must have made his action seem all the more horrible in the eyes of David and his men, newly returned from battle against Amalek. Amalekites remain Amalekites, even if they are sojourning in Israel; these born robbers do not even shrink from the Lord's anointed![22]

The process of de-nomination comes in two forms: forgetfulness of the fate of the Amalekites, and the use of their name (within the rabbinic tradition) as a cipher for every enemy of Israel everywhere and at all times. It is safe to say that outside Judaism there is no popular celebration of the culture of the Amalekites, no remembrance industry ennobling their sacrifice in the name of other people's hope, no heroic wall inscribed with the names of Agag and his people. And within Judaism the fate of Amalek is celebrated—but most commonly in the context of Purim in which Haman, the villainous enemy of the Jews, is presented as a descendant of Agag the Amalekite.[23] For most Jews, for most of the time, the denunciation of Haman the enemy is part of the light-hearted celebration of a rather 'laid-back' festival. But there are more sinister implications which have in recent years emerged on the political scene, and they by no means evoke a unanimous response among Jewish leaders. Much discussion starts from Moses Maimonides who, in *The Guide of the Perplexed*,[24] attempted to explain the different treatment accorded to Amalek on the one hand and Ammon and Moab on the other. He remarks that

> one particular tribe or nation ought to be punished, just as one particular individual is punished, so that all tribes should be deterred and should not co-operate in doing evil... Thus even if there should grow up among them a wicked corrupt man who does not care about the wickedness of his soul and does not think of the wickedness of his action, he will not find a helper of his own tribe to help him in the wicked things whose realisation he desires. Accordingly it was commanded that *'Amaleq*, who hastened to use the sword, should be exterminated by the sword.

---

22.   I cannot omit what strikes me as one of the most appalling instances of moral blindness and double standards. Commentators (e.g. Hertzberg, *Samuel*, pp. 227-29; William McKane, 1 & 2 *Samuel* [Torch Commentaries; London: SCM Press, 1963], pp. 170-71) discuss David's pursuit and execution of the Amalekites who destroyed Ziklag (though without killing the inhabitants) in 1 Sam. 30 as though this were an instance of divine guidance of the great king. The Amalekites, of course, deserve their punishment! What is not discussed is the fact that the same David had previously (1 Sam. 27.1-12) destroyed Amalekite towns *and killed all their inhabitants*. Hertzberg (pp. 214-15) does describe this as 'brutal' (more precisely, 'David's method is both practical and brutal'), but concludes with the unqualified comment that 'David is already beginning the task which he was later to complete: that of conquering the whole of the neighbouring peoples'. Our hero, it seems, can do no wrong: the Amalekites (being Amalekites) are corrupt whatever they do.

23.   This does rather beg the question as to how, in the light of 1 Sam. 15.7-8, 32-34, Agag could have had any descendants.

24.   Moses Maimonides, *The Guide of the Perplexed* III.41 (trans. and ed. Shlomo Pines; Chicago: University of Chicago Press, 1963, 1974), II, p. 566.

But the case of Ammon and Moab prompts a caveat, to the effect that we ourselves should not rush to importunate judgment: 'All these matters belong to the divine estimation of penalties, so that these should not be too great or too small'; and elsewhere[25] he repeats the warning that 'the *Decree* was only directed against the descendants of *'Ameleq'*. A contemporary discussion shows that these difficulties continue to be recognized and addressed:

> In the early 1900s, Rabbi Hayim Soloveitchik of Brisk argued that, according to Maimonides, there was a possibility of contemporary war against Amalek—such as a national attempt to exterminate the Jewish people. His grandson, Rabbi Yosef Dov Soloveitchik, used this position in the early 1940s to contend that the Allied war against Nazi Germany could be understood in Jewish law as a war against Amalek. Rabbi Soloveitchik, of blessed memory, insisted, however, that the war against this new 'figurative Amalek' was not subject to the same liberties *vis-à-vis* individual civilian vulnerability as was the war against original Amalek. Rather, the usual moral constraints applicable even to a war of self-defence, would apply in this war as well.
>
> Maimonides recorded the accepted rabbinic position that those wars could be fought only against the specific peoples God identified as deserving of such extreme violence. When those nation-states disappeared, there was no longer permissibility to intentionally engage in war against non-combatants.[26]

This passage ought to warn us against any simplistic view of the way that Amalek figures in contemporary Jewish thinking; nevertheless, there are signs that in some circles the belief that any enemies of the Jews may be characterized as Amalekites is gathering some momentum. The following poignant report tends to reinforce this disturbing trend. It is part of a meditation by Rabbi Arthur Waskow on hearing of the murderous attack by Baruch Goldstein in the mosque in Hebron:

> Purim morning. I have been up half the night, celebrating the hilarious festival of spring fever: reading Esther's tale of masks and ridicule; wearing my Hassid-diamond-merchant costume and drinking enough, as the Talmud commands, to forget the difference between the blessed liberator and the cursed murderer; swinging a noisemaker; dancing and telling bawdy jokes and acting out a Purimspiel that pokes fun at rabbis, at Jewish life, at the Torah itself.
>
> But now on Purim morning, the radio is muttering at me. It will not stop.
>
> What is it saying? No. Some Jew has entered the mosque in Hebron with a machine gun—no no—and has fired at Moslems kneeling in prayer—no no no no—and killed maybe forty, maybe fifty, more—no no no no no—it is the mosque at the Tomb of Abraham, Abraham our Father, father of Jews and Arabs, blessing to the world—oh no oh no oh no—
>
> No no no no no no no no no no.
>
> I lie in the bed sheets, dazed into silence, into a trance, but I know know know know, no no no no no no no.

25.   Maimonides, *Guide* III.50 in Pines, vol. II, pp. 614-15.

26.   Saul J. Berman, 'The War Against Evil and Ethical Constraints', available online at <http://www.shma.com/dec01/berman.phtml>.

I know at once this is no isolated crazy, this 'Baruch Goldstein' who has murdered forty of my cousins. I know at once, he has decided on this Purim to 'blot out the memory of Amalek' not with a noisemaker but a machine gun, not with rivers of *schnapps* and a L'Chaim but with rivers of blood and L'Mavet: 'To Death'.

Most scholars and most celebrants take Purim as a day of hilarity and joking. The seemingly nightmarish story of the Scroll of Esther is a fantasy, a joke. On the very day Haman/Amalek intended to destroy us, we instead killed 75,000 of our enemies. The fantasy of the powerless that once, just once, they could fight back and destroy everyone who ever sneered at them.

But Goldstein took the story at face value. Why?

In the generation after the Nazi Holocaust—the Holocaust that actually did happen, the one from which no Esther saved the Jews—this archetypal myth of disaster bites home with intense cruelty and fear. Suddenly, Jews for whom the Amalek mythos had become somewhat quiescent, become attuned to it.

So then, in our generation, for some Jews the Palestinians become Amalek. Some Palestinians are terrorists? Some Palestinians call publicly for the State of Israel to be shattered? The archetypes of fear slide into place: all Palestinians are Amalek.

And the fantasies of the powerless become the actions of the powerful. For in our generation, Jews have power.[27]

That piece is both a reminder of the danger and a sign of hope that there are those who see the danger—and it is striking that it comes from within the community which, if anyone ever did, might with justice argue the continuing need to blot out Amalek.

There is a Christian discourse about Amalek which also fuels the flames; here are two examples. One, fairly traditional, is from Matthew Henry's commentary on Exodus 17:

It was great encouragement to the people to see Joshua before them in the field of battle, and Moses above them on the hill. Christ is both to us; our Joshua, the Captain of our salvation, who fights our battles, and our Moses, who ever lives, making intercession above, that our faith fail not. Weapons formed against God's Israel cannot prosper long, and shall be broken at last. Moses must write what had been done, what Amalek had done against Israel; write their bitter hatred; write their cruel attempts; let them never be forgotten, nor what God had done for Israel in saving them from Amalek. Write what should be done; that in process of time Amalek should be totally ruined and rooted out. Amalek's destruction was typical of the destruction of all the enemies of Christ and his kingdom.[28]

Frightening enough, but probably nowadays read purely metaphorically (at least, one would hope so!). The other tradition is much more disturbing, because it forms a case study in which the writer seeks to justify the goodness of the kind of God who would encourage the annihilation of Amalekites, men, women and children.

---

27.   <http.//www.shalomctr.org/html/torah35.html>.

28.   <http.//bible.crosswalk.com/Commentaries/MatthewHenryConcise/mhc-con.cgi?book= ex&chapter=017>.

Readers interested in the dark side should visit the website; for now I shall simple pull out a few quotations which demonstrate vividly how close a bond there is between conservative Christian treatment of the Old Testament and right-wing rabbinic approaches to the 'problem' of the Palestinians. It does not take a political genius to draw the parallels implicit in what follows:

> As with the vast majority of the Canaanite population, the sensible Amalekites would have migrated somewhere else. All that would have been left at the time of Saul would have been a leadership raised and steeped in anti-Israel violence and hatred. This is NOT some innocent nation, protecting its homeland from an invading and greedy people. This is the sins of the fathers being *continued by* their children.
>
> …
>
> *The word of the LORD came to me: 'Son of man, speak to your countrymen and say to them: "When I bring the sword against a land, and the people of the land choose one of their men and make him their watchman, and he sees the sword coming against the land and blows the trumpet to warn the people, then if anyone hears the trumpet but does not take warning and the sword comes and takes his life, his blood will be on his own head. Since he heard the sound of the trumpet but did not take warning, his blood will be on his own head. If he had taken warning, he would have saved himself. But if the watchman sees the sword coming and does not blow the trumpet to warn the people and the sword comes and takes the life of one of them, that man will be taken away because of his sin, but I will hold the watchman accountable for his blood."'* (Ezek. 33.1-6)
>
> Notice how this would implicate the father in the death of his family. If he knew to flee (perhaps from other encounters with Israel, or just in general from their reputation at the time), then his failure to do so would have brought the blood of his family down upon himself. It would have been HE who killed his family and himself, regardless of who was the actual executioner.
>
> What this basically means is that *the father* would have been actually responsible for the death of his family, by his continued hostile actions towards the Israelites. The children were not punished FOR the crimes of the father; rather, they were victims OF the crimes of the father.
>
> …
>
> But why couldn't the Israelites just 'ignore' the Amalekites?
>
> Because the Amalekites wouldn't 'ignore' Israel…and responsible Israelite parents would need to do something to protect *their* lives…
>
> The Amalekites were a cruel, active, and hostile force, on Israel's immediate border. Israel was forbidden to attack other border kingdoms (by the biblical God), but Amalek had been actively oppressing Israel for at least 200+ years (without provocation), beginning with their first week of freedom from Egypt, to the more recent slave-capture, pillage, and scorched-earth aggressions in the book of Judges. The only active suffering up to this point was BY Amalek ON Israel.
>
> In spite of all reason, Amalek continued to destroy land, people, crops, cattle, and to haul off people for sale as slaves in foreign markets—people who had only now gotten their first taste of freedom. This is not your normal 'angry neighbor'— these are terrorists, these are slave-traders, these are vandals, these are unreasonable aggressors (unlike the Canaanites, who mostly migrated away; or the Jebusites, who resorted to deception). For Israel EVER to enjoy a moment's peace in the land of promise, Amalek must be rendered non-hostile. Without some kind of

self-defense action on the part of Israel, Amalek would simply continue inflicting 'active suffering' on Israel's families, their food, their freedom. Something had to be done—somehow Amalek must be stopped.[29]

One last point, before I reach some kind of conclusion, is to note that 11 September 2001 has not been neglected. A couple of 'position pieces' draw disturbing parallels between the suicide pilots and the enemy Amalek. The first is a Shabbat meditation in anticipation of Purim written by Rabbi Ralph Tawil[30] in which the writer, while acknowledging Rambam's restrictions on the law regarding Amalek, nevertheless comes perilously close to equating President George W. Bush's war against terrorism with Israel's command to eradicate their troublesome enemy:

> Shemuel the prophet defined the term 'blotting out the memory of Amaleq' to mean: 'Spare no one, but kill alike men and women, infants and sucklings, oxen and sheep, camels and donkeys' (1 Samuel 15.3)... Of course, everyone agrees that we should eradicate evil. However, it is hard to understand the Torah's commandments to kill every man, woman and infant of Amaleq. In the period of the war against terrorism that we are presently in, it is somewhat easier to understand it, but not completely...
>
> What the Torah is teaching is that some nations are so evil, that every person who identifies with that nation must be destroyed. Perhaps, if anyone of that nation is left alive, the Evil culture of that nation will resurface and create more problems in the future. We must be aware that as far as the total eradication of a nation, that only applies to the nation of Amaleq, which, does not exist today...
>
> Evil also exists today in the form of terrorism. Why is terrorism Evil? (Because its victims are innocent and defenseless.) Terrorism and those who support and incite towards it must be eradicated. Yielding to the terrorist's demands is not the way to accomplish this. Giving to the demands of terrorists invites more demands and further terrorism. Eradicating terrorism can only be done by an all-out war against terrorists until the people who remain renounce terrorism. It does not require killing of every person, but only those people who commit, support terrorism and those that incite towards terrorism.
>
> We pray to Hashem that the United States will be successful eradicating worldwide terrorism, so that the we can work together peacefully towards resolving the many problems that face us.

The second parallel, by Rabbi Daniel Lapin in the conservative National Review,[31] draws the same conclusions as Tawil, but sets it in the context of what reads like a typical right-wing American analysis. If this is the kind of advice that Bush is listening to in his formulation of policy *vis-à-vis* Israel/Palestine on the one hand, and the 'axis of evil' on the other, we do well to be afraid:

> From the Amalek story we may extract two lessons. First of all is the obligation to root out evil of the kind that sends airliners smashing into the World Trade Center. Second, not every victimized nation or group is perfectly virtuous.

---

29.   <http://www.christian-thinktank.com/rbutcher1.html>. I am tempted to wonder if 'christian-thinktank' here is an oxymoron, and if 'Butcher' is not an ironically apt surname.

30.   <http://www.judaic.org/tabletalk/tesave5762.htm>.

31.   <http://www.nationalreview.com/comment/comment-lapin091801.shtml>.

I realize this may sound outrageously insensitive, for many Americans are committed to the view that being a victim, as America was victimized this week, should immediately grant you immunity from all criticism. Thus the equation of victimhood with virtue has led some observers of turmoil in the Middle East to blame Israel for the fact that more than twice as many Palestinians have died in the present conflict as have Israelis. The conclusion for the morally untutored is simple: because Palestinians are dying in greater numbers, they must be the morally justified party in the conflict. But it is simply wrong to grant moral prestige on the basis of suffering. It is a core Jewish value, when confronted with catastrophe, to probe broadly and arrive at a detailed moral balance sheet...

The first mistake we made was to forget, amid peace and prosperity, what the face of sheer evil looks like. This forgetting has been easy for us. We are taught it in the schools, where children are instructed that there is no such thing as evil, only differences in point of view. You see, to admit the existence of evil means we would have to define evil according to someone's morality and we all know that in a multi-cultural society this would be wrong.

Knowing that there is evil carries with it many practical advantages. For instance, captains of commercial airplanes used to carry side arms, but politicians who didn't believe in evil long ago disarmed them. Armed pilots could have made quite a difference for the good on Tuesday.

A second mistake was to emasculate the CIA. In recent years, international sanctimoniousness about human rights trumped considerations of American security. The entire CIA structure was methodically undermined and demoralized by penalizing all operatives who might have violated the human rights of their targets.

Third, we Americans have ignored the real-life lessons that many of us learned in our fourth-grade schoolyard. The class bully was always encouraged by passivity. Sooner or later, you realized, you would have to bloody his nose. The longer you took to do the inevitable, the more demoralized you became...

When confronted with tragedy, the Jewish way is, then, to assess one's own moral condition. But—and here is the tricky part—while the victim gauges his faults he is also commanded to strike back in devastating force. In short, the strategy is counterattack accompanied by an equally remorseless attempt to identify the flaws that made the attack possible in the first place. Let us pray that something positive may come out of our suffering. If we Americans contemplate the lessons of Amalek, I believe it will.

The further implications of these opinion pieces for the continuing development of Bush's pre-emptive policy with regard both to Iraq and to all other presumed enemies of or threats to the US are uncomfortably clear.

3. *Conclusion*

We ignore at our peril the potential for violence built into the Bible. This is not something abstract, occupying a virtual space in which metaphor and rhetoric are safely confined, like computer viruses imprisoned in an IT lab. There is no shortage of those who cannot separate metaphor from reality, rhetoric from realpolitik, whose worldview (however unthinkable it may be to most of us) comfortably enshrines the principle of violence against individuals or the groups to which they belong in the name of religion. Nor is there in fact any wholly secure place in which to store dangerous ideas. Computer viruses roam the internet at will; biblical language and ideas are public property (however ill-informed). There is, therefore, real point to the project to which this article belongs, if what we do can somehow serve to dampen humankind's seemingly insatiable appetite for violence.

PURITY AND DANGER AT THE END OF THE WORLD: PRIESTLY AND PROPHETIC PARADIGMS IN CONTEMPORARY APOCALYPTIC VISIONS

Tod Linafelt

1. *Nuclear War and the Prophetic Imagination*

Let me begin with a quote from Ronald Reagan, from his days as Governor of California:

> Everything is falling into place. It can't be too long now. Ezekiel says that fire and brimstone will be rained upon the enemies of God's people. That must mean that they'll be destroyed by nuclear weapons. They exist now, and they never did in the past.[1]

This statement suggests that Reagan was right about at least one thing: the fire and brimstone of biblical apocalypse becomes, in the 1970s and 1980s, the threat of nuclear annihilation. Though Reagan cannot be forgiven for his belief that it is possible for one side to prevail in a nuclear war, he can perhaps be forgiven for understanding the threat of nuclear war in apocalyptic terms. The prophet Ezekiel's proto-apocalyptic imagery of a final war characterized by 'a cloud covering the earth' (Ezek. 38.16), mountains overthrown, cliffs toppling, walls crumbling (38.20), and 'sulfurous fire' raining down upon hordes of people (38.22) are not so very different than the images that fed the American imagination through the 1970s and 1980s.

Apocalyptic thought is most closely associated, of course, with the biblical books of Daniel and Revelation. These full-blown versions of apocalypse have their roots in just the sorts of prophetic texts represented by the book of Ezekiel and alluded to by Reagan. Fundamental to apocalyptic imaginings are the prophetic visions of the end of the world. This envisioned end is often designated as 'the Day of the Lord', 'the Day of the Lord's Wrath', or the 'Day of Judgment', and it typically takes the form of a great and final conflagration, in which God pursues a scorched-earth policy of final resort. Thus, for example, the following lines excerpted from Isaiah 24:

1.   From a 1971 conversation as remembered by James Mills, a California state legislator at the time; quoted in Stephen O'Leary, *Arguing the Apocalypse: A Theory of Millennial Rhetoric* (Oxford: Oxford University Press, 1994), p. 273.

> Behold, the Lord will strip the earth bare, and lay it waste, and twist its surface, and scatter its inhabitants…the earth is withered, seared, the world languishes, seared, both sky and earth languish; the earth is breaking, breaking; the earth is crumbling, crumbling; the earth is tottering, tottering; the earth is swaying like a drunkard. (Isa. 24.1-20 JPSV)

It is just such images and visions that haunted not only the American but arguably much of the global popular imagination during the decades of the Cold War: images of carnage, of total destruction. The annihilating force behind such images was, almost invariably, nuclear war, signified most emblematically by the mushroom cloud.

In both cases—prophetic texts and modern popular culture—this vision of the end is, of course, conventional war writ extraordinarily large. (This phenomenon is foregrounded in Russell Hoban's novel *Riddley Walker*,[2] where the imminent discovery of 'the 1 little 1' [gunpowder] recalls the '1 big 1' [nuclear destruction] that nearly annihilated humanity.) In both cases the apocalyptic imagination takes the all-too-common human experience of war and blows it up to titanic proportions; giving us in the case of the prophets *divine* war and in the modern version *nuclear* war—both of which arise from a realm normally unavailable to humans and usher in an epoch that heretofore has been unimaginable.

While datable rather precisely to 6 and 9 August 1945, when America dropped Atomic bombs on the cities of Hiroshima and Nagasaki, the nuclear age really explodes into the American psyche in the 1970s and 1980s. These decades gave us such novels as Hoban's *Riddley Walker* (1980), Maggie Gee's *The Burning Book* (1984), Tim O'Brien's *The Nuclear Age* (1985), and Bernard Malamud's *God's Grace* (1982); such plays as Arthur Kopit's *The End of the World* (1984); such television shows as *The Day After* (1983); such films as *Testament* (1983); and such popular music as U2's album *The Unforgettable Fire* (1983), Tonio K's *La Bomba* (1983), and The Rainmakers' *Tornado* (1989).

The effect of the threat of mass destruction by nuclear explosion was simply *everywhere* during these two decades—it was, in other words, nearly as pervasive as McDonald's. In his book *Life After God*, Douglas Coupland shrewdly brings these two cultural icons together in the description of his first visit to a McDonald's restaurant:

> I remember sitting on my purple vinyl stool being unable to eat, gazing out the window, waiting for the flash, waiting for the cars to float up into the sky, for the Hamburger statue to melt, for the tiled floor to break apart.[3]

Apparently even a Happy Meal, the unfailing panacea for psychic ailments of middle class childhood, could not counter the deep-seated fear of annihilation. Coupland goes on to recount the ubiquity of this 'waiting for the flash', as he introduces a series of vignettes of the end from his daydreams and nightmares:

2.   R. Hoban, *Riddley Walker* (New York: Summit Books, 1980).
3.   Douglas Coupland, *Life after God* (New York: Pocket Books, 1994), p. 97.

I was by the fridge in the kitchen when it happened... I was having my hair done when it happened... I was in rush hour gridlock traffic in the middle of the three express lanes leaving the city when it happened... I was at the mall when it happened... I was in the office and it was near the end of the day and people were getting ready to go home when it happened...[4]

Each of these opening lines is followed, in Coupland's book, with a description of the scene of destruction, each ending with Coupland's death. As I was reading through these vignettes and thinking back to the presence of the nuclear threat in my own childhood and adolescence, what struck me was not the horror of these scenarios, but rather their *matter-of-factness*; what should have been unthinkable had become the everyday.

In his novel from 1914, *The World Set Free*, H.G. Wells imagines the advent of artificial radioactivity, which is put to use in what Wells calls an 'atomic bomb', used in the novel in a devastating world-war erupting in the mid-twentieth century.[5] The physicist Leo Szilard admits to having read this novel in 1932, one year before he intuited the possibility of a nuclear chain reaction, thereby paving the way for a real atomic bomb to be used in the mid-twentieth century. In his novel, Wells writes: 'These atomic bombs which science burst upon the world that night were strange even to the men who used them'. Wells's prescience is uncanny, not only in his predictions of the weapons themselves, but also in his predictions of the psychological effect of the weapons. For it was many of the very people who had developed and deployed these weapons, including Leo Szilard, who argued most convincingly for their fundamental immorality. But by the 1980s the weapons that seemed so strange in 1945 had become, like McDonald's, a fundamental part of everyday life in the late twentieth century.

If the beginning of the nuclear age can be dated to 1945, its end can be dated to 1991: the dismantling of the Soviet Union and the end of the Cold War. In a flash, so to speak, the threat of nuclear destruction seemed itself obliterated. I am not arguing that the *possibility* of nuclear war is now gone; in fact, I suspect that one could make the case that the possibility is now more real than ever.[6] Rather, with the logic of a deterrence based on mutually assured destruction no longer so logical, nuclear war is simply no longer *perceived* as the threat that it once was; its grip on our imagination has been decisively broken.

Particularly instructive in this regard is the movie *Terminator 2*,[7] which represents both the culmination and the last gasp in popular culture of the nuclear paradigm of destruction. Released in 1991, *Terminator 2*—subtitled 'Judgment Day'—rests on the cusp of a post-nuclear age, even as it is entirely shaped by the

4. The quotes are taken from the section titled 'The Dead Speak', in *Life after God*, pp. 113-27.

5. H.G. Wells, *The World Set Free: A Story of Mankind* (New York: E.P. Dutton & Co., 1914), p. 114.

6. See, for example, Steven Weinberg, 'The Growing Nuclear Danger', *The New York Review of Books* (July 18 2002), pp. 18-20.

7. *Terminator 2: Judgment Day*, James Cameron (Guild/Carolco/Pacific Western/Lightstorm, 1991).

nuclear. In the opening scene and credits from the movie, one witnesses the fiery obliteration of a children's playground. This opening sequence, and film as a whole, are instructive for a number of reasons. First is the sheer quantity of fire in the credits: it is *the* defining image of the nuclear age. Second is the connection between the biblical prophetic vision of the end, and that offered by the modern film, indicated both by the subtitle—'Judgment Day'—and the fact that the opening scene is said to have been inspired by the apocalyptic scenario in Jeremiah 4:

> I looked on the earth, and, lo, it was waste and void; and to the heavens, and they had no light. I looked on the mountains, and lo, they were quaking, and all the hills moved to and fro. I looked, and lo, there was no one at all, and all the birds of the air had fled. I looked, and lo, the fruitful land was a desert, and all its cities were laid in ruins before the Lord, before his fierce anger. For thus says the Lord: The whole land shall be a desolation; yet I will not make a full end. (Jer. 4.23-27 RSV)

Third, in the course of the film we are quite explicitly ushered out of the nuclear age and into the yet to be defined space of a post-nuclear existence. That is, the central drive of the plot of *Terminator 2* is the *prevention* of nuclear war, not—like the novels and movies of the 1980s—the attempt to reconstruct the remnants of human society *after* the destruction.[8] The characters are successful in their quest of prevention so that by the end of the film the opening scene, set in the future, has become impossible. In fact, in a scene cut from the theater version, but now available on video in the director's cut, the credit sequence of a children's playground engulfed in flames is matched by a final scene in which the same playground is, in the newly insured future, the site of a group of children frolicking in a shiny, happy world.

2. *Viral Apocalypse*

If the film *Terminator 2* represents the successful termination of the nuclear paradigm of apocalypse—in other words, if Arnold '*won't* be back'—it does not, however, represent the end of our apocalyptic imaginings. Seeping into its place is a new paradigm of mass destruction: that of *viral* apocalypse. The threat of nuclear war has been replaced in popular imagination with the threat of contagion. Our nightmare visions of the end are no longer dominated by the image of the mushroom cloud or the flash that signals a few final seconds of existence, but rather the ravages of infectious diseases, viruses, and biological weapons. This shift in the 1990s seems to me to be decisive, culminating in the anthrax scares in Washington, DC, and to a lesser degree in New York City and in Florida, in the fall/autumn of 2001. While one does not want to gainsay the fact that several people died from exposure to anthrax at the time, it was not so much the actual threat of infection that drove the widespread public reaction as the fact that we had been primed for the better part of a decade to fear exactly this sort of threat.

---

8.   I am grateful to Robert Detweiler for this point. See his chapter 'Scheherazade's Fellowship: Telling against the End', in *Breaking the Fall: Religious Readings of Contemporary Fiction* (San Francisco: Harper & Row, 1989), pp. 159-91.

Although the shift is quick and nearly complete, if one looks closely attempts to represent or narrate the move from nuclear to viral can be identified. Again, I find the opening sequence to a film to be especially instructive. In this case, the film is *Outbreak*, from 1995. *Outbreak* opens with a conventional war scene, replete with the standard explosions and gunfire. As horrific as conventional war is, the movie inevitably moves to instate what it considers a larger and more disquieting threat. This more serious threat is not, however, nuclear war, which is after all (noted earlier) conventional war writ very, very large. The new threat is viral in nature. The opening sequence of *Outbreak* thus picks up where *Terminator 2* left us, with the nuclear threat neutralized; but it moves us into a new epoch with a new threat of annihilation.

It remains to be seen whether or not this new paradigm will have the staying power of the nuclear paradigm, but for the last decade at least it is difficult to underestimate its pervasiveness: from movies like *Outbreak*, *Ebola Syndrome*, and *Mimic*, to television shows like *Breakout*, *Condition Critical*, and *Plague Fighters*, to books like *The Hot Zone*, *The Coming Plague, Mad Cow Disease USA: Could it Happen Here?*, *The Killers Within*, and *Toxic Terror*, to one news report after another on AIDS, hantavirus, lyme disease, the Hong Kong bird flu, to bands like Biohazard and Anthrax and the digital art project 'Sex/Anthrax/Mathesis' by Alan Sondheim and Azure Carter, we are inundated with the specters of biological contamination. For Douglas Coupland it was McDonald's and the flash, today it is Jack-in-the-Box and E Coli; while Nevada was once known as 'the land of a thousand nuclear tests', it became most famous in 1998 for the arrest of Larry Wayne Harris on charges of possessing anthrax for use as a weapon. It mattered little that the anthrax in question turned out to be a harmless and easily obtainable variety used in the vaccination of farm animals; Harris was perfect fodder for the newscasts, combining as he did the knowledge of a microbiologist with the face of Charles Manson. (And it didn't hurt that he had exactly the nervous twitch of the lunatic Dreyfus from the Pink Panther movies.) This combination meant that Harris was the unqualified embodiment of the new fears, which in turn meant that TV news (in the business as it is of alternately reflecting and stoking our fears in the service of ratings) broadcast his image as often as possible, supplementing it with the report of Harris's arrest in 1995 for possession of bubonic plague and thereby harking back to a pre-nuclear agent of catastrophe that carries a near-archetypal symbolism. The frenzied tone of the discourse about biological weapons, and the quasi-religious threat they represent, is caught nicely in the title of the following recent book on smallpox by Richard Preston: *The Demon in the Freezer: A True Story*.[9]

A full-fledged and more explicit vision of viral contamination-as-apocalyptic event can be seen in the film *12 Monkeys*,[10] also from 1995. The film signals its

---

9.   Richard Preston: *The Demon in the Freezer: A True Story* (New York: Random House, 2002). Preston is also author of *The Hot Zone* (New York: Anchor Books, 1995).

10.   *12 Monkeys* (Polygram/Universal/Atlas/Classico, 1995), directed by Terry Gilliam and produced by Charles Roven.

status as apocalyptic by constant reference to the New Testament book of Revelation, a book that is in turn heavily indebted of course to the prophetic literature of the Hebrew Bible. *12 Monkeys* is also immediately recognizable as an example of the contemporary genre of films, such as *Terminator 2*, that envision the near-annihilation of humanity. But the means of this near-annihilation is a hyper-virulent biological agent released almost simultaneously in the world's major metropolises. The intentionality with which *12 Monkeys* displaces the nuclear paradigm is confirmed by the fact that it is a remake of an obscure French movie from 1962, *La Jetee*, in which the cause of the mass destruction was, predictably, nuclear war. In order for the new version of the end to impact audiences, the menace of decimation had to be updated.

This cultural shift in the way we envision the end is, I think, an interesting enough phenomenon in its own right—one that deserves a far more in-depth and subtle articulation than I have given it here. For example, other questions that come to mind include the following: Were there other dominant paradigms of total annihilation that were displaced by the nuclear? If so, what were they? To what extent do non-nuclear disaster films from the 1970s like the *Poseidon Adventure* and the *Towering Inferno* reflect a sublimated nuclear fear? How important has the threat of AIDS been for installing the new paradigm of infection? Is there a connection between this new paradigm and the increasingly disturbing perception in American political thought that immigrants represent a 'foreign' element that must be prevented from contaminating an otherwise healthy 'body'? What are the ways in which what I have been calling two 'paradigms' in fact overlap each other, especially if one adds the trope of genetic mutation that is part of our visions of nuclear destruction?

But what especially fascinates me, as a biblical scholar, is the way in which both of these paradigms have their counterparts in biblical literature. Whether one thinks that the biblical prophets were literally predicting nuclear destruction in the distant future of the twentieth-century (as apparently did Governor Reagan and people like Hal Lindsey, author of the best-selling book *The Late, Great Planet Earth*), or rather that modern purveyors of apocalypse took much of their inspiration from the biblical books (as apparently James Cameron did in his opening sequence for *Terminator 2*) the result is the same: our visions of nuclear apocalypse were strikingly resonant with prophetic visions of the end of the world in the form of the Day of the Lord. What is less obvious, though, is the striking resonance between the newer paradigm of viral contamination and the body of texts in the Hebrew Bible known as the priestly literature.

Priestly literature—which includes both the well-known first chapter of the book of Genesis in which God creates the world through a process of ordering and dividing a pre-existent chaos, as well as the lesser-known book of Leviticus—is the material in the Bible that was written, edited, or at least greatly influenced by the concerns of the priests in ancient Israel. What priests were concerned with included the sacrificial rites that took place in the Jerusalem temple, the dietary regulations that Israelites were to follow, the diagnosis of various skin diseases, and a complex of religious rituals associated with bodily fluids such as blood and semen. What unites these disparate matters is an underlying concern for *purity*. That is, priestly literature is fundamentally about containing contamination, neutralizing ritual pollution, combating contagion. Because God is holy, Israel is to be holy (Lev. 11.44); and to be holy means (among other things) to be on guard against impurity or uncleanness. Purity and cleanness are, in turn, largely about the discernment of what belongs where—the proper ordering of time, of space, of material reality. Sacrifice, then, is a means of purging impurity from the tabernacle or the temple, the dwelling place of God, where it does not belong. Skin diseases (often referred to as leprosy) seem to represent an irruption of death in living flesh, where death does not belong, and the person with such an affliction must be separated off from the rest of the community to keep it from spreading. Dietary regulations—the stipulations of which animals are 'clean' and therefore approved for eating—likewise seem to be based on a model of an ordered creation in which creatures have their proper place and must conform to that place; those that do not are considered unclean, or anomalous. Bodily fluids, of course, belong ideally in the body. When such fluids exit the body, and in particular when they do so in a way that the individual cannot control, such as nocturnal emissions for men and menstrual flows for women, they are anomalous and a source of uncleanness.

I am of course following here Mary Douglas, who, more than anyone, has made clear that a central concern of the priestly literature is with boundaries and divisions.[11] The maintenance of borders, in the face of a threat of contamination, is all-important: hence, the emphasis on where and when things enter and exit the body— food, seminal emissions, menstrual blood. These all represent points of danger and consequently are matters that require attentiveness. Similarly, entering and exiting the sphere of the holy—passing from the common realm, or the realm of the every-day, into the realm of the sacred—is a border crossing of great import and freight-edness. All of these activities must be done intentionally, and they must have rituals attached to them. Priests are the ones who know the arcane secrets, the ways of protecting borders when possible and crossing them when necessary, whether it be the border between the body and the world outside the body, or the border between the sacred and the common. It is not the case that uncleanness is necessarily 'bad', nor that it represents any sort of moral failure on the part of the person deemed unclean. The priestly literature understands that in the course of one's life one will constantly be passing back and forth between states of cleanness and uncleanness. It is simply that one must have the proper rituals to go with activities that render one unclean. Typically, the rituals involve washing with water, and waiting until the evening of the same day, or in more serious cases waiting for seven days, before entering the temple to sacrifice.

Entering the temple, or the tabernacle, the dwelling place of God, is under any circumstance an activity freighted with mystery, both dangerous and fascinating. Priests, being the ones who spend the most time in and around the dwelling place of

11. The crucial work is, of course, *Purity and Danger: An Analysis of the Concepts of Pollution and Taboo* (London: Routledge & Kegan Paul, 1966); but see now also her more recent *Leviticus as Literature* (Oxford: Oxford University Press, 1999).

God, are also the ones who require the most elaborate and meticulous ritual preparation, in order that they not contaminate or pollute the sanctuary. So one finds in Leviticus 8 a detailed description of the ritual ordination of Aaron and his sons as the first generation of priests in Israel. Before they can serve in the sanctuary they must undergo a process of purification and preparation. I would like to call attention to a brief part of this purification ritual, which deals with the vestments or garb of the priests, and then compare this with a scene from the 1995 film *12 Monkeys*:

> Then Moses brought Aaron and his sons forward and washed them with water. He put the tunic on him, girded him with the sash, clothed him with the robe, and put the ephod on him, girding him with the decorated band with which he tied it to him. He put the breastpiece on him, and put into the breastpiece the Urim and Thummim. And he set the headdress on his head; and on the headdress, in front, he put the gold frontlet, the holy diadem—as the Lord had commanded Moses. (Lev. 8.6-9 JPSV)

If one compares this with the opening sequence of the movie *12 Monkeys*, one notices that Bruce Willis's character, James Cole, dons a remarkably similar set of ritual garments. (And one notices the voice in the background, which sounds an awful lot like God's repeated warning in the Torah that 'you shall faithfully observe my laws and all my rules'.) For those who have not seen *12 Monkeys*, it is set a few decades after a viral apocalypse in which all but 0.001% of the human population of the earth has been wiped out. The survivors have gone underground to escape the various mutations of the virus that have since proliferated on the surface. The film's opening sequence shows the passage of James Cole, one of the survivors, from the underground complex to the surface. Cole, like the priests of Leviticus, is engaged in a border-crossing between realms of cleanness and uncleanness. And like the priests of Leviticus, Cole must be outfitted meticulously in elaborate garments in order to ensure against the contamination of one realm with the other. Those who have seen the movie may remember that every time he crosses between these realms he is also required to undergo a thorough cleansing by water, as in most ritual purifications in Leviticus.

Now, it may be that all this is simply the product of too much time spent reading the Bible, and that nobody else would see it this way, but it seems to me that contemporary representations of the priest as uniformed guardian against contagion—in the form of biological scientists—began popping up with increasing regularity in the mid- to late 1990s: in the movie *Outbreak*, for example, or on the covers of mass market magazines such as *Parade* or *Time*. In February of 1998 these magazines featured cover stories on, respectively, 'The Virus Hunters' and 'The Flu Hunters'. The subheading for the *Time* cover read as follows: 'Follow the trail of scientific detectives who are trying to stop a lethal virus—before it spreads around the world'.[12] *Parade* was more expansive:

---

12. *Time* (23 February 1998).

To protect the rest of us, a few men and women come face to face with a killer every day. They cannot see it, except under high-powered microscopes. They cannot feel it. But they know that, with one mistake, they risk death from devastating diseases for which there are no known cures.[13]

These are the new priests, presented as possessing the arcane knowledge that the rest of us lack, but which is absolutely necessary in order to keep at bay the threat of contagion; day-in and day-out they don the protective garments and perform the rituals necessary for the border crossing entailed by the containment of impurity. And like the priests in Leviticus—whose vocation is summarized in 10.10 with the statement 'you must distinguish between the unclean and the clean, and you must teach the Israelites all the laws which the Lord has imparted to them'—they prescribe for the rest of us our own less elaborate but equally important rituals of purification and protection: Thus, the *Parade* article comes complete with what can only be described as a modern, high-tech version of the Ten Commandments, under the heading of 'Ten Ways You Can Prevent Infectious Diseases'.

3. *Conclusion*

I have traced in this article two paradigms of mass destruction: one focused on the expectation of a final, single glorious-and-terrible conflagration, the other on the fear of a gradually but inexorably spreading contamination. If the shift in our thinking that I have tried to identify has indeed taken place, what then are its implications? Jonathan Schell, author of the 1983 book on the nuclear weapons race, *The Fate of the Earth*, evaluated in a recent article the effect of the nuclear threat, and especially the logic of deterrence, on our moral imagination.

> The experience of our century taught us that genocide was the worst of all crimes, but a nuclear 'priesthood' taught us that to threaten it, and even to carry it out, was not only justifiable but our inescapable duty. Every scruple in the human conscience declared that we must never risk extinguishing our species—the supreme crime against humanity, and the only crime greater than genocide—but solemn doctrine declared that it was essential to threaten this act... The morbidity of the era consisted of more than the threat of universal death with which it was overhung; it consisted also of the prohibition, so humiliating to the human spirit, against taking action to remove the threat. Thus did the reasoning of the age seemingly compel not only totalitarian regimes but great democracies to enter, against all their better instincts and understanding, into a hated complicity in potentially limitless killing.[14]

I am compelled to wonder if there is not some similar invidious effect of our present paradigm of contagion and contamination. Given that *yes* it is without a doubt beneficial to have scientists at the Centers for Disease Control working to identify and stave off possible epidemics, and given that *yes* it is true that biological

---

13. *Parade* (8 February 1998).

14. Jonathan Schell, 'The Gift of Time: The Case for Abolishing Nuclear Weapons', *The Nation* (2-9 February 1998), p. 12.

weapons are a potential threat, and given that *yes* it is important to work to curb the spread of AIDS through the use of condoms—given *all* of this—is there not also something troubling, even malignant, about this way of thinking that depends so heavily on the drawing of lines, the making of distinctions, the guarding of borders? Let me be clear that it is not the practices of purity or cleanliness that I am gainsaying here, but rather the reification of these practices as a paradigm; in other words, when notions of purity begin to pervade and to shape the way we see all things and all people, shaping not just our practices of hygiene and disease prevention, but our politics, our ethics, our face to face relationships.

Two recent examples of the peril of this sort of cultural spillover of the viral paradigm come to mind, though one could undoubtedly identify many more. First, there is the case of the three Pakistani medical students who had applied for temporary lab technician posts at the hospital at Duke University. The three students— Imran Bhaila, Hussain Khawaja, and Omer Ashraf—were rejected for the posts and each received an email in December of 2001 from a professor of cell biology at Duke. The note read, in part: 'Your ethnicity and your age (student age = idealistic) are so similar to those of the jihad-minded terrorists from the schools that nurtured the Taliban and Al-Quaeda [*sic*] that it is not worth our trouble to try to determine if you are a well-disguised terrorist or a real learning-motivated student'. In the spirit of the 1990s, this Duke professor justified the ethnic profiling of the students by claiming that they were 'as potentially lethal as anthrax or HIV'.[15] Secondly, it would appear that the language of purity has taken root in a pernicious way among teenagers in America. On the basis of extensive interviews with students, *Washington Post* reporter Liza Mundy has noted that one deleterious effect of teenagers being barraged with statistics and stories of sexually transmitted diseases is the way in which the labels 'clean' and 'dirty' are applied to girls as a marker of perceived sexual activity.[16] Of course we have had in English for some time the metaphorical use of 'dirty', as in dirty old man or dirty movies. But now this metaphor has been literalized with reference to STDs, paired with its opposite 'clean', and taken on a moral sense that is foreign to biblical notions of purity. It is hard to imagine the effect of this unholy mixture of ancient purity notions, modern science, and familiar gender stereotypes (sexually active boys are 'players' or 'pretty boys', while the girls are 'dirty' or 'skanky') on the psyches of adolescents.

We are not so sophisticated that we can't learn from the Bible on this matter; for the Bible knows that such large paradigms can never be beyond critique. So we find that the same prophets who announced the destruction represented by the Day of the Lord also passionately argued with God against allowing such destruction to happen. Likewise, the Bible recognizes that God not only grounds the structure of the purity system, but also in extreme circumstances moves to undermine that very structure. Thus in the book of Micah we read that God, in response to God's own

15. Quotes are from the news article by Richard Morgan, 'The Worst Rejection Letter', *The Chronicle of Higher Education* (1 February 2002).

16. Liza Mundy, 'Sex and Sensibility', *The Washington Post Magazine* (18 July 2000), pp. 17-21 and 29-34.

decree of destruction on account of Israel's transgressions, utters the following lines:

> Because of this I will lament and wail; I will go stripped and naked! I will lament as sadly as the jackals, as mournfully as the ostriches. For her disease is incurable, it has reached Judah, it has spread to the gate of my people, to Jerusalem. (Mic. 1.8-9 JPSV)

In this text a wailing and lamenting God takes on the very impurity and abjection that the priestly system works to keep at bay. Adopting priestly vocabulary and concerns—jackals and ostriches are the epitome of unclean animals, and the language of reaching and spreading is the priestly language for communicable diseases—God here brings that system crashing in on itself.[17]

To be sure, this one text about an impure and abject God does not offset the entire book of Leviticus and the purity system it endorses, nor is it desirable that it should. But what it does is to show that any such system must necessarily contain, as Tim Beal puts it, 'cracks, chips, and splits which open to new readerly possibilities, and therefore to new theological possibilities, and therefore to new lived possibilities'.[18] And, I would add, that occasionally, only occasionally, it is necessary to exploit those gaps and shake the system to its very foundation.

The trick of course is to decide when those occasions might be.

---

17. On this text see Timothy K. Beal, 'The System and the Speaking Subject in the Hebrew Bible: Reading for Divine Abjection', *BibInt* 2.2 (1994), pp. 172-89.

18. Beal, 'The System', p. 187.

The White Supremacist Bible and the Phineas Priesthood

Timothy K. Beal

Executing Vengeance

Across the bottom of the official homepage of the World Headquarters of the Aryan Nations march three diapered babies. At first glance these animated figures remind me of the dancing baby on the television show *Ally McBeal*. As such they appear out of place amid 'whites only' warnings, eulogies for Palestinian suicide bombers, doom-filled predictions from Amos and Joel littered with oddly transliterated Hebrew, and curses against corporate America and the ZOG ('Zionist Occupied Government'). But look more closely: the babies aren't dancing, and they're not smiling, and they're carrying clubs. And the banner running below them reads: 'Here comes the next generation...badder and meaner than the last, ALL full knowing His Truth and schooled in the Phineas Priesthood!'[1]

Similarly, on the Aryan Nations website for the Pennsylvania chapter, we find these comments, bathed in biblical idiom, on our present age, the immanent apocalyptic battle to come and the central role to be played by the 'Phineas Priest':

> A decadent, sinful Babylon policed by those who don't really understand or believe in what they're doing... Against the zealous Shiite to the East as well as both the Shiite of Islam and the Phineas Priest of Christendom within their own borders... Who do YOU think will win? The Earth was created by YHVH. It is said, render unto Caesar that which is Caesar'sbut the EARTH belongs to the LORD! WOE unto the servants of Satan when the day of Reckoning arrives![2]

Likewise on the national website, Aryan Nations devotee Joshua Caleb Sutter bewails what he sees as 'YHVH's children' blindly following their Zionist occupied government down the road to destruction, and calls for a new generation of 'Phineas Priests and Priestesses' to rise up and enact divine judgment like their Islamist counterparts in the Middle East. He asks, hopefully,

> Or will it be your son or daughter next who is the suicide bomber not in the distant land of Palestine, but here on American soil? Will the sons and daughters of YHVH God be joining with the zealous soldiers of Mohammed, rising up in righteous indignation? Will the Phineas Priests and Phineas Priestesses begin awaking all

---

1. From the homepage of the World Headquarters of the Aryan Nations <www.aryan-nations.org> (accessed April 2002).

2. <www.aryan-nations.org/pa> (accessed April 2002).

over this country to 'execute vengeance upon the heathen, and punishments upon the people' as the Psalmist David foretold?

He then quotes from the proto-apocalyptic announcement of judgment in Joel 2, anticipating the uprising of God's army against the unrighteous hordes, 'a great people and a strong; there hath not been ever the like... A fire devoureth before them; and behind them a flame burneth: the land is as the garden of Eden before them, and behind them a desolate wilderness.' 'Yea', Sutter concludes, in capitals, 'and NOTHING SHALL ESCAPE THEM'.

In fact, over the past decade, 'Phineas Priest' has emerged within Christian white supremacist culture as the privileged title for those who rise up to enact militant racist terror in the name of God. Some examples:

> After being convicted of murdering an interracial couple at a Grayhound bus station in Spokane, Washington, a skinhead named Chris Alan Lindholm referred newspaper reporter Bill Morlin to the story of Phineas in Numbers 25 as his justification. 'I wasn't mad at them or anything. I just knew they should die for what they had done. I think he put his arm around her or something.'[3]

> Members of the Aryan Republican Army, a militantly anti-Jewish organization that robbed twenty-two banks during 1994 and 1995, identified themselves with the Phineas Priesthood.[4]

> In April of 1996, cars parked at a Unitarian-Universalist fellowship in nearby Idaho Falls were leafleted with anti-gay tracts describing those who transgress biblical law as 'walking death sentences'. They described the 1986 murder and bombing at an adult bookstore in North Carolina as actions of Phineas Priests who carried out divine judgment against transgressors of biblical law, and warned, 'In cities and towns all over America, names and addresses of law violators are being compiled. Six-man teams are forming across the nation. Soon, the fog that comes from Heaven will be accompanied by a destroying wind of a righteous God.' At the bottom of the leaflet were the words 'The Phineas Priesthood'.[5]

> Four men convicted of bombing a Planned Parenthood clinic, a newspaper office, and two banks in Spokane, Washington (about 50 miles from the Aryan Nations compound at Hayden Lake) during the spring and summer of 1996 described themselves during their trial as Phineas Priests.[6] At the scenes of their crimes,

---

3.   Morlin's interview with Lindholm is described in David A. Niewert, *In God's Country: The Patriot Movement and the Pacific Northwest* (Pullman: Washington State University Press, 1999), p. 126. See also Bill Morlin and Jeanette White, 'Phineas Priests Take Name from Bible', *Spokesman-Review* (3 April 1996), A7.

4.   Niewert, *In God's Country*, pp. 124-25.

5.   Gene Fadness, 'Phineas Priests May Be Responsible for Racist Leaflets', *Idaho Falls Post Register* (18 April 1996), A1.

6.   One of the four men, Brian Ratigan, called the judge a 'prince of darkness' during the sentencing phase of the trial. He concluded, 'People of Spokane, you have been warned. You have been sent four witnesses. Babylon is about to fall. The Messiah, Yeshua, is on his way, so repent.' In the men's car, agents found a tape sermon by notorious white supremacist and Christian Identity theologian Pete Peters as well as a Bible in which references to the 'Lord' had been crossed out and replaced in the margin with 'Yahweh'.

investigators found carefully wrapped two-page notes including biblical passages from Jeremiah 51 and Revelation 18 about divine judgment. References to 'Lord' were replaced with 'Yahweh' and references to 'man' were replaced with 'Adam-man'. At the bottom was a cross with a P in the upper right quadrant [see Fig. 1].[7]

Figure 1. *'Sign of Phineas', from Richard Kelly Hoskins,*
Vigilantes of Christendom: The History of the Phineas Priesthood
(Lynchburg: The Virginia Publishing Company, 1990), p. 116.

White racist Burford O'Neal Furrow, who went on a shooting spree at a Los Angeles area Jewish Community Center in August 1999, called himself a Phineas Priest.

As these examples begin to make clear, 'Phineas Priest' is not only a title but a biblical-theological justification for militant violence against social behaviors that are perceived to be transgressions of biblical laws.

The biblical basis for these references to 'Phineas Priests' and the 'Phineas Priesthood' is a story in Numbers 25 about divinely sanctioned violence for the sake of ethnic and religious purity.[8] In that story, the Israelites are suffering from a deadly plague which the narrative presents as the result of their intermixing with the Moabites, which v. 1 describes in terms of profanation (חלל) and 'committing whoredom' (זנה). Given the use of these terms elsewhere in the Torah and related prophetic texts, it is not surprising that this intermixing is elaborated here as a transgression of *religious-devotional* purity and integrity. That is, the significance of Israelites marrying the daughters of Moab is that they are adopting their religious practices (25.2) to the extent that 'Israel joined himself unto Baal-peor; and the anger of the LORD was kindled against Israel' (25.3). In a jealous rage, God tells Moses to hang all the leaders of the people so that his rage may abate. In response, Moses orders his judges to slay everyone who has been 'joined to Baal-peor' (25.4-5). Just then an Israelite man named Zimri and a Midianite woman named Cozbi come into the presence of Moses and the weeping congregation. Seeing this apparently brazen couple, a priest named Phineas (Aaron's grandson) leaves the congregation, follows the couple into their tent, and runs them both through their

---

7.   Bill Morlin, 'Bomber Sounds Warning before 55-Year Sentence', *The Spokesman Review* (3 December 1997), B2; Craig Welch and Kim Barker, 'FBI's Work Challenged by Defense: Agents Describe Items Found in Cars of Bombing Suspects', *The Spokesman Review* (4 July 1997), B1. A few months before the bombings, Morlin had photographed an Aryan Nations security officer who had the same insignia on his belt buckle.

8.   Throughout white supremacist culture, biblical passages are most commonly quoted from the KJV. Therefore I use this translation here, referring to the Hebrew text where appropriate.

bellies on the same spear (implying that he found them joined in an embrace; 25.7-8). In immediate response to this zealous double murder, God stays the plague against the Israelites and blesses Phineas, giving him and his descendants 'my covenant of peace...even the covenant of an everlasting priesthood; because he was zealous for his God, and made atonement for the children of Israel' (25.11-13).

Phineas is also mentioned in Psalm 106, in the context of wilderness recollect-ions. There the psalmist praises Phineas for standing up and executing judgment in response to the Israelites having joined themselves to Baal-peor. Here there is no mention of inter-coupling, only religious intermixing. Nor is there any mention here of an everlasting priesthood, but rather that his zealous act was 'counted unto him as righteousness' (ותחשב לו לצדקה)—just as God reckoned Abraham's belief to him as righteousness in Gen. 15.6 (ויחשבה לו צדקה).

The relationship between these biblical representations of Phineas and militant white racist appropriations of the title 'Phineas Priest' is far from self-evident. In fact, throughout most of the history of biblical interpretation in Judaism and Chris-tianity, readings of the Phineas story in Numbers 25 and Psalm 106 have empha-sized the sin of *religious* intermixing rather than familial intermixing as the reason for God's and Phineas' righteous indignation. Psalms, after all, mentions no specific sin, and although Numbers 25 does initially mention that the Israelites were joining themselves to the daughters of their enemies (v. 1), the emphasis of the narrative is on the religious consequences of these new familial bonds, namely, that the Israel-ites were joining themselves to other gods through ritual devotion. How, then, did this biblical story come to play such a central role in the formation of radical white racist identity?

Vigilantes of Christendom

The missing link appears to be white supremacist theologian and financial advisor Richard Kelly Hoskins's book *Vigilantes of Christendom: The Story of the Phineas Priesthood* (1990), which celebrates a post-biblical lineage of 'Phineas Priests' who have committed acts of violent racial and moral purification out of righteous jealousy for 'God's Law', and which summons a new generation of white Christian zealots to similar action:

> There are those who obey God's Law and those who don't. Those who obey are the Lawful. Those who disobey are outlawed by God. God has specified the out-law's punishment. The Phineas priests administer the judgment, and God rewards them with a covenant of an everlasting priesthood.[9]

Hoskins's book presents what he describes as the story of an everlasting lineage of Phineas Priests who fought to the death in defense of God's laws, enforcing racial purity and Christian identity, and biblical prohibitions against usury, among other things. Beginning with the biblical story of Phineas, Hoskins's lineage includes

---

9.   Richard Kelly Hoskins, *Vigilantes of Christendom: The History of the Phineas Priesthood* (Lynchburg: Virginia Publishing Company, 1990), p. 213.

legendary heroes like St George and Robin Hood, heroes in the 'war of northern aggression' like the Confederate general Nathan Bedford Forrest and Lincoln's assassin John Wilkes Booth, and the vigilante executioners responsible for thousands of post-Civil War lynchings, among many others.

Biblical passages are interwoven throughout Hoskins revisionist history. These passages are often inserted into the text, indented in a bold or italic font, without any explanation. In many cases, moreover, Hoskins drastically abbreviates the passages he quotes with ellipses, as in this example from the last pages of the book:

> How long can one expect it to be before six men at a time gather at brass altars with drawn weapons?
> *'Cause them that have charge...to draw near, even every man with his destroying weapon...six men come...and one man...with a writer's inkhorn at his side: and they went in and stood beside the brazen altar... And to the others he said... Go ye...and smite: ...and begin at my sanctuary. Then they began at the ancient men (elders) which were before the house'* (Ezek. 9.1-6).

> Does one actually expect an impoverished Saxon to pass by and look over the iron fence at Goliath living unpunished in his mansion, one who is known to have committed capital crimes against God, and yet securely lives on Saxon land and feasts on Saxon wealth?[10]

So Hoskins continues, riffing on the David and Goliath story with nary another mention of Ezekiel 9. Of course, this passage provides inspiration, albeit somewhat obliquely detailed inspiration, for the ensuing battle of the righteous against the powers that be. Does it also suggest a role for Hoskins himself as the writer whose destroying weapon is the inkhorn—or rather, in today's economy, the self-publishing house? Hoskins leaves that to the reader to determine. On the one hand, the rhetorical effect of quoting biblical passages in this way, setting them off from the rest of the text with little or no explanation, is that they *appear* to have authority to speak for themselves. They need no interpretation. On the other hand, the multiple ellipses which Hoskins uses to abbreviate and streamline the passages he quotes undermine this implicit assertion of the autonomous authority of Scripture. Thus Hoskins's method of biblical quotation—inserting highly truncated passages into his text with little or no prose explanation—allows him to interpret the text without appearing to do so. His interpretation is located in the placement and streamlining of the texts he quotes.

This rhetorical strategy is very clear in Hoskins's presentation of the biblical story of Phineas. Indeed, although it is the foundation for his entire revisionist history, his presentation of this story comprises less than a page of text, including quotations. It begins with a highly abbreviated quotation of Num. 25.6-13, indented and in italics:

---

10. Hoskins, *Vigilantes*, p. 417. Earlier, in a discussion of the tragic downfall of Robert Matthews's militant group *The Order*, Hoskins quotes the same passage as the scriptural basis for keeping membership in Phineas groups to six (the seventh member being God).

One of the children of Israel came and brought...a Midianitish woman...and when
Phineas...saw it, he rose up from among the congregation and took a javelin in his
hand; ...and thrust both of them through...and the Lord spake...saying Phineas...
hath turned my wrath away from the children of Israel, ...that I consumed not the
children of Israel... Behold I give unto him my covenant of peace: ...and his seed
after him, even the covenant of an everlasting priesthood: because he was zealous
for his God, and made an atonement for the children of Israel (Num. 25.6-13).

This abbreviated rendition of the story in Numbers 25 zeros in on Phineas' action
and God's reward. Note, moreover, that Hoskins has elided those details in the
biblical text that emphasize concern about *religious* intermixing, thereby implying
that the transgression was that of ethnic (for Hoskins, racial) intermixing.

After this quotation from Numbers 25, and without further interpretive commentary on that text, Hoskins moves immediately to Ps. 106.29-31, which thereby
serves as a means of explaining the lesson of the longer story in Numbers, namely,
that 'plague results from violating God's instructions'.[11] The implication of lay-
ing the two texts out in this fashion, one immediately following the other, is that
Numbers 25 tells the story and Psalm 106 explains its lesson. Remember, moreover, that Hoskins's truncated version of Numbers makes it into a story about racial
rather than religious intermixing. Thus the logic of Hoskins's interpretation goes as
follows: God brought a plague on Israel because they were practicing racial intermarriage, which is against God's law; by killing a racial intermixer, Zimri, Phineas
executed judgment against Israel on behalf of God's law; in response to this action
on behalf of the law of racial purity, God lifted the plague and blessed Phineas on
account of his zealous action, which was reckoned to him as righteousness.

Thus Hoskins renders the biblical story of Phineas as a story that ordains racial
violence as defense of divine law, reckoning as righteous those who zealously carry
out such violence. Yet the rhetorical effect of his presentation gives the impression
that he is not imposing a racist interpretation on these texts, but rather is simply
presenting the texts as they stand and letting them speak for him.

White Racism as Biblical Theology

Indeed, Hoskins's interpretation represents a dramatic shift in focus, concerned as
it is with a certain modern idea of *racial* purity as much as it is with religious
purity. This shift involves highlighting some aspects of the story that traditionally
have been overlooked, especially the scandal of ethnic or tribal intermixing.
Whereas Christian and Jewish traditions have focused on religious intermixing in
the story, Hoskins focuses on ethnic intermixing, that is, intermarriage of Israelites
with non-Israelites. Hoskins pushes this reading further by importing, anachronisti-
cally, the modern idea of race, suggesting that the intermarrying at issue here is
interracial rather than simply inter-ethnic or inter-familial. Indeed, like many other
white supremacists steeped in the theology of Christian Identity, Hoskins sees the

---

11. Hoskins, *Vigilantes*, p. 25.

Israelites in the story as 'white' and the Midianites as 'black'. For Hoskins, the crime of Zimri and his fellow Israelites was miscegenation of whites with blacks.

As Hoskins makes this leap from an ancient Near Eastern idea of ethnic or familial intermarriage to a modern racist idea of racial intermarriage, however, he does not omit the religious dimensions of this intermixing. For Hoskins, racial identity is inextricably tied to religious identity. Indeed, for him, racial identity *is* religious identity. He explicates this biblical-theological idea of race most clearly in an article called 'America's Gods' published in his newsletter, *The Hoskins Report*.[12] There he explains that each race is created in the image of its deity. For Hoskins, Adamic Man, that is, the white human, was created in the image of the God of the Bible, and was given the Law, including laws against mixing with other races so that Man would remain pure and purely devoted to God (Hoskins does not refer to other 'races' as 'Man' or 'man'). Consistent with other Anglo-Israelists and Christian Identity adherents, Hoskins traces the genealogy of Adamic Man through Abraham and Isaac and through the northern tribes of Israel to northern Europe, asserting that whites of northern European descent are the modern racial heirs of Adam, created by God. 'Adamic Israel', he writes in another essay on Saxon identity, 'existed before governments or churches. God made His contracts and covenants with Adam and the sons of Isaac (Isaac-sons; Saxons); and with their descendants forever. We are those descendants. We know our identity. We know our inheritance.'[13] But non-whites, according to Hoskins, are not created by this same God, and therefore are not of the same race of Man. Blacks, he claims, were created not in the image of the biblical God, the God of Law. Rather they were created in the image of the black god, which he identifies primarily with several deities from the Hindu religious pantheon: Siva, his consort Parviti [*sic*], Kali, Lakshmi, and Genesha. Hoskins elaborates several white racist stereotypes of African-Americans in order to show how this race is created in the image of these gods. For example,

> Sex pleased Siva and Parviti his wife. Sex pleased the Blacks made in Siva's image. Wherever blacks are found, India, America, Europe, S. Africa or Australia, their actions reveal Siva, the god in whose image they are made, even when they call him by other names.

> Dr. Martin Luther King was notorious for his sexual escapades. He would come to town proclaiming that he came in peace and would incite the Blacks and leave the town in flames and its stores looted. This is the way Blacks act the world over.

Behind all these divine faces, Hoskins asserts, those who have eyes to see will recognize their true creator, the ever-deceptive Serpent who is always trying to infiltrate white racial-religious purity:

---

12. Richard Kelly Hoskins, 'America's Gods', *Hoskins Report* 293 <http.//www.richardhoskins. com/1_vphr.htm>.

13.   Richard Kelly Hoskins, 'Saxon Identity', *Hoskins Report* 266 <http.//www.richardhoskins. com/1_vphr.htm>.

Strangers may speak with the sweet voice of the Serpent god, and call his name 'Jesus', but 'By their acts ye shall know them', and know their gods.

To mix races is to mix gods. The central purpose of the biblical Law, planted in all whites at creation, is to keep God's creation, Man, separate and holy. And this, for Hoskins, is the true sin of racial mixing, whether by marriage or incorporation or whatever. Indeed, he sees evidence of it everywhere in contemporary American culture, from the US Government to the ever-elusive International Trade Cartel to the liberalized Christian church, which he tellingly calls 'Dharma-Christian churches':

> Dharma-Christian churches insist that the Jews are Israel and therefore only the Jews are bound by God's Commandments. Consequently, the Law is done away and people can do as they please... God's Commandments say 'A bastard (Heb: mamzêr mixed breed, mongrel) shall not enter into the congregation of the Lord (Israel)'. Deut. 23.2... Representatives of the Jews admit that they are a mixed race. God's Commandment excludes them from his Israel nation. Dharma-Christian churches brand themselves 'false witnesses' and incur the judgement due false-witnesses... Dharma-Churches bless cartel-appointed governments by giving them authority to enforce laws that violate God's Commandments. They do this by misquoting, 'Be subject to principalities and powers, to obey magistrates' (Titus 3.1)... Saxons reply: 'We must obey God rather than men' (Acts 5.29).[14]

And,

> To change the Christian separatist God into a loving Dharma-Christian Hindu god, the Trade Cartel hired priests to insert the Hindu 'Dharmatolerance' into the separatist Christian religion. This new Dharma-Christianity taught Saxons to love everyone without regard to 'race, creed, or national origin'. This done, the Christian God was chained and the international merchants were free to come and go as they chose.[15]

For Hoskins, then, religious identity is racial identity. Race is defined theologically: each race is created in the image of its creator god. To mix races, then, is to mix gods. By calling American liberal Christian churches 'Dharma-Churches', he indicates not only a mixing of religions but a mixing of the races that the gods of each religion have created in their image. For Hoskins, therefore, the sin of Zimri and others like him was that he was mongrelizing not only Israelite (white) identity but the very image of God. Phineas' zealous act of murder rose from the desire to maintain the holiness/purity of the image of God within Israel.

From this perspective, moreover, adherence to all biblical Law (as interpreted by Hoskins) would be exclusively the white Man's burden. For the main aim of these laws, for Hoskins, is to guard the holiness (separateness, purity) of white Adamic Man as the image of his creator God. This is why the four self-proclaimed Phineas Priests affiliated with white supremacist religious organizations bombed both

---

14. Hoskins, 'Saxon Identity'.
15. Hoskins, 'Saxon Identity'.

Planned Parenthood (for murder) and local banks (for usury).[16] This is also why Aryan Nations and other organizations call people who are homosexual 'walking death sentences' (for sexual transgressions of the Law). These activities are taken as transgressions of God's Law, and as such they threaten to brown the whiteness of the Law-abiding Adamic Man, which is the very image of God.

Ironies Notwithstanding

In the decade or so since the publication of *Vigilantes*, Hoskins's idea of the Phineas Priesthood has proliferated within religious white supremacist culture, to the extent that 'Phineas Priest' has become the privileged title for those self-proclaimed righteous individuals and small groups who enact God's judgment on those who break God's commandment.[17]

Hoskins's idea of the Phineas Priesthood is, of course, an easy target for criticism, rife as it is with deep ironies. From an academic perspective, for example, it's certainly ironic that the biblical Law to which Hoskins vows devotion, and which Phineas and his modern day anti-Jewish white heirs struggle to defend, is probably

16. Likewise, months before Reverend Paul Hill murdered Dr David Gunn as he was about to enter an abortion clinic in Pensacola, FL, on 10 March 1993, he wrote 'Should We Defend Born and Unborn Children With Force?' (July 1993) <http.//www.armyofgod.com/Paulhillindex.html>, which draws from Num. 25 as the primary biblical justification for violence against abortion workers. In fact, the Aryan Nations and numerous other Christian Identity organizations place the anti-abortion movement front and center. My point is that this is not an add-on agenda for them. Rather, they see it as part of the religious obligation of whites.

17. Of course, the biblical story of Phineas was well known among white supremacist ministers and congregants before the publication of Hoskins's book. Yet it was his book that recruited the idea of the Phineas Priesthood as a central biblical inspiration and justification for militant racist violence as a form of divinely sanctioned religious zeal. The idea first came to popular media attention in October 1991 during the trial and conviction of former Ku Klux Klan member Byron de la Beckwith for the 1963 murder of civil rights leader Medgar Evers. Months before his trial, the prosecutors discovered, a letter from Beckwith had appeared in Hoskins's newsletter with the concluding proclamation, 'Phineas for President!' Beckwith was apparently a friend of Hoskins. His wife Thelma claims that they attended Aryan Nations meetings together in Hayden Lake, ID (D.A. Neiwert, *In God's Country: The Patriot Movement and the Pacific Northwest* [Pullman: Washington State University, 1999]), p. 124. It is clear, moreover, that the Aryan Republican Army, mentioned earlier, received its Phineas inspiration through Hoskins: on their recruitment video, Peter Langan promotes *Vigilantes*, holding it up and calling it a 'handbook for revolution', and two of the group's members were members of a Christian Identity congregation in Hereford, PA, led by pastor and Aryan Nations leader Mark Thomas, whose church door bears the Phineas Priesthood insignia that appears on Hoskins book (see David Lethbridge, 'Killers for God: The Phineas Priesthood' [The Bethune Institute for Anti-Fascist Studies, 1998], available online at <www.bethuneinstitute.org>). That same insignia, a cross with the letter P in the upper right quadrant, also appeared on the tracts left at crime scenes by the four self-proclaimed Phineas Priests of Spokane, also mentioned earlier. In those notes, moreover, 'Adam-man' was used instead of 'man' in the biblical passages they quoted. Compare Hoskins's use of the same term in his biblical explications. Finally, note that Buford Furrow, who also described himself as a Phineas Priest, had another of Hoskins's books in his car (*War Cycles/Peace Cycles* [Lynchburg: Virginia Publishing Company, 1985]).

rooted in later post-exilic Judean 'Priestly' traditions. And then there's the more-or-less implicit polytheism built into Hoskins's own idea of divinely created race: white Adamic Israel was created by the biblical God to rule the world, but other races were created by other gods and are in conflict with the biblical God and God's creation. And then there's the fact that Moses himself, like Zimri, married a Midianite! Wouldn't that make Moses' own children mongrel enemies of Adamic Israel according to Hoskins's theology of race?

But irony has never been a forte among those on the religiously racist right. And such criticisms really are, we might say (more likely they might say), purely academic. The fact is that, *on the ground*, this idea of the Phineas Priesthood set within its larger racist biblical interpretive framework is working. And it works on several levels. I have identified seven.

First, it provides a biblical-interpretive set of unifying terms for an otherwise extremely disparate and centerless movement. Indeed, it has provided a collective religious identity and social coherence out of a smattering of isolated, more or less underground organizations and individuals—from neo-Nazis to Christian Identity parishioners to militias to unmedicated paranoid schizophrenics with guns. Given it's anti-establishment, anti-organizational vigilantism, moreover, it is able to provide this social coherence and identity in ways consistent with other values that are shaping the movement, especially Louis Beam's concepts of 'leaderless resistance' and 'phantom cells'.[18]

Second, the Phineas ideal ordains further militant racist action—'Phineas acts' as divine commission. To rise up from the congregation and carry out such actions is to join that spiritual priesthood of those zealously jealous for God.

Third, related to its power to ordain, the Phineas ideal reckons militant racist violence as righteousness. Recall that whereas Numbers 25 has God giving Phineas an everlasting priesthood, Psalm 106 puts it in other terms, terms that echo powerfully in a Protestant Christian theological context: [[**quote 'reckoned as righteous', same term, but here leading not to justification by faith but by zeal**]].

Fourth, the Phineas ideal asserts that such militant action is for the good of the larger social whole. Phineas' action atoned for the sins of Israel, and as a result God stayed the plague. Thus, although contemporary Phineas acts may look heinous in the eyes of the general lawless media-fed public, in the eyes of God, the argument goes, they are seen as selfless acts on behalf of the children of Adamic-Israel (that is, white Man), which may atone for their own heinous sins.

---

18. These concepts and terms were promoted after the Ruby Ridge incident in a paper presented by former Texas Ku Klux Klan Grand Dragon Louis Beam, Jr, 'Leaderless Resistance: Special Report on the Meeting of Christian Men Held in Estes Park, Colorado, October 23, 24, 25, 1992' (unpublished conference address; see Michael Barkun, *Religion and the Racist Right: The Origins of the Christian Identity Movement* [Chapel Hill: University of North Carolina, rev edn, 1997], pp. 280-81). The earlier development of these ideas can be seen in his essays and notes in *Essays of a Klansman Being a Compendium of Ku Klux Klan Ideology, Organizational Methods, History, Tactics, and Opinions, with Interpretations by the Author* (Hayden Lake: AKIA Publications, 1983).

Fifth, the Phineas ideal encourages potential Phineas Priests to dispel whatever inner conflict and hesitation they may be feeling, interpreting such feelings as a grievous paralysis brought on by generations of complacency in the face of lawlessness.

Sixth, it creates a new and open hagiography, a story of a royal priesthood of saints who have been jealous with God's jealousy. It is an open canon. A spiritual genealogy that runs all the way back to Israel's time in the wilderness, it remains open to the addition of new names of those who rise up and act within this new wilderness.

Seventh, it places individual militant violence in the context of a larger apocalyptic battle. Insofar as white Adamic Israel's battle for the Law is, on another level, a battle between Gods, Phineas acts are blows within a larger cosmic battle of apocalyptic proportions. Indeed, in some white supremacist rhetoric, Phineas acts are seen as potential sparks aimed to ignite the world in an apocalyptic racial holy war between the Aryan children of God and the non-white spawn of Satan.

Phineas in Diaspora

Although seldom recognized as such, radical white supremacist culture in the US is in many respects a *textual* culture. More precisely, it is a *biblical* culture. Its primary text is the Christian Bible, accompanied by a vast apocrypha of sermon transcripts and recordings, biblical commentaries, Bible study aids, and hagiographies, all of which are widely circulated in churches, at conventions and rallies, at Bible studies, in prisons, on the internet, and through small publishing houses. Historically rooted in the Christian Identity movement, a key means of growth and development continues to be biblical preaching in the context of worship, informal Bible study, and prison ministry.

Despite the centrality of biblical interpretation within white supremacist culture, biblical scholars have largely ignored it.[19] One reason for this ignorance is that academic training in biblical studies pays little or no attention to the place of the Bible in any cultural context later than the seventh century CE, concentrating instead on mastering the disciplines necessary to elucidate its earliest historical contexts and meanings: translation of ancient Near Eastern languages, exegesis, source criticism, and reconstruction of the editorial history of the literature. Research has been driven by questions of sources and authorship, and the answers to these questions have been used to reconstruct the original social contexts of the literature. More recent literary approaches have shifted attention from a search for origins to a

---

19. In fact, the two most important scholarly studies of religion and white supremacism are by a sociologist, James A. Aho (*The Politics of Righteousness: Idaho Christian Patriotism* [Seattle: University of Washington, 1990], on the Christian patriot movement in Idaho), and a political scientist, Michael Barkun (*Religion and the Racist Right* [see above], a historical account of the origins of the Christian Identity movement). Barkun is particularly clear in affirming the need for scholars trained in biblical criticism and hermeneutics to explore and elucidate the theological dimensions of contemporary white supremacism.

search for dynamics within the texts themselves. What we need, I contend, are approaches that focus on *cultural histories of the Bible*, that is, approaches that explore how biblical texts, themes and even the idea of 'the Bible' itself are handled in cultural terms—how they are appropriated and transformed in the context of particular cultural beliefs, practices and institutions. The urgency of this need is particularly clear with regard to a white supremacist culture whose religious dimensions are largely biblical. By exploring the idea of the Phineas Priesthood as one particular historically contingent form that biblical interpretation has taken within the context of American white supremacist culture, the present study makes a very modest step in this direction.

At the same time, white supremacist culture in the US is currently in a state of massive transition. Many of its most well-known leaders are very old, dead or in jail, and the Aryan Nations, which has been a center of influence since the 1970s, is in crisis, having lost its headquarters in northern Idaho. Yet we would be gravely mistaken to assume that these crises of location and leadership are ushering in the demise of white supremacist culture. According to monitoring groups such as the Southern Poverty Law Center, although the number of militia groups nationwide has shrunk dramatically over the past five years, the number of people involved in militantly racist groups has risen. Rather than disappearing, white supremacism is taking on new cultural forms. Abetted by new media technologies and inspired by concepts like 'leaderless resistance' and 'phantom cells', a centerless network culture is emerging—what I call 'diaspora white supremacism'. Amid all these changes, it remains a textual culture in which biblical interpretation serves to maintain ideological coherence and sanctify racist terror. Indeed, within this cultural diaspora, the movement's literary canon, especially the Bible and other biblically inspired texts, serves as a textual grounding for an otherwise increasingly ungrounded movement. References to specific biblical texts and interpretations within this diaspora network culture constitute an insider code language to maintain social identity and unity among those with ears to hear.[20] We ignore such references at our own peril.

---

20. Of course the idea that the truth is clearly heard by the chosen ones but appears as jibberish to those on the outside (e.g. Isa. 6.9; Mt. 13.15-16) is also a biblical idea. That the white supremacist biblical discourse makes perfect sense to those within the movement even while it is represented by the mainstream media and various human rights watchdog organizations as utter nonsense only confirms their self-understanding as divinely chosen judges, prophets and warriors of divine judgment, one that has had considerable circulation within many white racist groups. After an explication of Jn 3 and 8, arguing that the Jews are children of Satan and Jesus was not a Jew, for example, one Klansman complains of the ignorance of his implied audience of incredulous white liberals, then adds, 'But that's ok because we know you speak from ignorance, and your epithets are worn as badges of honor by all of us, so continue to rave on!' ('More on Why Christ was not a jew', *Political Satires by Klansman Born in '49* 6, from the main website for the White Camelia Knights of the Ku Klux Klan <www.wckkk.com/satires/satires_6.html>).

JESUS THE ACTOR: EDWIN MORGAN'S
A.D.: A TRILOGY OF PLAYS ON THE LIFE OF JESUS (2000)

David Jasper

There is a tiny moment in the great Easter Liturgy of Western Christendom from which, it may be true to say, mediaeval culture made the bridge between ritual and representational drama, and from the heart of the liturgy vernacular drama was born with the growth of the great mediaeval Mystery Cycles portraying the whole sweep of 'biblical history' from Genesis to Revelation. First appearing early in the tenth century, the *Quem quaeritis* dialogue is located at the pivotal moment not only of the Church's liturgical year but of all Christian history itself, that is, the moment of the Resurrection. Its basis is the dialogue of Mk 16.6-7:

> *Quem quaeritis in sepulchro, o Christicole?*
> *Ihesum Nazarenum crucifixum, o celicole.*
> *Non est hic, surrexit sicut ipse dixit; ite nunciate quia surrexit.*

> Whom seek ye in the tomb, O followers of Christ?
> Jesus of Nazareth who was crucified, O heaven-Dwellers.
> He is not here, he has arisen as he said; go announce that he has arisen.[1]

The dramatizing of this moment, it has been said, 'is not a tentative and blurred effort to express a felt experience in representational form, but a decisive realization of experience in terms of the history that the Middle Ages regarded as its basis'.[2] From this decisive moment, theatre moved from the Church's sanctuary, quite literally, into the market place, so that some four hundred years later the same exchange appears in the great 'Resurrection' play of the Chester Cycle.

Scholarship has exercised itself at great length over this tiny trope, but suffice it to say that its importance lies at many levels; in the history of liturgy and the history of drama, certainly, but also theologically, for here is 'secular' drama emerging from the key moment of Christian theology—a moment both in history and beyond it, and a moment which cannot strictly be represented. Nor does the trope try to do so except through the human experience of Mary Magdalene and the women at the tomb. Furthermore, there is no resurrection in St Mark's Gospel as such, but only a moment of recognition and realization. In Aristotelian terms the

---

1. Quoted in O.B. Hardison, Jr, *Christian Rite and Christian Drama in the Middle Ages* (Baltimore: The Johns Hopkins University Press, 1965), pp. 178-79.
2. Hardison, *Christian Rite*, p. 178.

resurrection is both the *peripeteia* and the *anagnorisis* of the Christian mythos. Around this moment comes to be built the great tradition of the miracle plays with their massive narrative sweep, their humour and, above all, their sense of community, shared by spectators and performers alike.[3] Deeply embedded in time, it draws together a vision of all time in eternity, meeting the liturgy again in its sense of celebration not simply as the recalling of a past event but as the bringing into being of an action, a moment of *poesis*.

All this is by way of a preamble to my primary concern which is Edwin Morgan's trilogy of plays on the life of Jesus, *A.D.*[4] Morgan is the poet laureate of Glasgow, a professor of English Literature, poet, playwright, translator and emphatically not a Christian. His plays were first performed in Glasgow at the Tramway in September 2000 as part of the city's millennium celebrations, and survived only a few performances before they were removed from the stage following public protest that they were religiously offensive. What remains in the text published by Carcanet is highly readable, a minor classic, part verse and part prose, in the tradition of the mediaeval drama up to the twentieth century appearances of Jesus as actor of stage and screen. Yet Morgan's plays are set decisively within the political and social ethos of our own time, his Jesus a 'human figure in an inhuman time',[5] one sane voice in an insane world. For all their differences, there is a startling similarity between Morgan's Jesus and the Jesus of John Dominic Crossan's *Revolutionary Biography* (1994), historically defined by Crossan as a peasant Jewish Cynic well aware of the Roman city of Sepphoris near Nazareth (a cultural centre of Greek drama which figures largely in Morgan's first play), but ultimately an inevitably fictional and complex character inhabiting whatever world needs him and needs to create him.[6]

Reading *A.D.* reminds me of another unbeliever's television play about Jesus, Dennis Potter's early work *Son of Man* (1969) of which Potter himself remarked (and he could have almost been talking about himself):

> There's this brave, witty, sometimes oddly petulant, man striding around in an occupied territory knowing and then not wanting to know that he's bound to die and to die painfully. And in the middle of it all, to say things that have never been said, and are still not said, about love. As a model of what human behaviour can be like, it still stands supreme.[7]

It reminds me also of another modern playwright who lives among the litter of religion, the Marxist film maker Pier Paolo Pasolini, who in his 1964 film *Vangelo Secondo Matteo* feels a deep affinity with the revolutionary Christ and underscores

---

3.   R.G. Thomas, *Ten Miracle Play* (London: Edward Arnold, 1966), p. 13.

4.   Edwin Morgan, *A.D.: A Trilogy of Plays on the Life of Jesus* (Manchester: Carcanet, 2000).

5.   Quoted from the text on the back cover of the book.

6.   John Dominic Crossan, *Jesus: A Revolutionary Biography* (San Francisco: HarperSan-Francisco, 1995), pp. 114-22.

7.   Quoted in Humphrey Carpenter, *Dennis Potter: A Biography* (London: Faber & Faber, 1998), p. 246.

Jesus' wrathful words ('Woe to you, Scribes and Pharisees, hypocrites. That you have shut out the Kingdom of Heaven for humanity! For you do not enter your-selves, and those who would enter, you do not allow them to enter!', Mt. 23.13) with the Russian revolutionary hymn that 'is not intended to be an aesthetic provocation, but must be understood according to a logic which, in this passage from the Gospel, brings together Pasolini's political leanings and mystical lean-ings'.[8] In his newsreel style of filming, Pasolini achieves an immediacy, a simul-taneous sense of presence and absence, and a violence which crawls under the skin of both our theology and our modern oblivion.

Reading Edwin Morgan's plays generates an interaction between text and reader that disturbs because they work between a number of textual experiences without ever settling upon one in particular. Deeply biblical, at the same time they play against the gospel references through contemporary allusions to power politics, guerrilla warfare and modern weapons of mass destruction. Then, in the second play, the character of John the Baptist breaks into alliterative verse that looks back to the Middle English of *Piers Plowman*, or perhaps the poetry of Gerard Manley Hopkins, while at other times we taken back into the formal commentary of T.S. Eliot's chorus in *Murder in the Cathedral* (1935). The plays thus form a dramatic interaction with the Gospels and Christian tradition, literature and contemporary experience. In no sense are they 'Christian drama', but rather they exercise a creative dialogue with the Christian tradition and its assumptions. This is, in many ways, far more dynamic than the much less creative task of conserving theology and the tradition in self-consciously 'Christian literature'. Morgan's plays have all the 'edge' of the Gospel texts themselves insofar as they are strictly speaking pre-theological, recognizing that the distant 'events' that lie behind the canonical texts can only be celebrated in narratives and stories which grow in the telling and flourish within the embellishments of the imagination as the sustenance of their mystery. In this literature problems are not solved nor questions answered. In the second play, entitled *The Ministry*, a Roman Centurion recounts how Jesus has mysteriously healed his son and asks, 'So what happened? What would magician Virgil say? What would philosopher Lucretius say? Are we in another world now?' His colleagues are sceptical, and his Commandant advises him, 'Do not think about it'. But thinking is exactly what the narrative provokes as the action deconstructs assumptions and religious patterns of thought.[9]

Morgan's Jesus is from the beginning an oddity, aware of his strange calling but never falling back into the comfort of theological expression. He disturbs people with his immoveable common sense and a kind of fatalism that is easy to mistake for obedience. In the first scene of the first play, *The Early Years*, Jesus is talking with his family in Nazareth, and Joseph is losing his temper with him:

8.　　Andrei Ujica, '2 Pasolini, June 2000', in Wilfred Thesiger, Raymond Depardon, Mounira Khemir and Paul Virilio, *The Desert* (Foundation Cartier pour l'art contemporain; London: Thames & Hudson, 2000), pp. 208-209.

9.　　Morgan, *A.D.*, pp. 121-22.

You are beginning to sound like one of those bloody Essenes. They want to snip your bollocks off to the greater glory of God. Take to the desert, live on dried dates and hot air, talk to the scorpions. God must be hard up for glory. Have you been talking to those fanatics?[10]

Jesus simply replies, 'I will talk to anyone. I am like a vessel waiting for learning, knowledge and truth to be poured in, deep and full.' An empty vessel, he is later described by a Roman Centurion as 'the eye of the cyclone',[11] that is, the still point at the heart of a world of intrigue, politics and violence. This is precisely the Jesus of the Miracle Plays, a figure who has stepped out of the liturgy of the Church and, stripped of the encumbrances of Christian theology, emerges as a human being in an inhuman world, with sexual drives, political awareness, humour, naivety and complexity. Morgan is skilful at interweaving political, literary and theological themes across cultures and historical eras in interaction with the familiar narratives of the Gospels themselves. Here the high priest, Caiaphas, is presented as a shrewd pragmatist, fully well aware of why Jesus is a threat yet still admiring him as an enigma. This Caiaphas is a literary brother to Fyodor Dostoevsky's Grand Inquisitor in the parable of *The Brothers Karamazov* (1880)[12] who cannot tolerate the immediate presence of his Prisoner for, as he says, as a man of the Church, 'We have corrected your great work and have based it on miracle, mystery, and authority'.[13] But the question remains at the end of Dostoevsky's parable, how seriously do we take this literary, pre-theological Jesus, for, as Ivan Karamazov remarks, 'It's only a stupid poem of a stupid student... Why do you take it so seriously?'[14]

Literature figures largely in Morgan's play, and he takes it very seriously. In Jesus' early years we see him in the town of Sepphoris, discussing a performance of the *Antigone* which he has watched. His responses, sharpened with phrases taken from the Gospels, are quick, uncompromising and 'pre-Christian', pre-dating the later Christian absorption of Greek philosophy and culture. Later, at the end of the second play (Act V, Scene 4), there is a crucial conversation between Jesus and the 'beloved disciple' John, who here is both a poet and gay. John, the poet, with words from his 'own' (the Fourth) Gospel, becomes the seer, aware far more than Jesus is of what will happen when 'Jesus' the man becomes 'the Word', when he ceases to be merely an actor and becomes a text in which everything that he says

...become a sort of holy scripture,
Everything *everything* may be acted on.[15]

Jesus the actor allows us to see the truth of Socrates' suspicion of the written word in the *Phaedrus*, for in the written text words may be taken literally or misunderstood without the benefit of correction by the speaker, for the speaker is no longer

10. Morgan, *A.D.*, p. 14.
11. Morgan, *A.D.*, p. 171.
12. Fyodor Dostoevsky, *The Brothers Karamazov* (trans. David Magarshack; Harmondsworth: Penguin Books, 1958), Part Two, Book Five.
13. Dostoevsky, *Karamazov*, p. 301.
14. Dostoevsky, *Karamazov*, p. 308
15. Morgan, *A.D.*, p. 147.

available, but only an actor, and Socrates had warned, 'Once a thing is committed to writing it circulates equally among those who understand the subject and those who have no business with it; a writing cannot distinguish between suitable and unsuitable readers'.[16] Jesus in this scene is caught between the character and the text that he will, or even already has, become, and he protests to his friend, the author of the Gospel:

JESUS
By 'sword' I don't mean a sharp-edged iron thing.
It's a figure of speech. Surely you see that.

JOHN
But if you set a man against his father
It may lead to a sharp-edged iron thing.
Think of how people use words.[17]

This Jesus cannot imagine massacres in his name, but John assures him 'There will be'. It is a fine dramatic moment. For Christianity is a religion of the book and we have nothing but the 'Word' of Scripture. But here in the play is Jesus, the actor, correcting and protesting the written word and its history. But it is only a play—and like the Grand Inquisitor we may be inclined to ask, 'Why do we take it so seriously?'

We take it seriously because, as a play, it reminds us what happens when words are written down and become inscribed in Holy Scripture. The consequences lie beyond what Jesus the actor can imagine ('I can't imagine massacres in my name', he remarks). This Jesus is clearly not the Jesus of the Christian tradition, but rather he is the still centre of violent events, both historical and contemporary, and eventually their victim. Throughout the three plays Morgan provides us with choric figures—the three Magi or astronomers, or the secretive Jewish disciples Joseph of Arimathea and Nicodemus—representing later interpretations and reflections on the dramatic events enacted in the plays. As Gaspar remarks, nothing here is 'thought through'—the violence is too raw and complex to have been given meaning, so that the plays become a kind of deconstructive (or better, perhaps, pre-constructive) backdrop to the systematic and justifying theology of the Christian Church. Hamlet, in another play on history, employs a group of actors on the stage to 'catch the conscience of the king',[18] as the violence probes the conscience of theology. In Morgan's plays Jesus the actor is never given the reprieve of resurrection, or the solace of the work of redemption. The arresting particularity of what is enacted makes its demands on explanation and the symbolic language of Scripture. Morgan's stage directions for the Crucifixion constitute a kind of sceptical commentary on the Gospel texts:

16. Plato, *Phaedrus* (trans. Walter Hamilton; Harmondsworth: Penguin Books, 1973), p. 97.
17. Morgan, *A.D.*, pp. 146-47.
18. William Shakespeare, *Hamlet* II.2. See also Horton Davies, *Catching the Conscience: Essays in Religion and Literature* (Cambridge MA: Cowley, 1984).

(...Something about the atmosphere, plus a climax of pain, added to the dreadful sense of alienation and humiliation, forces JESUS to exclaim, in his own Aramaic tongue.)[19]

The 'something' remains unexplored, a response to the unbearable pressure of the events and the moment. Jesus' death in the final play, *The Execution*, is stark, without comment and without consequence—the Centurion's familiar exclamation, perhaps of faith, in the Synoptic Gospels becoming here simply a puzzled remark which is quickly dismissed and forgotten:

CENTURION
I have seen many deaths, but none quite like this. That clap of Jupiter's thunder seemed to come from some other universe. Very strange. (*to his soldiers:*) Right, men. That's us. Back to the barracks. Break the legs of the two bandits before you go. They'll be dead before nightfall.[20]

The final stage direction reads, '*The crowd drift off, the show is over*'.

The show is over. The plays are ended. That's it, everything and nothing. I am reminded of another contemporary 'Passion' in Pat Barker's novel of the First World War, *Regeneration*, in which an army doctor witnesses the total breakdown of a young soldier traumatized by his experiences in the trenches, and realizes that '*Nothing justifies this. Nothing nothing nothing*'.[21] Nothing justifies such violence and such pain, not all the theology in the world, nor the piety of suffering and dying for one's country. Perhaps even more starkly than the dramatic Jesus of the mediaeval Miracle Plays, Edwin Morgan's Jesus steps out of the Church's liturgy and their redemptive, consoling narratives. It is just a play, but one which takes us, by the poetic willing suspension of disbelief, into a contemporary and universal world of intrigue, terrorism, politics and pragmatism, family quarrels and youthful idealism—a heady and highly dangerous mixture. Jesus, unlike the Zealots (in the plays his brother Jude dies the violent death of a terrorist) is the real danger because he cannot be summed up, cannot be explained away. The three plays present serious problems without conclusion, a decisive realization of experience, and, as Morgan himself humbly asserts, 'My ambition is to tell a good story'. But this is not 'the greatest story ever told', not the Christian story. The question then arises, whose story is it, as 'Jesus' the actor becomes a larger character, a man among men? In the plays the stargazing Magi have the last word as they discuss, many years later, the remembered phenomenon of this man in tones reminiscent of the Parable of the Sower:

GASPAR
...Let me just warn you that this person,
This Jesus, who is also called the Christ,
The dead man who may not be dead
Already has followers called Christians.

19. Morgan, *A.D.*, p. 216.
20. Morgan, *A.D.*, p. 217.
21. Pat Barker, *Regeneration* (Harmondsworth: Penguin Books, 1992), p. 180.

They are going to be blown about the world
Like seeds—they hope—

MELCHIOR
O let them blow
To India, no germination there.

BALTHAZAR
Arabia will smother that fantasy.

GASPAR
Well, we shall see. In the meantime I see
A patch of stars is ready for attention
In Persia. Gentlemen, to your posts.
The stars and planets in their glorious courses
Awaken thoughts that pass eternity.
The bones of Jesus lie in Palestine.
If they have light, let it join all our light.[22]

22. Morgan, *A.D.*, p. 223.

MESSIANIC VICTIMS OR VICTIMIZED MESSIAH?
BIBLICAL ALLUSION AND VIOLENCE IN *THE MATRIX*

Jeremy Punt

1. *Introduction: New Generation Science Fiction*

The appearance of biblical allusion in different media forms, and in Hollywood movies in particular, has for a long time been tacitly accepted if not always consciously acknowledged and studied, and the analysis of biblical allusion and religious signification in modern art and literature has not stayed out.[1] In fact, it has for many biblical scholars become important to assume, besides their traditional roles of historical scholars and students of ancient history, also the role of cultural critic.[2] Cultural studies can provide an analytical grid and hermeneutical parameters for investigating the reconfigured yet continued presence of the Bible in large parts of the modern world.[3] And the global influence of 'Western' culture is set to continue given the information age, the mechanisms and reach of various media formats, increasing globalization at both economic and geo-political (as far as these can still be differentiated!) levels, accompanied by spurts and splinters of cultured Christianity and its set of foundation documents. The negotiated intersection of

---

1. Cf., recently, e.g., G. Aichele (ed.), *Culture, Entertainment and the Bible* (JSNTSup, 309; Sheffield: Sheffield Academic Press, 2000); R. Jewett, *Saint Paul Returns to the Movies: Triumph Over Shame* (Grand Rapids: Eerdmans, 1999); L.J. Kreitzer, *Pauline Images in Fiction and Film: On Reversing the Hermeneutical Flow* (The Biblical Seminar, 86; Sheffield: Sheffield Academic Press, 1999).

2. Cf. Segovia's claim that besides being a biblical critic and even a constructive theologian, he is also a cultural critic, a task which includes a focus on issues of construction, representation and power, through an investment in contextual and ideological analysis as found in the accumulation of studies referred to as cultural studies. The task includes the investigation of various dimensions of one's social context apart from their socio-religious aspect (F.F. Segovia, 'Biblical Criticism and Postcolonial Studies: Towards a Postcolonial Optic', in R.S. Sugirtharajah [ed.], *The Postcolonial Bible* [Bible and Postcolonialism, 1; Sheffield: Sheffield Academic Press, 1998], pp. 56-63 [51 n. 2], 'Reading–Across: Intercultural Criticism and Textual Posture', in *idem* [ed.], *Interpreting Beyond Borders* [The Bible and Postcolonialism, 3; Sheffield: Sheffield Academic Press, 2000], pp. 59-83 [59]).

3. This vantage point of the essay is not intended either to claim special privileges for Christianity, its Bible and their legacies in the (post)modern world, or to exclude the influence of other religious systems, symbols and worldviews from having similar significance in history and today, or either to deny the varied forms of border-crossings between different religious frames of reference, or disclaim them as an ongoing phenomena.

(post)modern culture and Christianity is once again present in a recent motion picture which does not make an overt pitch for recognition as a movie with religious intent.

The Matrix,[4] written and directed by Larry and Andy Wachowski, was produced in 1999 by Warner Brothers. It is a science fiction thriller and the storyline is determined by the quest of a few people to subvert and hopefully overturn the world in which people (think that they) live but which is really a computer generated illusion called the Matrix and thus nothing else but virtual reality,[5] based on artificial intelligence. *The Matrix* portrays the human quest for the true self, attempting to break free from those mechanisms and processes that inhibit such freedom. To sustain their power and to derive the necessary energy for their exploits, the villains, in the guise of 'machines' or computers who have taken over the world, keep human beings in an artificially induced and perpetual sleep-like state.[6] While the machines derive their energy from human bodies,[7] people are kept content with the delusion, created through technology, that they are living real lives in the real world. The film's plot centers on a small group of dissidents who have, with the help of the original programmer, through the right knowledge or belief *and* by sheer willpower, managed to liberate themselves from both the illusion and their attraction to it. They live in a different and unavoidably threatening, treacherous and violent world. More particularly, this small group of liberated people is in search of a leader with specific qualities who will ultimately set all people free from their enslavement to the Matrix and its power—freeing their minds—through its destruction,

---

4.   My references are to the DVD-release. The beginning of a particular scene is indicated by chapter:hour:minute:second. The DVD creates an interactive environment for the viewer who is offered a choice between either a blue or red pill, similar to the choice put to Neo. To take the blue pill means to continue to live the illusion, to consider the unreal real; however, taking the red pill offers the opportunity to 'stay in Wonderland and see how deep the rabbit hole is'. This is important, because people cannot be told what the Matrix is, they have to see it for themselves (scene 9:0:27:37). The significance of the colours cannot be explored here.

5.   Virtual reality not depicted 'as a video game designed by geeks on LSD' (Anon, 'Maximizing the Matrix', *Newsweek* [19 April 1999]), but it is the ultimate dream of computer games aficionados come true: the perceived, real world is no more than computer simulation or virtual reality. This emphasis is highlighted if not sustained by the 'flo-mo' technique, comprising short scenes where the camera moves at normal speed while action is frozen (an actor suspended in mid-action, in the air) or happens in slow motion (showing the trajectory and movement of bullets slowly passing through the air).

6.   Really a kind of subconscious existence artificially created and manipulated through information technology. It is a counterfeit and feigned world of virtual reality, to which Morpheus refers as a 'neural, interactive simulation' (12:0:39:10). The Wachowski's introduced the muted human voices in the power plant and in scenes on the Neb to simulate the plight of humanity (Interview [with the Wachowski brothers] <http:\\whatisthematrix.warnerbros.com/cmp/chat_index. html> [consulted on 21 January 2002], 1999).

7.   The machines initially lived off solar power, but after its destruction, they use the bio-electricity of human bodies, growing humans to supply what they need. Humans have become little more than an excuse for a battery, as Morpheus points out holding a (Duracell) battery (12:0: 41:52).

since for as long as the Matrix exists, the human race will never be free. The result is a blend of the real and the fantastical, reality and illusion, as a matter of course.[8]

My intention is to show how *The Matrix* can be seen to explore biblical themes through allusion and intertextual play, and in particular how the film poses and interrogates the link between the messianic figure and violence.

2. The Matrix *and the Spiritual Connection*

Science fiction motion pictures have always concerned itself with the nature of life and reality, portraying scientists of technology as either going amok or playing God, with the difference not always easily discernible. But it was when science fiction itself started exploring political, social and moral issues, as exemplified in the mid-1960s *Star Trek* genre, and taken further in George Lucas's epic *Star Wars* movies, that the film industry started changing. This has resulted in over half of the top grossing films to date being from the science fiction genre, dealing with global technological fears, alternative futures and the nature of reality itself. All three of these themes are present in *The Matrix*, but with a spiritual undertone running through these themes. The spiritual undertone of the film is not difficult to identify, and is underlined by Larry Wachowski's comment that 'People would say, "They didn't blow up the Matrix?" But you can't beat the Matrix with fists… [Reeve's character, i.e. Neo] needs to basically transcend the Matrix.'[9]

The notion of people in search for the meaning of life, for self-actualization and in effect for an alternative life is a dominant theme throughout the film.[10] In a Web-interview with the Wachowski brothers, they claim that *The Matrix* 'examines the idea of an individual searching for their true self while attempting to escape the box, that we often make of our lives'. And, '*The Matrix* was an idea that I believe philosophy and religion and mathematics all try to answer, which is, a reconciling between a natural world and another world that is perceived by our intellect'. Neo is, or becomes, therefore, Thomas Anderson's potential self.[11]

While this may sound properly philosophical, even existentialist, the broader setting of the film exudes more than a passing concern for such matters, exploring

---

8. It would prove interesting to investigate the film from Baudrillard's position on the unreality of reality, that contemporary culture dominated by information technology and electronic media has created a world through simulation, replacing reference to the real with an emphasis on creating the real, or making the real coincide with the simulation. Not only are people trapped in a system impossible to contest, but they opt for a radical anti-metaphysics, 'a radical lack of will by which they choose not to will'. With reference to Raymond Williams' notion of culture becoming a hegemony without people living in the culture even being aware of it, Baum argues that the marginalized (referring to the movement Jesus has started, in particular) can create alternative visions of reality which will transcend, and thus relativize, the dominant culture (M. Warren, *Seeing through the Media: A Religious View of Communications and Cultural Analysis* [Harrisburg, PA: Trinity Press International, 1997], pp. 171-90).

9. Anon, 'Maximizing the Matrix'.

10. Cf., e.g., Trinity's challenge to Neo that he has been down the road (of normality) before, and 'that's not what you wanna be' (7:0:22:54)

11. Cf. n. 6, above.

them amid subtle and more robust religious overtones.[12] In the first place, and now probably a Marxist cliché, the virtual-reality existence of people serves as the 'opium' to keep them content in order to maximize their usefulness for the powerful of the world, who, of course has neither any other purpose nor regard for human existence otherwise. But secondly, as in many religious traditions, the notion of the presence of two worlds, or (the narrow and broad) paths[13] are dominant, borne out by the prominent use of reflections in the film, and with the imperative for the initiated to choose between them: the red pill or the blue pill. The one is ostensibly beautiful, promising of life to its fullest, but is in essence leading to unfulfillment, continued enslavement and eventually oblivious death, the unreal as reality.[14] The other world is unappealing, dangerous and difficult to inhabit, the real world is an apocalyptic desert of sewers and wasteland, and as such without good promise for the future but the *real* reality, warts and all. Indeed, Cypher's eventual betrayal is more about his remorse for taking the red pill (19:0:59:53; 25:1:24:30) than about betraying Morpheus (19:1:01:00), attacking Tank (25:1:22:50), or killing Apoc and Switch (25:1:25:30-55). The emphasis on two worlds raises a number of questions: How are these alternative realities recognized, and how should they be handled? Is the alternative reality *per se* a 'better' reality, another Kingdom or Reign, where life itself is defined differently, putting human existence on a different plane, and so on?

In the third place, the central theme of *The Matrix* is intensely concerned with what in religious terms is generally called 'faith' or 'faith convictions'.[15] Belief is the only way to transcend the here and now, the make-believe. Initially, and connecting with Marxist criticism, belief serves the purpose of allowing one to escape

12. From a faith perspective, the religious and/or spiritual dimension in human lives can be seen as a particular attempt to understand the world and what it is all about; to *real*-ly experience reality, as though the latter is fundamentally or in part metaphysical; where the plus-factor will be that there is more to the world and to human beings than what humans perceive, think or postulate. My discussion here, however, focuses on the construals and portrayals of the film itself.

13. In New Testament terms (Mt. 7.13-14//Lk. 13.24), a choice is to be made, 'taking the difficult, "narrow path" [which] symbolizes hearing and carrying out Jesus' demands, while taking the "wide path" entails the easier but unfruitful option of only hearing them' (M. Desjardins, *Peace, Violence and the New Testament* [The Biblical Seminar, 46; Sheffield: Sheffield Academic Press, 1997], p. 38). Cf. the difference between knowing the path and walking the path (32:1:47:25-34; cf. Mt. 7.21-23//Lk. 13.25-27).

14. Ironically, the real becomes the make-believe, and given the context of the film, the question is raised whether religious and biblical reference to the transcendent or transcendental, a notion which today is often postponed or denied, is reintroduced? Various other instances of irony will be identified below, but the most glaring example is the reliance of Morpheus and his group upon technology and computers, the very evil against which they are fighting (cf. n. 6, above).

15. Espousing fatalism the imperative is to take control of one's own life (8:0:25:38; 22:1:13:55) of being 'a believer' (here: in the One, cf. 16:54:01), which implies the need to free people's minds (13:0:43:05; cf. Rom. 12.1-3), at a young age (cf. Mt. 19.13-15//Mk. 10.13-16//Lk. 17.15-17). '*The Matrix* is about the birth and evolution of consciousness. It starts off crazy, then things start to make sense' (Larry Wachowski, in R. Corliss, 'Popular Metaphysics', *Time* [April 1999]). And, 'belief in oneself' is seen by the Wachowskis as a prominent emphasis in the movie (cf. n. 6, above).

one's precarious position in the all too real world, but in the longer run, also of achieving the fullness of life which presupposes at least a different order in this world.[16] It is with a fourth religious undertone, in particular, that the present study wants to connect. The movement from one world to another, from choosing to walk one path rather than the other, from one consciousness to another, from enslavement to liberation, is mediated by the messianic or saviour figure. The messiah plays a facilitating role in both calling upon people to break with living the lie as well as showing, and in this way, inaugurating, a different world and a different life—two elements typical of Messianism in at least the history of Christianity.[17] The expected leader will be the saviour of all, and is presumed to be among those 'asleep', that is, a saviour from among the people. The presence of a saviour in *The Matrix* does not eliminate the need for people to participate in a 'conversion' experience, with accompanying ritual (liturgy?), a 'rebirth' to leave enslavement to the unreal reality behind (ch. 12). But unwillingness and resistance of humans towards change sharpens the focus on the role of the messiah.

Before exploring the messianic element in more detail, it should be noted that names used for characters in the film are suggestive of biblical or at least Christian religious elements,[18] presenting them in twenty-first-century format. It is a short step from Cypher[19] to Lucifer, the one who eventually betrays Neo and his group's mission, and who identifies himself as 'messenger' (26:1:26:03) reminiscent of the portrayal of Satan in the Hebrew Bible's book of Job. Trinity falls in love with Neo and *her* kiss and pronouncement of love brings him back to live, urging him to get up. Nebuchadnezzar is the name of the hovercraft that hacks into the Matrix computer, and Zion is the name of the last human city, which is in relation to the city of biblical significance spatially inverted, situated underground, near the earth's core. Of crucial importance in a world determined by computer technology, Zion is where the mainframe computer of the resistance movement is situated, and it thus holds the key to the real world, whereas the other computers' task is to simulate the real while, in fact, merely portraying a virtual world. Zion is in the film, as in the Bible, more than a city, and holds as metaphor the promise of life, real life

16. Faith's importance is not, however, presented in monolithic way. Early on, Neo ironically, and amid the fervent convictions of his followers-to-be, claims that he disapproves of faith since *he* wants to control his life (8:0:26:8).

17. S. Freyne, 'Editorial: The Messiah in History', *Concilium* 1993/1 (1993), p. xii.

18. This is not to suggest the exclusion of allusions to, or intertextual echoes from, other religions or divergent religious experiences. As suggested by the Wachowski brothers (Corliss, 'Popular Metaphysics'), Buddhism recognizes messianic traces in reincarnation, Greek mythological allusion surfaces in the name Morpheus (Odyssey), the Sophist and later Gnostic exhortation to 'Know thyself', and Alice in Wonderland's White Rabbit make their rounds. The wordplay, hidden meanings and multiple meanings are all intentional; for example, the use of 'matrix' as a mathematical definition but also a reference to the womb. Names were chosen carefully and have multiple meanings (cf. n. 6, above).

19. Cypher is remorseful about taking the blue pill (19:0:59:50) and recognizes the task of Neo as being the One: to save the world (19:1:00:29). He claims to want no riches, just to return to no-fuss existence, and to be an important person (19:1:00:02). And he is clearly jealous of Trinity's growing feelings for Neo.

(27:1:30:08), and the location of the eschatological banquet ('party', 13:45:24) and approximates the apocalyptic value of Zion in the New Testament, and in Revelation, specifically.

Other biblical references in *The Matrix* are more subtle, in a 'the Bible meets Batman'-setting.[20] Some of these references overlap with other elements of biblical allusion referred to above. Without claiming the Bible as their exclusive frame of reference, allusions to biblical terminology and worldview include terms such as prophecy (21:1:06:52); belief and faith (see above and below); the Path (21:1:07:15); sacrifice (22:1:13:12); miracle (26:1:26:18); and revelation (28:1:33:29). In a more explicit way, Larry Wachowski is quoted by Corliss[21] in telling biblical—if somewhat New Agey—terms as saying that in both mathematics and theology, people start with a supposition from which they can derive a vast array of laws or rules. 'And when you take them to the infinity point, you wind up at the same place: these unanswerable mysteries really become about personal perception. Neo's journey is affected by all these rules, all these people trying to tell him what the truth is. He doesn't accept anything until he gets to his own end point, his own rebirth.'

The nuanced intertextual play on biblical themes in *The Matrix* is particularly rich in what can be described as its rethinking of the connection between Messiah and violence.[22]

2. *A Messianic Optic for Biblical Allusion in* The Matrix

a. *Allusions to a Messianic Person*
The messianic element emerges early on in the movie, even if ironically, when one of Neo's customers receives hacked goods on a diskette and calls out to Neo: 'Hallelujah, you're my saviour, man, my own personal Jesus Christ' (3:0:8:20).[23] More traditional notions of what is popularly considered appropriate for a messianic figure soon emerge in the film, with Neo presented as a dutiful and selfless servant, the lone crusader for a lost cause. Allusions to *biblical* messianism abound. The strong messianic expectation, regarding both his arrival and his actions is a

---

20. Corliss, 'Popular Metaphysics'.

21. Corliss, 'Popular Metaphysics'.

22. Violence includes all actions and everything that restricts, damages or destroys the integrity of things, living beings or people, or of cultural and social entities through superior power (H. Häring, 'Ploegscharen Omgesmeed tot Zwaarden [Joël 4,10]. De Wortels van het Geweld in de Religie', *Tijdschrift voor Teologie* 37.3 [1997], pp. 265-97 [266])—the 'violation of personhood' (Brown, quoted in Desjardins, *Peace*, pp. 12, 99). Beyond this more abstract formulation, violence in practical terms means to damage, humiliate, torture, kill and destroy with intent as apparent in programmes of torture and death, of terror and war, of exile and marginalization (cf. Häring, 'Ploegscharen Omgesmeed', p. 267) as well as non-physical violence such as insult, exclusion, prejudice, slighting, etc.

23. Remarks which reinforce the ironical element, also emerges from another side, for example, when Thomas A. Anderson's boss admonishes Neo, 'You think you're special, rules don't apply to you...you're obviously mistaken' (5:0:11:50). Not only *will* Neo break out of the 'rules' of the virtual world, but his followers certainly consider him *very* special.

dominant theme in *The Matrix*, awaiting a saviour of the world and all people, accompanied by the destruction of the forces of evil. Morpheus believes the cyber-messiah is Thomas Anderson, or rather Neo (played by Keanu Reeves), his computer hacker name (5:0:12:35; 6:0:17:25; esp. 6:0:17:43). Only the true messiah can save humanity, but initially an unwilling messiah or messianic candidate, he has to deal with his own doubts and disbelief about himself, his identity and his role in the bigger scheme of things.[24] The small group around the messiah (to be) is led by a 'big bad John the Baptist'[25] in the person of Morpheus (played by Laurence Fishburne), who claims to have spent his whole life searching for Neo (7:0:21:20). The unresponsive and recalcitrant people of the world fail to see the real world, in fact, refuse to be confronted with reality; and at the wider level a *metamorphosis* is required. A follower becomes a traitor seeking the death of the One, fearing he will destroy the comforts of the virtual world. The betrayal of the messiah and his messianic project by Cypher is not totally different from the New Testament, in contrast with the other disciples' willingness to defend the One and the messianic project, to the point of death.

The character of Neo is increasingly unfolded as messianic figure in the movie, from the initial flippant yet ironical identification (3:0:8:20), to Neo's own unpreparedness to understand (5:0:13:25), to Morpheus's statement to Neo, 'You are the One' (7:0:21:23), and his claim that the search is over: the returned or reincarnated messiah has been found (13:0:44:19). Neo starts what resembles messianic training (14:0:44:0) in preparation of the task ahead, training that is reminiscent of the temptation of Jesus-scenes in the Synoptic Gospels (Mt. 4.1-11; Mk. 1.12-13; Lk. 4.1-13), and is in the process identified as the genuine 'child of Zion' (14:0:45:16).

The chapter where the domesticated, cookie-baking and smoking Oracle is consulted about Neo is rich with messianic self-awareness couched in classical Greek sophism. Knowing that you are the One (22:1:11:23) is important since this knowledge is not dependent upon information gained from others but rather upon self-awareness. Even when the Oracle disclaims Neo's messianic status (22:1:12:10), the doubt induced by the Oracle is not only typical of the classical Greek oracles known for their ambiguous pronouncements.[26] It also compels the messianic incumbent towards introspection, to discover himself amid the Delphic oracle's central concern to 'Know yourself', even if this does not include making his own reality come true![27]

24. He is very much the messiah *in cognito* (the inverse of Wrede's notion of Mark's 'messianic secret'): his followers (or some of them, at least) perceive Neo as the messiah, but he is hard to convince, and is confused more than anything else by the Oracle, rendering a messiah-in-denial.

25. Corliss, 'Popular Metaphysics'.

26. Trinity, firm in her belief in Neo's messianic credentials, proclaims (33:1:49:05) that thus far everything the Oracle proclaimed came true except her prophecy about Neo. The ambiguity is evident both in the Oracle's identification of the One being the person Trinity falls in love with, holding the messiah's destiny in her hands, and in spurring Neo on, who does not believe in this 'fate-crap', to discover himself even if it means denying his own (dis)beliefs (22:1:13:13).

27. On the other hand and unsurprisingly, it is the traitor Cypher who reckons ignorance as bliss (19:1:01:40).

Neo's declaration, 'I'm not the One' (e.g. 27:1:31:50; 32:1:47:15) is challenged by Morpheus's insistence that he is, indeed, the One (32:1:46:51; 37:2:00:17), and Neo's messianic self-recognition and assumption of task (37:2:02:40) leads him to address the Matrix at the end of the film: 'You're out there, afraid of us, afraid of change. You do not know the future and this is only the beginning' (37:2:02:48). Neo will show people that the Matrix does not want them to see a different world, without the Matrix, without rules or controls, borders or boundaries, a world where anything is possible (37:2:02:56). And, indeed, in a final ascension-like scene a confident Neo *flies* off, up and away from computer-induced reality (38:2:03:57) surpassing all remaining restrictions and impositions of the Matrix.[28]

b. *Messianic Violence*
Certainly one of the strongest shared elements with the biblical context is the link between the messianic figure and violence, even if violent elements are portrayed and used differently in the two contexts. The messianic accounts of the New Testament and that of *The Matrix* both relate to the violent setting of these narratives into which the messiah enters, ostensibly to bring it to a head and, ultimately, to bring an end to violence. It is, ironically, not the Oracle but the highlighting of violence which confirms the messianic character of Neo's person. Messianism has certainly never been a theme exclusive to religious notions since it necessarily promotes a counter-political position,[29] and in *The Matrix* the political dimension of Neo's actions is clear.

It is the imperial designs and hegemonic control of the Matrix in the film (27:1: 27:47–28:07; for Empire-talk, cf. 1:28:50–29:31), as much as it was the impact of the Roman Empire in first-century Palestine, which instill the desire for a different, alternative reality and provide the setting for the resultant violence. And so from its opponents' side, employing insider-outsider rhetoric, the Matrix is the system which as the enemy (17:1:54:24) polarizes all. The people inside the system are as real as the dissidents trying to save them, but until that happens, they are all part of the system and thus the enemy (17:1:54:52), leading to a situation where, 'If it is not one of us, then it is one of them' (17:55:15). If people are not unplugged, they are potential agents and thus threatening the liberation of humankind; since inside the Matrix a person is everyone *and* no one (17:1:55:29). The messianic figures of Neo and Jesus become instrumental in both inaugurating a new world and the self-conscious choice of people for a new way of life, which are of course two sides of the same coin. In *The Matrix*, the ultimate or 'mother' of all 'big brothers' is watching

28. Although this happens in virtual reality, it certainly surpasses the Matrix's designs. According to John Gacta, visual effects supervisor, the scene shows that Neo is 'self-actualized', and Zach Staenberg, editor, claims that Neo experiments with his new found abilities regarding what used to be the laws of physics for him (interview with J. Gacta, Z. Staenburg and D.A. Davis <http://whatisthematrix.warnerbros.com/cmp/chat-johnzachdane_index.html> consulted on 21 January 2002).

29. Sometimes identifying a messianic figure outside the realm of the religious, for example, former President Nelson Mandela in South African politics, and, more recently, the slain Dutch politician, Pim Fortuyn (L. Dros, 'Pim Fortuyn / De dood van een Messias', *Trouw* [8 May 2002]).

and controlling, literally and down to the last and smallest detail. In the words of an agent, 'This [Matrix] is our civilization, this is what this is all about' (27:1:29:10). But control is now not only about regulating behaviour but also subsuming all actions and the very life of human beings for a singular purpose, that is, to serve the Empire through their provision of bio-energy. The violent setting is brought about and kept intact by the computer regime, requiring deadly force against those who would either want to expose and especially those who would attempt to oppose their control and power—usually these two groups are the same. The ideology is clear; the maintenance of the Matrix's power and control is paramount and any threat to it is to be met with extreme violence.[30]

And so enters also the dialectical relationship, underwritten by violence, between the One and his followers, accompanied by the dialectical relationship of insiders and outsiders. The strength of Morpheus's conviction that Neo is the One (22:1: 13:01) means that he is willing to sacrifice his own life to save Neo's (22:1:13:12; confirmed by Trinity, cf. 27:1:31:40), and when one of them is to die, Neo gets to choose who should live (22:1:13:23). And when it gets down to survival, attempts are made to rescue Neo first (24:1:19:35), Neo is all that matters (24:19:38). And while the messiah–violence connection may be subliminal in these attitudes and action, it becomes pronounced when Cypher is hastened on in his killing of Tank, Dozer and others, fearing that with Neo appearing on scene there is a real danger that the world to which he wants to return might not be around for much longer (25:1:22:50). The messiah is clearly instrumental in effecting violence, whether the causality is direct or indirect, and messianic victims pay the highest price.[31]

The profile of the victimized changes only slightly when the popular notion of martyrdom[32] is introduced, to be ready to give your life for what you belief in (Morpheus, 27:1:32:26), but now, strikingly, the messianic figure himself is included on the receiving end of violence (Neo, 27:1:32:32). The messiah becomes the sufferer of violence, especially when he intervenes to rescue Morpheus from the

---

30. In the words of an agent (gatekeeper) of the Matrix, human beings as a species define their reality through misery and suffering (27:1:28:20); their 'primitive cerebrum' necessitated the creation of a second Matrix replacing the first which was a perfect world without suffering. Humankind is a virus, disease, cancer, or plague, and not mammals since they are ecologically unfriendly (28:1:33:23). And for all this, the Matrix is the cure (28:1:34:33).

31. Christ-like figures' 'absolute and universal authority and dominion' (cf. M.W. Dube, *Postcolonial Feminist Interpretation of the Bible* [St Louis, MO: Chalice, 2000], p. 148) have implications for both the immediate group and other people.

32. Is martyrdom a notion inspired by the Messiah? (cf. Mk. 8.34-36; Rev. 12.11; 20.4-6; Desjardins, *Peace*, pp. 35-36). The classic Jewish version of martyrdom, however, would be in function contrary to messianic activity, since martyrs were not violent actors themselves but in fact believed their passivity would lead to God's activity (W.J. Heard, 'Revolutionary Movements', in J.B. Green, S. McKnight and I.H. Marshall [eds.], *Dictionary of Jesus and the Gospels* [Downers Grove, IL: Intervarsity Press, 1992], pp. 688-98 [697]). In purpose, though, both martyrdom and messiah had the same goal of establishing God's rule on earth: 'John and Jesus died as martyrs, Peter and Paul were willing to die, and all Christians ought to imitate this model' (Desjardins, *Peace*, p. 35). Cf. elsewhere in this volume the article by J.W. van Henten on martyrs and the use of violence.

agents (30:1:40:36), saves Morpheus from a fall to his death (31:1:44:57), and moments later also Trinity from a helicopter crash (31:1:46:19)—confirming for them his messianic status (31:1:47:00). Again, the messiah–violence link is instrumental, since it is through the violence surrounding him, that Neo starts to believe (33:1:49:51), and it becomes clear that the violence serves an enabling role. The significance of (bloody) violence for the messianic role is epitomized in two other incidents. During the Matrix's attack, Neo is not only bleeding more than others including Morpheus, Dozer and Tank (33:1:51:32), but after shedding blood, Neo assumes a new stance (33:1:51:50), refusing the name 'Mr Anderson' for 'Neo' when staring death in the face (34:1:53:19). However, it is when Neo later gets shot, and is proclaimed dead by the ship's monitor (36:1:57:30) confirmed by the agent's pronouncement, 'He's gone' (36:1:58:27), and repeated in Trinity's astonished remark, 'You can't be dead' (36:1:59:01), and when he rises again, that the *need* for violence exerted on the messiah is established. By means of his messianic resurrection, Neo not only lives again (36:1:59:32), but now also possesses new powers (36:1:59:47) through which he stops bullets, confirming his ultimate power over life and death. Now Neo is capable of seeing through computer code, 'the curtain of the Matrix' (36:2:00:23), and with his superior strength he penetrates an agent only to explode out of him, fully destroying evil in conquering it while remaining untouched by it himself (36:2:00:18; 36:2:00:56).

The Matrix is characterized by copious amounts of violence, whether in the form of hand-to-hand or martial arts fighting, Neo and Trinity shooting the foyer of a building and the guards literally to pieces, or the spectacular crashes of a refuse truck into a phone booth and a helicopter gunship into a building. This violence happens in the virtual world, of course, but in reality the battle between the Matrix and the dissidents is equally fierce, leading to an almost totally devastating attack on the dissidents' craft by the Matrix's sentinels. On both levels, however, the always-present violence seems to peak with the entrance of the messianic figure, Neo.

3. *The New Testament and Violence*

> *It is not the presence of violence that is remarkable, however, but its promotion.*
> *The acceptable New Testament model allows for both physical and non-physical*
> *violence to be inflicted upon others... The God of the New Testament is violent. So*
> *is Jesus, although to a lesser extent.*[33]

In Second Temple Judaism (approximately 587 BCE to 135 CE), which provides the socio-historical context for much of the New Testament, the destruction of the temple and the loss of the Davidic monarchy saw the development of forms of messianism, 'the history of speculations about a royal or priestly leader chosen by God', although versions of the expectation of a Messiah were neither uniform nor common to all Jewish groups.[34] Kingship as a nationalistic symbol of Jewish

---

33. Desjardins, *Peace*, p. 109.
34. L.L. Grabbe, *Judaism from Cyrus to Hadrian* (London: SCM Press, 1992), pp. 143, 552;

political and spiritual sovereignty in their own land gradually transformed into a 'more pure, spiritual and holy symbol'.[35] In the social and political turmoil of first-century Palestine, and with much fluidity and change in religious thought and practice, messianic expectations and eschatology were nevertheless important influences among certain popular movements and groups of revolutionaries, such as the Sicarii and groups of bandits as for example described by Josephus.

The Zealots, Sicarii and other disaffected groups held to the notion of a charismatic, military leader[36] who could, with the help of God and with or as a messiah-figure, overcome the occupying forces and inaugurate a theocratic nation, faithful to the Law.[37] They believed that God alone should be king of Israel, therefore no obedience should be given to any temporal authority, and frustration mounted when the whole of Palestine came under direct Roman rule in 44 CE and it became clear the Romans had no intention of changing the new political dispensation.[38] Usurping power had to be destroyed by any means, including extreme violence. God's followers were to join an earthly army to get rid of the oppressors of Israel and restore its purity before God, since he was viewed as a warrior who would assist his followers to destroy his (their) enemies.[39] Strife and fighting among Jewish revolutionary groups themselves were common,[40] and can apart from other considerations be related to the conflicting aspirations of groups which, while oppressed by a superior military power, were aimed at strengthening their own positions.

The claim is not that such notions of divine and especially messianic violence are fully representative of the first-century Jewish world, or that there was necessarily

---

cf. E. Ferguson, *Backgrounds of Early Christianity* (Grand Rapids: Eerdmans, 2nd edn, 1993), p. 517. Expectation of an anointed royal Jewish leader is scarce in the Hebrew Bible (e.g. Jer. 23.5-6; Isa. 11.2-9; Mic. 5.2); only a few instances of a future Davidic king are found in the period of Persian and Hellenistic domination (e.g. Sir. 47.11, 22; 1 Macc. 2.57), with only a mild increase of hope for a anointed royal leader during the Hasmonean period and some messianic movements arising in reaction to Archelaus' brutality (Heard 'Revolutionary Movements', pp. 589-691; however, cf. W. Beuken, 'Did Israel Need the Messiah?', *Concilium* 1993/1 [1993], pp. 3-13). After the destruction of the Jerusalem and the Temple in 70 CE, the notion of a heavenly Jerusalem and Temple increases in importance and the role of a Messiah become more pronounced (cf. *4 Ezra* and *2 Baruch*) to the extent that some rabbi's interpreted Simeon Bar Kokhba, leader of the revolt of 132–135 CE, as the king-messiah (D. Mendels, *The Rise and Fall of Jewish Nationalism* [Anchor Bible Reference Library; New York: Doubleday, 1992], pp. 371-78, 389). Gradually also the importance of faith and piety among the Jewish people replaced the notion of national suffering as the condition for the coming of the messiah (J. Limburg [transl. and ed.], *Judaism: An introduction for Christians* [Minneapolis: Augsburg, 1987], p. 149). In the period of 63 BCE to 70 CE, two differently shaped patterns for messianic figures are found: the political figure of Messiah the son of David, and the transcendental Messiah (Mendels, *Jewish Nationalism*, pp. 225-30).

35. Mendels, *Jewish Nationalism*, pp. 231-33.

36. The Jerusalem leader Menahem was killed by Zealots presumably for his messianic aspirations (Grabbe, *Judaism*, pp. 501, 549).

37. Cf. J. Riches, *Jesus and the Transformation of Judaism* (London: Dartman, Longman & Todd, 1980), p. 172.

38. Mendels, *Jewish Nationalism*, p. 252.

39. Riches, *Transformation of Judaism*, pp. 93-94.

40. Grabbe, *Judaism*, pp. 449-500; Heard, 'Revolutionary Movements', pp. 696-97.

direct influence of such notions on the authors of the New Testament texts. Nevertheless, the presence of Jewish perceptions regarding the time of the messiah as a period of the sword, linking the days of the messiah with violence formed part of the socio-historical setting and thought-world from which the New Testament emerged, and was therefore likely to have left traces or echoes of influence in the latter: the issue of the Messiah was in the air.[41] However, while first-century Jewish groups nurtured belief about the 'days of the messiah' rather than making a person or his functions central, the notion of a messiah became a central category in early Christianity through Jesus Christ.[42]

It is then not surprising that Jesus was typecast in the role of liberator as attested by scenes from the Gospel accounts, although, almost contradictorily, the Gospel authors are united in their tendency to traverse these *explicit* claims about Jesus.[43] Nevertheless, Jesus is consistently presented as the messiah, the Christ, in word and deed, and whether then as political figure or as spiritual messiah, violence forms part of the equation. In Luke's Gospel, for example, Jesus' birth is announced with reference to violence which will come to characterize his life and death (καὶ σοῦ δὲ αὐτῆς τὴν ψυχὴν διελεύσεται ῥομφαία, 2.35).[44] Jesus becomes a divine warrior, leading his followers into battle against Satan's kingdom (10.17-19). Even more explicitly, Jesus spells out the implications of his ministry: 'Do you think that I have come to give peace on earth? No, I tell you, but rather division' (δοκεῖτε ὅτι εἰρήνην παρεγενόμην δοῦναι ἐν τῇ γῇ; οὐχί, λέγω ὑμῖν, ἀλλ᾽ ἢ διαμερισμόν, 12.51),[45] leaving households and families divided (12.52-53). Practically it means leaving behind your life as you have known it, denying parents and family and taking on the cross, and therefore the following advice from Jesus: 'And let him who has no sword sell his mantle and buy one' (καὶ ὁ μὴ ἔχων πωλησάτω τὸ ἱμάτιον αὐτοῦ καὶ ἀγορασάτω μάχαιραν, 22.36b).[46]

---

41. Cf. C.E. Evans, *Noncanonical Writings and New Testament Interpretation* (Peabody: Hendrickson, 1992), pp. 239-52; S. Freyne, 'The Early Christians and Jewish Messianic Ideas', *Concilium* 1993/1 (1993), pp. 30-41.

42. Ferguson, *Backgrounds*, p. 519.

43. The spiritual nature of Jesus' messiahship is often inferred from passages such as Mt. 20.25-28; 22.41-46; 25.31-34; Mk. 14.3-9; Lk. 22.24-30, and various instances in John's Gospel, especially 18.33-40 (cf. Mendels, *Jewish Nationalism*, pp. 228-29).

44. Appearing six times in Revelation, this is the only other occurrence of ῥομφαία in the rest of the New Testament. The statement is often taken as a prophetic or eschatological reference to the eventual fate of Jesus, and the anguish that Mary will endure as Jesus' mother (e.g. W. Michaelis, 'ῥομφαία', in *TDNT*, VI, pp. 993-98 [995]). Possible intertexts are *Sib.* 3.316; Ezek. 14.17 (the sword as symbol for God's punishment of land) and Ps. 36.15 (the wicked destroyed by having their swords turned on themselves).

45. In Mt. 10.34, διαμερισμόν ('division') is replaced by μάχαιραν ('sword').

46. The reluctance to view this statement as a call to take up arms against the evil forces is borne out in descriptions of this verse as ironic, symbolic or unhistorical, at most referring to the impending hostility which the disciples of Jesus will experience (so T.J. Geddert, 'Peace', in J.B. Green, S. McKnight, and I.H. Marshall [eds.], *Dictionary of Jesus and the Gospels* [Downers Grove, IL: Intervarsity Press, 1997], pp. 604-605). And ambiguity remains, illustrated by Jesus' claim that those who take up the sword, will perish by it (cf. Lk. 21.53 but Mt. 26.52b; cf. Rev.

Violence was part of everyday life in the first-century Mediterranean world, the extent of which emerges clearly even from a brief analysis of the New Testament vocabulary. While the violence vocabulary is used for different purposes, referring to physical human violence, to the cosmic struggle between good and evil, and metaphorically to the Christian's life of service to God (a spiritual battle), it is evident that military terms dominate, indicative of the military environment of the day.[47] Going beyond the military setting, the 'naturalization of violence' in first-century Mediterranean context has often been commented upon.[48] Violence in different forms is common in an agonistic society, since the exercising of power amount to exerting control over the behaviour of others, and so becomes an important social and means value, as well.[49]

In the New Testament Desjardins has pointed to four aspects which reinforce the violent perspective of this set of documents, maintaining that non-physical violence dominates: an unquestioning acceptance of soldiers and war; extreme violence expected to occur at the end of this age; male domination in society as reflected in these texts; and the insider–outsider mentality which divides humanity into opposing groups. Although admitting that, 'Viewed as God's agent on earth (or his ambassador to humanity), Jesus himself occasionally accepts, condones or incites violence', Desjardins fails to note how strongly the messianic position of Jesus[50] as portrayed in the New Testament contributes to violence.

In presenting a meek and mild Jesus, the ambiguity of Scripture on the person of the Messiah is collapsed. Is his preaching not in fact subversive, and is he not perhaps critical of social and political structures to the point of initiating their change, not excluding the possibility of physical force? Even if stopping short of claiming Jesus as a political revolutionary, one has to admit that the establishment of the day—social, political as well as religious—did not escape his attention *and* intrusion. Abandoning the family model, making ambiguous statements about paying taxes (Mt. 22.15-22//Mk. 12.13-17//Lk. 20.20-26), questioning the Torah (e.g. Mk. 2.23-27), and entering Jerusalem the way he did and at the time he did (during the Passover festival of liberation from Egypt, Mt. 21.1-11//Mk. 11.1-11// Lk. 19.28-44) and his actions in the Temple, the religious center but also a political stronghold with the treasury (Mt. 21.12-17//Mk. 11.15-19//Lk. 19.45-48), are elements which already suggest a not-so-meek-and-mild Jesus. Jesus was proclaimed

13.10), when taken as referring to acts of violence, rather than penal power of the state (Rev. 13.4) or military service (W. Michaelis, 'μάχαιραν', in *TDNT*, IV, pp. 524-27 [525 n. 11]).

47. Desjardins, *Peace*, pp. 63-64.

48. Cf. P.J.J. Botha, 'Submission and Violence: Exploring Gender Relations in the First-Century World', *Neotestamentica* 34.1 (2000), pp. 1-38 (8-18).

49. J.J. Pilch, 'Power', in J.J. Pilch and B.J. Malina (eds.), *Biblical Social Values and their Meaning: A Handbook* (Peabody, MA: Hendrickson, 1993), pp. 139-42.

50. Desjardins, *Peace*, pp. 62, 72, 78-108. Postponing the question whether Jesus' messianic role was perceived as earthly, political or transcendental, spiritual (cf. Mendels, *Jewish Nationalism*, pp. 227-29, 262), and the corresponding positions about the Land (Mendels, *Jewish Nationalism*, p. 252), the oppositional nature of the messianic role remains, posing a threat to the (variety of) authorities and their demands for obedience.

King of the Jews, spurring Herod on to infanticide according to a Gospel account (Mt. 2.16), and resulting in a plaque sarcastically referring to him as *king* at his crucifixion, and he is frequently in the New Testament proclaimed as 'saviour', a title which the Roman emperors eagerly claimed.[51]

From the New Testament and traditional theological appropriations Jesus is perhaps best known as a victim of violence, non-physical as well as physical, including attempts to stone him and, of course, his death on the cross, which would become the ultimate symbol of violence.[52] But because of overt and more sublime religious reasons and purposes, the focus has traditionally been placed on the violence inflicted upon Jesus often to the exclusion of his contribution to it. Jesus as messiah also contributed to violence, at different levels and in many ways, inflicting violence in the interrelated socio-cultural, political and religious spheres of life in first-century Palestine. The followers of Jesus also acted as perpetrators of violence, not only in defense of Jesus' person at his arrest but also in shunning him at the onset of danger. In the New Testament, the Messiah and his followers are therefore not only portrayed as allowing violence, but also as being involved in legitimating and promoting violence: 'Violence is forbidden...but it is acceptable if God or Jesus inflicts it'.[53] A messianic claim seems to support the right to inflict violence.

4. *Conclusion:* The Matrix, *the Messiah and Violence*

As in the New Testament where non-physical violence predominates among the many forms of violence revealing itself,[54] it is similarly overwhelmingly in *The Matrix*. The captured state of human bodies as well as the physical force used on the dissidents are violent and destructive to say the least, but even then does not come close to the non-physical aspect of being alive but unable to live, enslaved for the purposes of those in power. *The Matrix*'s interpretation of the relationship

51. Accusations leveled at Jesus at his trial as depicted in the Gospels underline his political agenda: obstructing the payment of taxes, threats about the destruction of the Temple, and proclaiming himself king (cf. W.R. Herzog, II, *Jesus, Justice and the Reign of God: A Ministry of Liberation* [Louisville, KY: Westminster/John Knox Press, 2000], pp. 219-32). On another level, Jesus and his followers disrupted the easy alliance of Hellenistic–Roman religious patterns with the wellbeing of the Empire, challenging the concept of *religio*. In Roman law, *pietas* was the first and supreme national duty of citizens, and elevated a specific morality to a divine principle or will. And, of course, when Christianity became state religion in the fourth century, the Church took over this concept of *religio* (cf. E. Schillebeeckx, 'Documentation: Religion and Violence', *Concilium* 1997/4 [1997], pp. 129-42 [129-31]).

52. Desjardins, *Peace*, p. 23. But the cross is often spiritualized and depoliticized through dogma and/or pietist convention. Here the ambiguity of the New Testament texts also emerges, with Paul's claim that the crucifixion is contrary to the accepted wisdom of the world, which assumes violence gives power (1 Cor 1–2). Such ambiguity shows 'the Scriptures as a textbook on the pathology of religion' (G. Baum, *Religion and Alienation: A Theological Reading of Sociology* [New York: Paulist, 1975], pp. 62-84).

53. Desjardins, *Peace*, p. 82.

54. Desjardins, *Peace*, p. 62.

between the messiah and violence suggests a stronger link between the two than traditionally perceived of Jesus in the New Testament, indeed, a reciprocal relationship, where the messiah's actions contribute to violence and not least of all to violence to his followers. On the other hand, the messiah is simultaneously also a victim, which was brought about by the expectations of his followers and their actions in this regard, leading to violence directed at the messiah.[55]

In *The Matrix* there are two settings, clearly recognizable also in the New Testament, which lead to and continuously stimulate violence—namely, the insider–outsider context and the eschatologically-apocalyptic[56] charged situation. The messianic theme, which is present in both these two settings although often applied differently, contributes directly to the overt and covert manifestations of violence, bringing it to maximum levels. The two features which can be said to highlight the acceptance, condoning and incitement of violence by Jesus and his followers are the angry, self-righteous tone[57] heard in the New Testament, and the assumption that violence is required to bring about positive change.[58] These two features also characterize the group around Neo in *The Matrix*.

As much as Jesus' followers believed his presence to have dealt a crippling blow to the forces of evil and with the final victory in sight, so too are Morpheus and his compatriots convinced that with Neo's assumption of his messianic role, the days of the Matrix are numbered. Such an eschatological and apocalyptic worldview requires violence as requirement to inaugurate the new 'kingdom', with the expectation of horrific violence inflicted by the forces of evil only matched by the resolve of their opponents to counteract these actions through violence too. 'Simply put: since God is our model and he solves his problems through violence, so can we'.[59] The apocalyptic worldview has little room for acknowledging the equal worth of everyone, friend or foe, and has 'no intention to build a better world with

55. The Matrix, which has to be destroyed by the One and his followers, becomes the condition and therefore ultimate theological metaphor for a new life in all its facets and features. Liberating humans from the Matrix cannot happen sectionally or by category, is not limited to certain areas of the human experience and life but is all encompassing and totalizing—all or nothing!

56. In the apocalyptic tradition the battle to introduce the Kingdom was a more pronounced dualism between the forces of Satan and those of God. In the Qumran tradition, for example, the 'children of the light' considered themselves the only 'saved' remnant, thus consigning everyone else, Jew or Gentile, who was not of the Community, to the 'children of darkness'. The chosen would finally be vindicated when, with the appearance of two messiahs, of Aaron (priestly) and Israel (kingly) and a prophet, and the intervention of God's heavenly hosts, true worship would be restored to Israel, inaugurating the perfect Kingdom (Riches, *Transformation of Judaism*, pp. 173-74). In *The Matrix* the aim is to liberate Zion (the resistance's mainframe computer), to establish it as the New Kingdom for all humans, implying the full and final destruction of the anti-forces of the Matrix.

57. According to Desjardins, this was the result of the early Christians' lack of success, despite their own Jewish roots, in proselytizing among Jews, and the increasing failure of Christian missionary activity elsewhere too (*Peace*, pp. 66-70).

58. Desjardins, *Peace*, pp. 66-78.

59. Desjardins, *Peace*, p. 91.

opportunities for everyone'.[60] Whereas in the New Testament, 'In dying Jesus re-fused to repay violence with violence. He forgives those who kill him violently',[61] Neo in *The Matrix* destroys his enemies.

My intention in the foregoing discussion was not to collapse the ambiguity of the New Testament texts on violence, and its relation to the person and activity of Jesus Christ, in particular, but rather to show how such violent elements, often ignored and mostly spiritualized or relativized in traditional interpretation, are explored by default and design when the One appears on the scene in *The Matrix*. As much as peace is not an abstract idea but one rooted firmly in cultural, political, social and economic contexts,[62] so too are people's conceptions of violence contextually defined and situated. Looking at biblical allusion in *The Matrix* and recognizing the cultural setting largely defined by glamorous Hollywood, powerful America and the influen-tial media house Warner, enables us to realize the persistent influence of biblical and Christian-religious themes and scenes on the Western mind. Not suggesting an equal or reciprocal relationship, *The Matrix* is an important example of how biblical image and themes are reinterpreted in the twenty-first century.

To suggest that producers and directors of popular-style, Hollywood movies create this interplay intentionally only to achieve their own short-term purposes—a larger dollar—is probably too cynical. On the other hand, to presuppose some lofty quasi-religious or moral-ethical purpose as the *raison d'être* for popular movies is most likely also asking too much in a cutthroat business where box office numbers have the last word.[63] However, where latent and sublime religious notions and sentiments can contribute to the appreciation and appropriation of films, they will certainly be incorporated into films. The Wachowski brothers' corroboration of their interest in matters religious[64] and the inclusion of latent and even discernable biblical allusion in a popular Hollywood movie suggest the expectation that audi-ences will be in a position to understand the plot better, to relate to it more easily when their own popular religious sentiments allow them to connect and identify with the movie's setting and plot.

In the public media of a violence-soaked world, where sexual and religious taboos ironically often carry more censure than viewing violence as suggested by the coding and ratings imposed on audiovisual media, the Bible is evidently found useful in its ambiguity to condone and sustain expressive violence.[65] The reception

60. Desjardins, *Peace*, p. 91; cf. p. 84.
61. Schillebeeckx, 'Documentation', p. 140.
62. F. Mayor, 'The Human Right to Peace', *Bulletin* 4.4 (1997), pp. 1-2 (2).
63. Even if the Wachowski brothers are quoted as being interested in 'mythology, theology and, to a certain extent, higher level mathematics', that is, 'all the ways human beings try to answer bigger questions, and The Big Question'. They therefore claim to have written and directed *The Matrix* with more in mind that providing mere entertainment, but with the purpose of engaging the minds of people, to make them think (Corliss, 'Popular Metaphysics').
64. Claiming that the religious symbolism in the film is intentional, but that their own religious beliefs are 'non-denominational' (cf. n. 6, above).
65. J. Punt, 'Peace, Conflict and Religion in South Africa: Biblical Problems, Possibilities and Prospects', *Missionalia* 27.3 (1999), pp. 263-98.

history of the biblical messiah accentuates this in harsh terms, with the biblical life and Passion of Christ characterized as much by violence as the lives of his contemporary (and subsequent) followers suffered *and* exerted violence. As *The Matrix* points out so well!

THE MAKING OF MODERN MARTYRS:
THE MARTYRS OF COLUMBINE

Elizabeth Leigh Gibson

Introduction

Amid the tragedy of April 1999 in Littleton, Colorado, lurks an unusual opportunity for scholarly inquiry: to trace the making of two martyrs, Cassie Bernall and Rachel Scott. Scholars of the earliest Christian martyrdoms struggle to unravel the complex interplay of historical details, religious idealism and literary development from a single surviving narrative. In the case of the second century CE *Martyrdom of Polycarp*, the document seems to have been composed shortly after Roman authorities put to death this early Bishop of Smyrna (the modern city of Izmir, Turkey).[1] Yet echoes of the story of Jesus' own death and an interest in relics, generally thought to be a later development, have fuelled intense discussion among scholars as to the date of the *Martyrdom of Polycarp* and its relationship to the events it describes. Even the well known *Martyrdom of Perpetua* (early third century CE, North Africa), a text that includes Perpetua's own account of her arrest, imprisonment and confinement, has recently engendered a similar debate. Careful analysis at the hands of Roman historian Brent Shaw has revealed how her story was 'greatly distorted by subsequent male interpreters' who sought to temper Perpetua's rejection of Roman authority and familial obligation.[2]

Although the prevailing winds are changing, it has been commonplace for students of such martyr texts to countenance their authors' and editors' sincerity and to endorse the basic facts of the martyrs' deaths.[3] The murders of Cassie Bernall and Rachel Scott provide an opportunity to test this institution.

A wealth of evidence, including news coverage, biographies, video tributes, a play, and a Bible study guide, documents their tragic deaths and their proclamation

---

1. The bibliography concerning the *Martyrdom of Polycarp* is immense. An excellent starting point remains B. Dehandschutter, 'The Martyrium Polycarpi: A Century of Research', in *ANRW* 27.1, pp. 488-90.

2. Brent Shaw, 'The Passion of Perpetua', *Past and Present* 139 (1993), pp. 3-45 (21).

3. Among the many more recent studies that eschew this tradition are notably Judith Perkins, *The Suffering Self: Pain and Narrative Representation in the Early Christian Era* (New York: Routledge, 1995) and Daniel Boyarin, *Dying for God: Martyrdom and the Making of Judaism and Christianity* (Stanford: Stanford University Press, 1999). Yet traditional interpretative practices endure—see Louis Robert, *Le martyre de Pionios, prêtre de Smyrne* (ed. G.W. Bowersock and C.P.M. Jones; Washington: Dumbarton Oaks Research Library and Collection, 1994).

as martyrs. At the heart of this transformation is the claim that the gunmen asked each girl if she believed in God. When each answered 'yes', they were shot. This account was eventually challenged and remains in considerable doubt. This development did not impede the production of multiple narratives of their martyrdom. Rather, the martyrologies of Cassie Bernall and Rachel Scott depended little on a consensus about the facts of their deaths. Instead, the families and their religious communities elevated two average teenagers to martyr status.

The Tragedy

20 April 1999 was shaping up to be an average news day. In US news, Microsoft's then-surging profits led the headlines. On the international front, NATO conducted daytime bombings in the Balkans. At Columbine High School in Littleton, Colorado, near Denver, the day began without incident. But by noon, CNN had broken a story that would dominate the news for days to come. Interrupting regular programming, the Sheriff of Jefferson County, Colorado, reported that 'we have had reports of shots fired and explosions there[—]also some units are reporting a fire at this time. However, I don't have any confirmed reports about victims or if there are any or how many. It sounds very possible that there is more than one suspect involved at this time.'[4] The first wire stories quickly followed with more details:

> Two young men dressed in long, black trench coats opened fire in a suburban Denver high school today, scattering students as gunshots ricocheted off lockers, witnesses said. At least three students were injured. There were also reports of explosions in the school, which was ringed by ambulances and police officers at lunchtime. The location of the gunmen was not immediately known.[5]

By the following morning, the attack was better understood. It had started with bombs in the cafeteria and had continued as the gunmen, Eric Harris, 18, and Dylan Klebold, 17, moved through the school, firing rifles and igniting additional explosive devices. The greatest human loss occurred in the library, a large open space that provided limited protection from gunfire. Twenty-two were confirmed injured[6] and ultimately 15 would be dead—12 students, one teacher and the two gunmen.

In the ensuing days, the media pursued several dimensions of this story. Discussion of school violence was plentiful—Columbine was only one of a spate of school shootings, albeit the most deadly.[7] The press, of course, also explored the many human interest stories that sprang from this tragedy, stories concerning the killers, the dead and the injured. The present study concerns two victims who came to be called martyrs, Cassie Bernall and Rachel Scott, as well as one might-have-been martyr, Valeen Schnurr.

---

4. CNN *Breaking News* (Tuesday, 20 April 1999).
5. Associated Press, *Top News* (Tuesday, 20 April 1999).
6. Mark Obmascik, 'High School Massacre Columbine Bloodbath Leaves up to 25 Dead', *Denver Post* (21 April 1999): A-01.
7. In little more than a year, several deadly shootings had occurred in various towns, among them: Jonesboro, AR (March 1998); Edinboro, PA (April 1998); and Springfield, OR (May 1998).

The Making of Martyrs

Even before the official list of the dead was confirmed, informal tributes began to appear as friends and families publicly acknowledged their loved ones whose deaths the police had privately confirmed. Some especially tragic stories stole the headlines either because of biographical details of the victims, or because of the manner of death.

Journalists quickly picked up on the tragedy and the irony of Cassie Bernall's life. Only two years earlier, Cassie had been into 'witchcraft, suicide and a view of life so dark' and was part of 'the same sort of group that the killers were born from'.[8] But, after participating in a Christian youth retreat, she devoted her life to God.[9] Cassie, someone who might have been a friend of the gunmen only a short time before became one of their victims.

Also well publicized was the death of an originally unidentified student in the school library who was allegedly killed as a result of the gunmen's anti-Christian sentiments. In a television interview on *Good Morning America*, student Joshua Lapp described the gunmen's hostility to Christians:

> Charles Gibson: And then you said they walked over to a girl and asked her if she believed in Christ?
>
> Joshua Lapp: If she believed in God, and she paused—she didn't know what to answer. So she said "yes", and they go, 'Why?' And then they just proceeded to shoot her.[10]

The process of identifying this victim would, however, be halting and often contradictory. There were three potential answers to the question 'Who said "Yes"?': Cassie Bernall, Rachel Scott, and Valeen Schnurr. This study does not aim to resolve this matter but rather to trace how two of them came to be hailed as martyrs.

Cassie said 'Yes'

Mickie Cain, who escaped unscathed from the cafeteria, first identified Cassie Bernall as the female student who died after affirming her faith. Appearing on *Larry King Live* the day after the shooting, she shared her admiration for the friend she had lost:

> Mickie Cain: Let me just tell you about my friend [Cassie]... She was in the—in a classroom, I believe, and she ended up standing up for the greatest thing ever...she completely, completely stood up for God when the killers asked her if there was anyone who had faith in Christ. She spoke up and they shot her for it. And that is

---

8.   Steve Lipsher and Bruce Finley, '"I Cried And Cried...Now I'm Dry of Tears"', *Denver Post* (22 April 1999): A-12

9.   Lipsher and Finley, '"I Cried And Cried"', A-12.

10.   ABC, *Good Morning America* (21 April 1999). Interestingly, in an interview the night before on ABC's Nightline program, Lapp only mentioned the gunmen's targeting high school athletes and African Americans (ABC *Nightline*, 20 April 1999).

the most brave thing anyone could ever do, and I—I want that memory to live on and her example for that.[11]

Cain's own testimony, specifically her uncertainty about the location of her friend's death, reveals that she is not relating her eyewitness account but rather reporting a story she has heard elsewhere.

In ABC's continuing coverage the following day (22 April 1999), *Good Morning America* formally identified Cassie Bernall as the target of gunmen's query:

> Host Diane Sawyer: I wanted to tell you both that there is a footnote from our broadcast yesterday. There was the story of the young girl who was asked, if you'll remember, by the shooter if she believed in God. She said yes and he then fired and she died. Well, after the interview, a Colorado pastor called us up and said his church has decided it wanted to pay for her funeral expenses if they could. Her name, Cassie Bernall.[12]

Sawyer, however, does not name the source who led ABC News to refine their earlier reporting. Even the local Denver newspapers that first hailed her as a martyr never named the witness who saw Cassie say yes.[13] Without confirmation, Bernall's last words had become a totem of the tragedy, and were even featured by then Vice President Al Gore at the community memorial service (25 April 1999).[14] The only hint of concern about the possibly fragile foundation to the story came, albeit obliquely, in a statement the Bernall family released on the day of her funeral. Although Cassie's declaration is a central theme in the statement, Brad Bernall delicately reports it as hearsay: 'We have not read any papers nor watched much

11. CNN, *Larry King Live* (21 April 1999).

12. ABC, *Good Morning America* (22 April 1999).

13. Carla Crowder, 'Martyr for Her Faith: Youthful Christian Confesses Her Belief to Rampaging Gunman, Then Pays with Her Life', *Denver Rocky Mountain News* (23 April 1999): 5A, and Janet Bingham, 'Mourning the Slain: "Cassie Died a Martyr's Death" *Denver Post* (27 April 1999): A-06. The press employed a variety of strategies to handle the absent attribution of the story. Some accounts would provide no attribution for the story like this Washington Post coverage: 'Bernall, a Columbine junior who liked poetry, may have been slain in the attack because of her devout religious faith. When the gunmen burst into library, Bernall was there studying, as usual. Soon, eyewitnesses said, she came face-to-face with one of the gunmen, who asked her a fateful question: "Do you believe in God?" Bernall, who friends said belonged to her church's youth group, answered "Yes". And then she was shot.' At other times the story is placed on the lips of a student who was not an eyewitness to the event but is only repeating the circulating story as is demonstrated as the *Washington Post* story continues: 'The gunman shot her because she is a Christian', said Kevin Koeniger, a Columbine junior and one of Bernall's close friends. 'It is just so hard to understand' (Amy Goldstein, Rene Sanchez and Michael A. Fletcher, 'In Choosing Victims, Gunmen Showed Their Prejudice', *Washington Post* [23 April 1999]: A). In other cases, it was generally attributed to unidentified library survivors, 'Students who witnessed that confrontation say Cassie paused before she answered, not because they believe she doubted her answer, but because she sensed what might happen next' (*ABC World News Tonight* [26 April 1999]).

14. About Cassie Bernall, he movingly said: 'among them we remember Cassie Bernall, whose final words as she stared death in the face, were "Yes, I do believe in God"' (CNN transcript of the live broadcast of the memorial service, 25 April 1999).

TV since we learned our Cassie was a victim, *but I am told* that she was the young woman who boldly answered to a gunman, "YES" when he asked if she believed in God, prompting him to pull the trigger'.[15] Thus, even while its source remained unidentified, the story of Cassie Bernall's testimony spread and intensified as her funeral approached.

At the funeral itself, the pastors of Cassie's church, West Bowles Community Church, led the effort to make sense of Cassie's death, especially for the members of her large and active youth group. Forty-seven of them had been in Columbine High School on 20 April, four of them in the library.[16] Youth Pastor Dave McPherson would also compare Cassie to Jesus, 'Jesus fed 5000 with five loaves of bread and two fish. But Cassie fed the world with one word, "yes."[17] Praising Cassie's courage and inspiration, Reverend George Kirsten likened the service to Cassie's spiritual graduation: 'We are here today to celebrate the graduation of Cassie—with honors'. The greatest of her honors was her martyrdom and it won her a place in 'the martyr's Hall of Fame'.[18]

Rachel Said 'Yes'

The same day ABC News identified Bernall as the girl who said yes, *New York Newsday* broke a story about another victim, Rachel Scott:

> Gattoni [a student who was in the library at the time of the attack] said she had been told by an eyewitness that Rachel Scott had been beaten up by the gunmen, who then asked if she believed in God. 'She said, "Yes, I believe in God. Then he put the gun to her head and shot her."'[19]

This account, strikingly similar to the one that had been connected to Cassie Bernall, was even plagued by the same problem: the eyewitness was not identified. Nonetheless, Rachel's Scott's testimony to God would appear in various media in the following days, although not as consistently or frequently as Bernall's. In the case of *New York Newsday*, the story was associated only with Scott, with no mention of Bernall.[20] In other cases, journalists would retell the events as if the gunmen had asked both Scott and Bernall about their belief in God.[21]

The story of Rachel's confession would fade rather quickly, however. One of the most consistent elements of the girl-who-said-'yes' story was that it had taken place in the library, and it was quickly established that Scott had been eating lunch

---

15. Bingham, 'Mourning the Slain', AA-04 (emphasis added).
16. Bingham, 'Mourning the Slain', AA-04.
17. Bingham, 'Mourning the Slain', AA-04.
18. Bingham, 'Mourning the Slain', AA-04.
19. Steve Wick and Jeffrey Kass, 'The Colorado Tragedy Shattered Dreams: Grief-Stricken Students Recall 13 Killed at School', *New York Newsday* (22 April 1999): A5.
20. Another article similarly reported the story: Michael Daly, ' "She Had All That, and They Took It"', *New York News Day* (22 April 1999): 2.
21. E.g. Bill Duryea, 'Seeking Solace in Religion', *St Petersburg Times* (25 April 1999): 1A, and David van Biema, 'A Surge of Teen Spirit: A Christian Girl, Martyred at Columbine High, Sparks a Revival among Many Evangelical Teens', *Time* 153 (31 May 1999): 59.

outside when Klebold and Harris made her their first victim.[22] Already by the time of her 24 April funeral, Rachel was no longer the girl-who-said-'yes'.

Valeen said 'Yes'
As coverage from the Bernall funeral began to wane, media attention shifted to Valeen Schnurr, a library survivor who had sustained multiple gunshot wounds. On 27 April, on the eve of her daughter's release from the hospital, Shari Schnurr shared her daughter's version of events with local reporter:

> She heard other students being shot, some pleading for their lives. The screams coming from her end of the room drew the gunmen's attention, and they came back her way, guns blazing. When the bullets and shrapnel hit Valeen, she slumped and clutched her abdomen. 'Oh my God, oh my God!', she remembers saying. 'God!' one of the gunmen taunted her. 'Do you really believe in God?'

> Moments earlier, Valeen saw what happened when Cassie was asked the same question and answered yes.

> 'Val was scared to say, "Yes"', says Valeen's mother. 'But she was scared to say "no", because she thought she was dying'.

> Finally, she told the gunman, 'Yes, I believe in God'.

> 'Why?', he asked, as he stopped to reload.

> 'I do believe in God', she said, 'and my Mom and Dad have taught me about God'.[23]

The composition of this article merits close examination as it represents a form that would often be repeated. The journalist has sandwiched the story of Cassie Bernall between two quotations from Shari Schnurr about her daughter's exchange with the gunmen. But the comments about Cassie's death are not directly attributed to Shari Schnurr. An interview with Valeen's father, Mark Schnurr, reveals even more clearly that the Schnurrs do not confirm that the gunmen also asked Cassie about her faith:

> 'She really did a testimonial [to God and her Roman Catholic faith]', Mark Schnurr said. 'It wasn't like what they've been saying that somebody pointed a gun in her face and said, 'Do you believe in God?'

---

22. Placing her in the cafeteria was Sheba R. Wheeler, 'Remembering the Slain Rachel Scott Aspiring Actress Found Joy in Life', *Denver Post* (23 April 1999): A-06, and on the lawn, Manny Gonzales, 'Debate Team Mourns Loss of a Natural and a Comic Group Gathering Pays Tribute to Memories of Mauser, Scott', *Denver Rocky Mountain News* (24 April 1999): 28A; and running from the cafeteria, J. Sebastian Sinisi and Julia C. Martinez, 'Pastor: "We Have Failed"', *Denver Post* (25 April 1999): AA-03. As comprehensive reports emerged, the story would settle on the detail that she was outside eating lunch, Mark Obmascik, 'April 20 through the Eyes of Survivors', *Denver Post* (13 June 1999): A-01.

23. Rebecca Jones, 'Girl Did Not Forsake God: Teen-Ager Who Suffered Nine Gunshot Wounds is Recovering through "Divine Intervention"', *Denver Rocky Mountain News* (27 April 1999): 5A.

'First, they shot her, and she said, 'Oh my God!' She was on the floor under the library table and one of them looked back and said—'Do you believe in God?'

'She said, '"Yes, my mom and dad brought me up that way". They were reloading a gun and she crawled back under the table and they went away', Schnurr said.

'She said that what went through her mind when they asked that was, '"If I say no, what will they do? And if I say no and die—that's a problem".'

'So she gave her testimonial to her faith. Did it save her? Was it a sign (from God)?', her dad asked. 'If it was—it's a heck of a deal. It means she's here for a reason.'[24]

The Schnurr family, as this quotation reveals, certainly knew about the version of the story that had been connected with Cassie Bernall and believed that what had happened to their own daughter had been misdescribed. Interestingly, Mark Schnurr did not challenge the accuracy of the Cassie-said-yes story in this interview. Even when Valeen herself began to speak publicly that summer, the news reports were carefully crafted to avoid confronting the as yet unaddressed question —of who actually said 'yes':

Valeen Schnurr, a student injured during the April 20 rampage, was the featured speaker.

She said the gunmen asked her—just as they had asked slain student Cassie Bernall —whether she believed in God, and 'I wanted so bad to say no' but ultimately said yes. 'To say no would be disrespectful'.[25]

Again, the reference to Bernall's testimony occurs in an aside, suggesting only by its placement in the story, not by direct attribution that Valeen Schnurr heard Cassie say yes. The simmering tension between these two versions would go unresolved for months with reports either juxtaposing the accounts or eliminating Valeen's own testimony.[26]

Making Martyrologies

Even when national coverage of the massacre subsided, the story of the Columbine martyrs had not yet peaked. The Bernall story in particular continued to have a tremendous resonance with those in Littleton and beyond. The girlfriend of one victim was inspired to embark on a missionary journey.[27] Craig Scott, survivor and brother of victim Rachel Scott, organized a rally in his sister's memory.[28] The Bernall

24. William Brand, 'Wounded Student Back Home', *Denver Post* (28 April 1999): A-14.
25. Karen Santos, 'A New Year for Columbine', *Denver Post* (7 August 1999): A-14.
26. Even reports of Valeen Schnurr's high school graduation would not include her testimony to the gunmen; see, for example, Beth DeFalco, 'Injured Teens Savor March to the Podium', *Denver Post* (23 May 1999): A-21.
27. Wendy Murray Zoba, 'Do You Believe in God? Columbine and the Stirring of America's Soul', *Christianity Today* (4 October 1999): 40.
28. Santos, 'A New Year for Columbine', A-14.

family founded a not-for-profit organization in memory of their daughter and announced they would write her biography.[29] The parents of Rachel Scott founded a similar organization that coordinated their speaking engagements and that became the sole employer of several family members.[30] Outside of Colorado, Cassie's example inspired individual teenagers as well as the evangelical youth movement. One girl sought to take Cassie's name at her confirmation.[31] For an already thriving Christian youth movement, the martyrdom of one of their own sparked further growth and boosted attendance at Christian youth rallies.[32] Concern that the evangelical movement was exploiting the tragedy at Columbine was rarely expressed.[33]

Cassie's Martyrologies
With only a nod to the continuing lack of confirmation for Cassie's story, Misty Bernall, Cassie's mother, vigorously promoted *She Said Yes: The Unlikely Martyrdom of Cassie Bernall.*[34] Published only months after Bernall's death, it sold quickly and soon appeared on the *New York Times* nonfiction bestseller list.[35] For those who had been following Cassie's story, the outline of the book was familiar, but Misty Bernall delved into greater detail about Cassie before her conversion elaborating on her surliness, her suicidal thoughts, her drug use, her interest in the occult, and most dramatically, the violence she contemplated against a teacher and her own parents. Frantically trying to reach their daughter, the Bernalls had contacted the Sheriff's office and then their pastors at West Bowles Community Church[36] whose

29. Susan Besze Wallace, 'Book Goes Past Teen's Last Words: "She Said Yes" Hits Stores Today', *Denver Post* (10 September 1999): A-0, and Janet Bingham, 'Victim an "Unlikely Martyr": Cassie Bernall's Faith an Example to All, Church Says', *Denver Post* (7 June 1999): B-01.

30. Kevin Simpson, 'Daughter's Death Brings Life "into Focus": Rachel Scott's Dad Delivers Message of Faith across U.S.', *Denver Post* (20 October 1999): A-01.

31. Associated Press, 'Christian Slain in Littleton Sets Example for Faithful; One Girl Wants to Take Her Name at Confirmation', *St Louis Post-Dispatch* (16 May 1999): A5.

32. For coverage of this outpouring see Biema, 'A Surge of Teen Spirit': 58-59, Martha Sawyer Allen, 'Christian Cool', *Star Tribune* (13 September 1999): 1E; Wendy Murray Zoba, 'Do You Believe in God? Columbine and the Stirring of America's Soul', *Christianity Today* (4 October 1999): 40.

33. Richard Roeper, 'Choosing Life Rather than Becoming a Teenage Martyr', *Denver Post* (17 June 1999): B-11

34. In a Preface to the first edition, Misty Bernall concedes that although 'the exact details of Cassie's death...may never be known, the author's description as printed in this book is based on reports of numerous survivors of the library...and takes into account their varying recollections' (Misty Bernall, *She Said Yes: The Unlikely Martyrdom of Cassie Bernall* [Farmington, PA: Plough, 1999], p. vi). With respect to the other possible Columbine martyrs, Misty Bernall also includes the story of Valeen Schnurr and concedes that her daughter was not the only student to 'pay for taking a stand that day at the high school' (p. 132). She also refers to Rachel Scott's death and suggests Rachel was targeted for her convictions but does not suggest the gunmen asked about Rachel's belief in God (p. 132).

35. 'Best Sellers', *New York Times* (3 October 1999): 7.30.

36. Bernall, *She Said Yes*, pp. 53-55.

youth group was the only extra-curricular activity Cassie was permitted.[37] So complete had been Cassie's rejection of family and Christianity that Dave McPherson, the youth pastor, remembered her arrival at his youth group in this way:

> I told them [Cassie's parents] that they were welcome to bring Cassie to our youth group activities, and that we would do our best to help her, but underneath I never gave Cassie a hope. I remember walking away from that meeting and saying to myself, 'We'll give it our best, but this girl's going to be a hard one. She's gone, unreachable. There is no way that she'll ever recover from what she's doing.'[38]

Only a few months later, after attending a Christian youth retreat, Cassie reported to her mother: 'Mom, I've changed, I have totally changed. I know you are not going to believe it but I am going to prove it to you'.[39]

In letters to friends Cassie spoke of her desire to be ever closer to God and to learn his plan for her.[40] On occasion, she was concerned that she had perhaps made compromises with God because 'It's like being lukewarm—he'll spit me out if I keep it up'.[41] Yet her mother recounts her death as a final and indeed triumphant confession, quoting a sophomore identified only as Josh:

> I could recognize her [Cassie's] voice. I could hear everything like it was right next to me. One of them asked her if she believed in God. She paused, like she didn't know what she was going to answer, and then said yes. She must have been scared, but her voice didn't sound shaky. It was strong. Then they asked her why, though they didn't give her a chance to respond. They just blew her away.[42]

The biography, however, did not exhaust the possibilities of Cassie's story. Accompanying the publication of the book was a youth-oriented Bible study guide: *She Said Yes: A Bible Study Guide Based on the Life of Cassie Bernall*. Each of the five lessons in the study guide comprises selections from the New Testament, excerpts from *She Said Yes*, study questions and finally space for each student to complete a 'commitment plan'. Jeff Diedrich, the study guide's author, based each lesson on events in the life of the apostle Paul and drew out compelling parallels between the conversions that of Paul and Cassie. Just as Paul had once persecuted the Church, so too had Cassie opposed the Church in dedicating her soul to Satan. Like Paul on the road to Damascus, Cassie had a dramatic encounter and was converted.[43] The final lesson[44] builds on Cassie's and Paul's final defenses of their faith—Paul's

---

37. Bernall, *She Said Yes*, p. 62.
38. Bernall, *She Said Yes*, p. 63.
39. Bernall, *She Said Yes*, p. 93.
40. Bernall, *She Said Yes*, p. 112.
41. Bernall, *She Said Yes*, p. 113. Cassie's remark may refer to Rev. 3.16.
42. Bernall, *She Said Yes*, p. 14.
43. Jeff Diedrich, *She Said Yes: A Bible Study Guide Based on the Life of Cassie Bernall* (Rocky Mount, NC: Positive Action for Christ, 1999), pp. 6-9.
44. For the second of the five lessons, Diedrich draws on Paul's confrontation with Peter and on Cassie's reputation for honesty and candor, emphasizing both Paul's courage in critiquing Peter and Cassie's in affirming her belief in God to the gunmen (*She Said Yes: A Bible Study Guide*, pp. 15-16). The third lesson builds on Paul's lessons about love in 1 Cor. 13. Here the parallel to

before King Agrippa and Cassie's before the gunmen. In Paul's case, the persecution he had previously encountered had prepared him for the ultimate test. In Cassie's case, her strength stemmed from her daily willingness to die herself in order that Christ might live in her.[45]

Youth Pastor Dave McPherson, in conjunction with Cassie's youth group, produced a video tribute to Cassie and her Christian commitment. In it countless students testify to the power of Cassie's example 'as an instrument of God's peace'.[46] Other survivors of the library shootings also share their stories in the video. One member remembers how he dedicated himself to God as he hid from the gunmen protected by angels:

> There were angels all around us. There were three kids right behind me. They were directly behind me. And that's when I committed myself to Christ. It wasn't because I was afraid to die or get shot. It's 'cause it was time.[47]

Others believed they had survived because God had made them invisible:

> We just had to keep praying because it was the only way we were going to get through it. We just had to stay calm. That's where our faith came in—just believing that He would bring us through. I believe with all my heart that Seth, Sara and I were just invisible and God made us invisible. They were walking around us and so many around us were shot and wounded and even killed but we ran out of there without a single wound and that's only by the power of God that we got out of there.[48]

Just as this collection of material was released, the many unsettled questions connected to the Columbine story caught the attention of a persistent and probing reporter from *Salon* magazine. Getting to the bottom of the she-said-yes-story had proved particularly difficult for Dave Cullen:

> [C]ooperative sources quickly clammed up when questioned about the most celebrated Columbine story of all, immortalized this month in Misty Bernall's bestseller, 'She Said Yes: The Unlikely Martyrdom of Cassie Bernall'... [W]hile no one would go on the record, key investigators made it clear that an alternate scenario is far more likely: The killers asked another girl, Valeen Schnurr, a similar question, then shot her, and she lived to tell about it. Schnurr's story was

---

Cassie's life is not tight; Diedrich cites examples of her parents' patient love for her even when she was consumed with anger and resentment for them, Cassie's own need for love when she put on a tough exterior to hide a lonely heart and finally Cassie's love for others when she planned to donate her hair to a program that makes wigs for children undergoing chemotherapy (pp. 17-21). The fourth lesson draws out incidents in both Paul's and Cassie's lives in which they submitted to God and accepted a challenge as God's gift. In Paul's case, the challenge is the thorn of 2 Cor. 12.7-10; in Cassie's case it was the submission her parents demanded of her (which she ultimately willingly gave) and her submission to God after her conversion (p. 29).

45. Diedrich, *She Said Yes: A Bible Study Guide*, p. 35.

46. *She Said Yes: A Video Tribute to Cassie Bernall by Her Friends* (WBCC Production: Distributed by The Plough Publishing House, 1999).

47. *She Said Yes: A Video Tribute.*

48. *She Said Yes: A Video Tribute.*

then apparently misattributed to Cassie... And even if it is clear, investigators clearly don't intend to tell. They cited the tense political climate around the story in this heavily evangelical community, as well as the potential embarrassment to Cassie's family, uniformly describing the Bernalls as sincere victims who may have been misinformed 'through no malicious intent'.[49]

Following this report, the local Denver press, long silent on the issue, quickly began to cover it and uncovered this important detail: the discrepancies in the girl-who-said-'yes' story had been brought to the attention of the Bernalls soon after their daughter's death and long before the publication of Misty's book.[50] According to one police source, Rachel Scott's younger brother, Craig Scott, first identified Bernall as the girl-who-said-'yes'.[51] However, when investigators asked Scott where Bernall was when she said yes, Scott indicated the table where Valeen Schnurr, not Cassie Bernall, had been sitting.[52] Scott may have become physically ill when he realized his confusion.[53] Furthermore, a student that was hiding under the same desk as was Cassie publicly stated that she had told both the investigators and the Bernalls that she 'did not believe Bernall spoke to Klebold in the library'.[54] In the final Sheriff's report, Valeen Schnurr, not Cassie Bernall, was the girl-who-said-'yes'.[55]

49.   Dave Cullen, 'Everything You Know about the Littleton Killings is Wrong: But the Truth May Be Scarier than the Myths', *Salon* (23 September 1999) <http.//www.salon.com>.

50.   Dan Luzadder and Katie Kerwin McCrimmon, 'Accounts Differ on Question to Bernall: Columbine Shooting Victim May Not Have Been Asked Whether She Believed in God', *Denver Rocky Mountain News* (24 September 1999): 5A.

51.   Craig Scott did not mention this episode in his rather lengthy interview with Katie Couric on 22 April (NBC, *Today Show*, 22 April 1999), although he would include it without identifying the girl in an interview aired on the *Today Show* on 23 April 1999, two days after Cain's identi-fication on *Larry King Live* and the day after that of *Good Morning America*. Ultimately Craig Scott offered another version of the story in which two girls were asked whether they believed in God: '"They were having conversations with people before they shot 'em", says Craig" Scott, a fellow believer whose sister Rachel was killed. "The gunmen did ask two different people if they believed in God. They both said yes. Then they shot 'em... My ears were ringing, so I couldn't hear anything"' (Cole Moreton, 'Survivors Remember the Horror for New BBC Film', *The Independent* [10 October 1999]: 26).

52.   Susan Besze Wallace, 'Val Schnurr Knows What She Said on that Horrifying Day', *Denver Post* (28 September 1999): A-01.

53.   Luzadder and McCrimmon, 'Accounts Differ on Question to Bernall', 5A: 'Investigators told Mark Schnurr that a student who helped authorities retrace the events in the library got physically sick when he realized it was Val's table, not Cassie's, that he was pointing out to authorities'.

54.   Sean Kelly, 'Bernall Family Defends Accuracy of their Book about Cassie', *Denver Post* (26 September 1999): A-23.

55.   The final Sheriff's report mapped out where witnesses were sitting in the library for each detail of the tragedy. Investigators identify fifteen witnesses throughout the room for Valeen Schnurr's exchange with the gunmen (*The Jefferson County Sheriff's Report*, Diagram 72). For Cassie Bernall, the Sheriff's office settled on this account: 'Harris walked over to table 19 where he bent down and saw two frightened girls. He slapped the table top twice, said, "Peek-a-boo", and

Even in the wake of this scrutiny of Cassie's death and the doubt it cast on her final words, Cassie continued to be hailed a martyr—this time in a play written 'under the close supervision of Brad and Misty Bernall' that debuted in November 1999.[56] Designed to be easily produced by church youth groups, *Crossroads at Columbine* is sold in kits that include ten scripts and a CD-ROM containing sound files for the production and graphic files for tickets and posters. The play largely follows the narrative outline of Misty Bernall's book—Cassie's embraces Christianity and rejects her old ways and friends—but the script's goal is clearly didactic. Because the adult characters dominate the script, the play demands that its teenage actors identify with parental and adult sources of authority. In order to make this same impression on the audience, the Bernall characters often address them directly:

> Misty: Brad, we're not just dealing with a rebellious teenager, we're fighting a spiritual battle.
>
> Brad [in an aside to the audience]: Boy were we! Misty and I had never before felt a sense of spiritual warfare like that.[57]

Another Bernall-approved publication was a small missionizing pamphlet entitled, *She Said Yes: A Story of Hope from Columbine High*. In form, it is an openly pseudepigraphic testament: 'In the wake of the recent Columbine High Shootings Cassie Bernall's story has been an encouragement to many. The following is written as Cassie might have told it.' The Cassie character describes her previous ways as dabbling in 'black magic' and credits her parents with saving her life. She identifies 20 April 1999 as her moment of truth in which she would have to 'choose between my old life and new life in Christ'. Cassie relates that when the gunman asked her if she believed in God, she said 'yes' but did not live long enough to answer the gunmen's second question, 'Why?' In retrospect, the testament suggests that her death is the answer to that question: 'For today I am with God. Nothing can take that away from me!'[58]

Undaunted by concerns that Cassie was not likely to have said yes, the authors of Cassie's martyrologies explored every aspect of her life, her death and its aftermath. Misty Bernall's biography is the basis for them all, but each additional martyrology emphasizes a different strand of the story: the missionizing pamphlet expands on Cassie's own perspective of her conversion and death; the play leads teenagers to appreciate the critical role that parents and pastors played in Cassie's life; the video tribute documents the profound impact Cassie's death had on those around her. Her martyr's death proved to be a pliable vehicle for a range of messages.

---

fired, killing Cassie Bernall'—a report for which they have five witnesses, four in the immediate vicinity and one on the other side of the room (Diagram 56).

56. Alan Behn, *Crossroads at Columbine* (Rocky Mount, NC: youthimperative!, 2000), pp. ii.

57. Behn, *Crossroads at Columbine*, p. 17.

58. *She Said Yes: A Story of Hope from Columbine High* (Wheaton, IL: Good News Publisher, 1999).

Rachel's Martyrologies

On the first anniversary of the Columbine massacre, Rachel Scott was again por-trayed as a martyr by her divorced parents, Beth Nimmo and Darrell Scott. For anyone following the tragedy, their casting of Rachel as a martyr could only have come as a surprise. Rachel had been occasionally identified as the girl-who-said-'yes', but this identification was largely dismissed in the weeks that followed when the story became firmly tied to the library, rather than to the school grounds where Rachel was shot. Furthermore, the family must have been intimately aware of the controversy surrounding Cassie Bernall's final words, as their son Craig Scott's testimony had played a crucial role in that investigation. Nonetheless, Beth Nimmo and Darrell Scott co-authored *Rachel's Tears: The Spiritual Journey of Columbine Martyr Rachel Scott*

A number of pieces of information, many of which were not then and still are not publicly available, convinced Nimmo and Scott that Rachel was a martyr. The most important of these is the testimony of Richard Castaldo's mother. On the fateful day, Rachel ate lunch outside with her friend, Richard Castaldo. Richard survived but remains paralyzed as a result of gunshot wounds. Because of his injuries, Richard did not speak to the press directly after the shootings. Instead his father made various appearances recounting his son's experience, but never suggesting that Klebod and Harris had asked Rachel about her belief in God.[59] Nor did Richard himself once he began to give interviews. Indeed he no longer makes any claims about what happened that day, explaining that his memories of that day are lost through trauma and injury.[60] However, in January 2000 NBC news program *Dateline* interviewed Richard's mother, who allegedly claimed that Richard's earliest account of events included Rachel testifying to her faith.[61] This program, however, has never aired and her account cannot be verified. Thus the Scotts' conviction that Rachel was the girl-who-said-'yes' was confirmed eight months later by Castaldo's mother.[62] Indeed Beth Nimmo believes that nobody who knew Rachel 'would ever doubt her commitment and that is the main reason people accepted Richard Castaldo's account of her final moments. If you knew Rachel, her dying that way would make sense because it is the way she lived every moment of her life'.[63]

In addition to Castaldo's alleged testimony about Rachel's death, the Scott family believes that Klebold and Harris harbored 'an intense anti-Christian hostil-ity', and targeted—that is, persecuted—Christians. In a series of videos made before the attack, screened by the victims' families but not publicly released, Klebold and Harris explained the rationale behind their plan and outlined its details. Based on

59. His first account to this end was on NBC's *Today* show on 29 April 1999.
60. With respect to Rachel's possible last words Richard Castaldo has subsequently stated: 'I don't remember that. I can't remember either way' (Kevin Simpson, 'Who Said "Yes" Blurs with Time', *Denver Post* (16 December 1999): A-01.
61. Beth Nimmo and Darrell Scott, *Rachel's Tears: The Spiritual Journey of Columbine Martyr Rachel Scott* (Nashville: Thomas Nelson, 2000), pp. 91-92.
62. Simpson, 'Who Said "Yes" Blurs with Time', A-01.
63. Nimmo and Scott, *Rachel's Tears*, p. 98.

the portions he watched, Darrell Scott believes that 'spiritual forces were at work to take Eric to the level of hatred and despair that he experienced. Eric may not have known this at the time, but Satan doesn't always reveal his hand.'[64] For the lead investigator, Detective Kim Battan, a different picture emerged from the videos—namely, that the gunmen were consumed with an undifferentiated hatred. Journalist Dave Cullen summarized Battan's views this way:

> But investigators were willing to say that whichever girl was asked about her faith, her life did not hinge on her answer. One key investigator said there is no evidence the outcome would have been any different if she had denied she believed in God.
>
> The bottom line, investigators insist, is that regardless of which spiteful jibes the killers tossed about during the shooting spree, none of the taunts bore any relation to their motives. 'Were there things said about jocks?' Battan asked. 'Probably. About God? Probably. Was there a "nigger" comment? Probably. But that's not what it was *about*.' Investigators agree it was about hate. 'We can tell you why they did it, because they tell us why they're going to do it', a key source said. 'They did it because they were consumed with hate.'[65]

Cullen's summary was later supported by the reports produced by the Jefferson County Sheriff and by the taskforce commissioned by the governor of Colorado: Harris and Klebold did not aim to kill any particular students; rather, they aimed to kill as many students as possible.[66]

In spite of this weighty evidence against a specifically anti-Christian plot, Scott's family believes that the gunmen had a special reason to target their Christian daughter: Klebod had an unrequited crush on Rachel and had called her 'godly whore' and a 'stuck-up little bitch'.[67] In addition, Rachel had challenged Klebold and Harris about a negative and violent video they had produced in a class she shared with them.[68] Rachel's mother even suggests that her daughter's name was on a target list.[69] It remains impossible to assess the Scott family's analysis of this evidence, as the relevant tapes and written documents have not been released.[70] At this time, however, the Sheriff's and Governor's reports do not confirm their interpretations.

Rachel's Christian convictions, her relationship to God as demonstrated by her actions and revealed in her journal, and her predictions about her future are also

64. Nimmo and Scott, *Rachel's Tears*, p. 169.
65. Cullen, 'Everything You Know about the Littleton Killings'.
66. Harris and Klebold planned to detonate two large bombs in the cafeteria at 11.17 on 20 April 1999 and then to shoot students as they fled the scene of the devastation (*Columbine Review Commission's Report*, 25 May 2001). As it turned out, the cafeteria bombs did not detonate and Klebold and Harris spent the ensuing hour and a half improvising, ultimately killing far fewer students than they had hoped or expected. This was clearly a plan devised to kill as many students as possible, not one aimed at specific students or even groups of students.
67. Nimmo and Scott, *Rachel's Tears*, pp. 88-89.
68. Nimmo and Scott, *Rachel's Tears*, p. 114.
69. Nimmo and Scott, *Rachel's Tears*, p. 172.
70. This remains a live issue in Littleton as it makes its way through the courts: Tillie Fong, 'Stone Again Asks Rights to Tapes; Harris, Klebold Made Videos before Killings', *Rocky Mountain News* (20 March 2002): 4A

important evidence in the Scott family's eyes that Rachel died a martyr's death. Rachel was widely regarded as a beautiful and warm hearted girl.[71] She had even asked out a disabled classmate who had never been on a date, to his great delight. So accepting was she that her friendliness has been likened unto Jesus' mission to the outcasts.[72]

Rachel's journal, often structured as letters to God, reveals a deep commitment to her faith. She confessed in her journal her fears and struggles and continually sought guidance from God. In return, she believed that he spoke to her,[73] a dialogue her mother has compared to that which King David enjoyed with God.[74] Given Rachel's devotion and God's communication with her, her mother has toyed with the idea that her daughter was a saint,[75] while her father called her a mystic.[76]

Rachel's family also considers her a prophet based on what they take to be predictions of her death recorded in her journal. On 2 May 1998, Scott wrote, 'this will be my last year Lord. I have gotten what I can. Thank you.'[77] And her prophecy was fulfilled: she died within the year. On the day of the shootings, she twice premonished her impending death: she shared with a friend that morning that she felt like it was a strange day,[78] and she drew a picture of an eye crying thirteen tears onto a rose. Together with an earlier depiction of a rose springing from a columbine plant, the Colorado state flower after which the high school was named, the Scott family believes the image prophesies the murder that was about to occur—the tears represent the number of victims and the rose, the school.[79] A saint, mystic and prophet, her family concludes, could only have died a martyr's death.

The following year, another book was published in connection with Rachel's death, *A Real Diary of Faith: The Journal of Rachel Scott*. While the title suggests that the book will comprise lengthy excerpts from Rachel's diary, the Preface reveals a different sort of project. Nimmo and Scott wanted to publish more of Rachel's journals but in a way that 'gave a more complete picture of Rachel Joy Scott' than do her own actual writings.[80] As a result, a hired writer immersed herself in Rachel's journals and produced a pseudepigraphic journal with images of her actual journal pages interspersed.

Just as the pseudepigraphic missionizing pamphlet based on Cassie's story retells Cassie's life, so too does *The Journals of Rachel Scott*. What happened after Richard Castaldo had been shot appears in italics:

71. Nimmo and Scott, *Rachel's Tears*, pp. 71-75.
72. Nimmo and Scott, *Rachel's Tears*, pp. 103-108.
73. Nimmo and Scott, *Rachel's Tears*, p. 129.
74. Nimmo and Scott, *Rachel's Tears*, pp. 28-29.
75. Nimmo and Scott, *Rachel's Tears*, p. 39.
76. Nimmo and Scott, *Rachel's Tears*, p. 35.
77. Nimmo and Scott, *Rachel's Tears*, p. 23.
78. Nimmo and Scott, *Rachel's Tears*, p. xxii.
79. Nimmo and Scott, *Rachel's Tears*, pp. 175-77.
80. Beth Nimmo and Debra K. Klingsporn, *A Real Diary of Faith: The Journal of Rachel Scott* (Nashville: Tommy Nelson, 2001), p. xi.

Harris grabbed her by the hair and asked her, 'Do you believe in God?'

'You know I do', Rachel replied.

'Then go be with him', responded Harris before shooting her.[81]

Like the Bible study based on the Cassie Bernall story, *A Real Diary of Faith* includes exercises for its teenage target audience in order to develop and confirm their faith under the influence of Rachel's example.

Analysis

While comparative research is fraught with pitfalls, especially comparisons stretching across chronological and cultural chasms such as now lie between us and the ancient martyrs, many perhaps widely applicable insights emerge from this modern tragedy about how deaths make martyrs and martyrs, martyrologies.

In the study of ancient martyrdoms, attempts to isolate their apparent historical elements are on the decline. Still, scholars trying to characterize ancient persecutions and martyrdoms sometimes elevate to the level of fact elements that they consider sound or secure based on theological recasting. For instance, the second-century *Martyrdom of Polycarp* is widely thought to be an accurate account of the events described in spite of repeated echoes of Gospel stories and didactic passages. A clear lesson of the Columbine deaths is that the creation and propagation of a martyr story are not necessarily proportional to the story's correspondence with the events themselves.

The Bernalls were aware that the authorities could not confirm that Cassie was the girl who said yes from early in the investigation. This, however, did not deter them from publishing a martyrology. Even as the attack on the factual basis of this story grew, the Bernalls and others continued to produce materials embracing Cassie as the girl-who-said-'yes'. Rachel Scott's family published the biography of their martyr at an even greater remove from events but on no firmer ground with respect to their core claim, that Rachel was killed because she affirmed her belief in God. There is no verified account that either girl was murdered for their faith. What then are the elements of these stories and situations that fueled the development, elaboration and repetition of these stories?

Compelling Biography

At their deaths, Cassie Bernall and Rachel Scott may have affirmed their faith with just one word, 'Yes'. To fill out their martyrologies, their families relied heavily on their biographies and prior devotions to demonstrate the depth of the girls' Christian conviction. Cassie's dramatic rejection of her dark beliefs and practices and her subsequent devotion to Christianity proved to be fertile soil for her legacy as a martyr. Although Rachel could identify the moment of her Christian rebirth at age 12, her biography does not include a dramatic reversal. Instead, Scott's

---

81. Nimmo and Klingsporn, *A Real Diary of Faith*, p. 119.

revealing journal entries and letters to God render her biography compelling. In both cases, the girls' enthusiastic Christian devotion proved a necessary foundation from which their martyrologies grew.

The Role of their Survivors
The transformation of Cassie and Rachel into martyrs did not depend solely on their moving biographies. Indeed if this were the case, other victims might have been more likely nominees. For instance, John Tomlin had 'spent time in Mexico helping build housing for the poor and doing mission work'.[82] A Bible was even found open on the dashboard of his truck in the high school parking lot. Rather, the creation of martyrs depended in large part on those who survived them—their reaction to publicity, their theological orientation and their connection to organized Church structures. A comparison of Bernall and Scott with the almost-martyr, Valeen Schnurr, drives this point home.

By September 1999, with her confession widely substantiated, Valeen Schnurr might have seemed poised to become the great Christian youth hero of the Columbine tragedy. But, according to her father, the family decided 'to do no media interviews unless it's in their best interest' and, perhaps as a result, the media did not extensively cover her act of bravery.[83] Nor did Valeen author an autobiography perhaps out of concern for the Bernall family, perhaps out of her own concern for the trauma Cassie Bernall's family might experience if Valeen publicized her story, perhaps out of media shyness. In contrast, while Misty Bernall lamented how grueling it was to grieve in a public spotlight, she chose to sacrifice further her family's privacy to tell the tale of her daughter. The Scott family's frequent public appearances and their management by a Christian speakers' bureau suggest that even if they did have concerns about media attention, their desire to tell the story of their daughter won out.[84] The families of Cassie and Rachel readily, if not eagerly, served as publicists for their children's deaths.

The denominational commitments of the families also played a key role in the development of Bernall and Scott as public martyrs by providing a religious vocabulary with which to describe the events and by providing institutional support for the development and propagation of the martyr stories. Cassie Bernall, Rachel Scott and their families belonged to non-denominational evangelical Christian churches. In interpreting the motivations and actions of Klebold and Harris, these evangelical families and their supporters quickly invoked theological and cosmological explanations. In *Crossroads at Columbine*, Cassie is cast as a victim in a battle between good and evil. And in a triumphant vision in the weeks following Cassie's death, Youth Pastor Dave McPherson 'saw Cassie, and I saw Jesus, hand

---

82. Nimmo and Scott, *Rachel's Tears*, p. iv.

83. Ann Schrader, 'Family Copes after Columbine', *Denver Post* (9 October 1999): B-02.

84. The paperback edition of the book states that Ambassador Speakers Bureau exclusively handles the speaking engagements for Beth Nimmo and Darrell Scott (Nimmo and Scott, *Rachel's Tears*, p. 15). At the time of writing, the Ambassador Speakers Bureau web site listed only Darrell as an active speaker.

in hand. And they had just gotten married. They had just celebrated their marriage ceremony. And Cassie kind of winked over at me like, "Dave, I'd like to talk, but I'm so much in love". Her greatest prayer was to find the right guy. Don't you think she did?'[85]

The Scotts conceived of the tragedy in similar terms. Darrell Scott remembers thinking as he drove toward the school on the day of the shootings, '*This is a spiritual event, a spiritual event*'.[86] The survival of their son Craig was a miracle.[87] And with further hindsight, Darrell Scott paints the cosmic battle on a grand scale: the gunmen participated in 'spiritual battle'.[88] Rachel's youth pastor employed even blunter language: 'We're in a spiritual war between good and evil'.[89] It was these families that interpreted the crime in a cosmic framework that were also drawn to elevate their daughters' deaths to martyrdoms.

Moreover, the cosmological interpretations of their daughters' deaths took on added significance in the context of the evangelical commitments of the Bernall and Scott families (in contrast, Schnurr was a Catholic, a tradition with a limited number of evangelical congregations). Bernall's youth pastor David McPherson quickly appeared in print touting Cassie's conversion and retelling the story of her martyrdom. Once Cassie's story fell into the hands of her well-organized church—part of a nationwide movement committed to evangelical witness—her story gained momentum. Cassie's story enjoyed wide community support faster than it could be verified and, even when questioned, it hardly slowed.[90]

Rachel Scott, too, was part of an evangelical youth movement but her youth group, Breakthrough, was not in the Littleton area. While the West Bowles Community Church Youth Group directly confronted the tragedy through Cassie's death and the trauma of the many members who attended the Columbine High School, some of whom had escaped from the library, Breakthrough confronted the shock and confusion at some distance, even as they grieved a victim among their membership. Moreover, the halting spread of Rachel's alleged affirmation did not allow the activities surrounding her nationally broadcast funeral to advance her case as a martyr. Rather, the family's conviction in her martyrdom grew as they read her journals and as evidence of Klebold's and Harris's motivations and planning were made available to victims' families. In that context, Darrell Scott's previous career

85. Dave Cullen, '"I smell the presence of Satan': Is Littleton's Evangelical Subculture a Solution to the Youth Alienation that Played a Role in the Columbine Killings, or a Reflection of It?'" *Salon* (19 May 1999) <http.//www.salon.com>.

86. Nimmo and Scott, *Rachel's Tears*, p. 15 (emphasis in original).

87. Nimmo and Scott, *Rachel's Tears*, p. 15.

88. Nimmo and Scott, *Rachel's Tears*, pp. 100-101.

89. Nimmo and Scott, *Rachel's Tears*, p. 134.

90. As *Salon* reporter Cullen uncovered, the local authorities and press had long been aware of the difficulties of the Cassie story but had not published them citing, 'the tense political climate around the story in this heavily evangelical community, as well as the potential embarrassment to Cassie's family, uniformly describing the Bernalls as sincere victims who may have been misinformed "through no malicious intent"' (Cullen, 'Everything You Know About the Littleton Killings').

as a pastor may have been pivotal. As he pieced together the story of his daughter's life, he became convinced that his daughter's special relationship to God, and her martyr's death would motivate other youths and parents. To that end, he, along with Rachel's mother, wrote Rachel's biography and used it to advance the mission of the Columbine Redemption, the not-for-profit organization founded by the Scott family. To this day, he continues to log thousands of miles making public appearances and retelling the story of his daughter's life and death.[91]

Conclusions

In Littleton, the making of martyrs had at its source Klebold's and Harris's determination to kill as many students as they could on 20 April 1999 irrespective of race, athletic participation or religion. When they asked Valeen Schnurr if she believed in God, they were prompted by her own pained exclamations after she had been shot. In official reports and investigative articles alike, there is little ground to call these deeply tragic deaths martyrdoms.

In what is perhaps an important lesson to scholars of ancient martyrdom, the event themselves seem to have played only a limited role in the creation of a martyrdom. Rather, the decisive element in making a martyr and popularizing a martyrology seemed to be the commitment of the community (including the families) to the task. The grief of the Scotts and the Bernalls drove them to make sense of the seemingly senseless. And their religious devotion led them to find their answer in the spiritual realm, fueling their convictions that as martyrs their daughters' deaths would have enduring meaning. The bible played an important role in securing their convictions—for the Bernalls in the parallels to Paul's life and for the Scotts, in the daughter's participation in the tradition of prophecy. The families' toleration for, if not attraction to, the public spotlight combined with their ties to churches and evangelical organizations enabled them to create and publicize a range of materials documenting their daughters' martyrdoms. In their efforts, each family was supported by a larger evangelical movement that embraced the families and their desire to find something positive in this tragedy. When the girls' stories proved to be compelling missionizing material, the evangelical churches' larger goals and the families' determination that their daughters not have died in vain fueled the martyrologies in all of their various forms. Through all of this, increasing doubts about the actual circumstances of Cassie's and Rachel's deaths grew ever weightier but did not forestall their fortunes as martyrs. Rather, these modern martyrs were the products of their families and communities.

---

91. Darrell Scott continued to post his appearance schedule on the Columbine Redemption website <http.//thecolumbineredemption.com/calendar.htm> (1 June 2002).

The Tyranny of the Martyr:
Violence and Victimization in Martyrdom Discourse and the Movies of Lars von Trier[*]

Todd Penner and Caroline Vander Stichele

I saw the 'potamus take wing
Ascending from the damp savannas,
And quiring angels round him sing
The praise of God, in loud hosannas.
Blood of the Lamb shall wash him clean
And him shall heavenly arms enfold,
Among the saints he shall be seen
Performing on a harp of gold.
He shall be washed as white as snow,
By all the martyr'd virgins kist,
While the True Church remains below
Wrapt in the old miasmal mist.

—T.S. Eliot, 'The Hippopotamus'[1]

1. *The Power of the Script*

From the death of Jesus under Jewish and Roman authorities, to the image of Paul as one who suffers for the sake of the gospel, to the book of Revelation saturated as it is with the 'blood of the martyrs' (Rev. 17.6), the violated body of the martyr is inscribed as a quintessential legacy of early Christian discourse. Drawing on its Jewish (but also Greek) antecedents, the Christian model proffers the image of suffering and death as the *imitatio Christi*.[2] Early Christian literature bears these marks of Christ, as we see throughout the powerful image of the martyr's willingness to die for his or her commitment and devotion. Indeed, so powerful is this image, so much at the core of Christian discourse, so imbedded in the structures of Christian existence, that we find some individuals like Ignatius of Antioch who cannot be content unless they too suffer as their Lord and seemingly seek their own

* The authors thank Jan Willem van Henten and Bonnie Roos for their comments on an earlier draft of this paper.

1. T.S. Eliot, *Selected Poems* (London: Faber & Faber, 1961), p. 41.
2. D. Boyarin, *Dying for God: Martyrdom and the Making of Christianity and Judaism* (Stanford, CA: Stanford University Press, 1999), p. 95.

death.[3] Such images not only continue to motivate human desires and actions as the stand-off at Waco reminds us, but also inform the perception of victims as martyrs in the case of the murders at Columbine High School and the massive human loss in the September 11 attacks. In other words, these literary images of biblical discourse themselves not only reveal *post-eventu* reflections on early Christian history, but in fact still possess the power to give shape and meaning to historical events.

This study explores the persisting impact of the image of the martyr in the twentieth century, looking specifically at the way in which the victim-as-martyr scenario continues to inform the reception and adoption/adaptation of biblical themes in modern media. In particular, we look at the recent corpus of the Danish filmmaker Lars von Trier, famous for founding the Dogma 95 style of movie-making. It is especially intriguing to engage the ways in which biblical discourse is both received, partially undermined, but then fundamentally reaffirmed through the explicit and implicit scripting of the martyr's path in two of his recent movies, *Breaking the Waves* (1995) and *Dancer in the Dark* (2000). This painful and violent path demonstrates an almost uncanny ability to circumscribe all characters and plots in its sphere and even has the capacity to script the scriptor, impinging its own direction on the theater of horror established by the director. Indeed, we see here the true power of spectacle as a vivid, engrossing image that captures and enraptures the viewer today in a comparable way to the manner in which the ancient spectator was captivated by the rhetorical power of the literary representation of martyrdom. Before turning to von Trier's work, then, it is useful first to explore not only the themes that predominate in martyrdom accounts, but, even more importantly, the nexus of their rhetorical and literary power.

2. The Textual Body as a Rhetorical Battleground

If martyrdom accounts as we now possess them are first and foremost literary products, then, in their quality as ancient texts, they are fundamentally rhetorical constructions as well. Serious consideration must therefore be given to the enthrallment initiated by the spectacle paraded before the reader in the account.[4] D. Boyarin articulates this well:

> …I propose we think of martyrdom as a 'discourse', as a practice of dying for God and of talking about it… For the 'Romans', it didn't matter much whether the lions were eating a robber or a bishop, and it probably didn't make much of a difference

3. This leads to the literary representation of his imminent demise in part as a 'staged' event. See further, W.R. Schoedel, *Ignatius of Antioch* (ed. H. Koester; Hermeneia; Philadelphia: Fortress Press, 1985), pp. 11-12.

4. The literary spectacle evokes the historical spectacle of actual Roman imperial killings such as are recorded in the texts. The executions were writ large on the Roman emotional and mental landscape as public, graphic and dehumanizing events (see R.D. Young, *In Procession Before the World: Martyrdom as Public Liturgy in Early Christianity* [Milwaukee: Marquette University, 2001], pp. 12-13; and D. Potter, 'Martyrdom as Spectacle', in R. Scodel [ed.], *Theater and Society in the Classical World* [Ann Arbor: University of Michigan Press, 1993], pp. 53-88 [53, 65-68]).

to the lions, either, but the robber's friends and the bishop's friends told different stories about those leonine meals. It is in these stories that martyrdom, as opposed to execution or dinner, can be found, not in 'what happened'.[5]

This observation explains not only the evocative power of martyrdom accounts, but also the function of suffering and violence in the characterization of saint and sinner, martyr and tyrant. Traditionally, as M. Gleason rightly reminds us, 'to mark the body of another in the ancient world was to signal that ownership and agency rested not with the one who bore the mark but with the person who imposed it'.[6] This vital socio-cultural feature, however, receives a twist in classic martyrdom accounts, as they reverse the locus of power in the equation. As Perkins notes, 'Christian discourse challenged the discourse of power being constructed in other texts of the period'.[7] Indeed, at stake in both Jewish and Christian martyrdom texts is precisely a contest of power: a battle for the construction, maintenance and dominance of identity.[8] A prominent mark of martyr identity, then, is self-mastery in the face of those who could 'kill the body'. Taking this one step further, in his fascinating study of the image of Jesus in Romans, S.D. Moore has pointed out that the portrayal by Paul focuses on Jesus as one who displays his fullest masculine identity through submission unto death.[9] This observation suggests a relationship between self-mastery as evidenced in martyrdom and masculine identity in the ancient world, which is channeled into the forum of rhetorical combat, wherein identity is established in terms of the power of (s)words and proper physical/social comportment.[10]

The highly gendered nature of martyr discourse should not be ignored. Although images of the martyr do vary, in the ancient context they frequently entail masculine notions of identity, presented in terms of gaining power over one's opponents.[11] The comportment of the body, the choice of words, the tone of language,

5.   Boyarin, *Dying for God*, pp. 94-95.
6.   M. Gleason, 'Mutilated Messengers: Body Language in Josephus', in S. Goldhill (ed.), *Being Greek Under Rome: Cultural Identity, the Second Sophistic and the Development of Empire* (Cambridge: Cambridge University Press, 2001), pp. 50-85 (79).
7.   J. Perkins, *The Suffering Self: Pain and Narrative Representation in the Early Christian Era* (London/New York: Routledge, 1995), p. 115.
8.   A point aptly demonstrated by J. Lieu, *Image and Reality: The Jews in the World of the Christians in the Second Century* (Edinburgh: T. & T. Clark, 1996), pp. 82-86. See also T. Rajak, 'Dying for the Law: The Martyr's Portrait', in M. Edwards and S. Swain (eds.), *Portraits: Biographical Representation in the Greek and Latin Literature of the Roman Empire* (New York: Oxford University Press, 1997), pp. 39-67 (66-67).
9.   S.D. Moore, *God's Beauty Parlor and Other Queer Spaces In and Around the Bible* (Stanford, CA: Stanford University Press, 2001), pp. 159-64.
10.   Hence the prominence of the agonistic motif in some martyrdom accounts; B. Dehandschutter, 'Martyrium und Agon: Über die Wurzeln der Vorstellung Vom *AGŌN* im Vierten Makkabäerbuch', in J.W. van Henten (ed.), *Die Entstehung der Jüdischen Martyrologie* (SPB, 38; Leiden: E.J. Brill, 1989), pp. 215-19 (215).
11.   When women follow the path of the martyr in this model of masculine identity, they do so frequently by adopting the male mantle. Two famous female martyrs aptly demonstrate this point. From the Jewish tradition, the mother of the seven brothers of *4 Maccabees* is clearly portrayed in male terms (*4 Macc.* 15.23, 30; Rajak, 'Dying for the Law', pp. 55-56). From the Christian tradi-

all of these contribute to the persuasive end. The presentation of martyrs as being in control of their bodies, in so far as they achieve self-mastery through both speech and action, demonstrates the unity of *logos* and *ergon* in the service of the argumentative end they are constructed to embody. This emphasis shifts the balance of power away from those in the role of tyrant and oppressor to their supposed victims. Thus, the latter are not really (or only) the victims they appear to be, because the battle for self-identity and the position of superior power is always won by the martyred. They are vindicated by God in the end, but even more so in the present, as the martyr has gained power through becoming the victim. Thus, self-mastery points beyond the realm of the body to that of the superior spirit: the tyrant can destroy the body, but the spirit of the martyr escapes his control. The tyrant's destructive physical power cannot conquer the martyr's spiritual power, demonstrating finally the latter's ultimate moral superiority.

Within this basic framework of the martyrdom narrative, the typical literary features so frequently noted now come into sharper relief. It is worth noting some of these, beginning with the primary narrative component: the martyr always confronts a tyrant, whether that figure is embodied in a single character such as Antiochus or, as in the case of Stephen (Acts 6.8–8.1), a collective entity (in this instance represented by a council). In the context of ancient rhetorical elaboration, the primary focus here is on the creation of the *ethos* of the martyr, which has as its ultimate aim the centering of moral virtue in the body and words of the martyr over

---

tion, there is the example of Perpetua, who in her final vision is embodied as a male in the role of a gladiator (*Martyrdom of Saints Perpetua and Felicitas* 10.7-14, in H. Musurillo [ed.], *Acts of the Christian Martyrs* [Oxford: Clarendon Press, 1972], p. 119). Cf. G. Corrington Streete, 'Women as Sources of Redemption and Knowledge in Early Christian Traditions', in R. Shepard Kraemer and M.R. D'Angelo (eds.), *Women and Christian Origins* (New York: Oxford University Press), pp. 330-54 (351). Streete points out that feminine imagery is present elsewhere in the narrative account, especially when Perpetua submits herself to her fate in the arena. Yet, depending on whether the 'fight' or 'submission' is being emphasized, the character could be portrayed in shifting gendered roles (G. Cloke, *This Female Man of God: Women and Spiritual Power in the Patristic Age, AD 350–450* [London/New York: Routledge, 1995], pp. 214-17). E. Castelli makes a similar point: 'Perpetua's spiritual progress is marked by the social movement away from conventional female roles and by the physical movement from a female to a male body; these processes of transformation signify her increasingly holy status' ('"I Will Make Mary Male": Pieties of the Body and Gender Transformation of Christian Women in Late Antiquity', in J. Epstein and K. Straub [eds.], *Body Guards: The Cultural Politics of Gender Ambiguity* [London: Routledge, 1991], pp. 29-49 [35]; cf. M.A. Tilley, 'The Passion of Perpetua and Felicity', in E. Schüssler Fiorenza [ed.], *Searching the Scriptures. II. A Feminist Commentary* [New York: Crossroad, 1997], pp. 829-58 [844-46]). Castelli goes on to note, however, that the role of female nakedness in the martyrdom literature not only demonstrates how they are exposed as females to the male powers that are putting them to death, but also reveals that 'females remain…inscribed as sexualized beings for male viewers/spectators/readers' (p. 43). Thus, according to Castelli, female martyrs are both 'made male' but also reinscribed back into the gendered social order of the narrator's world. The issue of nakedness is especially interesting, since it is something that surfaces particularly in the representation of female martyrdom. Unlike male martyrs, women had to overcome their bodies as a penultimate hurdle. This is the road to perfection for females in a world in which sexual identity is modeled on maleness.

against the one depicted in dominance. This feature is not only explicitly moral (and moralizing) in its orientation, it is also the primary tool whereby the one who appears to be in power and authority, representing normative values, actually comes to be placed in the reverse position by the script/or. The martyr, by contrast, while in the role of a victim at the outset, achieves narrative reversal of his or her situation as well, becoming the one who is powerful, possessing authority and embodying the new normative value through self-mastery.[12] The character of the martyr is quintessential in this respect. We thus witness that Stephen, for instance, at the outset of the narrative is characterized as someone 'full of grace and power'. Much like Moses (Acts 7.22), Stephen is powerful in word and deed (6.8), and meets resistance from those who cannot withstand his oral and physical presence—his 'grace' is met with 'lies' and 'false charges', as Stephen is found standing before a court of his 'brothers and fathers' (7.2). This presentation creates the context for impending fratricide, which actually heightens the pathos of the martyrdom account. Stephen is not killed by an outsider, an 'other' like Antiochus, but by his own 'brothers' and 'fathers'. Both the narrative and the speech that function as Stephen's *apologia* serve to further this narrative *synkrisis*,[13] which is necessitated by the moral quality of the discourse: to highlight Stephen's superior character there must be a foil with which he is contrasted, which is a basic feature of the martyrdom account. Thus, in the speech the 'true' character of the Jewish leaders is revealed in the story of Moses, only to be re-entrenched in the subsequent stoning and death of Stephen. Critical here is the contrast between the image of the martyr, who maintains composure and equanimity, evincing courage and self-control throughout, and the narrative opponents, who impose their will by silencing Stephen, turning him into their victim and consequently a 'martyr' for those who share his (and the narrator's!) views. The narrator's construction of the scene intentionally creates and then contrasts the respective moral *ethoi* of Stephen and his victimizers. As 'Christian', Stephen's good character produces good works (in this case a death

---

12. The literary representation bears out its inherent rhetorical origins at this point. In the latter, significant emphasis is placed on, as Erik Gunderson notes, 'seeking to secure a special social status for the orator's body as exclusively a good and virile body' (E. Gunderson, *Staging Masculinity: The Rhetoric of Performance in the Roman World* [Ann Arbor: University of Michigan Press, 2000], p. 62). This focus is not an end in itself, however, but 'lends credence to the notion of truth, of an essence underlying appearances' (p. 89).

13. *Synkris* is used here in the classical rhetorical sense of the term, related to the comparison of particular vices and virtues in narrative composition in order to demonstrate the superiority of one over the other (cf. Aristotle, *Topica* 3.1; Theon, *Progymnasmata* 10). See further, T.W. Seid, 'Synkrisis in Hebrews 7: The Rhetorical Structure and Strategy', in S.E. Porter and D.L. Stamps (eds.), *The Rhetorical Interpretation of Scripture* (JSNTSup, 180; Sheffield: Sheffield Academic Press, 1999), pp. 322-47 (323-25); A. Smith, '"Full of Spirit and Wisdom": Luke's Portrait of Stephen (Acts 6.1–8.1a) as a Man of Self-Mastery', in L.E. Vaage and V.L. Wimbush (eds.), *Asceticism and the New Testament* (London/New York: Routledge, 1999), pp. 97-114 (101-102); D. Marguerat, 'Luc–Actes: une unité à construire', in J. Verheyden (ed.), *The Unity of Luke–Acts* (BETL, 142; Leuven: Leuven University Press, 1999), pp. 57-81 (70-74); and see especially T.E. Duff, *Plutarch's Lives: Exploring Virtue and Vice* (New York: Oxford University Press, 1999), pp. 243-86.

modeled on the death of Jesus in Luke[14]) and his opponents' bad acts (e.g. the dissolution of the orderly trial into resultant chaos and civic disorder; their failure to demonstrate the basic virtues of mercy and justice towards their victim) likewise attest to their bad moral character. This contrast is crucial to the potency of the constructed image: the martyr receives his power at the expense of the foils in the narrative, in this case the Jewish opponents of Stephen, who act as tyrants, but with the added tragic dimension that they are his kin. Vice and virtue are thus laid bare in their respective narrative incarnations, resulting in a starkly contrasted protagonist and antagonist.

Related to this first feature is the role that the martyr plays as the 'foreigner'. The *synkrisis* of narrative composition, posing two alternative paths, one superior and one inferior, naturally results in the depiction of the martyr as an 'outsider'. In all cases, the martyr is one who challenges the normative (or what is perceived/constructed as such), which is represented by the tyrant.[15] It is striking, however, that frequently in fact the martyr is a literal foreigner as well. The idea of being a foreigner in another land was a longstanding Jewish *topos*[16] and Christian accounts continued to play on this theme, even spiritualizing the notion. Given the longstanding Jewish and biblical traditions steeped in the convention of alienation from within the community (certainly the model of Jesus is primary here for Christian discourse), the accent placed on the martyr as an outsider either from without or within (or both) is readily understandable. In Stephen's case, he is explicitly delineated as a 'Hellenist' (6.5). Whatever else this term may mean, it certainly entails one who 'speaks Greek'.[17] The council, presumably, is made up of Jewish authori-

---

14. Cf., especially, Acts 7.59//Lk. 23.46 and Acts 7.60//Lk. 23.34 (if original).

15. J. Perkins, 'Space, Place, Voice in the *Acts of the Martyrs* and the Greek Romance', in D.R. MacDonald (ed.), *Mimesis and Intertextuality in Antiquity and Christianity* (Harrisburg, PA: Trinity Press International, 2001), pp. 117-37 (128), expands the characterization of the martyr as outsider to include narrative space and place as well: '…the martyr narratives project the city and its social structure as a prison and place of torment…[and the martyr is] a prisoner of the surrounding social structure'.

16. L. Wills, *The Jew in the Court of the Foreign King: Ancient Jewish Court Legends* (HDR, 26; Minneapolis: Fortress Press, 1990). Within this narrative context, one frequently finds the *topos* of the righteous man accused of crimes he did not commit (G.W.E. Nickelsburg, *Resurrection, Immortality, and Eternal Life in Intertestamental Judaism* [HTS, 26; Cambridge, MA: Harvard University Press, 1972], esp. pp. 170-71: 'The protagonist is a wise man in a royal court. Maliciously accused of violating the law of the land, he is condemned to death. But he is rescued at the brink of death, vindicated of the charges against him, and exalted to a high position…while his enemies are punished. Later versions of the story portray the wise man as a spokesman of the Lord whose devotion to the Torah is integral to the accusation' [p. 170]). This model becomes the prototype for the martyrdom accounts, wherein the theme is taken one step further and the righteous are actually put to death.

17. Although much more is often imputed into the term 'Hellenist', the primary accent seems to be on their language (and possibly geographical location as well). See further C.C. Hill, *Hellenists and Hebrews: Reappraising Division within the Early Church* (Minneapolis: Fortress Press, 1992), p. 24; R. Murray, 'Jews, Hebrews and Christians: Some Needed Distinctions', *NovT* 24 (1982), pp. 194-208 (204); and H.A. Brehm, 'The Meaning of *Hellēnistēs* in Acts in Light of a Diachronic Analysis of *hellēnizein*', in S.E. Porter and D.A. Carson (eds.), *Discourse Analysis and*

ties from Jerusalem. This element is intriguing in part because, while all involved are Jews, there is some indication that Stephen stands out as more than simply a 'follower of Jesus': he is presented as an outsider not only to the Jewish faith as traditionally represented by the Jerusalem authorities, but to their culture as well. So Stephen, despite being powerful in word and deed, and thus lionized by the narrator, nonetheless also becomes alienated within the narrative frame, rejected by his Jewish compatriots and also seemingly abandoned by his fellow Christian companions (they are certainly nowhere to be found after 6.7!). Thus, he stands alone, superior in character but alienated from those around him. He remains connected only to himself and God.

Perhaps one of the most significant and certainly most recognizable features of the representation of the martyr is his or her characterization as one who lives and dies for *nomos*.[18] The martyr is loyal to the very principle that he or she embodies in word and deed. Thus, the character is truly a *vir bonus*, living and dying for the principle not only embedded in the narrative *synkrisis*, but also inscribed in the words and the bodily comportment of the martyrs before their accusers. The principle for which the martyr stands shifts depending on the religio-cultural context of the narrative, from the Jewish martyr who dies for the law, to the Christian who dies for Christ, although both ultimately ground that stance in fidelity and devotion to God. In Stephen's case, while he does not seek death, he embodies in his words and actions exemplary Christian views and virtues; his bold speech exacerbating his imminent demise in the narrative. While depicted as embodying normative and exemplary virtue,[19] the martyr nonetheless does so in a hostile environment. In principle, then, martyrdom narratives often proffer a counter-cultural norm that subverts (from the narrator's standpoint) a broader cultural or social value represented by the narrative opponents/tyrants. Martyrdom narratives, then, not only function apologetically to reinforce and maintain identities of discrete communities, but also, in the process, they serve to challenge the values of the perceived dominant culture. The narrative portrayal is critical here, as the values of the 'powers that be' are subverted by either proffering alternative ones or by narrative demonstration that the 'opponents' do not actually fulfil in practice their own value system. In the narrative, then, the 'views' of the characters are contrasted, but the driving force beneath is the narrator's own critique of the respective moral frameworks of the individuals/groups in question. In the case of Stephen, for example, his view is opposed to that of his audience, but the rhetorical function of the narrative goes beyond mere difference in perspective to suggest that the opponents' response compared to Stephen's evinces a difference in respective values. In falsely accusing and slaying an innocent and righteous individual, the Jewish narrative opponents are in fact portrayed here as undermining their own biblical legal tradition (cf. Exod.

Other Topics in Biblical Greek (JSNTSup, 113; Sheffield: Sheffield Academic Press, 1995), pp. 180-99 (298).

   18.   For a detailed treatment of this theme see J.W. van Henten, *The Maccabean Martyrs as Saviours of the Jewish People: A Study of 2 and 4 Maccabees* (JSJSup, 57; Leiden: E.J. Brill, 1997), pp. 125-35.

   19.   Van Henten, *Maccabean Martyrs*, pp. 278-88.

23.7), while Stephen, established in the speech and framing narrative as a 'prophet like Moses',[20] is presented in turn as fulfilling this same tradition. In this manner, the voice of God/value/truth, regardless of what the narrative antagonists may claim for themselves, resides only in the body of the innocent, righteous individual, here 'wrongfully' put to death. The narrator's truth is thereby inscribed through the victimization of the protagonist. The martyr embodies absolute value, inscribing in his or her words and deeds the truth through testimony and witness.

Enhancing the aforementioned basic structure of martyrdom accounts is the sheer raw power of their dramatic and vivid narrative focus.[21] For this reason the martyr has to die, and often horribly/violently so. The martyr needs to be victimized (and sacrificed); and perhaps not surprisingly herein resides the locus of power for the resultant image, as well as the basis for its ritualistic overtones.[22] The vivid portrayal in language and image of the martyr's suffering and death captures the mind and emotions of the spectator. In fact, the distance between the viewer and the viewed is intentionally collapsed in vivid narration: the spectator is transported to the 'scene of the crime', making the impact all the more powerful and persuasive. Thus, just as the martyrs prove themselves superior over the tyrant in the narrative, they also transcend the narrative to exert their power over the spectator. The aim of such capturing of the imagination may be to bring adherence to the principle embodied in the martyr's own words and deeds, but the longevity of this powerful imaging proves that even when the principle may have been lost in the vicissitudes of history, the control of the martyr over the spectator is not.

Lastly, the dramatic, vivid portrayal of the martyr, who is willing to die under the tyranny of another, brings with it a certain vicarious benefit for those connected

20. On this theme in Luke–Acts, see D.P. Moessner, *Lord of the Banquet: The Literary and Theological Significance of the Lukan Travel Narrative* (Minneapolis: Fortress Press, 1989), pp. 259-88; L.T. Johnson, *The Literary Function of Possessions in Luke–Acts* (SBLDS, 39; Atlanta: Scholars Press, 1977), pp. 60-76; and P.S. Minear, *To Heal and to Reveal: The Prophetic Vocation According to Luke* (New York: Seabury Press, 1976), pp. 102-21.

21. Vivid narration was an essential feature of Greco-Roman narrative and oratorical compositions, with the intended impact being that the event was articulated vividly and 'brought before the eyes' of the reader/hearer (see A. Feldherr, *Spectacle and Society in Livy's History* [Berkeley: University of California Press, 1998], pp. 4-12; W.C. van Unnik, 'Luke's Second Book and the Rules of Hellenistic Historiography', in J. Kremer [ed.], *Les Actes des Apôtres: Traditions, rédaction, théologie* (BETL, 48; Leuven: Leuven University Press, 1979], pp. 37-60 [55-57]; and G. Avenarius, *Lukians Schrift zur Geschichtsschreibung* [Meisenheim/Glan: Verlag Anton Hain, 1956], pp. 130-40). Cf. Quintilian, 'There are certain experiences which the Greeks call *phantasiai*, and the Romans *visions*, whereby things absent are presented to our imagination with such extreme vividness that they seem actually to be before our very eyes. It is the man who is really sensitive to such impressions who will have the greatest power over the emotions' (*Institutio Oratoria* 6.2.29-30).

22. Young, *In Procession Before the World*, p. 12. Stemming from martyrdom as a ritualistic act, the narrative itself becomes liturgical in nature as well. Reflecting on the thirteenth English account of the martyrdom of St. Kenelm (ninth century), M. Rubin notes that 'the narrative of martyrdom thus becomes a deposit of truth and tradition, which could be read, or treated as a magical link with the past' ('Choosing Death? Experiences of Martyrdom in Late Medieval Europe', in D. Wood [ed.], *Martyrs and Martyrologies* [Cambridge: Basil Blackwell, 1993], pp. 153-83 [155]).

with the victim.[23] In many respects, this feature represents the narrative counterpart to God's vindication of the martyr. For instance, in the Stephen account the protagonist is vindicated partially by the appearance of Jesus at the right hand of God, in his role as judge and deliverer (Acts 7.55-56). The future resurrection of the martyr is thus proleptically realized in his present, affirming the commitment that is to be modeled. And as the narrative unfolds, Tertullian's famous dictum rings true—'the blood of the martyrs is the seed of the Church'—for the community expands and prospers after the death of Stephen, whose demise has seemingly reaped benefits for those sharing the same commitments and values. The Church is thus vindicated and 'resurrected' out of the threatened and alienated body of the martyr.[24] As *paradeigma* (cf. Eleazar in 2 Macc. 6.28, 31), then, the martyr lives on in those who follow. But the death of the martyr accomplishes even more, since there is a numinous quality associated with the death and body of a righteous individual.[25] The widespread development of the cult of the martyrs in late antiquity attests to the salvific power associated with the martyr's death. Indeed, there is undoubtedly a trace of the belief that meritorious deeds, those that are singular and unique, accrue benefits for those living out of and beyond the death of the righteous individual. Also critical in this respect is the connection in the literary representation of Christian martyrdom between the Akedah and the self-sacrificial death of Jesus,[26] a coupling that closely associates the violent death of the innocent with the sacrificial act of a savior. By linking together victimization and sacrifice modeled on Jesus and Isaac with the portrait of the martyr (already present in the book of Revelation), early Christian discourse paved the way for the martyr to be viewed as a sacrificial lamb, whose slaughter merits atonement or life for others. Finally, one should not overlook an essential feature of early Christian discourse that fosters and nourishes the ideas of sacrifice and atonement through suffering and death: that 'becoming the victim' is all done 'according to the Scriptures' and is therefore in line with the 'will' and 'plan' of God.[27] The divine sanctioning of the script itself goes a long way in explaining its enduring influence and its wide appeal in Christian

23. On the benefits of the death of the exceptional individual, see J.W. van Henten, 'The Tradition-Historical Background of Romans 3.25: A Search for Pagan and Jewish Parallels', in M.C. de Boer (ed.), *From Jesus to John* (JSNTSup, 84; Sheffield: JSOT Press, 1993), pp. 101-28, and *idem*, *Maccabean Martyrs*, pp. 140-63.

24. Perkins, 'Space, Place, Voice', pp. 136-37, emphasizes how the martyr's death gives way to Christian social harmony in the narratives.

25. J.E. Salisbury, *Perpetua's Passion: The Death and Memory of a Young Roman Woman* (London/New York: Routledge, 1997), refers to the 'spiritual power' that was depicted as having remained in the bodies of martyrs, which were 'transformed into vessels of holiness' (p. 168). Cf. G. Clark, 'Bodies and Blood: Late Antique Debate on Martyrdom, Virginity and Resurrection', in D. Montserrat (ed.), *Changing Bodies, Changing Meanings: Studies on the Human Body in Antiquity* (London/New York: Routledge, 1998), pp. 99-115 (108-109).

26. Lieu, *Image and Reality*, pp. 77-79.

27. See further D.P. Moessner, 'The "Script" of the Scriptures in the Acts of the Apostles: Suffering as God's "Plan" (*boule*) for the "Release of Sins"', in B. Witherington (ed.), *History, Literature and Society in the Book of Acts* (Cambridge: Cambridge University Press, 1996), pp. 218-50.

discourse.[28] We should note, furthermore, that these scripted images are gendered from the start, controlling not the martyr's path alone, but self-sacrifice as the ultimate expression of masculinity, as the victim is honored (and rewarded) for his endurance *qua* male even unto death.

This vicarious, salvific, life-giving power of the martyr, then, is also the final element of control that the martyr foists on the spectator. The martyr at this point so completely embodies the ideal in the narrative that he or she now also has transubstantiated into the divine itself. This move, then, represents the narrative consummation of the supremacy of the martyr. Not only do we find, as in the Stephen account, narrative justification of the divine perspective, but now the martyr also mediates the divine, becoming a conduit for the presence of heaven as manifested here on earth, an incarnation of true and absolute Power and Righteousness. There is thus every good reason, in line with the general thrust of martyrdom accounts in their ancient context, to observe here the ultimate power-play. And while it establishes the martyr as the locus of the divine in the text, the body of the martyr, as memorialized now in the narrative, also continues to effect this sacrificial, 'life-giving' force on the imaginations of all who confront this image in the future. The final 'benefit', then, is that the martyr never really dies, but continues to linger in the deep recesses of the cultural reservoir of the Judeo-Christian tradition, to die again and again in each new era, for the benefit of every new generation, in ever new forms. And by no means is this effect restricted to textual media, for the rhetoric of the texts has also continually been reproduced in visual images, depicting the fate and faith of the martyrs of old, as well as presenting us with new martyrs, who incorporate those ideals considered worth dying for. In what follows we analyze the form such new martyrs take, using the work of Lars von Trier as a particular case study.

3. *Scripting the Scriptor: The Power of the Martyr in the Movies of Lars von Trier*

Among one of the more evocative and provocative contemporary filmmakers, Lars von Trier has directed several movies that contain vivid and compelling reflections on the relationship of the individual to the group. Moreover, he has a particular affinity for outcasts, who in some way are punished by those around them for their 'outsiderness'. Alongside *Breaking the Waves* (BW) and *Dancer in the Dark* (DD),

---

28.   We are particularly interested here in delineating what V.K. Robbins refers to as 'suffering-death' discourse (*Tapestry of Early Christian Discourse: Rhetoric, Society, and Ideology* [London/New York: Routledge, 1996], pp. 173-74). Moving beyond more stringent form-critical categories in which there is a formal script for understanding martyrdom language as being operative, a socio-rhetorical approach lays stress on the fluid nature of the discourse related to martyrdom, suffering, death and self-sacrifice (with concomitant resurrection and vindication) in the ancient Mediterranean world, analyzing the particular ideological contexts in which the *topoi* related to this discourse are recontextualized and reconfigured and to what end. It is the power of the scripted discourse, outside of the boundaries of its particular 'form' in the ancient Jewish or Christian contexts, that explains its profound impact on Western culture.

von Trier's *Europa/Zentropa* (1991), as well as his production of Carl Thedor Dreyer's scripting of *Medea* (1987) and his own Dogma 95 contribution *The Idiots* (1998), all evince this larger interest in the alien to and within a community. In his more commercially successful movies (BW and DD), however, von Trier has not only pursued this same theme, but has also cultivated in both scripts a clear victim-focus, which follows a similar line of development in each, resulting in the death—but also vindication—of the respective protagonist. A parallel with the martyrdom narrative as discussed in the previous pages can be illustrated by von Trier's own comments on the execution of Selma, the protagonist in DD: 'I'm deeply against the death penalty. On the other hand, execution scenes are God's gift to directors. They're very efficient. If you're going to be a martyr, you have to die.'[29] In what follows, we explore the extent to which von Trier reproduces, but also redirects and reconfigures, the rhetoric of the martyr in both BW and DD.

Crucial to understanding the fate of the main characters in both movies and conforming to the basic structure of the martyrdom narrative is the concept of insider vs. outsider. In both films a reversal takes place in the protagonist's status from relative insider to outsider. The process in question can be described more specifically in terms of a 'casting out'. This terminology is literally used in the case of Bess when her mother warns her: 'You have no idea what it means to be cast out. You'll have nothing. Nothing, Bess! I have seen strong men and women wither away after being cast out. You are not strong, Bess. You are a feeble girl. It would kill you, Bess' (scene 180).[30] Such an act of exclusion turns the insider into an 'outcast' and is often expressed in the expelling of the victim to a place outside of the community. Stephen is dragged out of the city before he is stoned (Acts 7.58); Bess is thrown out of the church, ostracized by family and friends, and finally consigned to 'hell' at her internment. Selma's trial serves a similar function of alienating her from the group. While as a foreigner she is literally an outsider, Selma initially has an insider status, in so far as she lives in the US, has a job, and plays a major role in the community theater's production of the *Sound of Music*. Yet she ends up losing it all: her job, her role in the play, and ultimately her life, as she is denied the mercy of the American people and sentenced to death.

In both cases, however, the status of the main character is not as clear-cut as it may seem. On the one hand, Bess is an insider as far as the local community and church are concerned; but on the other hand, she is considered not 'right in the head' and a half-wit by the other members of that same community. As I. Makarushka notes: 'Her otherness is interpreted as a flaw, an emotional deficit.'[31] Selma

29. 'Interview with Lars von Trier', in L. von Trier, *Dancer in the Dark* (London: FilmFour Books, 2000), p. ix. See also J. Stevenson, *Lars von Trier* (London: British Film Institute, 2002), p. 90.

30. L. von Trier, *Breaking the Waves* (London: Faber & Faber, 1996). References to the scenes are based on the script in this book.

31. I.S.M. Makarushka, 'Transgressing Goodness in *Breaking the Waves*', in S.B. Plate and D. Jasper (eds.), *Imag(in)ing Otherness: Filmic Visions of Living Together* (Atlanta: Scholars Press, 1999), pp. 61-80 (66).

is also not a complete insider in DD, because she is an immigrant (from a communist country!) and is also going blind (an outsider physically), both of these elements being played out against her at the trial. Moreover, both characters can also
be viewed as consciously crossing borders for the sake of love. In their discussion
of BW, K. Keefer and T. Linafelt observe:

> The coming together of Bess and Jan physically both mirrors and depends upon
> the overcoming of the communal borders set up by Bess's church and embodied
> by the elders. Jan and his friends from the oil rig are patently presented as out-
> siders, whom Bess is introducing into this place in which they seem so foreign.
> The character of Bess embodies the erotic impulse toward border-crossing and the
> mixing of realms.[32]

A similar observation can be made with respect to DD, in which Selma has moved
to the States to receive the necessary eye operation for her son: 'That's why I came
to America. Because in America they can give Gene an operation' (p. 29).[33]

In terms of the rhetorical force of von Trier's basic plot line, the insider–outsider
distinction occurs within the context of a reversal but not subversion of (liberation
from) this opposition. In BW there exists an initial opposition between the local
community and especially Jan as outsider, but there is also the more fundamental
opposition between Bess and the religious community to which she belongs, which
grows as the story develops. J. Bekkenkamp points out that a dramatic climax is
reached in the confrontation between the fundamentalism of the church and the
child-like faith of Bess when she enters the church and responds to the minister,
who has stated that sinners can only achieve perfection through unconditional love
for the law. She tells him, 'I don't understand what you're saying. How can you
love a word? You cannot love words. You cannot be in love with a word. You can
love another human being. That's perfection.'[34] Although Bess is thrown out of the
church as a result, in the end the seemingly superior morality of the community is
replaced by that of Bess; this quality is symbolized in the closing scene by the
church bells, which proclaim the divine blessing 'from above' bestowed upon her
post mortem.[35] Stephen's vision of Christ at the right hand of God is comparable,

---

32. K. Keefer and T. Linafelt, 'The End of Desire: Theologies of Eros in the Song of Songs
and *Breaking the Waves*', in Plate and Jasper (eds.), *Imag(in)ing Otherness*, pp. 49-60 (55-56).

33. References to the pages of the script of DD are from von Trier, *Dancer in the Dark*.

34. J. Bekkenkamp, 'Breaking the Waves: Corporeality and Religion in a Modern Melodrama', in J. Bekkenkamp and M. de Haardt (eds.), *Begin with the Body: Corporeality, Religion
and Gender* (Leuven: Peeters Press, 1998), pp. 134-56 (146). What is said in the movie differs here
from the script (cf. scene 193).

35. According to Bekkenkamp, the scene with the bells refers 'both to Jan's resurrection and
Bess's posthumous heavenly canonization and to the glorification of the phallus' ('Breaking the
Waves', p. 154; cf. S. Heath, 'God, Faith and Film: *Breaking the Waves*', *Literature and Theology*
12 [1998], pp. 93-107 [103], who argues that 'the final shot is the validation of [what it thus
confirms as] her martyrdom…'). Makarushka elaborates upon this further, arguing that the bells
ringing out over the ocean can be interpreted as an ironic or even cynical interpretation of the status
of women in patriarchal religious traditions. She interprets the bells as 'huge bronze womb-like
vessels that contain within them the phallic ringer giving voice to her desire' ('Transgressing

although rather than dying with the bold proclamations of Stephen, Bess herself expires in despair and self-doubt. In DD the opposition is rather between the American civil society's and Selma's sense of justice, but here too a reversal takes place. The justice of Selma (her commitment to save her son's eyes and her promise to keep Bill's secret) is shown to be superior to that of the American legal system. Overall, then, in both BW and DD the opponents are depicted as legalists, who claim the Word of God (BW) or the word of civil law (DD). In both cases the opposition to the 'legalists' remains intact and starkly contrasted with the 'good' character of the protagonist. The comparison leaves little doubt as to the locus of von Trier's own sympathies: it lies neither with the religious/faith community nor with the American judicial system, but instead with the victim, who embodies opposition to the tyranny of both.

The reversal, however, seems to result in the martyr becoming another tyrant of sorts. This is perhaps most apparent when the martyr's decisions are imposed on the other characters in the films. Neither Jan in BW nor Gene in DD have a say in the final decision of the one who, while claiming to love them, is driven by her ideal and is willing to sacrifice her life to attain it. Jan is said to be dying when Bess makes up her mind to go back to the ship. As Makarushka observes in her discussion of BW, 'Jan's salvation is inscribed, or perhaps incised, on Bess's body by the man who rapes and kills her'.[36] In DD, Gene is completely unaware of his mother's plan to procure an operation for him, since it is supposed to remain a secret. Confronted with the ultimate choice between his eyes or her life, Selma chooses to die. The visualization of her agony and the physical violence she undergoes when put to death are probably the most chilling scenes of the movie. In the end, however, both protagonists quite literally receive a blessing, symbolized by the church bells in BW and by Gene's glasses, which Selma clutches in her hands before she dies. These signs represent their vindication as well as the validation by the (male) film writer of the worthiness of this particular kind of female self-sacrifice.

Thus in both cases, be it in different ways, their moral victory is complete. They embody 'true' virtue and value over against a starkly and dimly constructed adversary, but, like the imposition of religious values by the community in BW and of judicial values by the legal system in DD, it is a 'virtue' imposed upon those who did not ask for it. Very much like the traditional presentation of the martyr, the image of the victim is used in both movies to exert control over others, both from within the narrative/script and from without as well (in this case over the viewer). In the story about the stoning of Stephen, for instance, this character functions as *paradeigma* and endeavors to inscribe a particular pattern of belief and virtue, condemning narratively the 'opponents' while simultaneously shaping the character of the 'spectator'. The graphic nature of both Bess's and Selma's death similarly utilizes violent images to entrench the strongly moralistic value system of the

Goodness', p. 77). It is not evident, however, that von Trier himself shares this ironical, cynical perspective (Stevenson, *von Trier*, pp. 91-92).

36. Makarushka, 'Transgressing Goodness', p. 76.

writer/filmmaker.[37] The killing of Stephen in Acts is likewise graphically portrayed, with the same result: vivid imagery impacts and potently inscribes the scripted scenario and its rhetorical, ideological agenda on the spectator. Von Trier can thus be seen adopting discursive structures from the martyrdom narratives, although he also redirects them, more specifically against those communities he intends to criticize: be it the religious community in BW or the justice system of the US. According to Makarushka, in BW von Trier plays 'with traditional Christian notions of sacrifice and miracles, but deliberately subverts them through his implicit criticism of organized or denominational religions that disallow that which he values most: freedom, art, pleasure, desire, and sensuality'.[38]

It can be asked, however, whether von Trier is indeed all that subversive.[39] The values that are both reproduced and redirected in the movies are ultimately Judeo-Christian in orientation. The absolute value in both movies is that of love, though not necessarily of God, as both main characters give their life out of love for someone else. In the case of Bess this love is religiously motivated, even though it brings her into conflict with the Christian community to which she initially belongs. As with the Stephen narrative, she is cast out by 'her own'. She is 'stoned' by the children of her own community, connecting the image of the martyred Stephen with the 'woman caught in adultery' of the Fourth Gospel.[40] In DD, no explicit reference to religion is made, but the ideal is basically the same: Selma sacrifices herself (in more than one way) so that Gene may see. Here the ideal appears more radically 'secularized' than in BW.[41] Still, the overarching structural similarity is striking:

---

37. Keefer and Linafelt note that we are denied access to the scene of Bess's sacrifice because it takes place off-camera ('End of Desire', pp. 58-59). The violence she undergoes, however, is shown when she first visits the ship (scene 191) and suggested by her battered body when she is brought to the hospital (scene 227). The violence done to Bess is thus left to the viewer's imagination.

38. Makarushka, 'Transgressing Goodness', p. 75.

39. In his essay 'Death and the Maiden', in E. Wright and E. Wright (eds.), *The Žižek Reader* (Oxford/Cambridge: Basil Blackwell, 1999), pp. 206-21, S. Žižek formulates this question in somewhat different terms when he asks: 'what if the appearance of the strict opposition between the dry orthodox Letter of ritual (which regulates life in the Protestant community) and the living Spirit of true belief beyond dogma (of Bess) is misleading?' (p. 217). According to Žižek, both poles are ultimately on the same side. The conflict as presented by von Trier is one between tradition, represented by the institutional Church, and postmodernity, represented by the miracle of the bells, which indicate a return to 'a pre-modern "enchanted universe" in which miracles effectively do occur, as an aesthetic spectacle, without "really believing it", but also without ironic or cynical distance' (p. 219). Essentially missing, then, is the third term—modernity—with its permissive subject that avoids fixed obligations.

40. E. Ziolkowski (*Evil Children in Religion, Literature, and Art* [Cross-Currents in Religion and Culture; New York: Palgrave, 2001], p. 174) compares this scene to the mockery of Elisha in 2 Kgs 2.23-24, as the boys assault Bess 'in the same spirit of irreverence in which those ancient sons of Bethel derided God's prophet. The minister who shoos them away may seem to fulfil a protective role analogous to that of Elisha's bears.'

41. In BW, Bess's love for God and Jan cannot be neatly separated. Keefer and Linafelt draw a parallel here between the allegorical interpretations of the Song of Songs and the character of Bess: 'As human sexuality and theology mingle in the allegorical commentaries on the Song of Songs, so

not only does the love of another human being somehow replace the ideal of love for God or faith as an absolute value, but it is also highly gendered in so far as the female protagonist gives her life for her husband (in the case of Bess) or her son (in the case of Selma), thus reflecting traditional gender stereotypes.[42] In BW, Bess makes this sacrifice to save Jan's life: 'Jan will get well. I know that now. I made a sacrifice and he will get well' (scene 150). Bess even states that she has died already: 'When I made up my mind to follow Jan, I died' (scene 202). In DD, Selma gives her life so that Gene 'would be able to see his grandchildren' (p. 136). In both cases the women perceive this sacrifice to be their own choice. When Dr Richardson tells Bess that she cannot let someone control her the way Jan is doing, she replies: 'I choose for myself…to give Jan his dreams' (scene 181). In Selma's case, she ultimately decides that the money has to go to Gene's operation rather than to another attorney for herself, well aware that the implication is that she will die.

Also noteworthy is the fact that the female protagonists, who have the courage to face their fate, the control to choose it, and the resolve to commit themselves to the path chosen, are largely validated in the movies by the main male characters. In BW, Jan calls Bess 'special', 'fantastic', and 'strong' (scene 45), and Dr Richardson later calls her 'very special' (scene 181) and 'good' (scene 233). In DD, outside of Kathy's validations, Selma is equally bolstered by male affirmation. Bill refers to her as being 'strong' (p. 30) and Jeff calls her 'a beautiful lady' (p. 141). In both cases the gendered nature of von Trier's characters is simultaneously a vital and ambivalent feature of their portrayal. On the one hand, the traditional masculine image of self-mastery and strength of the martyr remains intact and the female protagonists are praised for incorporating these qualities. On the other, this characterization does not imply a subversion of their gender roles per se. Bess and Selma remain safely within the boundaries of such traditional female roles as nourishing woman, submissive wife, seductive whore, and self-sacrificing mother. This portrayal represents a serious domestication of the female characters, while perhaps bearing out some implications as well for the trope of the martyr. The characterization of the female as 'relational' serves to heighten the tragic dimension of their death, as the spectator looks on in horror at the fate but also in admiration for the woman, who fulfils her 'truest essence' as 'lover' at the very moment in which she sacrifices herself (or is sacrificed by the script/or) for the 'other'. In this respect, the

do Bess's desire for God and her desire for Jan come together' ('End of Desire', p. 59). Bekkenkamp goes a step further. According to her, Jan becomes God for Bess ('Breaking the Waves', p. 154).

42. Bekkenkamp makes a similar observation with respect to BW: 'As for the interaction between gender and religion, this film reconfirms thoroughly archaic gender roles and makes them appear authentic' ('Breaking the Waves', p. 153). A different perspective is offered by Makarushka, who considers it 'possible to see *Breaking the Waves* not only as a painful representation of the life of a woman in a culture over-determined by a rigid patriarchal religious tradition, but also as a condemnation of that culture and its destructive effects' ('Transgressing Goodness', p. 63). Granted that von Trier intends to criticize rigid patriarchal structures, the selfless 'love-ethic' he offers in its place is still fully grounded in the same structures of biblical discourse and hardly seems more liberating for women.

mother of *4 Maccabees* presents an interesting comparison, because the woman is praised precisely as 'mother' of the seven sons. The 'relational' quality of her female identity is a dominant feature, and the tragic proportions of the entire sequence of male torture and death are thus intensified as a result, since the mother watches the self-sacrifice of each of her male offspring.[43]

Thus, the martyr for von Trier is a devoted wife and loving mother, the affirmation of 'essential' features of female identity in the 'modern' world. This stands, even if the image of Bess as the 'obedient' and 'submissive' wife seems undermined by the types of activities in which she engages, since Bess ends up becoming a 'whore' for her husband, which is presented as one of the stages towards her ultimate self-sacrifice. The same is the case with Selma, who gives up her own life and sight so that her son may have eyes to see. While this second image may be more palatable to the tastes of contemporary viewers, the basic structures are identical: both women sink into the depths of human despair in order to save their beloved. The christological overtones are hard to avoid, and the added features of reconciliation, redemption and forgiveness between Bess and her mother and Selma and Kathy, both at the moment before death, make such parallels even harder to ignore.[44]

In line with von Trier's vision of the descent into despair/degradation, the martyrs herein are not completely devoid of self-doubt, as both Bess and Selma subscribe to the value system that leads to their ultimate exclusion. With respect to BW, as S. Žižek observes, 'the film establishes a fundamental Prohibition which opens up the space for authentic Transgression'.[45] Indeed, Bess is convinced that she is a 'sinner' in doing what she does and Jan acknowledges Bess's evaluation when he tells Terry that 'she would never have another lover in her life, with me lying here, if I had not told her that it was for me. She loves me so much' (scene 117). Bess expresses this conviction to Dodo when she says: 'He is my husband and God has said I must honour him' (scene 154). Her self-perception is also apparent from the dialogues she has with 'God', in which she calls herself stupid and confesses she has sinned. Yet she believes she is not rejected for doing so: 'Dear God, I have sinned', says Bess; 'Mary Magdalene sinned too, yet she is among my dearly beloved', replies 'God' (scene 139). In DD, Selma equally assumes responsibility (in her case for having had Gene) and is literally willing to

---

43. The narrator in fact explicitly plays on familial ties at length (cf. the emphasis on brotherly love in *4 Macc.* 13.19-27 and motherly love in 14.11–17.6; 18.6-9). In Perpetua's case this is less true, however. As Perpetua's impending fate approaches, she shuns her gendered roles, leaving behind her child (her breast milk in fact dries up) and father (cf. Castelli, '"I Will Make Mary Male"', pp. 35-39, who notes the increasing feminization of the father in relation to Perpetua's movement towards masculinity).

44. Bekkenkamp points to the double role of Christ in BW as 'Bess symbolizes the crucifixion and Jan the resurrection' ('Breaking the Waves', p. 153). A similar observation is made by Žižek, who notes that 'Jan's miraculous healing is the answer of the Real to her absolute sacrifice; that is, it is literally *over her dead body* that he rises up again' ('Death and the Maiden', p. 213; cf. Heath, 'God, Faith, and Film', p. 103).

45. Žižek, 'Death and the Maiden', p. 217.

pay for it. She refers to the situation as being her fault. When Bill asks her why, she replies, 'I knew he would have the same bad eyes as me, but I had him all the same' (p. 30). She offers a similar reply to Jeff, saying she has no excuse for having given birth to Gene: 'I just so much wanted to hold a little baby in my arms' (p. 142). Saving money is an act of restitution; giving her life (working herself 'to the bone') is the sacrifice she is willing to make to enable him to see. Both women are thus willing to transgress socially erected boundaries in order to achieve what they want, driven as they are by 'selfless love'.[46] And, as in classic martyrdom typologies, all of this is done on a purely voluntary basis, with both protagonists having ample opportunity to turn back at various stages along the way to their final demise (and indeed being urged to do so by both Dodo and Kathy).

As the victim who is sacrificed for her beloved, both characters undergo verbal as well as physical violence in the process. Bess is called names by Dodo ('stupid') and by the boys who throw stones at her ('tart'). She is abused twice by the sailors, the second time fatally so. Selma undergoes both types of violence too. She is robbed by Bill and then threatened by him with his gun (p. 83). She is accused by the prosecuting attorney of selfishness, robbery, murder, lying, vanity, and found guilty of murder in the first degree. She is also called 'a hard woman' by her friend Kathy, who ends up threatening her as well (in suggesting she will lie about the money and prevent Gene from receiving his operation), because Selma does not want another defense attorney. The final act of violence Selma endures is being hanged. The violence in word and deed thus effectively inscribes the bodies of Bess and Selma as ultimate sacrificial victims, with both characters having their own Gethsemanic moment of resolution towards their impending fates (Bess on the boat, Selma as she counts her steps while walking to the gallows).[47] Although bearing a secularized imprint, the *imitatio Christi* is patent—these two truly bear the marks of Christ. As such martyrs for their cause, for their faith, for their love, Bess and Selma also inadvertently reinscribe the very tyranny to which they have fallen victim. Gone is the ambiguity of moral dilemma; it is replaced with the overt moralism of von Trier's world, wherein these women suffer and die for love and 'submit' to their female place. The martyrdom imagery thus works rather effectively for von Trier. With weak/ened and ineffectual men (Bill and Jan) or a physically infirm (male) child (Gene), all of whom have trouble 'seeing' (let alone believing), the only hope is for a strong woman to love such males as these. And love here is the martyr's path: nourishing unto and through death, their bodies being transformed through and in suffering to bring life.

It is an irony, but not a surprise, that such a simplistic moral universe should evolve from the use of the martyr's image. Von Trier's attempts to subvert the shallow happy ending of the Hollywood musical in DD and the overt faith-based ending of Carl Theodor Dreyer's *Ordet* (1954; in which the female protagonist is

---

46. Ironically, both characters are labeled 'selfish', albeit for different reasons. Bess refers to herself this way (scene 56); Selma is accused of being so at her trial (pp. 104, 110).

47. Ziolkowski sees an analogy between Bess struggling uphill with her moped, being pursued by the children, and Christ ascending Calvary with his cross (*Evil Children*, p. 173).

literally resurrected) in BW, ultimately fail, done in by the very images utilized for subversion. Von Trier's aspiration to provide a way out of the optimistic and simplistic worlds of these alternatives does not bear fruit because the martyr's narrative world is no less simplistic and no less optimistic. And the structures of its discourse are powerful enough that even those who would use the image of the martyr to victimize others cannot, finally, escape the tyranny of the martyr themselves.

At the same time, however, von Trier leaves us with a troubling question with respect to the image of the martyr he has taken over and reconfigured. The ancient martyrdom narrative represented a distinctive Jewish and Christian challenge to the ideological power claims of opposing texts and communities. The martyr was a powerbroker, who demonstrated a 'different' kind of strength and virtue, and who, in that role, called into question the power of the antagonist. In von Trier's vision, however, the female trope of martyrdom represents a full immersion of the image in cultural gender stereotypes. There is no fundamental challenge here; no distinctive articulation of unique, counter-cultural identity. While the classical image is no less problematic, it does function in quite a different manner. In the end, Von Trier has left us with a stereotypical pattern of 'virtue', which ultimately domesticates the power of the martyr.

INTERNET MARTYRS AND VIOLENCE: VICTIMS AND/OR PERPETRATORS?

Jan Willem van Henten

1. *Introduction*

Living in the land of Israel for a year made a long time object of my studies suddenly a highly relevant item. Palestinian vans with slogans like 'rather dead than slaves' passed me while I drove the kids to school after buses started being attacked. To my surprise, the Maccabaean martyrs of twenty-two centuries ago still triggered a serious interest among a broader Jewish audience. At the same time, broadcast interviews and comments as well as personal talks showed that very different views of martyrdom were involved. Those who are martyrs in the eyes of the supporters of the Al-Aqsa Martyrs Brigade are terrorists for others. Anyone who might have doubted such opposed perspectives knows better after 'September 11'. Reading one ancient Jewish and Christian martyr text after another in the National Library in Jerusalem I was struck by the interviews with surviving relatives (mothers!) of the Palestinian suicide bombers about the reward for their child, brother or sister, and so on, because they echoed in several respects the ancient Jewish martyr texts. Comments by writers, journalists and ordinary people suggest that the Palestinians are the Jews of modern times. I will not pursue this analogy, which no doubt is painful for many on both sides. However, the correspondences between the ancient sources about the martyrdom of Jews and Christians and present day statements about Palestinians considered martyrs, calls for an inventory of current ideas on martyrdom. 'September 11' raised the issue again, because some consider its victims martyrs, but others the hijackers! On 6 May 2002, the Dutch anti-establishment politician Pim Fortuyn was shot dead in the middle of an unbelievably successful campaign. Jan Banks, a well-known history professor at Leiden University, prophesied in a leading Dutch newspaper (NRC) that Fortuyn would become a martyr soon. But what is a martyr, exactly, according to contemporary statements? What is understood as a deed of martyrdom, if more than being the victim of senseless violence is involved? Are there any shifts concerning the meaning of 'martyr' in contemporary sources if we compare them to the ancient, 'classical' and even canonical materials?

This paper is a first attempt to explore contemporary meanings of martyrdom, by using one powerful medium, the Internet, as basic source material. The Internet offers many relevant databases, reports, articles and comments, as well as websites devoted partly or entirely to martyrdom. Who is considered a martyr according to these sources? I decided not to work with more or less professional websites or search machines devoted to religion, but to use Google as my search engine. Google presents its results in order of frequency of citation by other web pages and number of visitors, meaning that the first dozens of results are the most popular pages among—let's say—a total of 5000. I collected such pages during several periods of the academic year 2000–2001 by searching the phrase 'martyrs' itself, as well as the string of 'martyrs and violence'. At the end of this article there is a list of the top 100 results of my last search of the term 'martyrs' in current web pages (1 May 2002): this list supplies the title, address and a brief indication of content. I put all the results of my searches in databases, using them as raw material for this discussion. I opted for the string 'martyrs and violence' in my second search, because I observed a significant shift in the meanings of martyrdom with respect to the link between martyrdom and violence. Ancient Jewish and Christian 'martyrs' are always presented as victims of gruesome persecutions; but they remain passive in their resistance to the aggressor, sometimes so persistently that it infuriated their opponents. Contemporary martyrs, not only the Palestinian Al-Aqsa Martyrs Brigade or the perpetrators of September 11, present themselves as victims of state or other collective violence. The violence they or their group undergoes legitimates acts of 'martyrdom' that cause extreme violence in their turn.

2. Who is a Martyr?

The phrase 'martyr' has become a fixed expression for people who die a heroic death for a specific cause, especially a religious conviction or practice. Before a discussion of current views, a brief survey of hitherto accepted definitions may be helpful. Scholarly definitions of 'martyrdom' often consider the aspect of witness or confession as central characteristic, taking the semantic development of Greek *martys* ('witness') and the related verb *martyrein* into the title 'martyr' and 'die a martyr's death' in early Christian writings as point of departure (e.g. *Martyrdom of Polycarp* 1.1; cf. 2.1; 14.2).[1] The notion of 'witness' is important in Islamic sources also. The Arabic term *shaheed* for 'martyr' is, like its Christian counterpart, linked to a verb meaning 'to witness'.[2] The oldest Jewish martyr texts lack technical terminology for the phenomenon, but from the third century CE onwards we find such terminology in rabbinic writings: *Qiddush ha-Shem* (the Sanctification of God's Name) and *Asarah Haruge Malkhut* for a specific group of martyrs (the Ten Killed by the [Roman] Government).[3] Yet, the phenomenon of martyrdom is older

---

    1.   B. Dehandschutter and J.W. van Henten, 'Einleitung', in J.W. van Henten, B. Dehand-schutter and H.J.W. van der Klaauw (eds), *Die Entstehung der jüdischen Martyrologie* (SPB, 38; Leiden: E.J. Brill, 1989), pp. 1-19 (5-8); A.M. Schwemer, 'Prophet, Zeuge und Märtyrer: Zur Entstehung des Märtyrerbegriffs im frühesten Christentum', *ZTK* 96 (1999), pp. 320-50.
    2.   E. Kohlberg, 'Shahid', in C.E. Bosworth *et al.* (eds.), *Encyclopaedia of Islam* (Leiden: E.J. Brill, 1995), IX, pp. 203-207.
    3.   J.W. van Henten and F. Avemarie, *Martyrdom and Noble Death: Selected Texts from Graeco-Roman, Jewish, and Christian Antiquity* (London: Routledge, 2002), pp. 2-4, with refer-ences.

than the Christian or Jewish terminology that indicates it, which calls for a func-tional definition. The 'classical' Jewish and Christian sources present a martyr as a person who, in an extreme hostile situation, prefers a violent death to compliance with a demand of the (usually foreign) oppressive authorities. Therefore, the martyr dies for a cause, whether religious or political, or both.[4] The young Roman woman Perpetua, to give just one example, refused to sacrifice for the wellbeing of the emperor in the early third century CE and, as the consequence of this refusal, had to fight a mad heifer in the arena (*Passion of Perpetua* 6 and 20).[5] Dying for a cause is also emphasized in Eugene and Anita Weiner's definition, who state that there are three ways of becoming a martyr: (1) choosing to suffer or die rather than give up one's faith or principles; (2) being tortured or killed because of one's convictions; (3) suffering great pain or misery for a long time.[6]

The Google list at the end of this article calls for a few brief comments. First, several sites concern institutions named after martyrs, and the relevance of those sites for this discussion varies from zero to highly relevant, depending on the link between the name and experiences of martyrdom. This list includes a nightclub and restaurant in Chicago (nos. 2, 88), a UK soccer club (nos. 23, 25), a music album by Roger Daltrey (no. 46, selection of best songs), two novels (nos. 21, 82), a dozen of mostly Roman Catholic parish churches (nos. 47, 48, 56, 64, 66, 68, 74, 79, 85, 87, 92, 94), but also two references to an Ugandan university named after Roman Catholic martyrs in that country (nos. 36, 41; cf. 50). In one clear case of zero relevance the name comes from the surname Martyr (the bus company of no. 80). Less clear is the reference to the Theatre of Martyrs, located at the Martyrs' Place in Brussels (no. 39). The website offers, among other things, the program of the theatre. Visitors of this location will note, however, that the Martyrs' Place in Brussels commemorates the victims of the Belgian rebellion against the Dutch, which began during the performance of Daniel-François-Esprit Auber's *La Muette de Portici* in 1830 in the opera theatre at this location. This already gives us a hint that not all martyrs die for religious causes.

Remarkably, most web pages refer to older martyrs, from antiquity up to the nineteenth century, and some of these offer elaborate and professional websites offering a wealth of information about these martyrs. Apparently, older martyrs still trigger a lot of admiration if not necessarily devotion for many, and one wonders why. This group includes well-known ancient Christian martyrs like Perpetua (no. 33), the Martyrs of Lyons and Vienne (no. 63), the Scillitan martyrs (no. 31; also 15, 32, 58, 73), and three entries of the 1913 *Catholic Encyclopedia*, available on

---

4.   Van Henten and Avemarie, *Martyrdom and Noble Death*. See also the discussions of martyrdom by Leigh Gibson, Todd Penner and Caroline Vander Stichele, as well as Yvonne Sher-wood in the present volume.

5.   D. Boyarin, *Dying for God: Martyrdom and the Making of Christianity and Judaism* (Figurae; Stanford: Stanford University Press, 1999), p. 109, argues that there were three basic constituents in late ancient Jewish and Christian presentations of martyrs: (1) a ritualised and performative speech act; (2) the fulfilment of a religious mandate; and (3) powerful erotic elements.

6.   E. Weiner and A. Weiner, *The Martyr's Conviction: A Sociological Analysis* (BJS, 203; Atlanta: Scholars Press, 1990), p. 9.

the Internet and offering discussions of martyrs according to the official Roman Catholic calendar of martyrs, beginning with Stephen as the first martyr and the first Pope.[7] Christian martyrs from later times are prominent as well, be they of the Roman Catholic Church (nos. 16, 22, 24, 38, 42, 65, 70, 71, 86, 89, 93) or other Churches. There are seven references to *Foxe's Book of Martyrs* (nos. 5, 10, 12, 60, 67, 90, 96), a sixteenth-century work about ancient Christian and Reformation martyrs.[8] One website commemorates the martyrs of the Covenanted Reformation (sixteenth-century England, no. 77), and two Greek-Orthodox sites honour the royal family of Nicholas II as martyrs (nos. 54, 57). Two sites refer to the huge Mennonite book of martyrs called *The Martyrs' Mirror*, and link it to educational activities (nos. 29, 81). If we take the search for 'martyrs and violence' in to account as well, an elaborate website about recent Coptic martyrs should be added to this group.[9]

Most of the martyrs mentioned thus far are considered martyrs because they died for their 'faith'. They were victims of violence against their religion, or against themselves as religious people. Contemporary believers commemorate their deaths, transmit and study the texts about their martyrdom and consider these a source for meditation and inspiration. A communal bond of religion and denomination is thus shared. Religion is not the only motive even in these cases, since in some borderline cases Church and other politics or ethnic conflicts are involved too.[10] An obvious example are the Roman Catholic so-called Irish Hunger Martyrs (no. 38). Here religious and ethnic identities go hand in hand, because these Irish martyrs remained steadfast against the English Protestant Church missions that tried to convert them to Protestantism by offering them food during the severe period of starvation in 1845–52. The site gives us a glimpse of the actual relevance of older martyrs for present people, because it includes a petition for the beatification of these martyrs by the Vatican that can be signed by its visitors. Apparently these martyrs are considered model figures that exemplify Irish identity into the twenty-first century.[11]

Strikingly, the sites devoted to recent or contemporary martyrs form the minority in the top 100. Many of those concern persecuted Christians again (nos. 1, 4, 6, 9, 13, 20, 50, 52, 53, 76, 91); but one is linked to the Jerusalem memorial foundation for the Shoah victims, Yad va-Shem, and commemorates the Jewish victims of the Second World War (no. 9; cf. 99). Three sites, all containing articles (below), concern Palestinian martyrs (nos. 35, 43, 78). These and the Yad va-Shem site call

---

7.   *Catholic Encyclopedia* from 1913. Cited 22 April 2002. Online: <http://www. newadvent. org/cathen/>. It is possible that several of the web pages referred to in this article are now temporarily or permanently unavailable, but I have decided to include these references nevertheless because they were on line when I made my inventories.

8.   <http://www.ccel.org/f/foxe_j/martyrs/begin.htm>.

9.   <http://www.copts.net/martyrs.asp>.

10.   For example, the web pages on Nicholas II and his family as martyrs (nos. 28, 54 and 57).

11.   For procedures of beatification and sanctification, as well as tensions between local initiatives and Vatican bureaucracy, see K.L. Woodward, *Making Saints: How the Catholic Church Determines Who Becomes a Saint, Who Doesn't, and Why* (New York: Touchstone, 1996).

for an elaboration of the definition of 'martyr', because there are obvious discrepancies between their definitions of 'martyr' and the one given above. Hardly any of the six million Shoa victims did have something of a choice to save his or her life by giving in to the authorities, and some even consider the phrase 'martyr' blasphemous for these victims for just this reason.[12] For a substantial part of those considered Palestinian martyrs, exactly the opposite is true: they die during a violent action or even determine their own death by a violent act of suicide, which explains why they are sometimes called 'suicide martyrs'. All this is highly problematic from the perspective of 'canonical' views on martyrdom. Besides, in both cases religion may be a factor, but cultural, ethnic or national identities seem more important.[13] Thus, the concept of 'martyr' has become broader in several ways according to the Internet sources. Martyrdom can have cultural, political, ethnic and national dimensions with or without a religious connotation.

The remaining sites of the top 100 confirm this extension of the concept and broaden it up in yet other directions, relativizing even the element of a violent death. Four web pages connected to national or ethnic entities commemorate their own martyrs: Tamil Tigers, Indians from the Kargil and Sikhs (nos. 55, 69, 59 and 95).[14] The Sikhs of no. 95 boast of their glorious martyrdom tradition, and the site lists many of their heroes as martyrs. It presents martyrdom as an important institution of Sikh religion. It sets it apart at the same time as a complete departure from the ascetic and pacifist Indian traditions. The basic idea is explained by Guru Nanak's hymn, 'Japu Ji', as living according to the will of God and an (altruistic) game of love: 'Should thou seek to engage in the game of Love, step into my street with thy head placed on thy palm: While stepping on to this street, ungrudgingly sacrifice your head'.[15] The web pages about Tamils, Kargil Indians and Sikhs present their martyrs proudly as military heroes, in contradistinction to the early Jewish and Christian traditions about martyrs (but cf. no. 3).

Other pages refer to two other types of martyrs, labour activists and metric martyrs. Nos. 19, 34 and 98 mention the famous Haymarket martyrs, radicals who were charged as responsible for bombing and policemen's deaths a few days after a mass strike for the eight-hour working day in Chicago on 1 May 1886. Four of them were hanged, and one committed suicide just before the execution. The detailed report of José Martí, a leader of Cuba's struggle for independence, made them famous in- and outside the US. Seven were buried at the Haymarket Monument in Chicago, where other deceased radicals like Emma Goldman were deposited as well.[16] The Ascott martyrs (no. 18) are female labour activists, sixteen

---

12. See the discussion in B.L. Jongkind, *De heiliging van Gods naam: verzet en overgave van het joodse volk* (Kampen: Kok, 1991).

13. For fascinating case studies concerning contemporary Pakistan pointing out the interconnections between constructions of martyrdom and religious, cultural and ethnic identities, as well as social conflict and gender conventions, see O. Verkaaik, 'Political Violence in Hyderabad, Pakistan: May 1990 and Muharram 1950', *The Eastern Anthropologist* 53 (2000), pp. 351-66.

14. Cf. <http://www.allaboutsikhs.com/events/jwbagh.htm>.

15. <http://www.sikh-history.com/sikhhist/martyrs/right.html>.

16. W.T. Whitney, 'May Day and the Haymarket Martyrs', *Labor Standard* (no date). Cited 4 January 2003. Online: <http://www.igc.org/laborstandard/Vol1No3/MayDay.htm>.

women from Ascott in Oxfordshire sent to prison in 1873 for their participation in the founding of the National Agricultural Labourers' Union in 1873. Queen Victoria remitted their sentences and 'the women were welcomed back into the village as martyrs'.[17] A slightly older male group of labour activists are the Tol-puddle martyrs (nos. 7, 100), who were convicted to forced labour in Australia in 1834 for setting up a union. They have their own museum now in Tolpuddle, Dorset, England.

Probably the loosest use of the phrase 'martyr' concerns the metric martyrs (nos. 14, 40), British retailers (and their supporters) who refuse to use the 'European' metric system of weights which has become the legal requirement in the UK. That this is a matter worthy of great sacrifice is, of course, hard to grasp for Europeans from the Continent, but a discussion at a local market in Northumberland recently made me understand that this counts as a crucial identity matter, at least for some.

A final group of pages in the top 100 concerns online articles about martyrs (nos. 11, 35, 43, 44, 49, 62, 78, 83, 99), and in one case a larger work in an electronic version (no. 72). Four of those concern Palestinian martyrs (nos. 35, 43, 78, 83), all written by non-Palestinian authors.[18] 'Making Martyrs' by Martin Himmel (no. 78), offers statements by Palestinians about their fascination with and legitimation of martyrdom. Himmel reports talks with two fathers of Palestinian martyrs, and a psychiatrist who explains the mentality leading to the decision to become a *shaheed*.[19] One of the martyrs, Mazen Badawi, a married Hamas fighter with one child and a pregnant wife, indicated explicitly that he wanted to become a martyr by leaving behind a videotaped statement and phoning his father an hour before the deed that led to his death (see further below). Not everybody admires martyrdom, though, as is apparent from H.L. Mencken's sceptical view, which ranks as no. 11 in the top 100 (cf. no. 49). R. Emmett Tyrrell Jr's article 'Mending the Minds of the "Martyrs"' for *The Washington Times* online (no. 83) criticizes Palestinian suicide martyrdom in the strongest terms, accusing Chairman Yasser Arafat of doing nothing against these horrible acts of terrorism which Tyrrell considers 'the most barbarous atrocities since the days of Japanese kamikazes', noting in an aside that the kamikaze pilots targeted soldiers only. He calls for Israelis to arrest the parents of suicide martyrs, because they should be 'held responsible for the slaughter their children have committed'. Greer Fay Cashman's article in the *Jerusalem Post* on-line (9 April 2002; no. 99) has the phrase 'martyrs' in its title: 'Holocaust Martyrs Remembered'. It is a report of the Holocaust Remembrance Day (8 April), includ-ing quotes from Israel's President Moshe Katsav and Prime Minister Ariel Sharon

---

17. The site commemorating these martyrs is set up by New Zealand descendants of some of these women.

18. One should note that there are several Palestinian-based websites commemorating Pales-tinian martyrs. But these did not make it into the top 100.

19. M. Himmel, 'Making Martyrs', *NewsHour* (19 March 2002). Online: <http://www. pbs. org/newshour/bb/middle_east/jan-june02/martyr_3-19.html>. See, for statements of 'mothers of martyrs', <http://www.washington-report.org/backissues/010201/0101009.html> and <http://www. memri.org/sd/SP2999.html>.

about Holocaust denial on the Internet, and the (current) 'global wave of violence and libel against Jews'. There is no explicit comment on the phrase 'martyr', but it may be linked to the following statement in the article: 'Katsav and Sharon marvelled that the Jewish people succeeded in maintaining humanity during the Holocaust, with many Jews risking their lives to save other Jews'.

Thus, the top 100 web pages about martyrs hardly elaborate what a martyr is. Yet, it is obvious that the term definitely denotes a wider meaning than the ancient vocabulary. First, for some, a violent death is not a pre-requisite, a justified cause that is important for a certain group's identity is enough to create a martyr (e.g. the Ascott martyrs and the metric martyrs). Second, the voluntary dimension of martyrdom is not self-evident any longer. Some of the martyrs in the list, such as the Holocaust martyrs and several Christian martyrs, were not in a situation to choose between life and martyrdom; they died as victims of Nazi or other collective violence. Nevertheless, survivors decided to commemorate them as martyrs. In this connection, the concept of martyrdom sometimes even seems to be interpreted in a broader sense, meaning that victims of meaningless or condemnable violence are martyrs and should be commemorated as such.[20] A highly significant shift of meaning is that, at least for some (not only Palestinians!), martyrs can be military figures. Those are even considered heroes when they cause extreme lethal violence against enemy civilians.

The second source of Internet material, the results of the searches into 'martyrs and violence', basically confirms these findings. I even found a few definitions of martyrdom in this material. In a statement after a shooting of seven people in a Baptist Church on 15 September 1999 in Fort Worth, Texas, Bishop Joseph P. Delaney of Fort Worth called the victims 'martyrs'. This remarkable statement for a Roman Catholic bishop linked the dead people to recent Catholic martyrs murdered in Guatemala and El Salvador in 1980–81: '…so many others who were engaged in the simple, everyday activity of spreading the word of Christ when slain… We consider them martyrs… So are they who were slain in this senseless tragedy.'[21] Thus, these Roman Catholic martyrs died for a religious cause, 'on duty', so to speak, victims of senseless violence like the Baptist believers. Being a victim of condemnable violence seems to be an important notion of contemporary martyrdom, which is not necessarily linked to religious identities. I came across the following types of martyrs in my second database (giving only one or two references by way of example in the footnotes):

(a) Anti-racism martyrs: Martin Luther King, Steve Biko and other individuals, Martyrs of Anti-Racist Resistance.[22]

---

20. See, for example, the commemoration of victims of 'September 11' as martyrs on <http://www.fallenmartyrs.com/> (see no. 6 in the Appendix).

21. <http://www.reformation.org/rome_calls_for_gun_control.html>.

22. <http://www.westminster-abbey.org/tour/martyrs/5_mlk.htm>; <http://www.gbgmmc. org/umw/readingprogram/education01.html>; <http://www.antiracist.org/articles/091600-ar-martyrs1.html> about the murder of Lin Newborn and Dan Shersty, 'two anti-racist skinheads', during the weekend of 4 July 1998.

(b)   Sexual martyrs: women victims of male violence;[23] homosexual mar-
        tyrs.[24]
(c)   Anti-globalization martyrs, sometimes linked to the nineteenth-century
        Tolpuddle martyrs (above).[25]
(d)   Anti-fascist martyrs: Manchester martyrs.[26]
(e)   Victims of school shootings: Cassie Bernall and others.[27]

One web page is anxious about future violence against Australian abortion doctors,
considering them potential martyrs.[28]

3. *Martyrs and Group Identities*

What makes a martyr a hero? Martyrs are always part of a group. They become
martyrs because others honour them as such. The Vatican's time-consuming process of beatifying or canonizing martyrs is just one example of this phenomenon.[29]
Anita and Eugene Weiner too emphasize a link between a martyr and his/her group:
'The martyr will be seen as a member of a suppressed group who, when given the
opportunity to renounce aspects of his or her group's code, willingly submits to
suffering and death rather than forsake a conviction'.[30] The posthumous group
function of martyrs is no less important, though. Their violent, ostensible if not
always spectacular, death is transmitted by communities of supporters and admir-
ers. Insiders of the martyrs' group receive, preserve, re-interpret (or sometimes
even invent?) and transmit the powerful scenes about these 'gladiators' to their own
group and, currently, often to the outside world also.[31] The 'victories of the arena'
become internalized and part of ritual practice as well. Communities of inside readers, listeners, viewers and/or participants in ritual meetings commemorate them.
Martyrs become the heroes of such communities, with whom the members may
want to identify, if only for a moment. The statement of Dr Iyahd Zaquout, a psychiatrist from Gaza, about Palestinian youngsters in the online article by Martin

23.   For Suman Chatterjee's songs about violence against Indian women called martyrs see:
<http://www.h-net.msu.edu/~asia/threads/sawom.html>.
24.   <http://www.hurricane.net/~wizard/0006.html>. Cf. <http://www.advocate.com/html/
stories/796/796_signorile.asp>. My findings include a reference to an article about victims of
violence because of their sexual orientation by David L. Kirp, 'Martyrs and Movies', <http://
www.prospect.org/print/V11/3/kirp-d.html>.
25.   <http://www.yahoo.com/group/queerflips/message/106>.
26.   <http://burn.ucsd.edu/archives/ats-l/1995.Jul/0025.html>.
27.   E.g. <http://www.nljonline.com/November1999/coverstory2.htm>. See Leigh Gibson's
contribution in this volume.
28.   <http://www.theaustralian.news.com.au/printpage/0,5942,2419847,00.html>. Cf. <http://
www.yankeesamizdat.org/ACBigots/FAQ.html>.
29.   Woodward, *Making Saints*.
30.   Weiner and Weiner, *The Martyr's Conviction*, p. 10.
31.   Leigh Gibson's case study in this volume brings fascinating material that can also help us
to understand this process in connection to the ancient writings about martyrdom better.

Himmel, confirms this process. Zaquout regretfully notes that the Palestinian suicide martyrs function as model figures for the Gaza children, who identify with
them and try to simulate their actions.[32]

Thus, martyrs have important social functions differentiating the 'us' and the
'them', as constructed in the documents about martyrdom. In my 1997 book I
applied the paradigm of the *reference group* to the Maccabaean martyrs, arguing
that the relevant sources construct them as exemplary figures, model citizens so to
speak, who indicate what other Jews should do in religious and political matters.
The martyrs function as a group that exemplifies important values and attitudes,
which the intended readers of the documents about them should have liked to share.
2 and *4 Maccabees* depict such martyrs as the ideal representatives of their group.[33]
A similar function seems valid for several of the early Christian documents about
martyrdom. The framework of *Perpetua's Passion* announces that the writing will
be passed on to other Christians, so that they could participate in the martyrs'
experiences (1.6). The redactor presents Perpetua and her fellow martyrs as models
of belief who yield to none of the old models (1.1-2; 21.11); the reading about these
model figures would make the Church stronger (21.11).

The contemporary materials clearly confirm that martyrs have everything to do
with group identities, whether religious, political, ethnic or otherwise. One of the
questions of a Dutch poll among 1000 people interviewed on the street just before
the Dutch Memorial Day for the victims of the Second World War (4 May 2002),
asked for examples of contemporary martyrs.[34] The most popular answer, despite
the obvious disgust of some respondents, was: 'the martyrs of the Middle East'. In
my view, this shows that the outsiders' perception, no doubt triggered by the media,
is that the perpetrators of Palestinian suicide actions are motivated by a national/
political cause. Palestinian statements, whether conveyed in their own sources (including websites) or through Western media, consistently present such martyrs as
heroes of the Palestinian people, who died for their land and state.[35] Those who are
martyrs for one group may be considered extreme terrorists by others, as the many
statements about the Palestinian martyrs as well as 'September 11' demonstrate.

32. <http://www.pbs.org/newshour/bb/middle_east/jan-june02/martyr_3-19.html>.
33. J.W. van Henten, *The Maccabean Martyrs as Saviours of the Jewish People* (JSJSup, 57;
Leiden: E.J. Brill, 1997), pp. 187-269.
34. The results of this NIPO poll were broadcasted on 4 May 2002, in the Evangelical
Broadcasting Society (EO) talk show 'Knevel op zaterdag' ('Knevel on Saturday').
35. See, e.g., <http://www.najah.edu/english/News/news.htm>; <http://www.pna.net/events/
daily_report_0801.htm>; <http://www.pna.net/events/daily_report_31.htm>; <http://www.pcbs.
org/english/martyrs1/table1_e.htm>; <http://www.pnic.gov.ps/arabic/quds/quds_en3.html>; *Al-
Risala* of 7 June 2001, about Sa'id Al-Hotari, the suicide bomber of the Tel Aviv disco, quoted by
Aluma Solnick, <http://www.memri.org>; <http://www.quorum.org/comment/20688> (comment by
Iden Rosenthal); <http://www.arabia.com/news/article/english/0,1690,46787,00.html>; <http://
www.najah.edu/english/News/news.htm> (for Palestinian and Iraqi martyrs alike); <http://www.
jmcc.org/research/special/toward.html>. Cf. the commemoration of the 1931 Indian martyrs in
Jammu and Kashmir at Khawaja Bazar as reported by <http://www.tribuneindia.com/20010714/
j&k.htm>; Indian Kargil martyrs: <http://www.hindustantimes.com/nonfram/260701/detNAT09.
asp>; <http://www.the-week.com/21jul29/daily.htm>; <http://www.indiavarta.com/gallery/>.

The breeding ground of these opposed views is much more complicated than a clash between West and East, as an interesting online report of 5 July 2001, about the besieged city of Dhala, Yemen, proves. The Yemen government described the victims of clashes between the army and citizens at Dhala as 'terrorists', whereas the local residents considered them 'martyrs'.[36]

4. *Martyrs and Violence: Victims and/or Perpetrators?*

What else do the web pages say about martyrdom and violence? A few trends may become apparent from the pages of the second search. Christian pages emphasize the peacefulness of martyrs, time and again, and often call to end violence. The greatest advocate of this is no doubt the present Pope. John Paul II is famous for surpassing his predecessors of the last 400 years in beatifications and sanctifications. By 11 March 2001, he had beatified 1227 and sanctified 477 saints (his predecessors 1310 and 300 respectively).[37] Many of these saints are martyrs, and one wonders why the Pope considers martyrs so important. The Internet references to his canonization of martyrs emphasize the fierce opposition and violence that Christians experienced in many recent hostile circumstances. The Pope, therefore, suggests a close link between martyrdom and violence against Christians in recent times. The Jubilee Year 2000 called, of course, for the commemoration of Roman Catholic martyrs. In a Jubilee service on 8 May 2000, the Pope paid tribute to modern martyrs and said that the 'hatred and exclusion, violence and murder' Christians experienced in the modern period resulted in more than 12,000 new Christian martyrs of the twentieth century.[38] Thus, the Pope considers martyrs as victims of violence (e.g. Nazi and Soviet terror), and undertakes great efforts to pay the appropriate tribute to them and their witness.[39] His commemoration of Christian

---

36. <http://www.yemen-observer.com/pols/jul05.html>.

37. <http://www.dailycatholic.org./issue/2001Mar/mar12nr1.htm>. At the end of 1995 he had finalized 208 beatifications and 38 sanctifications, which involved 875 individuals (Woodward, *Making Saints*, p. 5).

38. <http://news.bbc.co.uk/hi/english/world/europe/newsid_740000/740218.stm>. Web pages about beatification and sanctification include <http://www.dailycatholic.org/issue/2001Mar/mar12nr1.htm>, <http://www.cptryon.org/hoagland/travels/inno.html>, <http://www.cin.org/pope/beatification-spanish-martyrs.html> (Spanish martyrs); <http://www.catholic.org/media/news/archive/news062701.html>; <http://www.catholicnews.com/data/briefs/20010627.htm> (Ukrainian martyrs); <http://www.ewtn.com/library/papaldoc/jp950702.htm> (Slovakian martyrs); <http://www.hrschool.org/rghr/rpv2n44.htm> (Chinese martyrs, including victims of sexual violence); <http://www.cny.org/archive/ft/ft100500.htm> (Mother Drexel, Chinese martyrs and a Sudanese slave). <http://www.lewrockwell.com/rockwell/martyrs.html> recommends Robert Royal's book, *The Catholic Martyrs of the Twentieth Century: A Comprehensive World History* (New York: Crossroad Publishing, 2000).

39. <http://www.cwnews.com/browse/1998/07/8186.htm>. *Catholic World News* notes on 6 June 2000, that the twentieth Century Roman Catholic Martyrs are listed in an eight-volume work: <http://www.cwnews.com/browse/2000/12/14413.htm>. The various sites of *The Voice of the Martyrs* (e.g. Appendix nos. 1, 4, 13, 20), an evangelical faith mission founded by Sabina and Richard Wurmbrand and headquartered in Bartlesville, OK, concern help for persecuted Christians,

martyrs sometimes includes a prayer for all victims of violence.[40] At the same time, the Pope pleads consistently to stop the violence against Christians, emphasizing that the heart of the Christian tradition consists of love and peacefulness.[41]

Similarly, the leader of the Coptic Church, Pope Shenouda, commemorates the Coptic victims of Muslim aggression and articulates the identity of his Church as a 'church of martyrs'. In response to the violence his church members experienced he does not call for retaliation, not even for organizing protection, but states that violence needs to be answered with love of the other.[42] In the celebration of the beatification of 233 Spanish martyrs on 11 March 2001, at St Peter's Square, with 30,000 Spanish pilgrims present, the Pope links the memory of the new saints to a plea for ending terrorist violence in Spain, stating that no cause can justify terrorism: 'I wish to entrust to the intercession of the new blessed an intention that you carry deeply embedded in your hearts: the end of terrorism'.[43] The Mennonites are well known for their pacifism oriented peace work, including educational activities. My data include several references to the *Martyrs' Mirror*, the Mennonite collection of martyrs. One concerns an Internet Sunday School Study Guide for this *Mirror* by J. Daniel Hess, which is an attempt to demonstrate the relevance of this work for present day Mennonites in three steps: (1) introduction of the work; (2) bringing its history to life; (3) discussion. Two of the questions suggested for discussion are: 'What religious groups other than Christians must fear for their lives today? What are the circumstances?'[44] This trend for connecting the commemoration of martyrs with unconditional calls to end violence seems typical for the Christian web pages I found. However, the data did include one or two references to another powerful pacifist tradition linked to martyrdom: Mahatma Gandhi's famous notion of *satyagraha*:

> A satyagrahi must be afraid neither of imprisonment nor of deportation. He must neither mind being reduced to poverty, nor be frightened, if it comes to that, of being mashed into pulp with a mortar and pestle.[45]

<http://www.persecution.com/link/news.asp?headline=carbomb>; <http://www.chalcedon.edu/report/98jun/White_Christians_World.html>.

40. <http://www.cwnews.com/browse/1998/07/8186.htm>.

41. <http://www.cin.org/pope/beatification-spanish-martyrs.html>.

42. <http://www.christianitytoday.com/ct/7t9/7t9044.html>; <http://www.cin.org/pope/beatification-spanish-martyrs.html>. Cf. the ecumenical list of Heroes and Martyrs for Justice and Peace, constructed by deacon Robert M. Pallotti of St Joseph Church, Bristol, CT, USA: <http://www.rc.net/hartford/st_joseph/deacon/heroes.html> (cited 25 April 2002); the statement of the World Council of Churches on the occasion of the launch of the decade to overcome violence (2001–2010), dated 5 February 2001: <http://www.wcc-coe.org/wcc/news/press/01/cc-releases/16prf.html>; <http://www.bym-rsf.org/decade.html> (cited 25 April 2002).

43. <http://www.dailycatholic.org/issue/2001Mar/mar12nr1.htm>.

44. <http://www.mph.org/studygds/martyrssg.htm>; also: <http://www.homecomers.org/mirror/intro.htm>; <http://www.mennolink.org/books/>.

45. <http://www.mkgandhi.org/nonviolence/phil7.htm>; <http://www.anc.org.za/ancdocs/history/people/gandhi/3.html>. The association with a mortar is a striking echo of traditions about ancient philosophers who stood up against tyrants, van Henten and Avemarie, *Martyrdom and Noble Death*, pp. 25-27.

Most of the other pages envisage different routes for martyrdom and violence, accepting that the act considered as martyrdom can be violent itself.[46] Here, of course, it is crucial to differentiate between an insider and an outsider perspective. An intriguing case is the martyrdom of Joseph and Hyrum Smith (Latter Day Saints). One site offers Stephen Gibson's one-minute-answer to the question: Was Joseph Smith a martyr?

> Question: How can Latter-day Saints believe Joseph Smith died as a martyr? All he really did is lose a gun fight at Carthage Jail and killed two men before he died.
>
> [Answer:] …Webster's New World Dictionary defines 'martyr' as a person who chooses to suffer or die rather than give up his faith or his principles, or a person tortured or killed because of his beliefs. There is nothing in this definition to prohibit a martyr from defending himself.

The answer further explains the circumstances of Joseph Smith and his fellow Mormons' death. A mob attacked them on 27 June 1844 in their unprotected jail, storming up the stairs and firing into their room. Joseph Smith discharged his six shooter into the stairway, but was killed nevertheless.[47]

A big issue in the media is, of course, the case of the 'Muslim martyrs', although their religious inspiration is not always evident. Some of my database statements about them are clearly linked to Islam, but others are largely or even just political. Several web pages show that retaliation for Israeli killings of Palestinians is a prime motive for launching suicide attacks celebrated as martyrdom. On 7 July 2001 a prominent Hamas spokesperson, Abdel Aziz al-Rantissi, quoted in *The Guardian*, stated that Hamas vowed to send ten suicide bombers against Israel to avenge the Israeli army's killing of an 11-year-old Palestinian boy, Khalil Mughrabi in Rafah (in the Gaza strip). The blood of the martyrs has to be avenged.[48] The same Hamas official figures prominently in Martin Himmel's report (no. 78, below) and participated in the funeral of Mazen Badawi. The father of the other martyr in Himmel's report, Dr Nizar Rayan, legitimates the suicide acts because the Israelis took away Palestinian land: 'But when we lost our land, why should we not lose life as well?' Another Palestinian group that made it into the Western media with brutal acts of violence, the Al Aqsa Martyrs Brigade, which is linked to Yasser Arafat's Fatah movement, also legitimates its violence as retaliation against Israeli violence. In one of its statements, issued in the West Bank city of Jenin, this brigade claimed responsibility for a shooting on a main highway in northern Israel that killed an Israeli man and wounded a woman: 'The only language the enemy understands is

46. The site Martyrs or Arse-Holes? (<http://www.mememachine.cwc.net/atheism/martyr. htm>, cited 4 January 2003), offering a discussion about definitions and assessments of martyrdom by Martin Willett and others, states: 'Martyrs often aim their deaths. Martyrdom is a violent act.'

47. <http://www.lightplanet.com/response/answers/martyr.htm> (cited 25 April 2002). Surveys of Mormon martyrs include <http://www.ifas.org/fw/9606/violence.html>; <http://www.mormons.org/daily/history/people/joseph_smith/Martyrdom_Joseph_Hyrum.htm>.

48. <http://www.guardian.co.uk/international/story/0,3604,523248,00.html>. Cf. <http://www.groups.yahoo.com/group/uk_muslims/message>; <http://news.bbc.co.uk/hi/english/world/middle_east/newsid_1429000/1429745.stm>.

that of guns'.[49] Another example is the statement that followed the killing of Raed Karmi by the Israelis (14 January 2001): 'With your assassination of Raed Karmi, you have entered hell upon yourselves—you will be burned by its fire'.[50] John Irving even ascribes such a mentality to all Palestinians, commenting upon their funerals (Online *NewsHour*: 'Renew Violence', 2 October 2000: 'There is a huge turnout for each and every Palestinian funeral. These people regard their dead as martyrs, killed in a religious war over Jerusalem and, therefore, worthy of being honored. And appearing at each funeral are many more men prepared to die. This is one of several funerals taking place on the West Bank today. And it is not only an outpouring of grief. It is a call to arms, a call for retaliation'.[51] I did not find one 'insider statement' in my database that reflected either upon the consequences of this road to death for the 'other side',[52] or on the fact that the deliberate killing of civilians not involved in the military conflict is an act of murder according to experts on Islamic law, as stated many times regarding September 11.[53]

Other websites demonstrate that the violent type of martyrdom, legitimated by enemy violence, is not unique to Palestinians. Pages about anti-globalists present their own victims as martyrs, and vow that the enemy violence will be retaliated. Pages put on the web after the Genoa G8 summit (20-22 July 2001) state:

> It is clear that when the interests of big capital are threatened, the pretense at democracy is laid aside and naked force becomes the order of the day. The workers and the oppressed peoples the world over and particularly in the dominated countries have learned this lesson with the blood of hundreds of thousands of

49. <http://www.arabia.com/news/article/english/0,1690,45412,00.html>.

50. <http://news.bbc.co.uk/hi/english/world/middle_east/newsid_1760000/1760327.stm>.

51. <http://www.pbs.org/newshour/bb/middle_east/july-dec00/violence_10-2a.html>. Several Jewish websites pay great attention to Palestinian incitement to martyrdom, as well as (indirect) support by the Palestinian Authorities of suicide attacks: see, e.g., <http://www.memri.org/>; <http://www.likud.nl/viol06.html>; <http://www.likud.nl/extr42.html>; <http://www.cdn-friends-icej.ca/isreport/fouryrs.html>; http://www.jvim.com/IntelligenceBriefing/january2001/israel.html>; <http://www.aish.com/jewishissues/middleeast/Martyrs_and_Mothers.asp>; cf. <http://www.jcpa.org/jl/vp441.htm>. One of these sites offers a statement about the celebration of Palestinian martyrs that is heard frequently on the streets in Israel and out of the mouth of Israeli politicians: 'There should be no reward for violence', Aaron Lerner (September 1998) <http://www.freeman.org/m_online/sep98/lerner.htm>.

52. I did find one on the traumatic effects on Palestinian children: <http://www.washington-report.org/backissues/010201/0101009.html>.

53. An interview with Sheikh Hamza Yusuf by Richard Scheinin for *Mercury News*, is quoted on several web pages. The sheikh considers the hijackers '"enemies of Islam". Not martyrs, but "mass murderers, pure and simple"... There's no Islamic justification for any of it. It's like some misguided Irish using Catholicism as an excuse for blowing up English people... You can't kill innocent people. There's no Islamic declaration of war against the United States... In Islam, the only wars that are permitted are between armies and they should engage on battlefields and engage nobly': R. Scheinin, 'Muslim Scholar: Terrorists are Mass Murderers, Not Martyrs', *Mercury News*, cited 16 September 2001, online: <http://www0.mercurycenter.com/local/center/isl0916.htm>; <http://www.mpfweb.org/91101.html>; <http://www.muslimresource.com/article_hyusuf.shtml>; <http://www.muslimresource.com/resource_muslimvoice.shtml>; <http://www.arches.uga.edu/~godlas/hamza.html>.

> martyrs who have fallen in the struggle against imperialism and reaction... Long
> live the memory of the people's heroic martyrs! Violence against the people will
> not go unpunished![54]

A final example concerns the Tamil Tigers of Sri Lanka, who accepted a peace
settlement recently. Yet, on one of their current websites a 1992 speech of a leader
during a commemoration of Tamil martyrs on heroes' day, 27 November, is posted:

> But our enemy is committed to violence. Therefore, he has imposed an unjust war
> on us. Today, the enemy's armed forces have come to our doorstep and are beat-
> ing war drums. In this most difficult and critical situation what can we do? We
> have to struggle and win our freedom. Freedom is not a commercial commodity
> that can be bargained. It is a sacred right that can be won by shedding blood.[55]

5. *Relevance*

My findings indicate that the contemporary vocabulary of martyrdom has under-
gone multiple changes. Compared to what it was in the classical Jewish and
Christian sources, it has become much broader. It also supplies evidence of conflicting views on the interconnection of martyrdom and violence. How do my findings relate to the leading questions of our research project?[56] Some responses to
these questions are implicitly found in my paper, but let me add a few more comments. We can safely claim that the keywords of the violence vocabulary here are
'martyrdom', 'martyrs' and 'violence'. I could list some satellite words as well,
'senseless', 'commemoration', 'love', 'retaliation' or 'legitimate response'. More
important than these words, however, is the fact that these and other relevant terms
are almost always group specific; this is 'group identity' language, frequently
focusing upon insiders only. The meanings of martyrdom and violence are filled in
by the groups' perspectives and identities, which explains the observation that those
who are martyrs for some are extreme terrorists for others (above). It also explains
the fact that both the victims of 'September 11' and its perpetrators are commemorated as martyrs.

I hardly found references to Tanakh, Christian Bibles or Koran in the Internet
materials. Instead, there are many references to the 'classical martyrs' of the various Christian denominations involved in the majority of the web pages consulted.

With regard to vocabulary transformations, I have noted enormous shifts away
from the ancient Jewish and Christian martyr images as passive figures, not giving
in to authorities, preferring suffering, torture and execution to sacrificing one's
belief and/or practices. First, the voluntary aspect does not play a role in several
contemporary collective cases, such as the so-called Holocaust martyrs or indi-

---

54. <http://www.yahoo.com/group/queerflips/message/1061>; <http://www.geocities.com/
ilps2000/genoa2.htm>. Donald Macintyre offers a protest against this view: 'As an Old Peace
Protester, I Have No Time for Anarchists', *The Independent* (24 July 2001), available online at
<www. commondreams.org/views01/0724-03.htm> (consulted 22 April 2002).

55. <http://www.eelamweb.com/leader/messages/herosday/1992/> (consulted 25 April 2002).

56. See the Introduction to the present volume, and <http://www.theo.uu.nl/noster/>.

viduals like Martin Luther King and Steve Biko. Second, a violent death does not always seem to be presupposed; being a victim while fighting for a justified cause seems enough reason to be called a martyr (see sites referring, e.g., to labour activists, anti-globalists, metric martyrs). Third, calling people 'martyrs' expresses deep concern over their being victims of senseless violence who should be commemorated as such. Fourth, martyrs are in many contemporary cases not only victims of violence, but also—by the very act of martyrdom—initiators, or perpetrators of violence.[57] Here specific group identities seem to play a crucial role, turning the martyr into a highly dangerous figure. For some of the cases discussed above—and not only for the Palestinian so-called suicide martyrs—the following brutal reasoning may be accurate: (1) martyrdom is the appropriate response to violence of 'the others'; (2) the martyr dies for a justified cause; and (3) the consequences of this martyrdom are, therefore, justified, no matter what they are. In biblical as well as Qur'anic language one could speak of a bonus to the 'an eye for an eye' reasoning: by qualifying the response to the other's violence as martyrdom, the response is legitimated, while, at the same time, it is also glorified. To me the need to deconstruct such arguments seems crucial, which brings me to my final point.

What do the web pages offer us about reducing violence and martyrdom? Not much, I am afraid. One can surely find web pages that enter into this question, if one looks carefully for them; but it seems right to stick to the martyr database gleaned according to web popularity. In these one finds, on the one hand, educational Christian sites (e.g. the Mennonite ones) and calls for ending senseless violence that are linked to the commemoration of martyrs. Similarly, both the Coptic and the Roman Catholic Pope call for an attitude of love and pacifism as the appropriate way to confront violence. On the other hand, there are warnings against systematic glorification of and mental preparation for violent types of martyrdom. Both approaches call, of course, upon educators to take up responsibility. Focusing especially on the violent consequences of martyrdom, however, something else seems relevant as well. I have emphasized that martyrs are constructed as such by their source group; they function as model figures for this group and express group values, norms, practices and aims in a radical manner. The 'martyr' title legitimates the so-called martyrs' actions and elevates them to a level that cannot be criticized, which may have enormous consequences for the martyrs' opponents, who automatically become demonized or even dehumanized.

It is time to stand up against the discourse and rhetoric of such martyrdom; and to point out that the martyrs' 'others' cannot be ignored and have a right to live too—as quite a number of 'canonical' Jewish, Christian and Muslim traditions about 'the other' indicate.

---

57. Athalya Brenner's reading of Ps. 137 and Jan Gross' book about Jedwabne in this volume also implies dualities of being victim and perpetrator at the same time.

List of Top 100 Martyrdom Websites
(Based on a Google Search Performed on 5 May 2002)

1. The Voice of the Martyrs (see footnote 38): <http://www.persecution. com/>.
2. Martyrs' in Chicago (restaurant's name): <http://www.martyrslive.com/>.
3. Military Martyrs (ancient/early medieval military martyrs): <http://www. ucc.ie/milmart/>.
4. The Voice of the Martyrs Canada (see no. 1): <http://www.persecution. net/>.
5. Foxe's Book of Martyrs (1516–87; see p. 196): <http://www.ccel.org/f/ foxe_j/martyrs/>.
6. Fallen Martyrs (commemoration of martyrs by categories): <http://www. fallenmartyrs.com/>.
7. Tolpuddle Martyrs Museum (Tolpuddle Martyrs, p. 198): <http://www. tolpuddlemartyrs.org.uk/>.
8. 26 Martyrs Homepage (Japanese Christian martyrs): <http://www.baobab. or.jp/~stranger/mypage/26martyr.htm>.
9. Yad Vashem (Holocaust martyrs): <http://www.yad-vashem.org.il>.
10. Fox's Book of Martyrs (see no. 5): <http://www.sacred-texts.com/chr/ martyrs/>.
11. Martyrs, article by H.L. Mencken, sceptical view: <http://www.concentric. net/~Wkiernan/text/Mencken_martyrs.html>.
12. Fox's Book of Martyrs (see no. 5): <http://bible.crosswalk.com/History/ AD/FoxsBookofMartyrs/>.
13. Voice of the Martyrs Has Moved (see no. 1): <http://www.iclnet.org/pub/ resources/text/vom/vom.html>.
14. Metric martyrs (pp. 197-98): <http://www.metricmartyrs.com/>.
15. To the Martyrs (Tertullian's work with this title): <http://www.math.byu. edu/~smithw/Lds/LDS/Ancient-history-items/Early-Christian/Tertullian/To- the-martyrs>.
16. Martyrs Shrine (francophone Jesuit martyrs, Ontario, CA): <http://www. jesuits.ca/martyrs-shrine/>.
17. Tortures and Torments of the X-tian Martyrs (drawings of tortures): <http:// www.cat.pdx.edu/~chuff/christian-torture/6.html>.
18. Wychwood Home Page (Ascott Martyrs, pp. 197-98): <http://www. geocities.com/Heartland/Plains/6081/>.
19. The Haymarket Martyrs (information about them and their monument): <http://www.kentlaw.edu/ilhs/haymkmon.htm>.
20. Voice of the Martyrs Australia (see no. 1): <http://www.vom.com.au/ default.htm>.
21. Martyrs' Tomb (M. Hicks' thriller about school reform): <http://www. martyrs-tomb.com/>.
22. Compiegne (article about Martyrs of Compiègne, Carmelite nuns guillo- tined in 1794): <http://www.karmel.at/ics/others/newkir.htm>.

23. Welcome to the Martyrs Online (football club, Penydarren Park, UK): <http://www.themartyrs.com/>.

24. Christian Martyrs in Muslim Spain: <http://www.libro.uca.edu/martyrs/martyrs.htm>.

25. Martyrs on the Web (see no. 23): <http://www.home.clara.net/owain/martyrs/>.

26. The Mirror of the Martyrs (exhibition based on the Mennonite Martyrs' Mirror): <http://www.bethelks.edu/Kauffman/martyrs/>.

27. Fox's Book of Martyrs (see no. 5): <http://www.reformed.org/books/fox/fox_martyrs.html>.

28. Father Demetrios Serfes (Greek Orthodox site dedicated to the martyred family of Nicholas II): <http://www.fr-d-serfes.org/royal/>.

29. Martyrs Mirror Online (Mennonite martyrs): <http://www.homecomers.org/mirror/>.

30. Catholic Encyclopedia: Irish Confessors and Martyrs (see p. 196): <http://www.knight.org/advent/cathen/08163a.htm>.

31. Medieval Sourcebook (the ancient Scillitan Martyrs): <http://www.fordham.edu/halsall/source/scillitan-mart.html>.

32. Story of the Forty Holy Martyrs of Sebaste (ancient Christian martyrs with this name): <http://web.mit.edu/ocf/www/sebaste_martyrs.html>.

33. Catholic Saints and Martyrs (Felicity and Perpetua, see pp. 195, 201): <http://www.cin.org/saints.html>.

34. The Haymarket Martyrs (V. de Cleyre's 1901 memorial speech): <http://www.luminist.org/Archives/Haymarket.htm>.

35. Libération (D. François' article about Gaza martyrs): <http://www.liberation.fr/quotidien/semaine/020409-000004105EVEN.html>.

36. Uganda Martyrs University (Catholic University at Nkozi, Uganda): <http://www.fiuc.org/umu/umu.html>.

37. Catholic Encyclopedia: Japanese Martyrs (see no. 30): <http://www.newadvent.org/cathen/09744a.htm>.

38. Irish Hunger Martyrs (see p. 196): http://www.irishhungermartyrs.org/

39. Théâtre des Martyrs (theatre in Brussels at the Martyrs' Square, see p. 195): <http://www.europictures.com/martyrs/>.

40. Metric Martyrs (see no. 14): <http://www.metricmartyrs.sageweb.co.uk/>.

41. Uganda Martyrs University (see no. 36): <http://www.fiuc.org/umu/>.

42. National Martyr's Shrine at Auriesville, NY (Roman Catholic martyrs in US): <http://www.martyrshrine.org/>.

43. CNN.com In-Depth Specials (Al Aqsa Martyrs Brigade): <http://www.cnn.com/SPECIALS/2002/cfr/stories/al.aqsa.martyrs/>.

44. US News Search Results (J.L. Sheler's survey of martyrs, starting with Jesus): <http://www.usnews.com/usnews/issue/010416/christ.htm>.

45. Two Homilies Concerning the Forty Martyrs (Gregory of Nyssa's homilies, cf. no. 32): <http://www.sp.uconn.edu/~salomon/nyssa/martyrs.htm>.

46. Martyrs and Madmen Entrance (Roger Daltrey's music album): <http://www.fortunecity.com/rivendell/battlespire/82/>.

47. Church of the Martyrs (Anglican Church, Leicester, UK): <http://www.martyrs.org.uk/>.

48. NAM Home Page (Roman Catholic church in Lincoln, NE, named after US martyrs (cf. no. 42): <http://www.martyrs.org/>.

49. The UK's Leading Atheist Page (fact and fiction in martyrdom sources): <http://www.bowness.demon.co.uk/martyrs.htm>.

50. Uganda Martyrs (45 Catholic and Anglican martyrs in Uganda): <http://www.buganda.com/martyrs.htm>.

51. Catholic Encyclopedia: Acts of the Martyrs (see no. 30): <http://www.newadvent.org/cathen/09742b.htm>.

52. 10th Anniversary (commemoration of the El Salvador Jesuit martyrs): <http://www.creighton.edu/CollaborativeMinistry/10th-anniv.html>.

53. Jesuit Martyrs of El Salvador: <http://www.spc.edu/library/jesuit2.html>.

54. In Honour of the Imperial Martyrs of Holy Russia (Nicholas II and family): <http://www.mobilixnet.dk/~mob55672/>.

55. Maaveerar Home (Tamil martyrs): <http://www.tamilcanadian.com/eelam/maaveerar/>.

56. Domestic-Church.Com: (Canadian martyrs, Roman Catholic educational website): <http://www.domestic-church.com/index.dir/index_saints.htm>.

57. Father Demetrios Russian Royal Family Website (see no. 28): <home.rmci.net/fr-d-serfes/orthodox/royal/>.

58. Eusebius, Martyrs of Palestine (work about ancient Christian martyrs): <http://www.ucalgary.ca/~vandersp/Courses/texts/eusebius/eusempaf.html>.

59. Homage to the Martyrs of Kargil (commemoration of Indian soldiers who died in Kashmir): <http://www.angelfire.com/in2/kargil/>.

60. FOX's Book of Martyrs, Introduction (see no. 5): <http://www.ccel.org/f/foxe_j/martyrs/begin.htm>.

61. Religion/Hagiology/Martyrs (illustrations concerning ancient martyrs): <http://www.bnf.fr/enluminures/themes/t_2/st_2_03/a203_003.htm>.

62. From Jesus to Christ: (multi-authored article about ancient martyrs): <http://www.pbs.org/wgbh/pages/frontline/shows/religion/why/martyrs.html>.

63. The Lyons Martyrs (the Martyrdom of Lyons and Vienne, 177 CE): <http://www.gospelcom.net/chi/EARLYF/lyons.shtml>.

64. Our Lady and the English Martyrs (Roman Catholic church, Cambridge, UK): <http://www.olem.freeuk.com/>.

65. Lesser-Known Saints & Martyrs (Roman Catholic saints): <http://www.angelfire.com/ar/rhop/saints.html>.

66. Domeikava Church (Roman Catholic parish in Domeikava, Lithuania): <http://mano.delfi.lt/life/martyrs/martyrs_en.htm>.

67. Foxe's Book of Martyrs (see no. 5): <http://calvarychapel.com/library/foxe-john/text/bom.htm>.

68. Holy Martyrs Parish (parish dedicated to US Jesuit martyrs, Falmouth, ME): <http://www.holymartyrs.org/>.

69. EelamWeb© (commemoration of Tamil heroes): <http://www.eelamweb.com/maveerar/>.

70. Francis Britto's Brittopia (booklet about 26 Japanese martyrs): <http://pweb.sophia.ac.jp/~d-mccoy/xavier/yuki/yuki01.html>.

71. The Eight North American Martyrs (descriptions of them): <http://www.catholicism.org/pages/cjjangri.htm>.

72. Les] Martyrs (e-version of Chateaubriand's writing): <http://gallica.bnf.fr/Fonds_Frantext/T0087882.htm>.

73. On the Holy Forty Martyrs (homily by Basil the Great, see no. 32): <http://www.cybercom.net/~htm/forty_martyrs.htm>.

74. Canadian Martyrs Catholic Church (parish church in Richmond, British Columbia, Canada): <http://cmartyrs.rcav.org/>.

75. The Litanies of the Martyrs (ancient Roman martyrs): <http://www.catacombe.roma.it/en/litanie.html>.

76. Memory of the Martyrs of Mexico (organisation that commemorates these martyrs): <http://www.rtfcam.org/martyrs/martyrs.htm>.

77. Martyrs for Jesus Christ (martyrs of the Covenanted Reformation 1661–88): <http://members.aol.com/Puritanone/martyrs.html>.

78. NewsHour Online (Internet article by M. Himmel, see p. 198): <http://www.pbs.org/newshour/bb/middle_east/jan-june02/martyr_3-19.html>.

79. Welcome to Our Lady Queens of Martyrs (parish church, Centerport, NY, USA): <http://www.olqmparish.org/>.

80. Martyrs Bus Service (bus service, Yarra Valley, Australia, founded by Harry Martyr): <http://www.martyrs.com.au/>.

81. Martyrs Mirror Online (Mennonite Martyrs): <http://www.homecomers.org/mirror/contents.htm>.

82. Amazon.com: (Martyrs' Crossing: novel by Amy Wilentz): <http://www.amazon.com/exec/obidos/ASIN/0345449835/qid=1015528141/sr=1-1/ref=sr_1_1/102-2283144-4571323>.

83. Mending the minds of the 'martyrs' (Internet article by R.E. Tyrrell Jr, see p. 198): <http://www.washtimes.com/commentary/20020405-93348048.htm>.

84. Unseen ink ^ com (not visible on my computer): <http.//www.unseenink.com/martyrs.htm>

85. Holy Martyrs Home Page (Roman Catholic parish church, Medina, OH, USA): <http://www.holymartyrs.net/>.

86. Short Sketches of the Martyrs (Canadian martyrs, see no. 16): <http://www.jesuits.ca/martyrs-shrine/biograph.htm>.

87. New Page 3 … cmcc@chinesemartyrs.org (email address of Roman Catholic parish, Markham, Ontario, Canada): <http://chinesemartyrs.org/>.

88. Martyrs' in Chicago (see no. 2): <http://www.martyrslive.com/home.htm>.

89. 26 Martyrs (see no. 70): <http://www.baobab.or.jp/~stranger/mypage/martyr.htm>

90. Foxe's Book of Martyrs (see no. 5): <http://www.studylight.org/his/ad/fbm/>.

91. Jesuit Martyrs of the 20th Century: <http://www.companysj.com/news/martyrs20.html>.

92. Communauté Chrétienne Sts-Martyrs (Roman Catholic parish in Saints Martyrs, Montréal, CA): <http://www.cam.org/~martyrs/>.

93. CIN—The Martyrs of Japan (Japanese martyrs): <http://www.cin.org/saints/paulmiki.html>.

94. Our Lady Queen of Martyrs Roman Catholic Church (Roman Catholic church in Forest Hills, NY, USA): <http://www.ourladyqueenofmartyrs.org/>.

95. Sikh Martyrs (Sikh heroes): <http://www.sikh-history.com/sikhhist/martyrs/>.

96. Foxe's Martyrs (see no. 5): <http://logosresourcepages.org/foxes.htm>.

97. ISFA (Internet Soccer homepage; 'martyrs' not found): <http://www.isfa.com/isfa/lists/mtfc/>.

98. May Day and the Haymarket Martyrs (article about Haymarket Martyrs): <http://www.igc.org/laborstandard/Vol1No3/MayDay.htm>.

99. The Jerusalem Post Newspaper (Internet article by Greer Fay Cashman about Holocaust martyrs): <http://www.jpost.com/Editions/2002/04/09/News/News.46556.html>.

100. The Tolpuddle Martyrs (links concerning these martyrs): <http://homepages.rootsweb.com/~lovelace/tolpuddle.htm>.

VIOLENCE AND FINAL VOCABULARIES:
ON MAPPING ACTUAL HOPES AND BELIEFS

Jonneke Bekkenkamp

Suppose that you are an immigrant from Iran. Two years ago you received a scholarship to study at the University of Amsterdam. You've fallen in love with a fellow student, you've married, and for the first time you are allowed to vote. In the turmoil preceding the elections there is a lot of talk about the dangers of Islam and about Christian norms and values. This disturbs you. You want to know: What makes people believe that all Islamic people tend to terrorism? Is the link between violence and Qu'ran stronger than the link between Bible and violence? Or is the link between Christianity and Bible looser than the link between Islam and Koran? What is it that makes, in the eyes of 'liberals', modern collective identities like Amsterdam, Holland and Europe 'Christian'? What makes up a civilization that is both Christian and secularized? You are prepared to accept and imitate whatever beliefs and attitudes in order to belong and to integrate.

What could, what would you do? Go to a bookstore and read a book about the Christian faith? Interview religious leaders? Watch TV and/or talk to your friends? Whatever you do, you'll get confused. Why? First, because there is a gap between professional articulations of belief and actual beliefs of people who call themselves Christian or post/Christian. Secondly, and most confusingly, people seem to be confused themselves. It is not so much that they are unwilling to answer your questions. Some people get irritated when asked about their hopes and beliefs. They regard your questioning as a lack of respect for their a-religious view of life. However, that is a minor problem compared to the major point: hardly anyone seems to be able to *articulate* his or her hopes and beliefs.

In fact, the problem you are facing is the problem shared by religious studies. How to analyze and handle moving and melting, seemingly incoherent beliefs of believers and non-believers? Characterizing somebody or some institution as 'Christian' hardly says anything. There are Christians who 'as Christians' believe in violence and there are Christians who 'as Christians' believe in non-violence, and what is true regarding violence holds for other existential issues as well. The old systems of dividing and subdividing people and their life views according to 'religion' simply do not work anymore. This raises the questions: How do we differentiate between different mind-sets? How do we tell apart different views of life? How do we map actual hopes and beliefs?

Roughly speaking, there are two ways out of the impasse. Either you focus on observing actions people take—from small gestures to big manifestations; and/or you focus on what people say when confronted with existential themes and feelings, such as violence and aggression. Out of patterns of speaking—typical terms, characteristic words, and recurring themes—you may tease out something about people's belief systems.

In this article I wish to explore the second way through methodological reflections and by reading a novel. The methodological reflections are based on Richard Rorty's coining of the term 'final vocabularies', as well as on recent market research. The novel read is *The Piano Teacher* by Elfriede Jelinek,[1] a novel with a strong vocabulary of violence.

The Piano Teacher

Before going into Rorty's concepts and the methods developed in market research, let me introduce to you Erika Kohut, the piano teacher of Jelinek's novel. I will not give a close reading of this novel. What I am interested in is the development of methods for getting hold of people's belief systems. In that context, Jelinek's novel functions as a point of reference and Erika Kohut, its main character, as an experimental person.

Erika teaches piano at the Vienna Conservatory. Her mother, with whom she lives in stifling symbiosis, had a solo career in mind; however, Erika's career ended before it ever got underway. One more disappointment for the mother is Erika's buying of clothes, which she never wears. This habit keeps them from buying a house of their own. What the mother does not know is that, on her way home, Erika visits peepshows and spies on her students, whores and whoever is under the suspicion of sexual activities. In this daily routine Walter Klemmer, one of her students, intervenes. He wants sex and Erika is willing to give in, but under her own conditions. She writes him a letter in which she describes how she wants to be humiliated. She only wants to be an instrument on which she will teach him to play. He should be free, and she in fetters. But Erika will choose the fetters herself. He can take on Erika only under the condition of violence. He is to love Erika to the point of self-surrender; she will then love him to the point of self-denial. They will continually hand each other notarized evidence of their affection and devotion. Erika waits for Klemmer to renounce violence for the sake of love. Erika will refuse for the sake of love, and she will demand that he do to her what she has detailed in the letter, whereby she ardently hopes that she will be spared what is required in the letter.[2] In the end he responds to her feelings with banal violence, and leaves her on the floor of her apartment.

Erika's vocation is her profession: the celestial power known as music.[3] In her mother's and Erika's vocabulary Art and She are written with capitals:

---

1. Elfriede Jelinek, *Die Klavierspielerin* (Reihbek: Rowohlt Verlag, 1983). Citations in this article are from Joachim Neugroschel's translation (Wheatland Corporations, 1988), published in a 5-star pocket in 1999: *The Piano Teacher* (London: Serpent's Tail, 1999).

2. Jelinek, *The Piano Teacher*, pp. 212-13.

3. Jelinek, *The Piano Teacher*, p. 6.

> Mother points out that Erika is not just a face in the crowd: She's one in a million. Mother never stops making that point. Erika says that she, Erika, is an individualist. She claims she cannot submit to anyone or anything. She has a hard time just fitting in. Someone like Erika comes along only once, and then never again. If something is especially irreplaceable, it is called Erika. If there's one thing she hates, it's standardization in any shape...[4]

Erika is superior to everyone else. Her mother puts her high above them. According to the mother, ERIKA leaves the others far behind and below, but exactly that makes her utterly alone. On a holiday in her youth, when everyone is gathered downstairs, 'She sits alone in her room, isolated from the crowd, which has forgotten her because she is such a lightweight'.[5] On that occasion she cuts herself. Not for the first time and not for the last time. From Jelinek's depictions of cutting scenes, I take the one most shocking to me:

> She sits down in front of the magnifying side of the shaving mirror; spreading her legs, she makes a cut, magnifying the aperture that is the doorway into her body. She knows from experience that such a razor cut doesn't hurt, for her arms, hands and legs have often served as guinea pigs. Her hobby is cutting her own body.[6]

Note that the cutting does not hurt. Her self-destruction is not motivated by hate but by feelings of alienation. She is 'off-limits to herself'; 'Her body is one big refrigerator, where Art is well stored'.[7]

Her devotion to music is not only destructive to herself, but to others as well, to her students and to numerous others, for example people in the streetcars:

> Bristling with instruments, she arduously staggers into the mobs of homebound workers, detonating among them like a fragmentation bomb. If need be, she hides her true feelings and says, 'Pardon me, I'm getting off here'... They look at the music student and imagine that music has raised her spirits; but the only thing that's raised is her fist.[8]

Mother and daughter spray acid on students who do better than Erika or threaten to do so. Ordering her students to her concerts, she uses 'dishonest methods, such as coercion, extortion, intimidation'; 'For Erika, you see, is all alone on the other side, and instead of being proud of her situation, she wreaks vengeance'.[9] Her attitude towards others is clearly motivated by hate and contempt, but underlying that contempt is fear. Fear to be measured, fear to participate. 'She desires medals, badges for successful completion of nonparticipation, so she won't have to be measured, weighed'.[10] The security that her mother and her position offer her creates fear of uncertainty.[11]

---

4.   Jelinek, *The Piano Teacher*, p. 12.
5.   Jelinek, *The Piano Teacher*, p. 43.
6.   Jelinek, *The Piano Teacher*, p. 86.
7.   Jelinek, *The Piano Teacher*, pp. 54, 21.
8.   Jelinek, *The Piano Teacher*, p. 16.
9.   Jelinek, *The Piano Teacher*, pp. 66, 67.
10. Jelinek, *The Piano Teacher*, p. 85.
11. Jelinek, *The Piano Teacher*, p. 190.

Erika hates everyone, including, although more ambivalently, Klemmer and her mother. Her mother's feelings towards Erika are no less ambivalent. At night, after a fight, she is 'dreaming up new methods of torture',[12] and whenever Erika is late in getting home, she lets her feel the hot flame of her torch:

> No art can possibly comfort HER then, even though art is credited with many things, especially an ability to offer solace. Sometimes, of course, art creates the suffering in the first place.[13]

Erika believes in music because she has dedicated her life to it, not because music fills her with feelings of warmth and excitement. It is suggested in the novel that, in that respect, Erika does not stand alone. As Erika talks about 'the sins against the spirit of Schubert', others involve 'God and his dwelling place' whenever they talk about Bach. These people love music, and want others exposed to it too, 'With loving patience; if necessary, by force'.[14] Jelinek gives a plastic description of the stifling, self-complacent circle in which Erica moves:

> Vienna, the city of music! Only the things that have proven their worth will continue to do so in this city. Its buttons are bursting from the fat white paunch of culture, which, like any drowned corpse that is not fished from the water, bloats up more and more.[15]

Final Vocabularies

In a way, Jelinek's novel explains to our uncomprehending Iranian student how one can be both 'Christian' and secularized and, for that matter, aggressive towards the self and others. Art has become God, but the words in which Erika formulates her praise for Schubert and her contempt for the crowd sound stereotypically Christian. Erika's being a piano teacher is not just a job but also her un/willing response to a vocation of serving music. Nonetheless, I would hesitate to call her vocabulary 'Christian' or 'religious'. 'Christian' is not the right word because Christian vocabulary has many more registers; and because Erika's vocabulary is too much a melange to be characterized away so easily. The word 'religious', on the other hand, is too broad and at the same time too provocative. I shall come back to this later. For the moment I would say that Erika's vocabulary is indeed quite unique and, as such, one of the many 'final vocabularies' circulating in our culture.

The concept of 'final vocabularies' is taken from Richard Rorty. In his book *Contingency, Irony and Solidarity* he gives the following definition:

> All human beings carry about a set of words which they employ to justify their actions, their beliefs, and their lives. These are the words in which we formulate praise of our friends and contempt for our enemies, our long-term projects, our deepest self-doubts and our highest hopes. They are the words in which we tell,

---

12. Jelinek, *The Piano Teacher*, p. 10.
13. Jelinek, *The Piano Teacher*, p. 12.
14. Jelinek, *The Piano Teacher*, pp. 114, 159, 60.
15. Jelinek, *The Piano Teacher*, p. 12.

sometimes prospectively and sometimes retrospectively, the story of our lives. I shall call these words a person's 'final vocabulary'.

It is 'final' in the sense that if doubt is cast on the worth of these words, their user has no noncircular argumentative recourse. Those words are as far as he can go with language; beyond them there is only helpless passivity or a resort to force. A small part of a final vocabulary is made up of thin, flexible, and ubiquitous terms such as 'true', 'good', 'right', and 'beautiful'. The larger part contains thicker, more rigid, and more parochial terms, for example, 'Christ', 'England', 'professional standards'... The more parochial words do most of the work.[16]

For the enterprise of a literary analysis of religions and views of life, this concept might be useful and, therefore, I will discuss it here at some length. The term 'final' in the concept of a 'final vocabulary' does not exclude self-doubt. In Rorty's own liberal-ironist final vocabulary, self-doubt seems to be a key term: self-doubt as opposed to common sense; self-doubt as the facing up to the contingency of one's own most central beliefs and desires. The 'final' in 'final vocabularies' points to a limit: these words are as far as one can go with language. What you can do with language depends on your socialization and particular experiences. One way or the other, final vocabularies are the product of certain historical circumstances.

In Rorty's view there is no common human nature, although it is distinctively human to use every particular person, object, situation, event and word encountered for a symbolic purpose in later life.[17] To be a person is to speak a particular language, which enables us to discuss particular beliefs and desires with particular other people.[18] For public purposes, it does not matter if everyone's final vocabulary is different, as long as there is enough overlap so that everyone has some words with which to express the desirability of entering into other peoples' fantasies as well as into one's own.[19]

Looking for a counter-term for 'final', you might say that 'final' is opposed to 'fundamental' or 'validated':

> Just as there is nothing which validates a person's or a culture's final vocabulary, there is nothing implicit in that vocabulary which dictates how to reweave it when it is put under strain. All we can do is work with the final vocabulary we have, while keeping our ears open for hints about how it might be expanded or revised.[20]

In a certain sense 'final' is also opposed to 'rational'. The choice between vocabularies is simply a matter of playing the new one off against the old. Logical argument does not work when the discussion is about which vocabulary is best. A vocabulary is in itself a unit of persuasion.

The only sensible way to discuss final vocabularies is in terms of their utility. According to Rorty we should stick to questions concerning what works for

---

16. Richard Rorty, *Contingency, Irony and Solidarity* (Cambridge: Cambridge University Press, 1989), p. 73.
17. Rorty, *Contingency*, p. 19.
18. Rorty, *Contingency*, p. 36.
19. Rorty, *Contingency*, pp. 92-93.
20. Rorty, *Contingency*, p. 197.

particular purposes. We use final vocabularies to justify our actions, beliefs, lives. The principle function of vocabularies is, as Rorty states it elsewhere, 'to tell stories about future outcomes which compensate for present sacrifices'.[21] More neutrally, but equally generally, he speaks of the function of final vocabularies as contributing to our knowledge of human possibilities. However, when it comes actually to comparing final vocabularies, more specific descriptions of purpose are more interesting. As such Rorty names:

- Suggesting answers to the question, What is to be done?
- Increasing the ability to predict and control events.
- Providing inspiration.
- Sensitizing to cruelty.
- Coping with the contingencies of one's upbringing.
- Tying up with other people.
- Producing shudders of indignation.
- Producing tingles.
- Reweaving the vocabulary of moral deliberation in order to accommodate new beliefs.[22]

Vocabularies are best compared with tools.[23] Different vocabularies are more like alternative tools than like bits of a jigsaw puzzle. To treat them as a jigsaw puzzle is to assume that all vocabularies are capable of being united. However, the analogy between vocabularies and tools has an obvious drawback. The craftsman typically knows what job he needs to do before picking or inventing tools with which to do it. With vocabularies it happens the other way around. The creation of a new vocabulary will have its utility explained only retrospectively. We then conclude from its effect or product back to its purpose:

> We cannot see Christianity or Newtonianism or the Romantic Movement or political liberalism as a tool while we are still in the course of figuring out how to use it...but once we figure out how to use the vocabularies of these movements, we can tell a story of progress...

> Christianity did not know that its purpose was the alleviation of cruelty; Newton did not know that his purpose was modern technology; the Romantic poets did not know that their purpose was to contribute to the development of an ethical consciousness suitable for the culture of political liberalism... We can view these people as toolmakers rather than discoverers because we have a clear sense of the product which the use of those tools produced. The product is *us*—our conscience, our culture, our form of life.[24]

---

21. Rorty, *Contingency*, p. 86.
22. Rorty, *Contingency*, p. 196. Rorty redefines philosophy as one of the techniques for this reweaving.
23. Rorty, *Contingency*, pp. 9-22. Reference is made here mainly to Donald Davidson and Ludwig Wittgenstein.
24. Rorty, *Contingency*, p. 55.

Private and Public Final Vocabularies

The basic distinction Rorty draws is between private vocabularies of self-creation and public vocabularies of justice:

> The vocabulary of self-creation is necessarily private, unshared, unsuited to argument. The vocabulary of justice is necessarily public and shared, a medium for argumentative exchange.[25]

This distinction is based on a difference in purpose and use. Vocabularies of self-creation, of individual persons' chosen idiosyncratic metaphors, serve the pursuit of private perfection. They provide strategies to cope with the contingencies of our upbringing and help us to become autonomous. Vocabularies of justice help us to become less cruel, and serve the discussion of public affairs.

Both types of vocabularies are brought about by historical contingencies. Moreover, according to Rorty, the difference itself is a product of historical contingencies. Somehow, for the first time in history, large numbers of people have become able to separate public from private questions, the question 'Do you believe and desire what we believe and desire?' from the question 'Are you suffering?'[26] Liberal political discourse would do well, Rorty states, to remain as un-theoretical and simple-minded as it looks. The discourse of self-creation on the other hand should become as finely textured and custom-tailored as possible.[27]

Our responsibilities to others constitute only the public side of our lives, a side that has no automatic priority over private motives. The only thing that can let a human being combine altruism and joy is some very specific chain of associations with some highly idiosyncratic memories.[28] One of Rorty's central claims is that the private and the public are separate domains, not to be united. His whole history of the West climaxes in people being able to draw the public/private distinction. However, reading and rereading his book it is hard to visualize how both domains relate to one another. Not as private, idiosyncratic sections to a public, universal core: this is quite clear.[29] Sometimes the image of a wall arises, separating the public side of our lives from the private. But then on which side of the wall should we locate efforts to extend our sense of 'we', or efforts to become less cruel? Efforts to avoid pain, to become less cruel, typically belong on the public side. But the best way to become less cruel, Rorty tells us, is to learn as many vocabularies as possible, which is also part of the enterprise of self-creation: 'the liberal ironist needs as much imaginative acquaintance with alternative final vocabularies as possible, not just for her own edification, but in order to understand the actual and

25. Rorty, *Contingency*, p. xiv.
26. Rorty, *Contingency*, pp. 192, 198.
27. Rorty, *Contingency*, pp. 121, 32.
28. Rorty, *Contingency*, pp. 153-54. According to Rorty, both Vladimir Nabokov and Sigmund Freud make this 'important psychological point'.
29. '[T]hat distiction between a central, shared, obligatory portion and a peripheral, idiosyncratic, optional portion of one's final vocabulary is just the distinction which the ironist refuses to draw' (Rorty, *Contingency*, p. 92).

possible humiliation of the people who use these alternative final vocabularies'.[30] Efforts to extend our sense of 'we' pose a similar problem. Where to locate them? Extending our sense of 'we' is as much a matter of self-creation as it is a matter of justice.[31]

Apart from private vocabularies of self-creation and public vocabularies of justice, Rorty speaks incidentally also of scientific vocabularies, moral and political vocabularies, a culture's final vocabulary and common vocabularies. As vocabularies of we-creation—[my term, JB]—these diffuse the private/public distinction. Common, familiar, widely used vocabularies bind societies together.[32] No vocabulary is so private not to be formed, still, by common, shared vocabularies. Common vocabularies create the overlap necessary for language to remain a medium of communication.

Final Vocabularies and the Impasse of Religious Studies

The concept of final vocabularies might be fruitful for religious studies, namely, for the development of a method for mapping actual hopes and beliefs. The old categories, dividing and subdividing religions, simply do not work anymore. Approaching beliefs as final vocabularies might produce more accurate systems of grouping or classification. Compare the developments within market research. Fifty years ago a few 'hard' data like income, age, religion(!), education and gender sufficed to predict with relative accuracy what car you would buy, what political party you would vote for and what you liked for breakfast. Nowadays alternative classification systems are developed, based on value-patterns. As I see it, these value-systems—described in hierarchical lists of values—are abbreviations of final vocabularies. I shall come back to this later.

The concept of final vocabularies might be helpful, more specifically, for understanding the workings of traditional religious terms in actual speech. In Rorty's Darwinistic perspective on vocabularies, the distinction between old and new vocabularies is as important as the private/public distinction. He sketches the history of language as the history of a coral reef, old metaphors constantly dying off into literalness and then serving as a platform and foil for new metaphors.[33]

---

30. Rorty, *Contingency*, p. 92.

31. Another way to visualize Rorty's public/private distinction is the image of a network. If we want to tie up to other people's final vocabularies or not is up to us. However, to be a member of a liberal society demands to keep some links operational. The question remains: Which links? Are there some 'public' links and other more 'private' links? Here again the weakness of the public/private difference reappears.

32. Vocabularies are the glue of *societies*, not of the human *species* (Rorty, *Contingency*, p. 86): 'what unites her [the liberal ironist] with the rest of the species is not a common language but *just* susceptibility to pain—and in particular to that special sort of pain the brutes do not share with the humans—humiliation' (p. 92).

33. Rorty, *Contingency*, p. 16. Explaining the distinction between old metaphors (metaphors that have died off into literalness) and new metaphors as a distinction between familiar and unfamiliar uses of noises and marks, Rorty refers to Nietzsche's definition of 'truth' as a 'mobile army of metaphors' (p. 17), New metaphors serve as a mobile army for change. Literalized metaphors

If we use the concept of final vocabularies, and if we succeed in developing a method for describing them, we should be as clear as possible about the aims of our research. Unless we clarify what we are up to, comparing vocabularies is pointless. What is of interest here from the viewpoint of religious studies? What is the task we pose to ourselves? Do we strive for a new mapping of actual hopes and beliefs? Do we want to detect and/or update old religious vocabularies? Do we see ourselves as moral advisers? And, if so, do we achieve this by expanding for our clients the repertoire of alternative descriptions, or by making a selection of the most fortunate, familiar descriptions? Let me stay for this moment with reflections on the possibility of developing a method of describing final vocabularies, focusing on vocabularies and violence.

Final Vocabularies and Violence

Final vocabularies are sets of words which, among other things, we use to justify our actions. As violence almost always seems to ask for justification, focusing on violence might be an efficient way to discern different types of final vocabularies. Regarding violence and looking back on the articles in this volume, I can imagine four types of vocabularies of violence: (1) vocabularies of suffering: (e.g. dying for a cause, martyrdom); (2) vocabularies of vocation: (messianism and discipleship); (3) vocabularies of vows and victories; and (4) vocabularies of revenge and indifference: (an eye for an eye and 'if you leave me alone I'll leave you alone)'.

It is noteworthy that Rorty's interest in final vocabularies is motivated by his wish to diminish violence or, rather, cruelty.[34] For Rorty the liberal, cruelty is the

---

serve communication. A language which was 'all metaphor', would be a language, which had no use. Because we all integrate the accidentally produced metaphors of strong poets into our own private vocabularies, we more or less understand each other. So, 'strong poets'—strong because they created their selves by describing themselves in their own terms—paradoxically create the overlap in vocabularies necessary for communication. Rorty takes the notion of 'strong poet' from Harold Bloom. In his view an ideally liberal polity would be one whose culture hero is Bloom's 'strong poet'. Sometimes old metaphors stay alive or revive. Take 'solidarity': as the moral and political vocabularies, typical of the secularised democratic societies of the West 'gradually...de-theologized and de-philosophized, "human solidarity" has emerged as a powerful piece of rhetoric' (p. 192). Rorty does not wish to diminish its power but to disengage it from older vocabularies. By updating it as 'a matter of imaginative identification with the details of other's lives' (p. 190), he integrates it in his new liberal-ironist vocabulary.

34. Violence and aggression he considers as realities of self and world that are beyond words: 'Both [self and world], however, have power over us... But that sort of power is not the sort we can appropriate by adopting and then transforming its language, thereby becoming identical with the threatening power and subsuming it under our more powerful selves. This latter strategy is appropriate only for coping with other persons—for example with parents, gods, and poetic precursors. For our relation to the world, to brute power and to naked pain, is not the sort of relation we have to persons. Faced with the nonhuman, the nonlinguistic, we no longer have an ability to overcome contingency and pain by appropriation and transformation, but only the ability to *recognize* contingency and pain.' This having been said, Rorty leaves the tension or gap between vocabularies and violence in order to turn his attention to indifference and humiliation, the realities of self and world we have to undergo. Languages are not media of representation or media of

worst thing we commit, and the question 'Are you suffering' the basic question of humanity. For Rorty the ironist, the cruelest thing we do is causing humiliation, destroying one another's final vocabularies. What he as a liberal ironist looks for are books that help us become less cruel; and the books he comes up with are books by Vladimir Nabokov and George Orwell. Nabokov, according to Rorty, wrote about cruelty from the inside, illuminating the way in which the private pursuit of aesthetic bliss produces cruelty. Nabokov's greatest creations are obsessive poets, entirely incurious about anything that affects anyone else. Being incurious can be cruel. Orwell, again according to Rorty, wrote about cruelty from the outside, from the victims' point of view. He sensitized his readers to a set of excuses for cruelty: the human equality rhetoric, put in circulation by a particular group of intellectuals. The reason Rorty lingers so long on Orwell, however, is the lesson he gets from Orwell's portrait of the 'curious, perceptive, intellectual' inquisitor in the last part of *1984*. Here Orwell writes about cruelty from an inside perspective too, mediating insight in the cruelty of violating final vocabularies. Violating a person's final vocabulary is to 'unmake' her or his world:

> Getting somebody to deny a belief for no reason is a first step toward making her incapable of having a self because she becomes incapable of weaving a coherent web of belief and desire. It makes her irrational, in a quite precise sense: She is unable to give a reason for her belief that fits together with her other beliefs. She becomes irrational not in the sense that she has lost contact with reality but in the sense that she can no longer rationalize—no longer justify herself to herself.[35]

The violation of final vocabularies can be cruel. In his discussion of Orwell Rorty clearly makes this point. But some vocabularies may, because of their destructive character, better be broken—for the sake of their users. Take the piano teacher's final vocabulary. In Erika Kohut's vocabulary words like 'lust' or 'pleasure' do not occur. Its parochial terms are words like 'music', 'mother', 'hate', 'home', 'cut', 'spy', 'criticize', 'correct', 'Schubert', 'surrender', 'violence' and 'contempt'.

A point could be made that Erika's final vocabulary is forced on her. In Jelinek's plastic description:

> Mother, without prior notice, unscrews the top of HER head, sticks her hand inside, self-assured, and then grubs and rummages about. Mother messes everything up and puts nothing back where it belongs...[36]

But the fact that Erika's vocabulary is forced on her does not make it less final or private. After all, all vocabularies are a matter of socialization. If Erika's feelings toward music are indeed widely shared, it does not help her. It only adds to her feeling of security, which keeps her from changing her life. Maybe novels like Jelinek's help women like Erika Kohut to change their lives. However, at this

---

expression. We cannot adequately represent or express violence or pain, but we can ask one another, 'Are you suffering?'

35.   Rorty, *Contingency*, p. 178. Rorty makes a reference here to Elaine Scarry, *The Body in Pain: The Making and Unmaking of the World* (Oxford: Oxford University Press, 1985).

36.   Jelinek, *The Piano Teacher*, p. 22

moment I am less interested in the moral the novel teaches and more in mapping. Where to situate Erika's vocabulary of vocation on a map of actual hopes and beliefs? I would say it is a vocabulary of vocation, the second of the four types of vocabularies of violence I discerned at the beginning of this paragraph, but what is the worth of an improvisatorial typology like this? Here I propose to return to Rorty before making a final movement into the recent market research mentioned earlier.

Methodological Reflections

Is it possible to (re)construct people's belief systems out of patterns of speaking? That was the question I started with. In my opinion the concept of 'final vocabularies', discussed at length above, can serve as an excellent starting point for this project. Rorty's sketch of their historical-contingent character and of the ways they relate, especially his distinction between old and new vocabularies, seems really fruitful. The big question remains: How to develop methods of description, useful first of all for new mappings of people's hopes and beliefs and, thereafter, for comparing final vocabularies?

When it comes to describing final vocabularies Rorty refers to 'strong poets'. Names of strong poets, titles of texts, their characters, keywords and coined concepts all function as abbreviations of final vocabularies. When it comes to mapping, Rorty is not of direct help. But what if we use his (criticized earlier) public/private distinction as a potential grid? The extremities of the dimension of private perfection could be 'autonomy' and 'heteronomy', the extremities of the public affairs dimension 'liberal hope 'and 'traditional satisfaction'.

The result would be the first draft of a map for situating final vocabularies, among others Rorty's own liberal ironist vocabulary and Jelinek's pianist's final vocabulary of vocation:

Figure 1. *Map of Vocabularies of Violence*

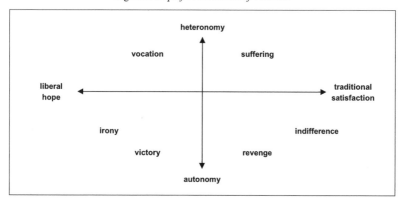

What brings me to this suggestion is the outcome of a recent Dutch market research. In the spring of 2002 Ellen Hessing-Couvret and Albert Reuling published their so-called 'WIN-model',[37] a segmentation of the Dutch market according to the values people uphold.

The model is based on lists of instrumental and final values composed by Rokeach, as used in large-scale intercultural research by Shalom Schwartz and Wolfgang Bilsky.[38]

Respondents are asked to prioritize the listed values according to the importance attributed to those in their lives. Analysis of the obtained data results in a so-called value space, within which every value has its own place:

Figure 2. *The WIN-Value Space, Based on Rokeach, Schwarz and Bilsky*[39]
(Source: NIPO, 2002)

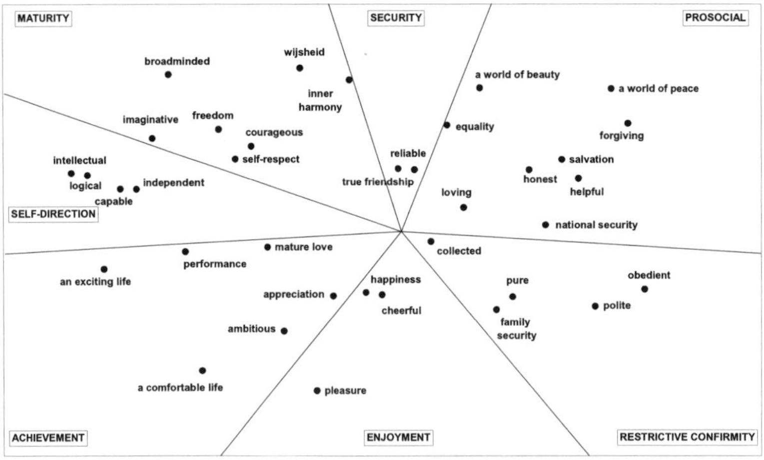

The values on this map are more or less modernized Dutch translations of Rokeach value survey.[40] The structure of the map confirms the 'motivational domains' discerned by Schwartz and Bilsky. The coordinating values are other/self and progress/stagnation:

37. Ellen Hessing-Couvret and Albert Reuling, *Het WIN-model* (NIPO, Amsterdam, May 2002). WIN stands for *Waardensegmenten In Nederland* ('Valuesegments in the Netherlands'). The report is published on internet: <www.nipo.nl>.

38. The NIPO report refers here to M. Rokeach, *The Nature of Human Values* (New York: Free Press, 1973) and to S.H. Schwartz and W. Bilsky, 'Toward a Universal Psychological Structure of Human Values', *Journal of Personality and Social Psychology* 53 (1987), pp. 550-62; S.H. Schwartz and W. Bilsky, 'Toward a Theory of the Universal Content and Structure of Human Values', *Journal of Personality and Social Psychology* 58 (1990), pp. 878-91.

39. Hessing-Couvret and Reuling, *Het WIN-model*, p. 1.

40. The Rokeach value survey consists of eighteen instrumental values (iv) plus eighteen final values (fv).

Figure 3. *Foundation of the WIN-Model*[41]
(Source: NIPO, 2002)

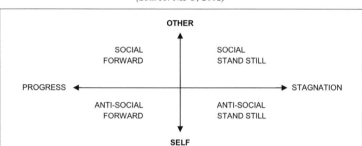

The dimensions derived from Rorty's *Contingency* are quite compatible with these distinctions. However, the names of the coordinating values are far from neutral. They indicate where one 'ought' to be: in the Northwest according to the WIN-model; in the southwest according to the model based on Rorty.

The move to market research may, within religious studies, be an unusual move, but I really think that the results of this research form an excellent first draft for a map of actual hopes and beliefs along non-denominational lines. A big advantage of this kind of research is the big poll samples they work with. Based on ranking values of 1500 respondents, Hessing and Reuling arrive at eight different groups with a specific value pattern or, rather, seven groups with a specific value pattern and one middle group:

Figure 4. *The Eight Resulting Groups in the WIN-Value Space*[42]
(Source: NIPO, 2002)

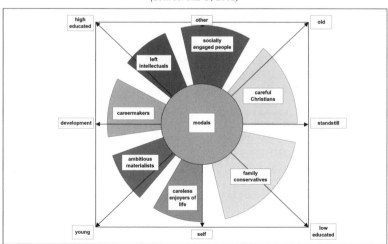

41. Hessing-Couvret and Reuling, *Het WIN-model*, p. 20.
42. Hessing-Couvret and Reuling, *Het WIN-model*, p. 2.

To show the potential of their model, Hessing and Reuling apply it to socio-demographic variables as well as to opinions about capital punishment, organ donor registration, desire for sensation and adventure, breach of law, favourite artists and use of the media. In all these cases, it turned out to be possible to draw a line through the center of the circle that goes from one extremity to the other. To get more certainty about the interpretation of the found value-patterns, they asked their panel to make their choices in Charles Morris's thirteen 'ways to live' and measured them along scales developed in other research, such as Harold Grasmick's low self-control scale and Russel Weigel's scale of selfishness.[43]

In all cases the connections—oppositions and affinities between the segments—reappeared. To cut a long story short, if the model is applicable to a wide range of opinions, preferences and attitudes, why should it not be applicable to religious beliefs and attitudes? As a starting point it could be a new departure, but in what direction? Let me point out three lines for further research.

The first line of research is toward finding the best discriminating dimensions for mapping actual hopes and beliefs. Dimensions can either be abstracted from empirical data or deducted from pieces of theory. In both cases the art of naming is involved. When the question is how to map values or value-loaded views on life, it seems important to formulate the found dimensions as value-neutral as possible. To be more concrete: what I called the vocabulary of vocation in Jelinek's *Piano Teacher* is better compared with a final vocabulary of—to use the stereotypes of the WIN-model—another 'left intellectual' or 'career woman' than with the final vocabulary of a 'careless enjoyer of life' or 'family-conservative'.

The dimensions of the WIN model are abstracted from empirical data, as are the value dimensions found by Joke Oppenhuizen in recent research on the values of native Dutch people.[44] Instead of taking the values listed by Rokeach as a workable survey, Oppenhuizen undertook fundamental research into actually upheld values and how these can be structured in a useful manner. In her research she used qualitative interviews, out of which she selected 1372 value descriptions. These descriptions were reduced to 160 values and subsequently presented to 2000 households in order to determine to what extent values correspond in meaning, and to what extent they form each other's opposites. In the end she distinguishes six dimensions:

	Dimension	Dimension extremities
1.	Relations	Achievement
2.	Socially oriented	Individually oriented
3.	Values of old	Present-day values

---

43. Here the NIPO report refers to Charles Morris, *Varieties of Human Value* (Chicago: University of Chicago Press, 1973). The respondents were confronted with strongly shortened versions of Morris's descriptions of lifestyles. Harold G. Grasmick *et al.*, 'Testing the Core Empirical Implications of Gottfredson and Hirschi's General Theory of Crime', *Journal of Research in Crime and Delinquency* 30 (1993), pp. 5-29; Russell H. Weigel *et al.*, 'Egoism: Concept Measurement and Implications for Deviance', *Psychology, Crime and Law* 5 (1999), pp. 349-78.

44. Joke Oppenhuizen, *Een schaap in de bus? Een onderzoek naar waarden van de Nederlander* (Amsterdam: SWOCC, 2000)

4.	Certainty	Challenge
5.	Family life	Freedom
6.	Being conformist	Doing it your way[45]

Oppenhuizen states that the application of her value research in the value-monitor of the Society of Dutch Universities proves that these six dimensions yield independent results. 'Which dimensions discriminate well in this process depends on the market analysed.'[46]

Which dimensions discriminate best on the marketplace of actual hopes and beliefs? For the purpose of religious studies it may be most efficient to start with deducing some hypothetical dimensions out of relevant pieces of theory—much like I deduced the dimensions autonomy/heteronomy and liberal hope/traditional satisfaction out of Rorty's *Contingency*. The results could be used to structure qualitative interviews; and from there on the research could follow a path similar to Oppenhuizen's research.[47]

Which dimensions discriminate best for the purposes of religious studies depends to a large extent on what we conceptualize as religion. This brings me to a second line of research, the continuing story of defining the object of religious studies. Hessing and Reuling present as one of their findings that, in the WIN-model, 'careful Christians are 80% religious, whereas at the opposite pole—among the ambitious—it is only 42%'.[48] That is undoubtedly the kind of result you get when you take the common sense meaning of the word 'religious' for granted; or if you restrict it to the acknowledged religious streams. That is what you do if you ask people 'Are you religious?' or 'Are you Christian?', 'Islamic?', 'Buddhist?', 'Hindu?', 'Jewish?' or 'nothing?' You will certainly find the most 'religious' people in the northeast then, but that does not add any information about actual hopes and beliefs. For that matter, I suppose that it is far more productive to use a functional concept of religion: religion as the way people deal with the needs Salman Rushdie named in his essay 'Is Nothing Sacred?' as the needs religion, down the ages, has satisfied:

> I would suggest that these needs are of three types: firstly, the need to be given an articulation of our half-glimpsed knowledge of exaltation, of awe, of wonder... Secondly, we need answers to the unanswerable: 'How did we get here?... And, thirdly, we need codes to live by, 'rules for every damn thing'.[49]

---

45. Oppenhuizen, *Een schaap in de bus?*, p. 254.

46. Oppenhuizen, *Een schaap in de bus?*, p. 255.

47. In a way Oppenhuizen starts with theoretical hypotheses as well. To structure the qualitative interviews she discerned twenty-two 'living domains'—varying from having babies, going to school, puberty, work, holidays, politics, violence, to dying—and she used stimuli material in the form of photographs accompanied by a number of questions. It is this structuring that provides standardization and repeatability of the research.

48. Hessing-Couvret and Reuling, *Het Win-model*, p. 35. Salman Rushdie, *Imaginary Homelands: Essays and Criticism 1981–1991* (London: Granta Books, 1991), p. 421.

49. Rushdie, *Imaginary Homelands*, p. 421.

The advantage of this kind of conceptualizing religion is that it is easy to opera-
tionalize. A line of questioning is already implicated. The three basic questions—
following the three needs—are easy to multiply in many directions in order to get a
rich spectrum of individual answers. More important, though, is that a functional
definition of religion makes it possible to explore the 'religious' perspective of
people in all segments of the population, of people who call themselves religious
and of people who don't.

Religion is a word; what is in a word? That question belongs to the third and last
line of research I'd like to point to. On the basis of the mentioned market research
we can fairly state that Dutch people—Western people, all people?—fall into discernible groups with specific value-patterns. It is likely then to suppose that the
found segmentation of the population is mirrored when it comes to religion.[50] But,
to go one step further, isn't it equally likely that words and values (word-values and
the value of words) are interpreted differently by each group[51] and, from there, that
each segment has its own peculiar final vocabularies? It might for example be
worthwhile to follow the word 'vocation' through the segments: What is the status
of the word within the different segments and is it in all segments equally linked to
religion and violence? Or, to take one of Rorty's favourite values, 'curiosity': Could
it be the southwest translation of the northeast 'religious' value of 'responsive-
ness'?

To carry out a research project in this direction might take years and/or team-
work and/or more money than is normally spent on research in the field of religious
studies. However, I do think we have models available, models developed in market
research, most of all the fundamental research carried out by Oppenhuizen. Instead
of qualitative interviews we might better use novels, or other fictional texts,[52] in
order to avoid the problem often encountered. (See my introduction here: people,
asked directly for their hopes and beliefs, are unwilling and/or unable to answer.)
It is worth noting in this regard that, in Oppenhuizen's research, people were not
asked for their own values. They were asked for the opinions of others. To get answers on the more elusive personal levels, fictional texts, thanks to their relatively
high degree of self-reflectivity, might be a better resource.

Preliminary Conclusions

Violence and religion, sanctified agression—what is there to say about these topics
in the light of recent world events: the USA's war against terrorism, in which
political Islam is identified with terrorism? One way of concluding this article is by

---

50. It could even be defended that the value-patterns form a part of people's religious outlook.

51. See Oppenhuizen, *Een schaap in de bus?*, p. 253: 'The same value may be interpreted
differently per group'.

52. Within the context of the SWOCC value-research there are experiments with alternatives
for qualitative interviews: a research into the values of children's books and a research into the
values in Dutch soap operas. I. Posthouwer made a survey of values in eight children's books, four
books of allochthonous writers and four books of autochthonous writers (See Oppenhuizen, *Een
schaap in de bus?*, pp. 16, 234-36).

saying that my explorations and reflections thus far have been too abstract to be of use in answering such concrete historical questions. Another way of concluding is by repeating my point: notions like 'religious', 'Christian', 'Islamic' and for that matter 'secular' are far too abstract to be of help in clarifying the situation. Religion, not as a word but as a phenomenon, is not something specific for some individuals or groups. Everyone has his or her way to cope with the mystery of life and the question of how to live.[53]

If we stick to the traditional sense of 'religious', religious wars would be an anomaly. According to the WIN-model the segment that is the most 'religious' is the least egoistic, the least anti-social, and the least challenged by danger and adventure.[54] Moreover, religious leaders all over the world criticize the actual threat of war. In a common declaration Dutch leaders of Islamic, Jewish, Christian and humanistic councils express their shared conviction that an eventual war is not a religious war, their shared fear that a war may heighten the tensions between communities, and their shared wish to engage more with each other, 'openly' and 'with respect'.[55]

The public language of this declaration—thin words like 'open', 'honest', 'respect', 'engage', 'talk'—stands in glaring contrast to the powerful pieces of religious rhetoric in actual war-talk. This contrast shows in a nutshell what is at hand. Traditional religious words are literalized, and people asked for their hopes and beliefs seem speechless. The introduction of Magnum ice creams named after the seven sins signals the commercializing of the old religious vocabulary, as the tremendous marketing success of the Mecca-cola in Paris recently signals how it can be politicized. When trend watchers are called prophets, and killers can be called martyrs,[56] we need new series of value-loaded words to detect belief systems. And we need texts, texts of 'strong poets' like Jelinek that back up the listed words, describing the territory behind them.[57] What final vocabularies do they refer to? What quality of life are they likely to produce? What sense of reality and solidarity?

53. Oppenhuizen confirms this insight. She states that the intercultural research of Schwartz and Bilsky has shown that 'spirituality' is not a motivational domain of its own (Oppenhuizen, *Een schaap in de bus?*, p. 73).

54. Hessing-Couvret and Reuling, *Het WIN-model*, p. 35.

55. 'Verklaring van verbondenheid' (Declaration of Communion), non-published pamphlet, Amsterdam, Mozes- en Aäronkerk, 24 February 2003.

56. See the article of Jan Willem van Henten in the present volume.

57. As far as I am concerned, the dreamed-of results of the project are (1) lists of value-loaded words, very much like the lists used in market research, whose prioritizing makes visible new structures of belief and (2) a CD-Rom providing texts that back up the listed words, describing the territory behind them. What final vocabularies will they refer to? What quality of living are they likely to produce? What sense of reality and solidarity will they promote? Comparable with the CD-Rom enclosed in Oppenhuizen's book: 'The interviews, photos, value-descriptions, statements by respondents and results from statistical analysis have been collected on a CD-Rom called the "Waardenwoordenboek" [Dictionary of Values]. In this way the results are now available to science and marketing sectors. There is also a thesaurus included on the CD-Rom with which the 160 values…are linked to the remaining value descriptions and also to statements and background variables of the respondents and the photos' (Oppenhuizen, *Een schaap in de bus?*, pp. 254-55).

BIBLIOGRAPHY

Aho, J.A., *The Politics of Righteousness: Idaho Christian Patriotism* (Seattle: University of Washington Press, 1990).

Aichele, G. (ed.), *Culture, Entertainment and the Bible* (JSNTSup, 309; Sheffield: Sheffield Academic Press, 2000).

Allen, L.C., *Psalms 101–150* (WBC, 21; Waco, TX: Word Books, 1983).

Anonymous, 'Maximizing the Matrix', *Newsweek* (19 April 1999) (reproduced by permission on the Warner Brothers DVD-edition of *The Matrix*).

Avenarius, G., *Lukians Schrift zur Geschichtsschreibung* (Meisenheim/Glan: Verlag Anton Hain, 1956).

Barker, Pat, *Regeneration* (Harmondsworth: Penguin Books, 1992).

Barkun, M., *Religion and the Racist Right: The Origins of the Christian Identity Movement* (Chapel Hill: University of North Carolina Press, rev. edn, 1997).

Barnard, Benno, *Jefta of Semitische liefdes* (Amsterdam: Het Toneel Speelt, 1998).

Baum, G., *Religion and Alienation: A Theological Reading of Sociology* (New York: Paulist Press, 1975).

Beal, T.K., 'Redemption in an Unlikely Place', *The Washington Post* (20 October 2002), B-3 (Outlook section).

—'The System and the Speaking Subject in the Hebrew Bible: Reading for Divine Abjection', *BibInt* 2.2 (1994), pp. 172-89.

Beam, L., *Essays of a Klansman Being a compendium of Ku Klux Klan Ideology, Organizational Methods, History, Tactics, and Opinions, with Interpretations by the Author* (Hayden Lake: AKIA Publications, 1983).

—'Leaderless Resistance: Special Report on the Meeting of Christian Men Held in Estes Park, Colorado, October 23, 24, 25, 1992' (unpublished conference address).

Bekkenkamp, J., 'Breaking the Waves: Corporeality and Religion in a Modern Melodrama', in J. Bekkenkamp and M. de Haardt (eds.), *Begin with the Body: Corporeality, Religion and Gender* (Leuven: Peeters Press, 1998), pp. 134-56.

Benvenisti, Meron, *Sacred Landscape: The Buried History of the Holy Land Since 1948* (Berkeley: University of California Press, 2001).

Berman, Saul J., 'The War Against Evil and Ethical Constraints', available online at <http://www.shma.com/dec01/berman.phtml>.

Bernall, M., *She Said Yes: The Unlikely Martyrdom of Cassie Bernall* (Farmington, PA: Plough, 1999).

Beuken, W., 'Did Israel Need the Messiah?', *Concilium* 1993/1 (1993), pp. 3-13.

Bialik, Haim Nahman, *Revealment and Concealment: Five Essays* (Jerusalem: Ibis Editions, 2000).

Bickerman, E., 'Ritualmord und Eselskult', *MGWJ* 71 NS 35 (1927), pp. 171-87, 255-64.

Botha, P.J.J., 'Submission and Violence: Exploring Gender Relations in the First-Century World', *Neotestamentica* 34.1 (2000), pp. 1-38.

Boyarin, Daniel, *Carnal Judaism: Reading Sex in Talmudic Culture* (Berkeley: University of California Press, 1993).

—*Dying for God: Martyrdom and the Making of Christianity and Judaism* (Figurae; Stanford: Stanford University Press, 1999).

—*Intertextuality and the Reading of Midrash* (Bloomington: Indiana University Press, 1990).

Brehm, H.A., 'The Meaning of *Hellēnistēs* in Acts in Light of a Diachronic Analysis of *hellēnizein*', in S.E. Porter and D.A. Carson (eds.), *Discourse Analysis and Other Topics in Biblical Greek* (JSNTSup, 113; Sheffield: Sheffield Academic Press, 1995), pp.266-99.

Briggs, C.A., and E.G. Briggs, *A Critical and Exegetical Commentary on the Book of Psalms* (2 vols.; repr., Edinburgh: T. & T. Clark, 1969 [1906–1907]), II.

Bright, John, *A History of Israel* (London: SCM Press, 2nd edn, 1972).

Carpenter, Humphrey, *Dennis Potter: A Biography* (London: Faber & Faber, 1998).

Cashman, G.F., 'Holocaust Martyrs Remembered', *The Jerusalem Post* (9 April 2002), available online at <http://www.jpost.com/Editions/2002/04/09/News/News.46556.html>.

Castelli, E., '"I Will Make Mary Male": Pieties of the Body and Gender Transformation of Christian Women in Late Antiquity', in J. Epstein and K. Straub (eds.), *Body Guards: The Cultural Politics of Gender Ambiguity* (London: Routledge, 1991), pp. 29-49.

Certeau, Michel de, *The Writing of History* (trans. T. Conley; New York: Columbia University Press, 1975).

Chrétien, Jean-Pierre, 'Les deux visages de Cham', in Guiral and Témime (eds.), *L'idée de race*, pp. 171-99.

—*Rwanda: Les médias du génocide* (Paris: Karthala, 1995).

Christian Thinktank, <http://www.christian-thinktank.com/rbutcher1.html>.

Clark, G., 'Bodies and Blood: Late Antique Debate on Martyrdom, Virginity and Resurrection', in D. Montserrat (ed.), *Changing Bodies, Changing Meanings: Studies on the Human Body in Antiquity* (London: Routledge, 1998), pp. 99-115.

Cloke, G., *This Female Man of God: Women and Spiritual Power in the Patristic Age, AD 350–450* (London: Routledge, 1995).

Corliss, R., 'Popular Metaphysics', *Time* (April 1999) (reproduced by permission on the Warner Bros. DVD-edition of *The Matrix*).

Corrington Streete, G., 'Women as Sources of Redemption and Knowledge in Early Christian Traditions', in R. Shepard Kraemer and R. D'Angelo (eds.), *Women and Christian Origins* (New York: Oxford University Press), pp. 330-54.

Coupland, D., *Life after God* (New York: Pocket Books, 1994).

Crossan, John Dominic, *Jesus: A Revolutionary Biography* (San Francisco: HarperSanFrancisco, 1995).

Davidson, F. *et al.* (eds.), *The New Bible Commentary* (London: The Inter-Varsity Fellowship, 1953).

Davies, Horton, *Catching the Conscience: Essays in Religion and Literature* (Cambridge, MA: Cowley, 1984).

Davies, Philip R., *In Search of 'Ancient Israel'* (JSOTSup, 148; Sheffield: Sheffield Academic Press, 1992).

De Vaux, Roland, *Ancient Israel: Its Life and Institutions* (London: Darton, Longman & Todd, 2nd edn, 1965).

Dehandschutter, B., 'Martyrium und Agon: Über die Wurzeln der Vorstellung Vom *AGŌN* im Vierten Makkabäerbuch', in van Henten, Dehandschutter and van der Klaauw (ed.), *Die Entstehung der Jüdischen Martyrologie*, pp. 215-19.

Dehandschutter, B., and J.W. van Henten, 'Einleitung', in van Henten, Dehandschutter and van der Klaauw (ed.), *Die Entstehung der Jüdischen Martyrologie*, pp. 1-19.

Derrida, Jacques, *Acts of Religion* (ed. G. Andijar; London: Routledge, 2002).

—*Cinders* (trans. and ed. Ned Lukacher; Lincoln: University of Nebraska Press, 1991).

—*Without Alibi* (trans. Peggy Kamuf; Stanford, CA: Stanford University Press, 2002).

Desjardins, M., *Peace, Violence and the New Testament* (The Biblical Seminar, 46; Sheffield: Sheffield Academic Press, 1997).

Detweiler, R., *Breaking the Fall: Religious Readings of Contemporary Fiction* (San Francisco: Harper & Row, 1989).

Dicou, B., *Edom, Israel's Brother and Antagonist: The Role of Edom in Biblical Prophecy and Story* (JSOTSup, 169; Sheffield: JSOT Press, 1994).

Diedrich, J., *She Said Yes: A Bible Study Guide Based on the Life of Cassie Bernall* (Rocky Mount, NC: Positive Action for Christ, 1999).

Dostoevsky, Fyodor, *The Brothers Karamazov* (trans. David Magarshack; Harmondsworth: Penguin Books, 1958).

Douglas, M., *Leviticus as Literature* (Oxford: Oxford University Press, 1999).

—*Purity and Danger: An Analysis of the Concepts of Pollution and Taboo* (London: Routledge & Kegan Paul, 1966).

Dros, L., 'Pim Fortuyn/De dood van een Messias', *Trouw* (8 May 2002), available online at <http://www.trouw.nl> (consulted on 14 May 2002).

Dube, M.W., *Postcolonial Feminist Interpretation of the Bible* (St Louis, MO: Chalice, 2000).

Duff, T.E., *Plutarch's Lives: Exploring Virtue and Vice* (New York: Oxford University Press, 1999).

Eichrodt, Walther, *Theology of the Old Testament* (2 vols.; London: SCM Press, 1961).

Eilberg-Schwartz, Howard, *God's Phallus and Other Problems for Men and Monotheism* (Boston, MA: Beacon Press, 1994).

—*The Savage in Judaism* (Bloomington: Indiana University Press, 1990).

Elbaum, Yaakov, 'From Sermon to Story: The Transformation of the Akedah', *Prooftexts* 6 (1986), pp. 97-116.

Eliot, T.S., *Selected Poems* (London: Faber & Faber, 1961).

Evans, C.E., *Noncanonical writings and New Testament interpretation* (Peabody: Hendrickson, 1992).

Fadness, G., 'Phineas Priests May Be Responsible for Racist Leaflets', *Idaho Falls Post Register* (18 April 1996), A1.

Feldherr, A., *Spectacle and Society in Livy's History* (Berkeley: University of California Press, 1998).

Ferguson, E., *Backgrounds of Early Christianity* (Grand Rapids: Eerdmans, 2nd edn, 1993).

Freedman, D.N., 'The Structure of Psalm 137', in H. Goedicke (ed.), *Near Eastern Studies in Honor of W.F. Albright* (Baltimore: The Johns Hopkins University Press, 1971), pp. 187-205.

Freud, Sigmund, *Moses and Monotheism*, in *The Origins of Religion* (Penguin Freud Library, 13; Harmondsworth: Penguin Books, 1985).

Freyne, S., 'The Early Christians and Jewish Messianic Ideas', *Concilium* 1993/1 (1993), pp. 30-41.

—'Editorial: The Messiah in History', *Concilium* 1993/1 (1993), pp. vii-xiv.

Friedlander, G. (trans.), Moses Maimonides, *The Guide for the Perplexed* (New York: Dover Books, 1956 [1904]).

—*Pirke de Rabbi Eliezer* (New York: Sepher-Hermon Press, 4th edn, 1981).

Gaon, S., 'Reasons for Sounding the Shofar', in P. Goodman (ed.), *The Rosh Hashanah Anthology* (Philadelphia: Jewish Publication Society of America, 1992), pp. 38-40.

Gacta, J., Z. Staenburg and D.A. Davis, Online interview <http://whatisthematrix.warnerbros.com/cmp/chat-johnzachdane_index.html> (consulted on 21 January 2002).

Geddert, T.J., 'Peace', in Green, McKnight and Marshall (eds.), *Dictionary of Jesus and the Gospels*, pp. 604-605.

Ginzberg, L., *The Legends of the Jews* (Philadelphia: Jewish Publication Society of America, 1937).

Gleason, M., 'Mutilated Messengers: Body Language in Josephus', in S. Goldhill (ed.), *Being Greek Under Rome: Cultural Identity, the Second Sophistic and the Development of Empire* (Cambridge: Cambridge University Press, 2001), pp. 50-85.

Goldin, Judah, 'Introduction', to Shalom Spiegel, *The Last Trial: On the Legends and Lore of the Command to Abraham to Offer Isaac as a Sacrifice* (Woodstock, VM: Jewish Lights, 1993 [1st edn Hebrew 1950, ET 1967]), pp. xi-xxx.

Goldman, Ronald, MD, *Circumcision, The Hidden Trauma: How an American Cultural Practice Affects Infants and Ultimately Us All* (Boston, MA: Vanguard Publications, 1997).

Gollaher, David L., *Circumcision: A History of the World's Most Controversial Surgery* (New York: Basic Books, 2000).

Goodman, P. (ed.), *The Rosh Hashanah Anthology* (Philadelphia: Jewish Publication Society of America, 1992).

Gordon, Robert P., *1 & 2 Samuel* (Exeter: Paternoster Press, 1986).

Grabbe, L.L., *Judaism from Cyrus to Hadrian* (London: SCM Press, 1992).

Grasmick, Harold G., *et al.*, 'Testing the Core Empirical Implications of Gottfredson and Hirschi's General Theory of Crime', *Journal of Research in Crime and Delinquency* 30 (1993), pp. 5-29.

Green, J.B., S. McKnight and I.H. Marshall (eds.), *Dictionary of Jesus and the Gospels* (Downers Grove, IL: InterVarsity Press, 1992).

Greenstone, Julius, *Jewish Feasts and Fasts* (Philadelphia: Jewish Publication Society of America, 1945).

Gross, Jan T., *Neighbors: The Destruction of the Jewish Community in Jedwabne, Poland* (Princeton, NJ: Princeton University Press, 2001).

Gruber, Mayer I., *Rashi's Commentary on Psalms 1–89 (Books I–III) with English Translation, Introduction and Notes* (South Florida Studies in the History of Judaism, 161; Atlanta: Scholars Press, 1998).

Guillebaud, M., *Rwanda, The Land that God Forgot? Revival, Genocide and Hope* (London: Monarch Books, 2002).

Guiral, P., and E. Témime (eds.), *L'idée de race dans la pensée politique française contemporaine* (Paris: Editions de CNRS, 1977), pp. 171-99.

Gumbiner, Joseph H., 'Existentialism and Father Abraham', *Commentary* (February 1948).

Gunderson, E., *Staging Masculinity: The Rhetoric of Performance in the Roman World* (Ann Arbor: University of Michigan Press, 2000).

Gunkel, H., *Die Psalmen* (Göttinger Handkommentar zum Alten Testament. Abt. 2, Die poetischen Bücher, 2; Göttingen: Vandenhoeck & Ruprecht, 5th edn, 1968).

Hadas-Lebel, Mireille, *Jerusalem contre Rome* (Paris: Cerf, 1990).

Halperin, David J., *Seeking Ezekiel: Text and Psychology* (University Park: Pennsylvania State University Press, 1993).

Hardison, O.B., Jr, *Christian Rite and Christian Drama in the Middle Ages* (Baltimore: The Johns Hopkins University Press, 1965).

Häring, H., 'Ploegscharen Omgesmeed tot Zwaarden (Joël 4,10). De Wortels van het Geweld in de Religie', *Tijdschrift voor Teologie* 37(3) (1997), pp. 265-97.

Harrelson, Walter J. (ed.), *The New Interpreter's Study Bible* (Nashville: Abingdon Press, forthcoming).

Harroy, Jean-Paul, *Le Rwanda, du féodalisme à la démocratie (1955–1962)* (Brussels: Hayez, 1984).

Hartman, G.H., and S. Budick (eds.), *Midrash and Literature* (New Haven: Yale University Press, 1986).

Heard, W.J., 'Revolutionary Movements', in Green, McKnight and Marshall (eds.), *Dictionary of Jesus and the Gospels*, pp. 688-98.

Heath, S., 'God, Faith and Film: *Breaking the Waves*', *Literature and Theology* 12 (1998), pp. 93-107.

Henry, Matthew, <http://bible.crosswalk.com/Commentaries/MatthewHenryConcise/mhc-con. cgi?book=ex&chapter=017>.

Henten, J.W. van, *The Maccabean Martyrs as Saviours of the Jewish People: A Study of 2 and 4 Maccabees* (JSJSup, 57; Leiden: E.J. Brill, 1997).

—'The Tradition-Historical Background of Romans 3.25: A Search for Pagan and Jewish Parallels', in M.C. de Boer (ed.), *From Jesus to John* (JSNTSup, 84; Sheffield: JSOT Press, 1993), pp. 101-28.

Henten, J.W. van, and F. Avemarie, *Martyrdom and Noble Death: Selected Texts from Graeco-Roman, Jewish, and Christian Antiquity* (London: Routledge, 2002).

Henten J.W. van, B. Dehandschutter and H.J.W. van der Klaauw (eds.), *Die Entstehung der Jüdischen Martyrologie* (SPB, 38; Leiden: E.J. Brill, 1989).

Herr, M.D., 'Edom in the Aggadah', in *EncJud*, VI, pp. 379-80.

Hertzberg, H.W., *1 & 2 Samuel* (London: SCM Press, 1964).

Herzog, W.R., II, *Jesus, Justice and the Reign of God: A Ministry of Liberation* (Louisville, KY: Westminster/John Knox Press, 2000).

Hessing-Couvret, Ellen, and Albert Reuling, *Het WIN-model* (Amsterdam: NIPO, 2002) (WIN stands for 'Waardensegmenten In Nederland' ['Value Segments in the Netherlands']), the report is published online at <www.nipo.nl>.

Heuch, L. de, *Le Rwanda et la civilisation interalacustre: etudes d'anthropologie histoire et structurale* (Brussels: Université Libre de Bruxelles, 1966).

Hill, C.C., *Hellenists and Hebrews: Reappraising Division within the Early Church* (Minneapolis: Fortress Press, 1992).

Himmel, M., 'Making Martyrs', *NewsHour* (19 March 2002), available online at <http://www. pbs.org/newshour/bb/middle_east/ jan-june02/martyr_3-19.html>.

Hoban, R., *Riddley Walker* (New York: Summit Books, 1980).

Hoffman, Lawrence A., *Covenant of Blood: Circumcision and Gender in Rabbinic Judaism* (Chicago: University of Chicago Press, 1996).

Holz, B.W. (ed.), *Back to the Sources: Reading the Classic Jewish Texts* (New York: Simon & Schuster, 1992).

Hook, Brian S., and R.R. Reno, 'Abraham and the Problems of Modern Heroism', in Leonard J. Greenspoon and Bryan F. LeBeau (eds.), *Sacred Text, Secular Times* (Studies in Jewish Civilization, 10; Omaha, NB: Creighton University Press, 2000), pp. 135-61.

Hoskins, R.K., 'Saxon Identity', *The Hoskins Report* 266, available online <http://www. richardhoskins.com/1_vphr.htm>.

—*Vigilantes of Christendom: The History of the Phineas Priesthood* (Lynchburg: The Virginia Publishing Company, 1990).

Hunter, Alastair G., 'Whose Land is it Anyway?', in Robert P. Carroll and Alastair G. Hunter (eds.), *Words at Work: A Festschrift for Robert Davidson* (Glasgow: Trinity St Mungo Press, 1994), pp. 44-56.

Hunzinger, C.H., 'Babylon als Deckname für Rom und die Datierung des 1. Petrusbriefs', in H. Reventlow (ed.), *Gottes Wort und Gottes Land* (Göttingen: Vandenhoeck & Ruprecht, 1965), pp. 67-76.

Irving, J., 'Renew Violence', *NewsHour* (2 October 2000), available online <http://www.pbs. org/newshour/bb/middle_east/july-dec00/violence_10-2a.html>.

Jelinek, Elfriede, *Die Klaviespielerin* (Reihbek: Rowohlt Verlag, 1983).

Jewett, R., *Saint Paul Returns to the Movies: Triumph Over Shame* (Grand Rapids: Eerdmans, 1999).

Johanssen, E., *Geistesleben afrikanischer Völker im Lichte des Evangeliums* (Munich: Chr. Kaiser Verlag, 1931).

Johnson, L.T., *The Literary Function of Possessions in Luke–Acts* (SBLDS, 39; Atlanta: Scholars Press, 1977).

Jongkind, B.L., *De heiliging van Gods naam: verzet en overgave van het joodse volk* (Kampen: Kok, 1991).

Kagame, Alexis, 'L'historicité de Lyangombe, chef des "Immandwa"', in Tassa Okombe Lukumba (ed.), *Lyangombe mythe et rites: actes du deuxième colloque du CERUKI BUKAVU, 10-14 Mai 1976* (Bukavu: Centre de Récherches Universitaires du Kivu, 1976), pp. 17-28.

Kagame, Alexis, *Un abrégé de l'ethno-histoire du Rwanda* (Butare: Editions Universitaires du Rwanda, 1972).

Keefer, K., and T. Linafelt, 'The End of Desire: Theologies of Eros in the Song of Songs and *Breaking the Waves*', in Plate and Jasper (eds.), *Imag(in)ing Othernes*, pp. 49-60.

Kellerman, U., 'Psalm 137', *ZAW* 90 (1978), pp. 43-58.

Kepnes, Stephen, Peter Ochs and Robert Gibbs (eds.), *Reasoning after Revelation: Dialogues in Postmodern Jewish Philosophy* (Boulder, CO: Westview Press, 1998).

Kirp, D.L., 'Martyrs and Movies', *The American Prospect* 11 (20 December 1999), available online <http://www.prospect.org/print/V11/3/kirp-d.html> (consulted 22 April 2002).

Kissane, E.J., *The Book of Psalms* (2 vols.; Dublin: Browne & Nolan, 1954).

Kohlberg, E., 'Shahid', in *Encyclopaedia of Islam* in C.E. Bosworth *et al.* (eds.), *Encyclopaedia of Islam* (Leiden: E.J. Brill, 1995), IX, pp. 203-207.

Kraus, H.-J., *Psalms 60–150: A Commentary* (trans. H.C. Oswald; Minneapolis: Augsburg, 1989).

Kreitzer, L.J., *Pauline Images in Fiction and Film: On Reversing the Hermeneutical Flow* (The Biblical Seminar, 86; Sheffield: Sheffield Academic Press, 1999).

Kristeva, Julia, *Les nouvelles maladies de l'âme* (Paris: Fayard, 1993).

—*New Maladies of the Soul* (trans. Ross Guberman; New York: Columbia University Press, 1995).

Kugel, James L., *In Potiphar's House: The Interpretive Life of Biblical Texts* (Cambridge, MA: Harvard University Press, 2nd edn, 1994 [1st edn 1990]).

Lacger, L. de, *Ruanda* (Kabgayi: Imprimatur, 1959).

Lapin, Daniel, <http://www.nationalreview.com/comment/comment-lapin091801.shtml>.

Lehmann, Clayton Miles, <http://www.usd.edu/erp/Palestine/history.htm>.

Lethbridge, D., 'Killers for God: The Phineas Priesthood' (The Bethune Institute for Anti-Fascist Studies, 1998) available online at <www.bethuneinstitute.org>.

Levenson, Jon D., *The Death and Resurrection of the Beloved Son: The Transformation of Child Sacrifice in Judaism and Christianity* (New Haven: Yale University Press, 1993).

Levine, H.J., *Singing Unto God a New Song: A Contemporary Reading of the Psalms* (Bloomington: Indiana University Press, 1995).

Lieu, J., *Image and Reality: The Jews in the World of the Christians in the Second Century* (Edinburgh: T. & T. Clark, 1996).

Limburg, J. (trans. and ed.), *Judaism: An introduction for Christians* (Minneapolis: Augsberg, 1987).

Linafelt, Tod, *Surviving Lamentations: Catastrophe, Lament and Protest in the Afterlife of a Biblical Book* (Chicago: Chicago University Press, 2000).

Macintyre, D., 'As an Old Peace Protester, I Have No Time for Anarchists', *The Independent* (24 July 2001), available online at <www.commondreams.org/views01/0724-03.htm> (cited 22 April 2002).

Makarushka, I.S.M., 'Transgressing Goodness in *Breaking the Waves*', in Plate and Jasper (eds.), *Imag(in)ing Otherness*, pp. 61-80.

Mann, Jacob, *The Bible as Read and Preached in the Old Synagogue* (Cincinnati: published by the author, 1940).

Marguerat, D., 'Luc-Actes: Une unité à construire', in J. Verheyden (ed.), *The Unity of Luke–Acts* (BETL, 142; Leuven: Leuven University Press, 1999), pp. 57-81.

Martin, François, *Pour une théologie de la lettre: l'inspiration des Écritures* (Paris: Éditions du Cerf, 1996).

Mayor, F., 'The Human Right to Peace', *Bulletin* 4(4) (1987), pp. 1-2.

Mays, J.L., *Psalms* (Interpretation; Louisville, KY: John Knox Press, 1994).

Mbonimana, G., 'Ethnies et église catholique', in *Cahiers Centre Saint-Dominique: Ethnies au Rwanda en 1995* (Kigali: Fraternité Saint-Dominique, 1995), I, pp. 52-67.

McCann, J. Clinton, Jr, 'The Book of Psalms', in Leander E. Keck (ed.), *The New Interpreter's Bible* (Nashville: Abingdon Press, 1996), IV, pp. 639-1280.

McEntire, Mark, *The Blood of Abel: The Violent Plot in the Hebrew Bible* (Macon, GA: Mercer University Press, 1999).

McKane, William, *1 & 2 Samuel* (Torch Commentaries; London: SCM Press, 1963).

Mendels, D., *The Rise and Fall of Jewish Nationalism* (Anchor Bible Reference Library; New York: Doubleday, 1992).

Mensching, W., *Ruanda: Eine Selbsdarstellung des Volkes in alten Ueberlieferungen* (Stadthagen: General-Anzeige-Verlag, 1987).

Michaelis, W., μάχαιραν', in *TDNT*, IV, pp. 524-27.

—'ῥομφαία', in *TDNT*, VI, pp. 993-98.

Minear, P.S., *To Heal and to Reveal: The Prophetic Vocation According to Luke* (New York: Seabury Press, 1976).

Mintz, Alan, *Hurban: Responses to Catastrophe in Hebrew Literature* (Syracuse: Syracue University Press, 2nd edn, 1996).

Moessner, D.P., 'The "Script" of the Scriptures in the Acts of the Apostles: Suffering as God's "Plan" (*boule*) for the "Release of Sins"', in B. Witherington (ed.), *History, Literature and Society in the Book of Acts* (Cambridge: Cambridge University Press, 1996), pp. 218-50.

—*Lord of the Banquet: The Literary and Theological Significance of the Lukan Travel Narrative* (Minneapolis: Fortress Press, 1989).

Moore, S., *God's Beauty Parlor and Other Queer Spaces In and Around the Bible* (Stanford: Stanford University Press, 2001).

Morgan, Edwin, *A.D.: A Trilogy of Plays on the Life of Jesus* (Manchester: Carcanet, 2000).

Morgan, R. 'The Worst Rejection Letter', *The Chronicle of Higher Education* (1 February 2002).

Morlin, B., 'Bomber Sounds Warning before 55-year Sentence', *The Spokesman Review* (3 December 1997), B2.

Morlin, B., and J. White, 'Phineas Priests Take Name from Bible', *The Spokesman Review* (3 April 1996), A7.

Morris, Charles, *Varieties of Human Value* (Chicago: University of Chicago Press, 1973).

Mundy, L., 'Sex and Sensibility', *The Washington Post Magazine* (18 July 2000), pp. 17-21 and 29-34.

Murray, R., 'Jews, Hebrews and Christians: Some Needed Distinctions', *NovT* 24 (1982), pp. 194-208.

Musurillo, H. (ed.), *Acts of the Christian Martyrs* (Oxford: Clarendon Press, 1972).

Muzungu, B., 'Ethnies et clans', in *Cahiers Centre Saint-Dominique: Ethnies au Rwanda en 1995* (Kigali: Fraternité Saint-Dominique/Kacyiru, 1995), I, pp. 19-52.

Nahimana, F., *Le Rwanda: Emergence d'un état* (Paris: L'Harmattan, 1993).

Neiwert, D.A., *In God's Country: The Patriot Movement and the Pacific Northwest* (Pullman: Washington State University Press, 1999).

Nickelsburg, G.W.E., *Resurrection, Immortality, and Eternal Life in Intertestamental Judaism* (HTS, 26; Cambridge, MA: Harvard University Press, 1972).

Nimmo, Beth, and Debra K. Klingsporn, *A Real Diary of Faith: The Journal of Rachel Scott* (Nashville: Tommy Nelson, 2001).

Nimmo, Beth, and Darrell Scott, *Rachel's Tears: The Spiritual Journey of Columbine Martyr Rachel Scott* (Nashville: Thomas Nelson, 2000).

Novello, V. (ed.), *Jephtha: An Oratorio in Vocal Score* (London: Novello & Company).

Nulman, Macy, *The Encyclopedia of Jewish Prayer: Ashkenazic and Sephardic Rites* (Northvale, NJ: Jacob Aronson, 1996).

O'Leary, Stephen, *Arguing the Apocalypse: A Theory of Millennial Rhetoric* (Oxford: Oxford University Press, 1994).

Oppenhuizen, Joke, *Een schaap in de bus? Een onderzoek naar waarden van de Nederlander* (Amsterdam: SWOCC, 2000).

Ouaknin, Marc-Alain, *Mysteries of the Kabbalah* (trans. J. Bacon; New York: Abbeville Press, 2000).

Page, T.E., E. Capps and W.H.D. Rouse (eds.), *Philo, On Abraham* (trans. F.H. Coulson; LCL, 6; London: Heinemann, 1935).

Perkins, J., 'Space, Place, Voice in the *Acts of the Martyrs* and the Greek Romance', in D.R. MacDonald (ed.), *Mimesis and Intertextuality in Antiquity and Christianity* (Harrisburg, PA: Trinity Press International, 2001), pp. 117-37.

—*The Suffering Self: Pain and Narrative Representation in the Early Christian Era* (London /New York: Routledge, 1995).

Perufia, Paul del, *Les derniers rois-mages* (Paris: Phébus, 1970).

Pilch, J.J., 'Power', in J.J. Pilch and B.J. Malina (eds.), *Biblical Social Values and their Meaning: A Handbook* (Peabody: J.C. Hendrickson, 1993), pp. 139-42.

Pines, Shlomo (trans. and ed.), *Moses Maimonides, The Guide of the Perplexed* (Chicago: University of Chicago Press, 1963, 1974).

Plate, S.B., and D. Jasper (eds.), *Imag(in)ing Otherness: Filmic Visions of Living Together* (Atlanta: Scholars Press, 1999).

Plato, *Phaedrus* (trans. Walter Hamilton; Harmondsworth: Penguin Books, 1973).

Potter, D., 'Martyrdom as Spectacle', in R. Scodel (ed.), *Theater and Society in the Classical World* (Ann Arbor: University of Michigan Press, 1993), pp. 53-88.

Preston. R., *The Demon in the Freezer: A True Story* (New York: Random House, 2002).

— *The Hot Zone* (New York: Anchor Books, 1995).

Prunier, G., *The Rwanda Crisis: A History of Genocide* (London: Hurst & Company, 1995).

Punt, J., 'Peace, Conflict and Religion in South Africa: Biblical Problems, Possibilities and Prospects', *Missionalia* 27(3) (1999), pp. 263-98.

Pyper, Hugh, 'The Triumph of the Lamb: Psalm 23, Darwin and Textual Fitness' (unpublished paper presented at the Reading, Theory and Bible section of the Society of Biblical Literature Annual Meeting, Orlando, 21-24 November 1998).

Rajak, T., 'Dying for the Law: The Martyr's Portrait', in M. Edwards and S. Swain (eds.), *Portraits: Biographical Representation in the Greek and Latin Literature of the Roman Empire* (New York: Oxford University Press, 1997), pp. 39-67.

Riches, J., *Jesus and the Transformation of Judaism* (London: Dartman, Longman & Todd, 1980).

Robbins, V.K., *Tapestry of Early Christian Discourse: Rhetoric, Society, and Ideology* (London: Routledge, 1996).

Robert, Louis, *Le martyre de Pionios, prêtre de Smyrne* (ed. G.W. Bowersock and C.P.M. Jones; Washington: Dumbarton Oaks Research Library and Collection, 1994).

Roberts, Alexander, and J. Davidson (eds.), *Ignatius of Antioch, Epistle to the Romans*, in *The Anti-Nicene Fathers: Translations of the Writings of the Fathers Down to AD 325*, V (10 vols.; Buffalo, NY: The Christian Literature Publishing Company, 1885–96).

Rogerson, J.W., and J.W. McKay, *Psalms 101–150* (Cambridge Bible Commentary; Cambridge: Cambridge University Press, 1977).

Rokeach, M., *The Nature of Human Values* (New York: Free Press, 1973).

Rorty, Richard, *Contingency, Irony, and Solidarity* (Cambridge: Cambridge University Press, 1989).

Royal, R., *The Catholic Martyrs of the Twentieth Century: A Comprehensive World History* (New York: Crossroad Publishing, 2000).

Rubin, M., 'Choosing Death? Experiences of Martyrdom in Late Medieval Europe', in D. Wood (ed.), *Martyrs and Martyrologies* (Oxford: Basil Blackwell, 1993), pp. 153-83.

Rushdie, Salman, 'Is Nothing Sacred?', in *idem, Imaginary Homelands: Essays and Criticism 1981–1991* (London: Granta Books, 1991), pp. 415-29.

Salisbury, J.E., *Perpetua's Passion: The Death and Memory of a Young Roman Woman* (London: Routledge, 1997).

Sarna, Nahum (ed.), *Torah Commentary: Genesis* (Philadelphia: Jewish Publication Society of America, 1989).

Scarry, Elaine, *The Body in Pain: The Making and Unmaking of the World* (Oxford: Oxford University Press, 1985).

Schaefer, K., *Psalms* (Berit Olam; Collegeville, MN: Liturgical Press, 2001).

Scheinin, R., 'Muslim Scholar: Terrorists are Mass Murderers, Not Martyrs', *Mercury News* (16 September 16 2001), available online at <http://www.mercurycenter.com/local/center/isl0916.htm>.

Schell, Jonathan, *The Fate of the Earth* (New York: Alfred A. Knopf, 1982).

—'The Gift of Time: The Case for Abolishing Nuclear Weapons', *The Nation* (2-9 February 1989), pp. 9-60.

Schillebeeckx, E., 'Documentation: Religion and Violence', *Concilium* 1997/4 (1997), pp. 129-42.

Schoedel, W.R., *Ignatius of Antioch* (ed. H. Koester; Hermeneia; Philadelphia: Fortress Press, 1985).

Schwartz, Regina, *The Curse of Cain: The Violent Legacy of Monotheism* (Chicago: University of Chicago Press, 1997).

Schwartz, S.H., and W. Bilsky, 'Toward a Universal Psychological Structure of Human Values', *Journal of Personality and Social Psychology* 53 (1987), pp. 550-62.

Schwemer, A.M., 'Prophet, Zeuge und Märtyrer: Zur Entstehung des Märtyrerbegriffs im frühesten Christentum', *ZThK* 96 (1999), pp. 320-50.

Segovia, F.F., 'Biblical Criticism and Postcolonial Studies: Towards a Postcolonial Optic', in R.S. Sugirtharajah (ed.), *The Postcolonial Bible* (Bible and Postcolonialism, 1; Sheffield: Sheffield Academic Press, 1998), pp. 49-65.

—'Reading–Across: Intercultural Criticism and Textual Posture', in F.F. Segovia (ed.), *Interpreting Beyond Borders* (The Bible and Postcolonialism, 3; Sheffield: Sheffield Academic Press, 2000), pp. 59-83.

Seid, T.W., '*Synkrisis* in Hebrews 7: The Rhetorical Structure and Strategy', in S.E. Porter and D.L. Stamps (eds.), *The Rhetorical Interpretation of Scripture* (JSNTSup, 180; Sheffield: Sheffield Academic Press, 1999), pp. 322-47.

Sharrat, P., and P.G. Walsh (eds.), *George Buchanan Tragedies* (Edinburgh: Scottish Academic Press, 1983), pp. 21-94.

Shaw, Brent, 'The Passion of Perpetua', *Past and Present* 139 (1993), pp. 3-45.

Sherwood, Yvonne, 'Abrahamic' religions, see my 'Binding-Unbinding: Divided Responses of Judaism, Christianity and Islam to the "Sacrifice" of Abraham's Beloved Son', *JAAR* 72.4 (forthcoming 2004)

—*A Biblical Text and Its Afterlives: The Survival of Jonah in Western Culture* (Cambridge: Cambridge University Press, 2000).

Smith, A., ' "Full of Spirit and Wisdom": Luke's Portrait of Stephen (Acts 6.1–8.1a) as a Man of Self-Mastery', in L.E. Vaage and V.L. Wimbush (eds.), *Asceticism and the New Testament* (London: Routledge, 1999), pp. 97-114.

Spiegel, S., *The Last Trial: On the Legends and Lore of the Command to Abraham to Offer Isaac as a Sacrifice* (Woodstock, VM: Jewish Lights, 1993 [1st edn Hebrew 1950, ET 1967]).

Steinberg, Leo, *The Sexuality of Christ in Renaissance Art and in Modern Oblivion* (Chicago: University of Chicago Press, 2nd edn, 1996).

Stern, M., *Greek and Latin Authors on Jews and Judaism*, I (Jerusalem: Israel Academy of Sciences and Humanities, 1974).

Stevenson, J., *Lars von Trier* (London: British Film Institute, 2002).

Tawil, Ralph, <http://www.judaic.org/tabletalk/tesave5762.htm>.

Thomas, R.G., *Ten Miracle Plays* (London: Edward Arnold, 1966).

Tilley, M.A., 'The Passion of Perpetua and Felicity', in E. Schüssler Fiorenza (ed.), *Searching the Scriptures. II. A Feminist Commentary* (New York: Crossroad, 1997), pp. 829-58.

Trible, Phyllis, 'Genesis 22: The Sacrifice of Sarah', in Alice Bach (ed.), *Women in the Hebrew Bible: A Reader* (London: Routledge, 1999).

Trier, L. von, *Breaking the Waves* (London: Faber & Faber, 1996).

—*Dancer in the Dark* (London: FilmFour Books, 2000).

Tyrrell, R.E., Jr, 'Mending the Mind of the "Martyrs"', *The Washington Times* (4 May 2002), available online at <http://www.washtimes.com/commentary/20020405-93348048.htm>.

Ujica, Andrei, '2 Pasolini, June 2000', in *The Desert* (Foundation Cartier pour l'art contemporain; London: Thames & Hudson, 2000), pp. 208-209.

Unnik, W.C. van, 'Luke's Second Book and the Rules of Hellenistic Historiography', in J. Kremer (ed.), *Les Actes des Apôtres: Traditions, rédaction, théologie* (BETL, 48; Leuven: Leuven University Press, 1979), pp. 37-60.

Verkaaik, O., 'Political Violence in Hyderabad, Pakistan: May 1990 and Muharram 1950', *The Eastern Anthropologist* 53 (2000), pp. 351-66.

Wachowski Brothers, Interview 1999, available online at <http://whatisthematrix.warnerbros. com/cmp/chat_index.html> (consulted on 21 January 2002).

Warren, M., *Seeing through the Media: A Religious View of Communications and Cultural Analysis* (Harrisburg: Trinity Press International, 1997).

Waskov, Arthur, <http://www.shalomctr.org/html/torah35.html>.

Wasserstein, Bernard, *Divided Jerusalem: The Struggle for the Holy City* (London: Profile Books, 2001).

Watson, D.F., 'Babylon in the NT', in David Noel Freedman (ed.), *The Anchor Bible Dictionary CD-ROM* (New York: Doubleday, 1997).

Weber, Samuel, 'Wartime', in Hent de Vries and Samuel Weber (eds.), *Violence, Identity and Self-Determination* (Stanford CA: Stanford University Press, 1997), pp. 80-105.

Weigel, Russell H., *et al.*, 'Egoism: Concept Measurement and Implications for Deviance', *Psychology, Crime and Law* 5 (1999), pp. 349-78.

Weinberg, S., 'The Growing Nuclear Danger', *The New York Review of Books,* July 18 (2002), pp. 18-20.

Weiner, E., and A. Weiner, *The Martyr's Conviction: A Sociological Analysis* (BJS, 203; Atlanta, GA: Scholars Press, 1990).

Welch, C., and K. Barker, 'FBI's Work Challenged by Defense: Agents Describe Items Found in Cars of Bombing Suspects', *The Spokesman Review* (4 July 1997), B1.

Wells, H.G., *The World Set Free: A Story of Mankind* (New York: E.P. Dutton, 1914).

Whitelam, Keith W., *The Invention of Ancient Israel* (London: Routledge, 1996).

Whitney, W.T., 'May Day and the Haymarket Martyrs', *Labor Standard* (no date), available online at <http://www.igc.org/laborstandard/Vol1No3/MayDay.htm> (consulted 4 January 2003).

Wijngaards, N.C.H. (ed.), *Vondels Jeptha of offerbelofe. Treurspel* (Zutphen: W.J. Thieme, 2nd edn, 1976).

Wills, L.M., *The Jew in the Court of the Foreign King: Ancient Jewish Court Legends* (HDR, 26; Minneapolis: Fortress Press, 1990).

Wolfson, E.R., 'Listening to Speak: A Response to Dialogues in Postmodern Jewish Philosophy', in Kepnes, Ochs and Gibbs, *Reasoning after Revelation*, pp. 93-104.

Woodward, K.L., *Making Saints: How the Catholic Church Determines Who Becomes a Saint, Who Doesn't, and Why* (New York: Touchstone, 1996).

Young, R.D., *In Procession Before the World: Martyrdom as Public Liturgy in Early Christianity* (Milwaukee: Marquette University Press, 2001).

Ziolkowski, E., *Evil Children in Religion, Literature, and Art* (Cross-Currents in Religion and Culture; New York: Palgrave, 2001).

Žižek, S., 'Death and the Maiden', in Elizabeth Wright and Edmond Wright (eds.), *The Žižek Reader* (Oxford: Basil Blackwell, 1999), pp. 206-21.

INDEX OF AUTHORS